TEACHER MANUAL

Glencoe

WORLD LITERATURE

TEACHER MANUAL

Glencoe

An Anthology of Great
Short Stories, Poetry, and Drama

DONNA ROSENBERG

 **Glencoe**

New York, New York   Columbus, Ohio   Chicago, Illinois   Peoria, Illinois   Woodland Hills, California

Cover art: *Femme assise dans un fateuil*, 1920. Pablo Picasso. Oil on canvas, 130 × 89 cm. Private Collection. © 2003 Estate of Pablo Picasso/Artists Rights Society (ARS), New York/Christie's Images Ltd.

Glencoe

The *McGraw·Hill* Companies

Send all inquiries to:
Glencoe/McGraw-Hill
8787 Orion Place
Columbus, OH 43240-4027

ISBN (hardcover) 0-07-860353-6
ISBN (softcover) 0-07-860352-8
ISBN (teacher manual) 0-07-860354-4

Printed in the United States of America.

1 2 3 4 5 6 7 8 9   069   09 08 07 06 05 04 03

CONTENTS

CONTINENTAL EUROPE 59

AFRICA 113

ASIA AND THE SOUTH PACIFIC 151

SOUTH AND CENTRAL AMERICA 219

GREAT BRITAIN AND IRELAND 299

INTRODUCTION

*T*HIS TEACHER MANUAL WILL FACILITATE your use of the *World Literature* text. The following section gives you an overview of the contents of this *Manual* and of the philosophy that shapes the instructional format of *World Literature*.

This Introduction begins with the criteria for choosing the selections in *World Literature*. It includes teaching objectives and suggestions for using the text in the classroom, as well as charts that organize the contents of *World Literature* by genre, by major themes, and by literary techniques.

The Introduction also includes a section that explains how to use the instructional format of *World Literature* and this *Manual* to enhance your students' literary experience. It explains the many elements of the student text and of the *Teacher Manual*. It includes a discussion of the Socratic method of questioning, which emphasizes open-ended questions and multiple responses. The Introduction concludes with suggestions for testing and evaluating students' knowledge and skills.

The main body of this *Manual* is devoted to a detailed treatment of each of the eighty-six selections in *World Literature*.

This *Manual* concludes with a Selected Bibliography of works related to the selections in *World Literature*.

THE SELECTIONS IN *WORLD LITERATURE*

The selections included in *World Literature* meet five important criteria:

1. **Global Scope** *World Literature* is a truly global anthology in that it contains short stories, poems, and plays from around the world. To emphasize the global aspect of its contents, the selections are organized in seven geographical sections: The Mediterranean, Continental Europe, Africa, Asia and the South Pacific, South and Central America, North America, and Great Britain and Ireland. Each geographical section contains many short stories and poems and one play. In addition to their global scope, the selections in *World Literature* include a variety of subjects and themes.

2. **Literary Quality** Each selection included in *World Literature* is an outstanding work by a world-famous author. As you peruse the contents of the student text, you will find many old favorites and—equally exciting—you can anticipate making many new friends.

3. *Appeal and Value* The selections in *World Literature* have been chosen to promote the enjoyment and appreciation of great literature from around the world. Until recently, the concept of "world literature" has meant European literature. However, we owe it to ourselves and our students to become aware of the literary treasures that exist in other world cultures as well.

These selections also reveal how, for all their cultural differences, human beings through time and across space are members of one universal family. Like all human beings, the characters in these selections experience joy, tragedy, and difficult challenges. For them as for us, life includes the despair of failed dreams and the triumph of perseverance, the frustration of prejudice and the power of friendship, the danger of impulsive behavior and the achievement of self-respect, the bondage of outworn tradition and the value of self-discovery, the devastation of war and the delight in nature's beauty, the loss of loved ones and the joy of love.

Finally, the experience of reading and discussing fine literature should be fun, informative, and intellectually stimulating. Therefore, in addition to its literary quality, each selection is interesting and enjoyable and provokes stimulating classroom discussion. By discussing the thoughts, feelings, conflicts, and choices of others, students become more sensitive to the human condition, more aware of their own relationships, and more knowledgeable about themselves.

4. *Complete and Unabridged* An important feature of *World Literature* is that, with the exception of "The Pardoner's Tale," which is part of Chaucer's *Canterbury Tales*, each selection in this anthology appears in its complete form. This approach respects the integrity of the work and also respects the need of readers to consider a work in its entirety to be able to form a thoughtful response that is based on a close reading of the text.

5. *Modern Translations* Each non-English selection appears in a fine modern translation. Translators must constantly balance remaining true to the literal word with preserving the intended effect of the original work. They also accommodate their translations to the prevailing literary styles of their age. Modern readers are accustomed to hearing and reading English that is clear, concise, and direct; consequently, given a choice of translations of literary classics, I favored translations that keep the spirit of the original in a modern idiom. Because modern translations emphasize the intended, rather than the literal, meaning of a work, I found it more appropriate to analyze these selections in terms of their meaning rather than in terms of the particular writer's use of language. Therefore, you will find a greater emphasis on connotative and figurative language in the questions that relate to the selections from North America and Great Britain and Ireland.

TEACHING OBJECTIVES

World Literature meets three primary objectives:

1. *To Foster an Enjoyment of Literature* A teacher's primary goal is to create or foster the love of learning in his or her students. Students should enjoy the experience of reading and discussing literature, whether because the

process is enjoyable or because the student finds it to be of personal value—or both. The variety of selections in *World Literature* provides something of interest and value for every student. I chose these particular selections because of their literary quality and because some aspect of each of them relates to students' own life experiences. In addition, each selection is interesting to read and stimulating to discuss. Students feel valuable and important when they can express their ideas in an accepting environment. Sharing their ideas with their classmates enables them to enrich their understanding of themselves and others.

2. **To Increase Awareness of Human Values, Attitudes, and Behavior** The second goal in teaching global literature is to encourage students to recognize a common humanity through time and across space. The selections in *World Literature* reveal that the human needs for love and friendship, for the respect of oneself and others, for a secure and beautiful environment, and for a sense of personal accomplishment know no boundaries. Students understand and sympathize with Antigone in ancient Greece, with Jade in eighth-century China, with Rosendo in Argentina, and with Nnaemeka in Nigeria. Their cultures differ from our own, but their stories teach us that the human bond that connects us is stronger than the differences that divide us. Equipped with this understanding, we no longer view what is foreign as necessarily threatening; instead, variety becomes stimulating and valuable and an opportunity to learn from others.

3. **To Analyze Literature** The third goal of teaching world literature is to analyze literature. This is valuable both as a way to appreciate each selection and as a means of learning to distinguish fine literature from ordinary writing. Students should be exposed to the best to learn how to distinguish it from what is ordinary or bad and, in the process, to develop a taste for the best. The Analyzing Literary Technique questions lead students to discover important keys to the artistic quality of each story, poem, and play in *World Literature*. Students will become aware of how a writer manipulates plot, narration, structure, and language to arouse particular reactions in the reader. As they learn to appreciate the writer's tools, students will become more discerning in what they read and more skillful in their own writing.

USING *WORLD LITERATURE* IN THE CURRICULUM

Because *World Literature* is an anthology of excellent short stories, poems, and plays, it is ideally suited for use as an integral part of the standard English curriculum or for a global literature elective. Moreover, it can be used in an English-social studies core program that focuses on the study of world cultures or as a literature supplement to a course in world history.

Student Materials

Each selection includes the following supporting materials in the student text:

- *An Introduction* highlights important biographical, historical, and literary information. It provides students with a framework for appreciating the selection while preserving their ability to discover and experience the work for themselves.

- *Footnotes* explain foreign words and allusions that appear in the selection to aid students' comprehension.
- *Interpretive and analytical questions* lead students toward an understanding of both content and style. These question are designed to stimulate class discussion and thoughtful analysis of important issues.
- *Essay and creative writing assignments* provide students with the opportunity both to analyze the work in depth and to enlarge upon it in an imaginative way. These writing assignments are also useful for purposes of evaluating students' knowledge and skills.
- The *Glossary of Literary Terms* at the back of *World Literature* defines terms and enriches students' appreciation of writing as an artistic pursuit.

Teacher Resources

This *Teacher Manual* includes the following supporting materials for each selection:

- An *Introduction* provides an authoritative literary analysis of the work.
- *Questions for Private Literary Journals* help each student relate in personal terms to an important theme in the selection.
- A *list of Literary Terms* alerts you to the importance of these techniques in the selection.
- *Comprehension questions and answers* test factual knowledge of each selection.
- *Answers to all Understanding the Selection and Analyzing Literary Technique questions* help you prepare for class discussion.
- *Notes about essay and creative writing assignments* help you prepare for students' writings.
- *AP icons* identify essay questions that may be useful in helping students prepare for the Advanced Placement exam.
- *Suggestions for Further Reading* enable you to guide interested students toward additional works by the same author.
- *Extending Your Reach questions* at the end of each unit offer you additional synthesis and Advanced Placement preparation questions to give students more opportunities to practice writing.

In addition to the materials that relate to each selection in *World Literature*, this *Manual* provides you with suggestions for discussing the selections, for teaching expository writing, and for evaluating and testing students' knowledge and skills.

Alternate Tables of Contents

The table of contents in *World Literature* organizes the selections by geographical location. The Appendix in the student text lists a thematic table of contents, which is echoed in this *Manual* in Chart B. The following three charts organize the selections by genre, by theme, and by literary technique.

CHART A

Selections Organized by Genre

	Short Story	Play	Poem
The Mediterranean			
Akhenaton			◆
David			◆
Sappho			◆
Sophocles		◆	
Catullus			◆
HaNagid			◆
Dante			◆
Pardo Bazán	◆		
Pirandello	◆		
García Lorca			◆
Hikmet			◆
Mahfouz	◆		
Continental Europe			
Schiller			◆
Andersen	◆		
Dostoyevsky	◆		
Tolstoy	◆		
Ibsen		◆	
Lagerlöf	◆		
Chekhov	◆		
Colette	◆		
Rilke			◆
Kafka	◆		
Akhmatova			◆
Sartre	◆		
Camus	◆		
Africa			
Dahomey			◆
Casely-Hayford	◆		

	Short Story	Play	Poem
Africa (continued)			
Paton	◆		
Senghor			◆
Dadié			◆
Lessing	◆		
Gordimer	◆		
Achebe	◆		
Ogot	◆		
Soyinka		◆	
Head	◆		
Asia and the South Pacific			
Li Po			◆
Jiang Fang	◆		
Li Qingzhao	◆		
Rumi			◆
Hafiz			◆
Nguyen Binh Khiem			◆
Tagore		◆	
Mansfield	◆		
Lu Hsün	◆		
Akutagawa	◆		
Kawabata	◆		
Shen Congwen	◆		
Ting Ling	◆		
Hayashi	◆		
Narayan	◆		
Desai	◆		
Grace	◆		
South and Central America			
de la Cruz			◆
Mistral			◆
Bombal	◆		
Borges	◆		

	Short Story	Play	Poem
South and Central America (continued)			
Neruda			◈
Rosa	◈		
Cortázar			◈
Paz			◈
Solórzano		◈	
Castellanos			◈
García Márquez	◈		
North America			
Zuñi			◈
Whitman			◈
Dickinson			◈
O'Neill		◈	
Hemingway	◈		
Eliot			◈
Hughes			◈
Welty	◈		
Munro	◈		
Hébert			◈
Walker	◈		
Great Britain and Ireland			
Anonymous			◈
Chaucer	◈		
Shakespeare		◈	
Wordsworth			◈
Arnold			◈
Barrett Browning			◈
Brontë			◈
Rossetti			◈
Conrad	◈		
Yeats			◈
Joyce	◈		

Selections Organized by Theme

	family	fantasy and imagination	friendships	the individual and society	justice and dignity	love and romance	the natural world	roots and origins	self-discovery	values and beliefs	war and peace	youth and age
The Mediterranean												
Akhenaton								◆		◆		
David								◆		◆		
Sappho			◆							◆		
Sophocles	◆			◆	◆							
Catullus	◆		◆									
HaNagid							◆	◆		◆		
Dante						◆						
Pardo Bazán						◆			◆	◆		
Pirandello	◆			◆					◆		◆	
García Lorca			◆						◆	◆		
Hikmet	◆			◆	◆					◆		
Mahfouz		◆		◆					◆			◆
Continental Europe												
Schiller							◆			◆		
Andersen		◆								◆		
Dostoyevsky				◆						◆		
Tolstoy	◆			◆						◆		
Ibsen	◆			◆	◆	◆			◆	◆		
Lagerlöf	◆		◆			◆						
Chekhov				◆		◆						
Colette						◆						
Rilke							◆			◆		
Kafka		◆		◆					◆			
Akhmatova				◆		◆					◆	
Sartre				◆						◆	◆	
Camus			◆		◆					◆		

	family	fantasy and imagination	friendships	the individual and society	justice and dignity	love and romance	the natural world	roots and origins	self-discovery	values and beliefs	war and peace	youth and age
Africa												
Dahomey								◆		◆		
Casely-Hayford	◆							◆				◆
Paton			◆	◆						◆		
Senghor								◆		◆		
Dadié							◆	◆		◆		
Lessing							◆		◆			
Gordimer							◆		◆			
Achebe	◆					◆						
Ogot	◆			◆		◆				◆		◆
Soyinka	◆			◆					◆			
Head	◆			◆		◆		◆				
Asia and the South Pacific												
Li Po				◆							◆	
Jiang Fang						◆				◆		
Li Qingzhao						◆						
Rumi							◆			◆		
Hafiz				◆						◆		
Nguyen Binh Khiem							◆			◆		
Tagore		◆	◆	◆						◆	.	◆
Mansfield	◆								◆		◆	◆
Lu Hsün	◆			◆	◆					◆		
Akutagawa								◆		◆		
Kawabata							◆			◆		
Shen Congwen	◆	◆		◆								
Ting Ling				◆	◆					,	◆	
Hayashi				◆	◆						◆	
Narayan	◆			◆	◆							
Desai	◆			◆						◆		◆
Grace	◆			◆					◆	◆		

	family	fantasy and imagination	friendships	the individual and society	justice and dignity	love and romance	the natural world	roots and origins	self-discovery	values and beliefs	war and peace	youth and age
South and Central America												
de la Cruz				◆		◆				◆		
Mistral							◆			◆		◆
Bombal	◆				◆	◆			◆			
Borges			◆		◆				◆			◆
Neruda							◆		◆			
Rosa	◆	◆		◆								◆
Cortázar	◆	◆	◆	◆								◆
Paz						◆				◆		
Solórzano						◆		◆				
Castellanos			◆			◆						
García Márquez		◆		◆	◆					◆		
North America												
Zuñi							◆			◆		
Whitman				◆			◆		◆			
Dickinson			◆							◆		
O'Neill	◆			◆			◆			◆		
Hemingway	◆			◆					◆	◆	◆	
Eliot				◆						◆		
Hughes				◆	◆		◆			◆		
Welty				◆	◆							
Munro			◆	◆	◆							◆
Hébert												◆
Walker	◆			◆		◆				◆		
Great Britain and Ireland												
Anonymous	◆			◆	◆							
Chaucer		◆								◆		
Shakespeare	◆		◆	◆	◆	◆			◆			
Wordsworth							◆					◆
Arnold						◆	◆			◆		

	family	fantasy and imagination	friendships	the individual and society	justice and dignity	love and romance	the natural world	roots and origins	self-discovery	values and beliefs	war and peace	youth and age
Great Britain and Ireland (continued)												
Barrett Browning						◆			◆			
Brontë				◆						◆		
Rossetti	◆	◆	◆							◆		
Conrad				◆					◆	◆		
Yeats							◆			◆		
Joyce				◆						◆		◆

CHART C

Selections Organized by Literary Technique

	allusion	antihero	apostrophe	characterization	comedy	connotative language	dialogue	doppelgänger or Shadow
The Mediterranean								
Akhenaton			◆					
David								
Sappho	◆		◆	◆				
Sophocles	◆					◆	◆	◆
Catullus	◆		◆		.			
HaNagid	◆							
Dante			◆					
Pardo Bazán				◆				
Pirandello				◆				
García Lorca	◆		◆					
Hikmet			◆					
Mahfouz				◆				
Continental Europe								
Schiller	◆							
Andersen				◆				◆
Dostoyevsky				◆				
Tolstoy				◆				
Ibsen				◆			◆	◆
Lagerlöf								
Chekhov				◆				
Colette				◆				
Rilke			◆					
Kafka								
Akhmatova	◆							
Sartre		◆		◆				◆
Camus		◆		◆				

	epiphany	figurative language	foreshadowing	free verse	hero	imagery	irony	leitmotif or motif	lyric	narrative perspective	paradox	reversal	satire	setting	sound device	symbolism	theme	tone	tragedy
									◆		◆							◆	
		◆							◆								◆	◆	
					◆				◆										
		◆	◆		◆		◆		◆	◆	◆	◆				◆	◆	◆	◆
		◆							◆							◆	◆		
		◆							◆									◆	
					◆				◆										
	◆	◆	◆													◆			
		◆					◆				◆	◆	◆			◆	◆	◆	
		◆				◆	◆								◆	◆	◆	◆	
		◆					◆		◆			◆				◆	◆	◆	
			◆				◆							◆		◆	◆	◆	
		◆					◆		◆		◆					◆	◆	◆	
							◆				◆		◆			◆	◆		
							◆			◆	◆		◆			◆	◆	◆	
		◆			◆	◆	◆				◆		◆			◆	◆		
		◆	◆		◆		◆				◆		◆				◆		◆
		◆		◆					◆				◆		◆				
							◆	◆		◆	◆		◆	◆				◆	
		◆					◆	◆			◆						◆	◆	
	◆			◆					◆									◆	
							◆	◆		◆	◆			◆		◆	◆	◆	
	◆								◆								◆		
							◆			◆	◆					◆	◆		
							◆			◆				◆		◆	◆		◆

	allusion	antihero	apostrophe	characterization	comedy	connotative language	dialogue	doppelgänger or Shadow
Africa								
Dahomey								
Casely-Hayford				◆				
Paton				◆				
Senghor								
Dadié								
Lessing						◆		
Gordimer				◆				
Achebe				◆				
Ogot				◆				
Soyinka	◆	◆		◆	◆		◆	
Head				◆				
Asia and the South Pacific								
Li Po						◆		
Jiang Fang				◆				
Li Qingzhao								
Rumi	◆		◆					
Hafiz								
Nguyen Binh Khiem								
Tagore								
Mansfield				◆				◆
Lu Hsün				◆				
Akutagawa				◆				
Kawabata			◆			◆		
Shen Congwen				◆				
Ting Ling						◆		
Hayashi				◆				
Narayan				◆				
Desai				◆				
Grace				◆				

epiphany	figurative language	foreshadowing	free verse	hero	imagery	irony	leitmotif or motif	lyric	narrative perspective	paradox	reversal	satire	setting	sound device	symbolism	theme	tone	tragedy
	◆					◆							◆			◆	◆	
						◆									◆	◆		
	◆	◆				◆			◆						◆	◆		◆
	◆			◆	◆							◆	◆	◆	◆			
	◆				◆			◆					◆		◆			
◆	◆					◆			◆			◆			◆	◆		
						◆			◆		◆	◆		◆	◆	◆		
		◆				◆						◆			◆	◆		
	◆					◆			◆		◆							
						◆				◆	◆		◆				◆	
	◆		◆			◆			◆			◆			◆			
	◆					◆		◆							◆			
		◆		◆		◆			◆			◆			◆			◆
			◆														◆	
			◆												◆	◆		
	◆		◆												◆			
			◆															
						◆			◆		◆	◆			◆	◆	◆	
◆		◆							◆						◆	◆	◆	
						◆			◆			◆			◆			◆
						◆			◆			◆			◆			
						◆			◆					◆	◆	◆	◆	
	◆					◆										◆	◆	
	◆					◆							◆	◆	◆	◆	◆	◆
		◆				◆						◆				◆	◆	
		◆				◆			◆	◆						◆		◆
	◆					◆			◆		◆	◆					◆	
		◆				◆						◆				◆	◆	

	allusion	antihero	apostrophe	characterization	comedy	connotative language	dialogue	doppelgänger or Shadow
South and Central America								
de la Cruz			◆					
Mistral						◆		
Bombal				◆		◆		
Borges	◆	◆		◆				◆
Neruda	◆							
Rosa		◆		◆				◆
Cortázar	◆							
Paz								
Solórzano					◆	◆	◆	
Castellanos								
García Márquez	◆			◆				
North America								
Zuñi			◆					
Whitman			◆			◆		
Dickinson						◆		
O'Neill				◆			◆	
Hemingway				◆				
Eliot	◆			◆		◆		◆
Hughes			◆	◆		◆		
Welty				◆	◆			
Munro				◆				
Hébert								
Walker	◆			◆				
Great Britain and Ireland								
Anonymous								
Chaucer				◆				
Shakespeare				◆	◆		◆	
Wordsworth								
Arnold	◆		◆			◆		

epiphany	figurative language	foreshadowing	free verse	hero	imagery	irony	leitmotif or motif	lyric	narrative perspective	paradox	reversal	satire	setting	sound device	symbolism	theme	tone	tragedy
																	◆	
	◆							◆									◆	
	◆					◆	◆		◆	◆			◆		◆			
		◆				◆			◆	◆					◆	◆		
	◆					◆		◆						◆				
													◆		◆			
	◆	◆				◆									◆			
	◆			◆				◆					◆	◆				
		◆				◆				◆			◆	◆	◆			◆
				◆		◆		◆						◆	◆			
						◆				◆	◆				◆	◆	◆	
	◆			◆				◆							◆			
		◆			◆			◆		◆			◆		◆			
										◆							◆	
		◆		◆		◆	◆			◆			◆	◆	◆	◆		◆
◆													◆		◆	◆		
	◆	◆		◆				◆		◆			◆	◆	◆	◆		
	◆	◆													◆	◆		
	◆								◆	◆			◆		◆		◆	
						◆	◆			◆					◆			
	◆			◆													◆	
	◆					◆	◆		◆					◆	◆			
	◆					◆			◆	◆			◆			◆	◆	
		◆				◆										◆		
	◆	◆				◆				◆	◆			◆		◆	◆	◆
	◆							◆		◆			◆			◆	◆	
						◆				◆			◆		◆	◆	◆	

	allusion	antihero	apostrophe	characterization	comedy	connotative language	dialogue	doppelgänger or Shadow
Great Britain and Ireland (continued)								
Barrett Browning								
Brontë						◆		
Rossetti				◆		◆		◆
Conrad		◆		◆				◆
Yeats						◆		
Joyce	◆							

TECHNIQUES FOR TEACHING SELECTIONS IN *WORLD LITERATURE*

This section of the *Manual* includes specific suggestions for using the many instructional aids that are included in *World Literature*.

Private Literary Journal

The use of a Private Literary Journal (P.L.J.) allows students to relate in a personal way to the principal issues and values in each selection while retaining their right to privacy. Consequently, these journals must remain the private property of their authors, and P.L.J. prompts should not become the focus of class discussion.

The P.L.J. concept is to be used after your students have read the introduction in the student text but before they read the selection itself. The open-ended P.L.J. writing prompts motivate students to think about their own attitudes and experiences before they encounter the protagonist's choices in the selection, thus providing an additional framework for understanding and appreciating the selection. To preserve your students' opportunity to discover and experience each selection for themselves, do not discuss the relationship that exists between the P.L.J. prompts and issues in the work that they are about to read.

Selection Introductions

Studies in the psychology of learning reveal that just as seeds strewn on cement will not sprout, people cannot understand, remember, and enjoy what they read without a background or framework that enables them to relate the selection to some aspect of their own experience. The two introductions to each selection— one in the student text and one in this *Teacher Manual*—provide this framework.

Introductions in the Student Text. The introductions in the student text provide you and your students with a framework for understanding and appreciating each selection and its author while permitting your students to discover and experience the work for themselves. These introductions contain information about the author's stature, the author's life, factors in the culture that influenced the author, and aspects of the author's literary focus that relate to the selection. Most introductions in the student's text are about a page in length; however, the discussions

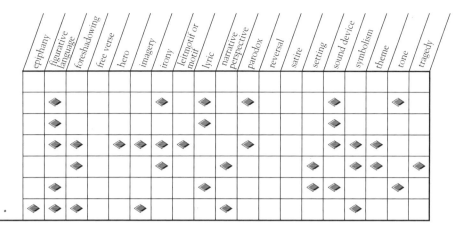

epiphany	figurative language	foreshadowing	free verse	hero	imagery	irony	leitmotif or motif	lyric	narrative perspective	paradox	reversal	satire	setting	sound device	symbolism	theme	tone	tragedy
	◆				◆		◆		◆				◆			◆		
	◆						◆						◆					
	◆	◆		◆	◆	◆	◆		◆				◆	◆	◆			
	◆				◆			◆				◆		◆	◆			◆
	◆							◆					◆	◆		◆		
◆	◆	◆			◆			◆						◆				

of *Antigone*, *Much Ado About Nothing*, "The New Year's Sacrifice," "Life," and "Voronezh" have been extended to provide additional information that will help students understand and appreciate the work.

Introductions in the *Teacher Manual*. The introductions that appear in this *Manual* provide you both with an authoritative literary analysis of each selection and with a way to relate the work to human behavior so that you can help your students gain insights into themselves and others. These are not the only possible literary analyses. Any analysis that can be supported with details from the selection and that is consistent with all of the details in that selection may be equally valid. However, these introductions will give you a foundation on which to build; they supply the framework for the possible answers contained in this *Manual* to the questions that you will find under Understanding the Selection and Analyzing Literary Technique in the student text.

List of Literary Terms
The list of Literary Terms that follows the P.L.J. assignment tells you the stylistic devices that you will find in a particular selection. The Analyzing Literary Technique questions involve a discussion of how most of these techniques are used in the work. In the student text, these terms are boldfaced the first time they are used for each selection, and each term is defined in the Glossary of Literary Terms. The writing assignment will often ask students to analyze what the writer achieves by using one or more of these techniques. Such assignments can also be used as part of an evaluation of your students' knowledge.

Reading for Understanding and Appreciation
One way to advise students to prepare for a discussion is the following. Ask them to read the selection twice, first quickly and then slowly. Their initial, superficial reading acquaints them with the general content of the selection and provides a framework for integrating the knowledge that they acquire from their careful reading. The second reading builds upon the first and increases your students' ability to understand and appreciate the selection's content, structure, and language.

Following their second reading, ask your students to write down their opinions of the selection, the reasons for these opinions, and any questions they might have about the work. Any response is acceptable as long as the student can support it with details in the selection, but a summary is unnecessary. Students should focus on the selection that is about to be discussed, not on other works or experiences. Finally, give each student a chance to contribute to the preliminary discussion before beginning the open discussion to allow each student an opportunity to contribute something personal. This approach validates each individual's response to the work before that response is influenced by the opinions of others.

Before beginning any discussion of the work, you may wish to use the Comprehension Questions that appear with each selection in this *Manual*. The Comprehension Questions are one way for you to be certain that your students have read the selection and have grasped its obvious points. You may use the questions for discussion or to evaluate the knowledge of your students.

Discussing Selections

As a teacher, I recommend conducting class discussions by using the Socratic method, a method of shared inquiry. This method involves asking open-ended interpretive questions to which more than one correct answer often exists, and it places the burden of the discussion and the answers on the students rather than on the teacher. Some answers are better than others in that they are consistent with all of the details in the selection. However, students will often have different opinions that are equally supported by details in the selection, and to close a discussion without resolving all differences of opinion is perfectly acceptable.

It often works best to open a discussion with a preliminary activity in which you call upon each student to read from his or her prepared response. Without being critical, question anyone whose response is based on incorrect facts or whose opinion needs clarification. Remember, however, that a response to a work of literature depends as much upon the experiences and attitudes of the reader as upon an accurate reading. It is important to give everyone the opportunity to contribute before the open discussion occurs.

This approach enhances students' self-esteem and encourages their active involvement in a literature program. The Socratic method enables students to become active and involved participants in their own education. Many among them will read the selection more than twice to be able to contribute to the discussion, and you will find that they will discover many of the issues that you choose to discuss.

You may find it useful to take notes on your students' responses. These notes may remind you of questions to discuss, and they enable you to give your students credit for their opinions and ideas.

When everyone has contributed, you are ready to discuss the selection. There are three sources of questions available to you: your students' questions, your own questions, and the questions that follow each selection in *World Literature*.

Understanding the Selection. The Understanding the Selection questions focus on understanding the content of the work on an interpretive level. They emphasize inferential thinking and open-ended class discussion, and they prepare students for thoughtful essay and creative writing. Because the questions may have more than one correct answer, this *Manual* provides a variety of possible answers. You and your students may find other answers, and you should accept any answer that is consistent with all of the details in the selection.

Certain answers in this *Manual* are marked with an asterisk. These asterisks relate to particular assignments in Writing About Literature. You may discuss these questions as preparation for the assignment, or you may use them to evaluate your students' knowledge. For example, the questions that relate to characterization and theme are excellent ways of evaluating your students' knowledge of a particular selection.

Analyzing Literary Technique. The Analyzing Literary Technique questions focus on the structure and style of the selection so that students will be able to appreciate it as a work of art. These questions deal with such aspects as narrative perspective, foreshadowing, irony, symbolism, and figurative language. Each term is defined in the Glossary of Literary Terms at the back of the student text.

Like the questions in Understanding the Selection, these questions prepare students for thoughtful essay and creative writing. They often have more than one correct answer, so this *Manual* provides a variety of possible answers. Here, too, your students may find other answers that are supported by specific details in the selection.

Once again, certain answers in this *Manual* have an asterisk preceding the question number. As with the Understanding the Selection questions, these asterisks relate to particular assignments in Writing About Literature. You may discuss these questions as preparation for the assignment or use them to evaluate your students' knowledge of the selection. For example, the questions that relate to narrative perspective and symbolism are excellent for evaluating your students' knowledge of a particular selection.

Glossary of Literary Terms

A Glossary of Literary Terms is located at the back of the student text. It defines the terms used in *World Literature*, including literary techniques, literary movements, and relevant psychological terms. At the end of each explanation, your students will find a sampling of the selections in *World Literature* that illustrate the use of that term. In this way, the Glossary prepares them to analyze the selections more thoughtfully and to write about them in greater depth.

Writing About Literature

Teaching Essay Writing. If your students need help with essay writing, and if you are not obligated to follow a particular method of instruction, you may find the following approach useful.

Begin the teaching of essay writing with a formal approach, because a specific format enables students to understand exactly what to do and how to do it. Try using the short stories and poems in *World Literature*, because these provide enough detail to allow students to learn how to write a structured essay. The three parts of a short, structured essay are: an introduction that states the subject of the essay and provides background material; at least one core paragraph that states the major point of the essay, discusses two or three examples, and uses direct quotations to support each of these examples; and a good conclusion. (These components are discussed in greater detail in Evaluating and Grading an Essay on page xxxvii.)

Once students are comfortable with the procedure, they move on to the complexity of longer works, such as novels and plays. These more complex essays support three or more core paragraphs, each of which discusses a major point, supported by three or more examples from the selection. Finally, students who have mastered this approach may discard the rigid structure and write interesting essays that, regardless of length, are both organized and scholarly.

Thinking must precede writing. Begin the writing assignment by giving students two concrete pre-writing activities as independent work in class. This allows you to supervise and evaluate each student's individual performance. First, ask students to brainstorm possible topics related to the assigned subject and to gather and make note of the direct quotations from the selection that support each topic. In this way, they will realize that some topics do not receive enough support in the text to be suitable for an essay, while other topics may be strengthened by grouping them. Close examination of the selection enables students to choose their major points and to be certain of their supporting details before they progress to their next step.

The next step in the writing process is developing an outline. An outline will reveal problems at the pre-writing stage, when it is easy to find and correct them. Each example that supports the major point of a core paragraph must have two subpoints: first, a direct quotation that supports that example; and second, the student's explanation of how or why that quotation supports both the example and the major point. When it is complete, the outline contains all of the ideas that each student will include in his or her first draft of the essay.

Since students now know exactly what they are going to say, they are free to concentrate on how well they can express their ideas and create smooth transitions in a first draft. Meanwhile, you will have been observing their work in process, answering their questions, asking leading questions, praising their strengths, and evaluating their progress.

Note that without proper planning, students' essays may be weak in two areas. First, students may not support their examples with direct quotations from the text, and consequently they may make statements about the selection that are wrong. Second, when they use direct quotations, they may not explain how each quotation relates both to the example it supports and to the point of the paragraph; consequently they may choose inappropriate quotations. Their analysis of these quotations is a major aspect of their essays, and it permits you, the instructor, to evaluate their intellectual growth.

Writing an Essay. Each selection in *World Literature* is accompanied by at least one suggestion for an essay that emphasizes critical thinking skills. These assignments may involve analyzing the author's use of a particular literary technique or the way in which the work is consistent with the principles of a particular literary movement; these terms are defined in the Glossary of Literary Terms. Suggestions for focusing or organizing the essays may also be included.

The explanations of these writing assignments in this *Manual* are often followed by such directions as "See **U.P.** (or **A.L.T.**) question X above." This direction refers you to the answers with the asterisks that relate to this particular assignment. (**U.P.** and **U.S.** refer to Understanding the Poem, the Play, or the Story; **A.L.T.** refers to Analyzing Literary Technique.) You may discuss these questions as preparation for the assignment, or you may use them to evaluate your students' knowledge of the selection.

Some of the essay assignments are marked in this manual with an AP icon **AP**. These icons indicate essay-writing assignments that may help your students prepare for the Advanced Placement exams.

Writing Creatively. Each selection in *World Literature* is accompanied by at least one suggestion for creative writing that invites students to enlarge on some aspect of the selection in an imaginative way. For example, some assignments involve continuing a story or telling it from the point of view of a different character. The instructions usually include the choice of writing in prose or in poetry and questions to help students focus their creative piece.

Students who are uneasy about writing poetry may find the following technique helpful. First, they should write their selection in prose, with attention both to detail and to descriptive language. Next, they should remove all but the essential words from each sentence and arrange these words in a poetic form that pleases them. (Many students find it easiest to write in free verse, without the constrictions of regular rhythm and rhyme.) Finally, they should revise to improve the poetic content and form of their work by sharpening the focus of their ideas and by improving their choice and arrangement of words.

The explanations of the creative writing assignments in this *Manual* are often followed by "(**P.L.J.**)," which refers to the students' Private Literary Journal. Students' responses to the P.L.J. prompts may lead them to imagine how another character might respond to the situation presented in the selection. Occasionally, the directions "See **U.P.** (or **A.L.T.**) question X above" refer you to the answers with the asterisks that relate to this particular assignment.

Extending Your Reach

New to this edition are questions called Extending Your Reach. These questions appear at the end of each geographical unit in this *Teacher Manual* and give you additional essay-writing options to offer your students, whether by asking students to compare and contrast the treatment of a theme in several selections or to analyze a literary technique across several selections. These additional questions may assist you in further evaluating your students' knowledge and writing skills or in helping them prepare for the Advanced Placement exam.

Evaluating Students' Knowledge and Skills

Using Tests for Evaluation. The Comprehension Questions and answers for each selection in this *Manual* are a fine way to evaluate whether students have read each selection and understood the facts. Many of the questions in Understanding the Selection, such as those devoted to characterization and theme, and in Analyzing Literary Technique, such as those devoted to narrative perspective, irony, and symbolism, are excellent for testing and evaluating more sophisticated knowledge. Depending on the ability of your students, you may use them as they are or expand upon them.

Using Essays for Evaluation. Essay writing is a superb test of the knowledge and skills that your students have acquired. In writing an essay, students must select, organize, analyze, and draw conclusions about some aspect of a work of literature. Many of the essay assignments that deal with characterization or with an analysis of a particular literary technique are excellent for this purpose. These are often very similar to the questions under Analyzing Literary Technique that support them, but they are expressed in a more complex form and demand a more complex response.

You may want to give one of these essay assignments as a test to be written in class. Allowing students to use their texts for such a test enables them to use direct quotations to support their ideas. You might remind your students to outline their points before beginning to write so that they will know what they are going to write and where to look for their documentation.

In a longer and more complex essay, you might evaluate students' critical thinking skills and knowledge by having them compare and contrast two selections that have already been discussed individually in class. While it is possible to write such an essay by discussing first one work and then the other, it is more effective to take one point at a time and to compare or contrast the two selections side by side.

Moreover, if you have exposed your students to a complete analysis of one selection in *World Literature*, you might evaluate their knowledge and skills by assigning them a similar selection in their text to read and analyze independently. To feel comfortable with this type of assignment, your students must know how to analyze a particular aspect of a selection, such as characterization, theme, or style, as well as how to write such an essay.

One approach to preparing students for this kind of essay is to assign the reading of the selection as homework and to use the next class period for pre-writing activities. In this way, you will be able to provide encouragement and support and evaluate how each student is progressing. You might make the outline the focal point of the assignment and evaluate that. Another approach is to assign the entire project as an independent activity. If your students know your expectations and have had enough experience in writing about literature, they will perform well without your direct supervision.

The three charts in this *Manual* that organize the selections by genre, by theme, and by literary technique (pages xvii–xxxi) will guide you to selections to compare and contrast. For example, the stories by Alan Paton and Nadine Gordimer deal with apartheid in South Africa, those by Fyodor Dostoyevsky and Lu Hsün focus on the plight of the outcast in society, those by James Joyce and Doris Lessing focus on initiation, and those by Fumiko Hayashi and Ernest Hemingway deal with the aftermath of war. The plays by Sophocles and Eugene O'Neill may be paired as tragedies, and the stories by Joseph Conrad and Franz Kafka may be paired as night journeys. Moreover, to focus on an analysis of literary technique, you might pair the story by María Luisa Bombal with the poem by Christina Rossetti to analyze leitmotifs or pair the poem by Friedrich von Schiller with the story by Jean-Paul Sartre to analyze paradox.

Evaluating and Grading an Essay. If you are not obligated to follow a particular method for evaluation and grading, you may find the following approach useful. Try assigning numerical values to components of an essay and make students aware of this grading system. As you mark each essay, keep a running tally of the score in the margins and base the student's grade on the total score. This method underscores how valuable a good outline is in writing a good essay.

You, as the teacher, create your own point system that reflects your priorities for the essay. The following example sets forth one method that you might use to evaluate and grade a five-paragraph essay, where a perfect score would be 100 points or an A. In this example, the points have been allocated so as to emphasize and reward the student's analysis of the selection. However, you might choose to allocate them to emphasize and reward the student's use of structure, language, and mechanics or to emphasize and reward the priorities that best suit your objectives for the essay.

In the sample essay, a good introductory paragraph (for a total of 10 points) contains a thesis sentence that states what the essay is going to be about (1 point); an organizing sentence that lists the three major points to be discussed in the three core paragraphs (3 points); and some background material on the subject (6 points). The background material might include a brief summary of related aspects of the plot if the focus of the essay is characterization or theme or a statement about the general importance of the particular literary technique discussed in the essay. The purpose of the background information is to interest readers in the subject and to give them a framework for understanding and appreciating the essay. Students are free to arrange this information in an effective way, usually beginning or ending with their thesis sentence.

The evaluation of the three core paragraphs focuses on ideas, supporting details, and analysis (25 points for each paragraph). Each paragraph contains a topic sentence that sets forth the main point of the paragraph and connects it with the thesis idea (1 point). Three examples from the text follow (1 point each), each with a supporting detail in the form of a direct quotation (2 points each). In turn, each quotation is followed by the student's analysis, in a minimum of two sentences, of why this particular quotation supports the topic of the paragraph (5 points each).

A good concluding paragraph (for a total of 10 points) briefly summarizes the subject (5 points) and expresses the student's evaluation of its importance in the literary work (5 points).

Finally, the essay is judged for its overall quality of expression (for a total of 5 points), including word choice (1 point), interesting sentence structure (1 point), use of transitions (1 point), correct spelling (1 point), and correct punctuation (1 point).

This is one example of using a point system to evaluate and grade a student essay. The points will change depending on the weight you give to each category.

Motivating Students. Nothing is more frustrating for a teacher than to spend an hour correcting an essay only to have the student look at the grade, ignore the instructor's comments, and make the same mistakes in the next essay. To give your students a sense of responsibility for their own progress, try keeping an anecdotal record of each student's work that is available to the student and that includes the type of errors the student makes on each assignment. This record tells you what to focus on and the extent to which you are succeeding; it tells students that you are watching to see if they are learning from their mistakes and that they are responsible to make sure that this learning occurs. If a student continues to make the same type of errors, you and the student should confront the problem together.

Additional Reading
One of the objectives of *World Literature* is to foster an enjoyment of good literature, and this *Teacher Manual* provides additional resources to give to students who want to further their knowledge of a particular writer.

Further Reading. At the end of the discussion of each selection in this *Manual*, you will find a list of other works, usually by the same author, that will interest you and your students. The selections are available in paperback or from the library. You might enrich your program by having a group of students read and discuss a particular selection or by having different students read different selections and then share their responses with the class as a whole.

Selected Bibliography. This *Manual* concludes with a Selected Bibliography of secondary sources. This Bibliography supplements the selections in *World Literature* and includes biographical materials, works of literary criticism, and, occasionally, autobiographical materials such as letters and diaries. The Bibliography correlates with the organization of *World Literature* and the writer to which each reference work relates. Since these works are continually being reissued or reprinted, more recent editions may be available. Moreover, new reference works continue to be published.

The Mediterranean

ANALYZING LITERARY TECHNIQUE: POSSIBLE ANSWERS

1. *Apostrophe* The use of apostrophe creates a sense of immediacy and a sense of intimacy between the speaker and the Aton. The speaker assumes that the Aton is present and that the god is listening to his hymn.

2. *Paradox* It is paradoxical that the sun is distant, yet its rays are near. It is also paradoxical that its rays are visible, yet its plans and strength are hidden. Both paradoxes reveal the great power of the Aton.

*3. *Contrast* Examples of contrast: life/death; light/darkness; day/night. The contrasts reveal the power and beneficence of the sun.

*4. *Tone* The tone is one of joy and well-being, achieved through numerous positive examples of the Aton's power.

5. *Lyric poem* This is a lyric poem in that it expresses the personal thoughts and feelings of the speaker and emphasizes descriptive detail.

WRITING ABOUT LITERATURE

1. *Essay analyzing use of detail* Call students' attention to the directions and suggestions in the textbook assignment. Note that stanzas 2, 4, and 5 provide excellent detail. The poet's use of elaborate detail reveals the poet's appreciation of the power and beneficence of the Aton and establishes the tone of joy and prosperity. (See **U.P.** questions 1 and 2 and **A.L.T.** questions 3 and 4 above.) **AP**

2. *Creative writing: hymn to a god of a people who live in an unstable environment* An area with unpredictable weather might have a storm god, who would be angry or temperamental. The tone might be pleading. An area with aggressive neighbors might have a war god, who would support warriors who possess courage, strength, and skill in battle against their country's enemies. The tone might be heroic, a call to provide strength and to reward courage and skill. **(P.L.J.)**

FURTHER READING

Psalm 104 in the Bible.

Psalm 8

DAVID

INTRODUCING THE POEM

Psalm 8 is an eloquent testimony to the psalmist's view of God's glory and human dignity. The psalmist praises God for creating the magnificent heavens, and he marvels that such a gifted Creator would take such care with His creations. Given human limitations, it is wondrous that God has put all other forms of life under human domination and has chosen humans to combat His enemies. According to the psalm, God has made mortals only a little lower than the angels and has given mortals power, honor, and glory. The psalmist praises God for His universe and for the special place of human beings in that universe.

The psalmist's striking contrast between the magnitude and beauty of the heavens and the fragile mortality of human beings dramatizes the irony and the glory of human stature. The vertical movement of the psalm from the heavens down to the forms of life beneath human feet creates a visual picture of the hierarchy of power from God down to sea life. The psalmist's parallel repetitive phrasing contributes to the appeal and power of the psalm. It is interesting to compare Psalm 8 with Sophocles's "Ode To Man" (a chant by the chorus in *Antigone*, lines 376–416). Both works portray the bond between God and human beings. Both Psalm 8 and Sophocles's ode consider the unique place that human beings occupy in the universe. The psalmist expresses the excellence of both God and human beings, but human beings occupy in the universe. The psalmist's primary focus is God. Human beings are God's creation; God has made them "a little lower than the heavenly beings." Sophocles, however, describes the physical power and intellect of human beings as inborn traits, not divine gifts. Human beings are limited by their inclination to error. When human beings act imprudently, they are rejected by their fellow human beings, not by the gods. Death is the only force that is beyond human ability to conquer.

Personal Literary Journal: In your opinion, what aspects of the universe are most awesome? What aspects of human beings are most remarkable? To what extent, if any, could aspects of either the universe or human beings be improved? List your ideas.

Literary Terms: Contrast, irony, lyric, ode, parallelism, theme, tone, voice

COMPREHENSION QUESTIONS

1. *According to the psalmist, what did God do for human beings?* God created them "a little lower than the heavenly beings" and gave them power and glory.

2. *According to the psalmist, what do human beings do for God?* fight His enemies

UNDERSTANDING THE POEM: POSSIBLE ANSWERS

*1. *The psalmist's attitude toward God* God created a wondrous universe. Most remarkable, He chose to give human beings an important role in this universe and to give them power, honor, and glory. Human beings praise God both for the universe and for their place in it.

*2. *The unusual aspect of the psalm* The psalmist places as much emphasis on what God has done for human beings as on what God has done in the universe, so the psalmist is glorifying humans as well as God. One might expect that the glorification of God would have resulted in an emphasis on the insignificance of human beings.

3. *Importance of human beings* The psalmist uses both content and structure to call attention to the importance of human beings. The psalm's structure involves a spatial arrangement that demonstrates the hierarchy of power— from God to human beings to creatures underfoot and in the seas. Human

beings are described as being only a little lower than the angels; they have been given power over all life on earth and in the seas. The psalmist may have taken his descriptions of nature from chapter 1 of Genesis.

*4. *Themes* The psalm contains two primary themes: the excellence of God and the glory of His name on earth and the excellence of human beings, who are only "a little lower than the heavenly beings."

5. *Psalm 8 and Sophocles's "Ode to Man"* Whereas the psalmist expresses the excellence of both God and human beings, human beings are the sole focus of Sophocles's ode. In Psalm 8, the psalmist's primary focus is God. Whatever the psalmist says about human beings glorifies God because God created human beings. The psalmist ignores the limitations of human beings and their inclination to error. In Sophocles's ode, the physical power and intellect of human beings are described as inborn traits, not divine gifts. When human beings cast aside good judgment and act imprudently and inhumanely, they are cast out by other human beings, not by the gods. Death alone is beyond man's ability to conquer.

ANALYZING LITERARY TECHNIQUE: POSSIBLE ANSWERS

1. *Irony* The psalmist uses contrast to create irony. By presenting the range of God's achievements—the heavens, human beings, and animals—the psalmist magnifies the awesomeness of God. Given the greatness of creation, it is ironic that God would care more about human beings and their inherent worth than He does about birds, fish, and other animals. God uses "children and infants" to defeat his enemies, and ironically the human beings are able to fulfill this task.

2. *Lyric poetry* The lyric derives its name from the lyre, a small stringed instrument in ancient Greece. Lyric poems were intended to be sung to the accompaniment of a lyre. In content, they are short expressions of the thoughts and the feelings of the speaker. In style, they emphasize pictorial imagery and sound rather than drama or narrative. Psalm 8 is a lyric poem in both style and content; it was probably sung in the Temple to the accompaniment of a lyre.

3. *Parallelism* Parallelism creates rhythm through the repetition of phrase patterns. Examples: "What is man . . . / the son of man . . ." "You made . . . / and crowned . . ." "everything under his feet: / All flocks and herds, / and the beasts of the field, / the birds of the air, / and the fish of the sea." The repetitions add a rhythmic quality to the poem.

*4. *Tone* The psalmist's tone is one of adulation and praise. It is achieved by listing God's great creative acts and the creatures that human beings are to dominate. Only positive attributes are mentioned. The psalmist does not discuss death, illness, cruelty, or injustice.

5. *Function of the "envelope" technique* The "envelope" technique creates a repetition that pleases the ear and emphasizes the theme. The central part of the psalm provides details that amplify the theme.

*6. *Lyric and Ode:* Psalm 8 is lyric poem; its expresses the personal thoughts and emotions of the poet. It may originally have been part of public worship in the Temple, with a chorus singing the opening and closing lines. The poet, focusing on the glorification of God, conveys his deep joy as he views the universe that God has created.

The "Ode to Man" in *Antigone* (lines 376–416) is a more formal type of lyric poetry. It is a serious philosophical commentary on the nature of human beings. It is chanted in a dignified manner by the members of the chorus. *Antigone* would have been performed for the public in ancient Athens, where drama was part of religious celebrations. Like Psalm 8, Sophocles's poem has a single focus. However, Sophocles presents a more objective view of human nature. He points out that human beings have both positive traits (physical strength and creative intelligence) and negative traits (the inclination to act imprudently, without considering the consequences of their actions). Sophocles's balanced view gives the poem an impersonal tone.

WRITING ABOUT LITERATURE

1. *Essay analyzing tone of Psalm 8* Students should focus their essay on the nature of God, the nature of human beings, and the relationship between God and human beings. (See **U.P.** questions 1, 2, and 4 and **A.L.T.** questions 4 and 6 above.) **AP**

2. *Creative writing: a psalm* A psalmist might ask God for help in making human beings respectful of those who are different from themselves or in making human beings wise enough to end poverty, cure illness, and create peace. **(P.L.J.)**

To an Army Wife, in Sardis

SAPPHO

INTRODUCING THE POEM

Sappho's poem is a love letter. It may be a letter from Sappho to a friend who is now married to a soldier, or it may be a letter from a soldier to his wife. Either way, the speaker argues that whatever one loves is the finest sight on earth.

The speaker's argument has a circular structure (a-b-c-b-a). The speaker argues as follows: (a) Others say [stanzas 1 and 2]; (b) I say [stanza 2]; (c) an example from days of old proves my point [stanzas 3–5]; (b) therefore, I say that I am correct [stanza 6]; and (a) the others are wrong [stanza 7].

The speaker alludes to Helen of Troy, who left her husband, King Menelaus, in Sparta to live in Troy with Paris (son of Priam and Hecuba, the Trojan king and queen). Rather than return Helen to the Greeks, the Trojans fought the Trojan War to defend their palace-state against the Greek siege. However, after ten years the Greeks entered the walled city by hiding inside the Trojan horse.

Troy fell in flames, Paris was killed by Achilles' son (the great warrior Achilles had died earlier), and Menelaus took Helen back to Sparta.

The appealing subject matter, the artful quality of the speaker's reasoning, the appropriate nature of the allusion, the pictorial detail, and the sincerity of the emotional component all contribute to the great charm of the poem.

Personal Literary Journal: If you want to convince someone that your opinion is correct and well founded, what do you do? Is it enough to state your opinion, or do you need to support your opinion with reasons? Explain your reasoning.

Literary Terms: allusion, apostrophe, contrast, lyric

COMPREHENSION QUESTIONS

1. *Who is the speaker of this poem?* probably Sappho, but possibly a soldier
2. *Where is the speaker?* probably back home, but possibly away from home
3. *What is the speaker's argument?* whatever one loves is the finest sight on earth
4. *What event in Greek mythology is alluded to in the poem?* the Trojan War
5. *What emotion is expressed in this poem?* love; longing

UNDERSTANDING THE POEM: POSSIBLE ANSWERS

1. *Speaker* a) The speaker is probably Sappho. The lines "although you / being far away forget us" imply that Anactoria has forgotten more than one person. It is possible that Anactoria has left Sappho and her friends to go off with her soldier-husband (as Helen went off with Paris) and that she has made no effort to communicate with those back home who love her. b) The major reason for believing the speaker to be the soldier-husband is the striking use of military details. However, Sappho lived through politically tumultuous times and was probably familiar with the sights that she describes. Viewing the speaker as the soldier-husband involves overlooking three problems: (1) the use of "us" in the lined quoted above; (2) the direct comparison between Anactoria and Helen, both of whom have gone off with a loving male and have left loved ones behind; and (3) the fact that Sappho usually wrote about her own experiences and emotions.

   Either choice of speaker is legitimate, because the emotion is what is most important in the poem; the emotion is conveyed regardless of who the speaker is.

2. *Opinions of others* The technique of contrasting the opinions of others sets the speaker apart and emphasizes the superiority of her or his opinion.

3. *Anactoria's forgetting the speaker* If the speaker is Sappho, it is likely that Anactoria has not forgotten the friends she left behind when she accompanied her husband; she has simply become very involved in her new life. If the speaker is Anactoria's husband (who is apart from Anactoria), it is unlikely that Anactoria has forgotten him, though he may feel lonely and homesick because he has received no word from her.

ANALYZING LITERARY TECHNIQUE: POSSIBLE ANSWERS

1. *Appeal to the senses* The poem comes alive with visual military images: cavalry corps on glittering Lydian horses, armored infantry, and the swift oar-powered naval fleet. The visual appeal is enhanced by the elaboration of the opening descriptions in the concluding lines.

2. *Contrast* Sappho uses contrast to dramatize the speaker's distinctive viewpoint that individuals determine what is most beautiful to them.

3. *Apostrophe* Apostrophe adds the personal touch of direct address. It creates a sense of immediacy, as though Anactoria were able to hear the speaker's words.

*4. *Allusion to Helen of Troy* Helen left her husband, King Menelaus, in Sparta to live in Troy with Paris. Anactoria is like Helen in that she has gone off with a loving male and has left other loved ones behind. The allusion to Helen also relates to the theme of beauty, since Helen was considered to be the most beautiful woman of her time.

WRITING ABOUT LITERATURE

1. *Essay on Helen of Troy* You will need to direct students to the resource center or to the neighborhood library for books on Greek mythology. If you prefer, you may bring an appropriate selection of books into the classroom. Possible authors include Alfred Church, Padraic Colum, Robert Graves, Roger L. Green, Edith Hamilton, and Rex Warner. The textbook *World Mythology*, Third Edition, by Donna Rosenberg (Glencoe, © 2000), includes the story of the *Iliad*. (See **A.L.T.** question 4 above.)

2. *Creative writing: Anactoria's response* Call students' attention to the suggestions in the textbook assignment. Note that background reading will enhance this assignment. **(P.L.J.)**

FURTHER READING

Sappho, *Greek Lyrics*.

Antigone
SOPHOCLES

INTRODUCING THE PLAY

Theater performances in Athens in the fifth century B.C. were given at the Great Dionysia, a religious and civic festival that occurred each spring in honor of the god Dionysus. The open-air theater was located in the area sacred to the god. The actors were all men, who wore robes and large masks that they changed when they changed roles. Actions were stylized, and violence always occurred offstage. In Sophocles's time, tragedy was a developing dramatic form that had originated with a Chorus that sang and danced in honor of Dionysus. Thespis added an actor, Aeschylus a second actor, and Sophocles a third. Sophocles also invented painted scenery.

Sophocles wrote his plays to be performed and judged in the dramatic competitions that were part of the festival honoring Dionysus. Each playwright would submit a group of four plays (three of them tragedies), and a committee would choose three groups of plays for performance in each day's competition. In these festivals Sophocles won first prize for twenty-four groups of plays.

Each day during the festival, seventeen thousand spectators would watch the day-long dramatic competition. They always knew the subject of each tragedy because playwrights were expected to choose their material from the well-loved stories that made up Greek mythic history (pre-seventh century B.C.). The Theban cycle of myths was so popular that several versions still exist: *Oedipus the King, Oedipus at Colonus*, and *Antigone* by Sophocles; *Seven Against Thebes* by Aeschylus; and *The Suppliant Women* and *The Phoenician Women* by Euripides.

The seven existing complete plays of Sophocles were found in Byzantine textbook anthologies. In modern times a large part of an eighth play has been found on papyrus in Egypt, where many Greek plays were imported between 300 and 200 B.C.

Antigone is a play about the conflicting rights of the state and the individual. Creon believes that the law must always be obeyed, whereas Antigone believes that one's religious duties are more important than civil laws. However, *Antigone* is much more than an "idea play." It is a play of conflicting personalities. If ideas were the only issue, it would have been possible to consider an acceptable compromise between the two positions. Instead, the personalities of Creon and Antigone do not permit compromise. As the drama evolves, worthy principles become secondary, both to Creon's pride and his growing hatred of Antigone and to Antigone's belief in the importance of being true to her personal values. No character escapes the tragic consequences of this confrontation.

Antigone is enjoyable because it appeals to the intellect as well as to the emotions. One group of intellectual issues involves questions such as the following: Is there anything or anyone more important than the good of the state? What takes priority when issues of state directly conflict with religious principles? What does the citizen owe the state? What does the state owe the citizen?

In the fifth century B.C., loyalty to one's city-state was a practical necessity. The frequent wars between city-states were a threat to life, freedom, and property. Massacre, pillage, and enslavement accompanied defeat. Thus, the welfare of the individual and the family was dependent upon the welfare of the city-state. The Athenians had seen their great city burned by the Persians, and they could understand Creon's attitude toward the burial of invading warriors.

However, far older values were still honored along with the newer ones. People were reared in a tradition that viewed family relationships as the strongest and most important ties. Proper burial and mourning rites, even of enemies, were required. This was primarily the women's domain, except that warriors on foreign soil were responsible for their own dead. People believed that they would live forever with the consequences of their behavior on earth.

Loyalty to the state clashes with loyalty to the family in this play. While Creon eloquently articulates what the citizen owes the city, he ignores what he as king owes the citizens. Antigone is determined to bury Polynices because it is important in her society to honor family ties and religious conventions and because she believes that these values take precedence over a royal edict.

A second group of intellectual issues involves questions about the role and value of women in society. Even in a society where a woman's primary roles are rearing children and burying the dead, her responsibilities are important to the welfare of her community. Is it ever right to treat a human being as an object—even if that person has a different political, economic, or social status? Creon places the rights and status of women on a par with the rights and status of slaves, whom he also treats as objects.

A third group of intellectual issues involves family relationships. What do fathers owe their sons and sisters owe their siblings? Do the living have more responsibility toward their living siblings or toward those who have died? In the fifth century B.C., authority in the family resided with the father, who expected unquestioning obedience from his children. Obligations to the dead simply involved proper funeral rites; then the family could devote its attention to the living.

While these intellectual issues provide the framework for the play, the characters in Antigone are not symbols of principles: They are real people with real strengths and weaknesses. Because they are inherently well meaning and they take positions that make sense, all of the characters elicit some degree of understanding and sympathy.

Sophocles introduces Creon and Antigone at a point where they are at odds with each other and they are under great stress. They are both so committed to the principles by which they live that they do not understand the other's point of view, and they ignore advice, even when it is in their own best interests to be flexible. In a masterful way, Sophocles dramatically plays these two characters off each other and off the minor characters who love them. The process gradually reveals what type of people Creon and Antigone are and how they are responsible for their own tragic fates. Even when they are not likeable, they are heroic. Their principles are admirable, and they stand up to their destinies with dignity.

Creon's actions fit the psychological pattern typical of many great people in Greek myth. Excellence in ruling Thebes after Laius's death (aretē) makes Creon excessively proud of his ability as a ruler (hubris). His pride leads him into rash behavior, the blind recklessness of atē. In his legitimate and admirable pursuit of justice, he issues an edict that defies conventional religious practices. In an important sense, this is Creon's fatal step, because respect for the gods reminds mortals of their human limitations. What follows is not surprising. Creon becomes inflexibly attached to the merit of the edict, imposes the death penalty on anyone who defies it, and then repeatedly ignores all suggestions that conflict with his ideas.

At the end of the play, Creon's behavior brings disaster on himself and his family (nemesis). Too late he sees that Antigone was partially correct when she criticized him for being motivated by hatred. Under stress, he has seen others only in terms of what they should do for him, and the only person he has respected and loved has been himself. Haemon's death makes Creon realize that although he is king, he is still only a human being. Finally, with dignity, he accepts responsibility for his behavior and his fate.

Antigone is the Sophoclean hero who is willing to die for her convictions. She is as concerned with justice as Creon is, but her concept of what is right differs dramatically from his. Whereas Creon focuses on the needs of the city-state and the obligation of citizens to obey the law, Antigone is preoccupied with the needs of family and the obligations of religion. Going to her death alone, Antigone suddenly realizes that she has acted as she has not only because of religious principles but because of feelings deep within her that go beyond religious duty.

The translation of *Antigone* in *World Literature* is complete and unabridged. It includes a passage (lines 995–1004) that has been omitted in the translation by Fitts and Fitzgerald on the theory that it is inconsistent with a traditional interpretation of Antigone's character (that she died for her religious principles) and that, therefore, Sophocles did not write it. Although its authenticity is still debated, many leading scholars accept this passage as the work of Sophocles and find it to be consistent with his ability to portray psychologically complex characters. Not only did Aristotle accept the passage (less than a century after Sophocles) and imply that it was well known, but he used part of it in his treatise on rhetoric.

In the disputed lines, Antigone reveals that her motive is not solely to fulfill her religious duties; she is acting in a way that is consistent with her love for her brother and her deepest personal values. This analysis is consistent with the fact that no one in the play indicates that religious law requires Antigone to risk martyrdom and that Ismene's attitude supports the idea that religious obligations do not require disobedience to civil law.

Sophocles dramatizes the virtues of "the golden mean" in human behavior by revealing the terrible consequences that may result from rigid attitudes and extreme actions. He was aware of the paradox that rigid adherence to an inherently good cause may produce evil results. This is true of both Creon's adherence to his belief that the citizen is obligated to be loyal to the state and Antigone's adherence to her belief that the citizen is obligated to be loyal to religious principles and family needs. Their self-righteous attitudes toward their own principles cause both Creon and Antigone to disregard the reality of conflicting loyalties; in the end, paradoxically, each of them wins a disastrous victory.

Sophocles emphasizes this important psychological lesson by creating Haemon as a foil for Creon and Ismene as a foil for Antigone. Both minor characters exhibit rational thinking and self-control and plead the virtues of these values against the destructive values of passion and inflexibility. Ismene's relationship to Antigone is particularly important because of its psychological dimension. The sisters, whom Creon treats as if they are twins, function as alter ego (literally, "other I") to one another and represent two sides of one human personality. Antigone functions as Ismene's darker, passionate, and unrestrained self (in psychological terms, as Ismene's doppelgänger), and Ismene represents the values that were prized by the ancient Greeks. Haemon and Ismene are unsuccessful in their efforts to influence Creon and Antigone, and the audience learns from the ensuing tragedy the danger of behavior that is based on uncontrolled passion.

No discussion of *Antigone* is complete without emphasizing the beauty of the lyric odes that are recited by the Chorus. In connotative and figurative language that no writer has ever surpassed in eloquence, the Chorus speaks about the nature of the human condition.

Personal Literary Journal: What qualities must a person possess to earn your respect? Would you ever disobey the laws of your community and country? If so, under what circumstances?

Literary Terms: allusion, alter ego, antagonist, *aretē*, *atē*, catastrophe, catharsis, characterization, chorus, climax, conflict, connotative language, contrast, crisis, discovery, doppelgänger, figurative language, foil, foreshadowing, *hubris*, irony, lyric, myth, *nemesis*, ode, paradox, protagonist, resolution, reversal, symbol, theme, tragedy

COMPREHENSION QUESTIONS

1. *What edict does Creon issue?* not to bury Polynices
2. *Why does he do this?* He considers Polynices a traitor.
3. *How does Antigone react?* She defies Creon and attempts burial.
4. *How does Ismene react?* helpless; offers to die; afraid to be alone
5. *What advice does Haemon give Creon?* The people sympathize with Antigone, so Polynices should be buried.
6. *How does Creon punish Antigone?* has her walled up in a vault
7. *What happens to Haemon?* After finding Antigone dead, he tries to kill Creon and then kills himself.
8. *What does Tiresias do in the play?* prophesies doom for Creon
9. *Why does Creon make the decisions he does?* thinks he knows best
10. *What is Creon's attitude toward women?* no respect; treats them like slaves

UNDERSTANDING THE PLAY: POSSIBLE ANSWERS

*1. *Antigone:*

a) *Antigone's attitude toward laws of Thebes* Antigone will not obey political laws that conflict with religious practices. She does not view herself as a traitor, because she feels that her cause is just.

b) *Why Antigone risks death to bury Polynices* She believes that displeasing the gods is worse than displeasing Creon; she loves Polynices; and she believes that it is essential for people to act on their beliefs.

c) *Why Antigone won't let Ismene join her* Antigone wants to be rewarded for her courage by a glorious death. She views Ismene as a coward who doesn't deserve to share her reward. Antigone also sees no reason for Ismene to die for a cause that Ismene does not believe in. Antigone wants Ismene to publicize her deed because she believes death with glory is better than life or death without glory.

The Hymn to the Aton

AKHENATON

INTRODUCING THE POEM

"The Hymn to the Aton" praises the beauty, goodness, creative powers, and universal presence of the sun. The Aton's light drives away darkness, with its danger and risk of death. With daybreak, all of nature flourishes and joyfully offers praise to the one god. The Aton creates all life and the reproductive capacities of all life. The Aton also provides what each form of life needs for sustenance. As the son of the Aton, only Akhenaton knows the Aton's plans and strength.

Through the use of contrast (day and night, light and darkness, life and death), repetition, and enumeration of examples, the poet creates a paean to the sun's awesome powers in a land of secure political borders and economic well-being.

In addition to its inherent appeal as a work of literature from the fourteenth century B.C., "The Hymn to the Aton" is interesting as it compares, in idea and wording, to Psalm 104 (lines 11–14; 20–26) in the Bible. Some scholars think that the psalmist knew "The Hymn to the Aton" and consciously patterned part of Psalm 104 on the earlier poem.

Personal Literary Journal: What aspects of nature do you find most powerful? Most worthy of praise? Most frightening? Explain the reasons for each of your choices.

Literary Terms: apostrophe, contrast, lyric, paradox, tone

COMPREHENSION QUESTIONS

1. *What is the Aton?* the sun
2. *What type of power does the Aton have?* power to create all life and sustenance
3. *What characterizes the Aton's absence?* danger and death
4. *What does Ahkenaton know about the Aton?* the Aton's plans and strength

UNDERSTANDING THE POEM: POSSIBLE ANSWERS

*1. *Nature of the Aton* The Aton is unique, universal, and beneficent. Functioning as a combined mother and father, the Aton creates and sustains all life. All of the Aton's creations are good and beautiful. Have students find examples of supporting details.

*2. *How life reacts to the Aton* Every living thing is conscious of its creator, revels in the sustenance and beauty of the Aton's light, and offers praise to it. Have students find examples of supporting details.

3. *What the view of the Aton reveals about the poet's world* The beneficent nature and accomplishments of the Aton reflect a satisfied and optimistic people living in a fertile, prosperous, peaceful, and secure environment.

d) *How Antigone would have fared if she had treated Creon with respect* On the basis of Creon's response to Haemon, Creon probably would have shown no mercy toward Antigone.

e) *Antigone's ambivalence about her sacrifice* On the way to the tomb, Antigone laments that her principles and her love of Polynices force her to give up love, marriage, and children. She is not ambivalent—she regrets her great loss.

f) *Antigone's heroic qualities* Antigone's motives are consistent with religious laws and are based on love and loyalty. She recognizes right and wrong, acts in accordance with her convictions, and accepts the punishment for her beliefs.

g) *Danger in behavior like Antigone's* Antigone's devotion to her principles and her attitudes toward advice and death make her a fanatic. Religious, political, and social fanatics are a danger to the established order because no prohibition can stop them from attempting to take the law into their own hands.

*2. Creon:

   *a) *Creon's edict as an emergency decree; Creon's right to issue such an edict* It is important that Creon's edict is an emergency decree because this reveals that the law breaks custom. According to Tiresias, who says that the laws of the gods take precedence over laws of a king, Creon has no right to issue such an edict. Creon later says, "It's best to keep the established laws / to the very day we die" (lines 1237–38).

   *b) *Greek concepts* Aretē (excellence): Creon is a good man who possesses the leadership qualities of a good king. *Hubris* (excessive pride): As king, Creon feels that everything is within his power. His *hubris* leads to *atē* (rash behavior based on excessive pride, which the Greeks called "blind recklessness"): He enacts his emergency decree making it illegal to bury those who attacked the city; the law applies to his nephew Polynices. Creon's *nemesis* (retribution), which occurs at the end of the play, is the suicides of his wife and his son.

   c) *Possible for Creon to honor Eteocles and still to bury Polynices* It would have been possible to honor Eteocles and still to bury Polynices. Creon could have given Eteocles a different ceremony and could have buried him in a different location. Because everyone is entitled to proper burial, Polynices' burial would not have been an injustice to Eteocles.

   d) *Important that Haemon is sole surviving son of Creon* Creon's behavior toward Haemon shows how harsh Creon is. One would expect that Creon would value Haemon's advice more highly and be more flexible in his response to his only son.

   e) *Creon's attitude toward disobedience* Creon's attitude toward disobedience reveals that he respects neither humans nor gods.

f) *Why Creon changes nature of Antigone's sentence* Haemon reveals to
Creon the Theban support for Antigone and reminds him of his obli-
gations to be sensitive to the needs and interests of his people. Burying
Antigone alive with food permits divine (or other) intervention, and
Creon does not have to risk further defiance by forcing the Thebans to
stone Antigone to death.

g) *Creon's responses to Tiresias show disrespect for gods* Tiresias speaks for
the gods and their values. When Creon accuses Tiresias of prophesying
for personal profit, he demeans Tiresias, his role, and his message.
Creon's statement that he is free to do whatever he chooses because
"we can't defile the gods— / no mortal has the power" (lines 1156–57)
is insulting and irreverent, revealing that Creon no longer recognizes
his place in the universe. Creon's responses reflect the psychological
pattern of *aretē*, *hubris*, and *atē* because it is his overestimation (*hubris*)
of his excellent qualities (*aretē*) and his feeling of omnipotence as king
(*hubris*) that lead him to criticize Tiresias (*atē*) and lose his perspective
in terms of his relationship to the gods (*atē*).

h) *Why Creon buries Polynices before rescuing Antigone* Creon buries
Polynices first because he puts duty to the state before duty to his
family. He realizes he has wronged the dead and offended the gods. In
addition, Creon has no reason to think that Antigone is in danger.

*i) *Creon motivated by hatred* Hatred of the enemy, particularly of Polynices
as the initiator of the attack, motivates Creon to issue the burial edict.
Hatred of anyone who defies his authority causes Creon to impose the
death penalty. Only after Haemon's death is Creon able to feel remorse
and to question his actions. Thus, Creon's feelings of hatred can be said
to have determined his fate. However, these feelings are not the sole
determinant. Creon's hatred is empowered by his political position,
and his excessive pride (*hubris*) motivates him to create and enforce
the edict (*atē*).

*j) *Creon as a tragic figure* Creon is a tragic figure in that he is a good man
who is qualified to be the king of Thebes. Unfortunately his excessive
pride in his ability and power as a ruler (*hubris*) leads to his rash action
of issuing the edict (*atē*), which in turn causes disaster for himself
(*nemesis*) and his family. Creon is also a tragic figure in that he causes
the tragedy within his family and he recognizes his errors too late to
make amends. The fact that he accepts his fate with dignity enhances
his tragic stature.

*k) *"Absolute power corrupts absolutely"* Creon is a capable leader who,
when he becomes king, treats criticism as treason and tramples on the
rights of the individual. These facts reveal the truth of Lord Acton's
principle as well as the truth of the Greek view that it is risky to be a
human being of great stature or power.

3. *Ismene:*

   a) *Different from Antigone* Ismene and Antigone are very different. Ismene is passive while Antigone is active. Ismene is subservient, accepting the conventional role of women in relation to Greek society and civil law, while Antigone is defiant of both. Ismene is fearful, while Antigone is courageous. Ismene is flexible, while Antigone is intransigent.

   b) *Ismene a coward* Those who would defend Ismene from the charge of cowardice would argue that if one obeys the state, perhaps the gods will forgive. Ismene is willing to die with Antigone. She questions Creon about the wisdom of his intent to kill Antigone and the effect of his ruling on Haemon. Those who would accuse Ismene of being a coward would argue that she lacks both convictions and courage. Ismene is afraid to die, but she is more afraid to be left without Antigone.

*4. *Haemon:*

   a) *Diplomatic elements in Haemon's speech* (1) Haemon accepts Creon's wishes; (2) Haemon says that another view is possible; (3) Haemon reveals the attitudes of the citizens but not his own; and (4) Haemon shows concern for Creon, not Antigone.

   b) *Haemon's concept of kingship* Haemon believes that rulers must consider the needs and attitudes of their people. A king must listen to advice, realize that he is not infallible, and demonstrate flexibility. Creon believes that a king always knows what is best for himself and for everyone else. Without the king's law, anarchy would occur; thus, the king's laws must be obeyed.

*5. *Chorus:*

   *a) *"For mortal men / there is no escape from the doom we must endure"* (lines 1457–58) Students might argue that Creon, Antigone, and Haemon could have chosen to behave differently: Creon and Antigone could have been more flexible; Haemon could have accepted Creon's behavior. Only Ismene has no choice, since her fate is determined by the actions of Creon and Antigone. However, given the personality of these characters, each could behave only as he or she did.

   *b) *"Love / you wrench the minds of righteous into outrage / swerve them to their ruin"* (lines 886–88) This concept applies to both Antigone and Haemon, each of whom commits suicide because of the death of a loved one. Haemon's suicide is complicated by his feelings about Creon's role in Antigone's suicide and by his own attempt to kill Creon.

   *c) *"No towering form of greatness / enters into the lives of mortals / free and clear of ruin"* (lines 687–89) This concept applies to both Antigone and Creon. Antigone is a loving sister who becomes the victim of her loyalty to Polynices. She disregards the loyalty she owes Thebes in favor of her obligation to give Polynices a religious burial. Yet no one indicates that religious law requires that Antigone become a martyr. On the contrary,

Ismene's attitude supports the idea that religious obligations do not require disobedience to civil law. Therefore, Antigone brings her fate upon herself, and in the process she inadvertently brings about Haemon's death as well.

Creon is a good man and a qualified ruler who becomes the victim of his kingship. Once he sees no limitation to the extent of his power, he is on a slippery slope toward destruction. He creates an unjust edict that defies religious principles and practices, and then he refuses to adapt it to extenuating circumstances or, better yet, to repeal it. As a result, he brings immediate disaster upon his family and himself and future disaster upon Thebes.

*6. *Themes at the end of the play* (lines 1466–70)

- "Wisdom is by far the greatest part of joy": One of the primary lessons of the Oedipus myth is that a lack of knowledge—especially self-knowledge—is destructive. In contrast, wisdom creates the possibility for happiness by revealing what may be a source of happiness.

- "Reverence toward the gods must be safeguarded": Whether or not people are religious, they must recognize that they are not free to behave just as they please, without regard for the rights of other human beings and the condition of the environment.

- "The mighty words of the proud are paid in full / with mighty blows of fate": The ancient concepts of *aretē*, *hubris*, *atē*, and *nemesis* remain a potential part of the human personality. People who act with too much pride still bring disaster upon themselves. Power still tends to corrupt, absolute power still corrupts absolutely, and human beings still have long memories when it comes to retribution.

- "At long last / those blows will teach us wisdom": People can learn from the experience of others, but it is a hard task to accomplish. The ancient Greeks did not learn from their history, although plays such as *Antigone* were designed to try to make the audiences more sensitive to these issues in their own lives.

ANALYZING LITERARY TECHNIQUE: POSSIBLE ANSWERS

1. *Function of minor characters*

a) Ismene is a foil for Antigone. She supplies the contrast of a sister who reacts in a significantly different manner to a crisis, and she represents the values that were important in ancient Greece. Ismene is the reasonable sister who exhibits rational thinking, self-control, and flexibility. Her attitude toward Antigone and Creon's attitude toward both sisters imply that Antigone and Ismene are alter egos for each other before Creon issues his emergency edict. The issue of Polynices' burial causes them to separate and to function as two sides of one human personality. Ismene's attitudes and behavior are characteristic of the Greek ideal of "the golden mean," while Antigone represents Ismene's darker, passionate, and unrestrained self that, in psychological terms, is called the double or the doppelgänger.

b) Haemon is a foil for Creon, revealing Creon's inhumanity. In addition, Haemon also reveals that the people support Antigone, and this foreshadows a tragic end for Creon.

c) Tiresias reveals the value of the gods to Creon and how the gods view both Creon and Antigone. The Chorus reveals the feelings and concerns of the people of Thebes and, by extension, of the audience. Both characters, therefore, represent forces in the world that are larger and more enduring than the personalities of the play's central characters.

2. *Late introduction of Antigone's engagement* This late information adds dramatic power, since it magnifies the conflict between Creon and Antigone. Antigone's engagement is not important either to Creon or to Antigone, only to Haemon.

*3. *Choice of title: the more important character* Antigone is the title because Antigone is the Sophoclean type of Greek hero, the one who dies for her convictions. Antigone is a more sympathetic character than Creon in that her motivation is more appealing than Creon's. However, Antigone and Creon are equally important. Creon is typical of many Greek tragic heroes, and the play does not end until he learns his lesson about life. However, Antigone's response to Creon creates the lesson. Much of the play's impact results from how Sophocles has interwoven Creon and Antigone so that they cannot be viewed as independent of each other. Students may disagree about which character is the protagonist and which is the antagonist; each character is both, depending on the perspective. Such a relationship between two kinds of heroes creates a taut, dramatic experience for the audience.

4. *Dramatic irony* For the informed audience, dramatic irony lends drama and suspense to the play. The audience knows something the character does not know and wonders how and when that character is going to learn it. Creon's certainty that a *man* has buried Polynices (beginning with line 277) reveals Creon's view of women as submissive, reinforces Ismene's amazement at Antigone's behavior, and reveals how unusual Antigone's defiance is. Creon refers repeatedly to a *man's* deed, with each repetition enhancing the drama of the situation. Because the audience knows the story—knows more than Creon does at the time—the suspense continues to build.

*5. *Paradox* Paradox is evident in the nature of the victories that Antigone and Creon win: Both victories are disastrous. Antigone persists in giving Polynices a symbolic burial despite Creon's decree, and she dies because of her defiance. Creon succeeds in killing Antigone, with the result that Haemon and then the queen commit suicide.

Paradox is also evident in the psychological concept that a person's greatest strength is often that person's greatest weakness. Both Antigone and Creon reveal the truth of this paradox. Antigone's devotion to her brother's burial is an admirable trait; however, when she persists despite the circumstances, her devotion becomes a fault of character. Creon's devotion to the state and his determination to enforce its laws are also admirable traits in a political leader; however, when Creon creates an unjust law and then kills anyone who defies it, these traits also become faults of character.

6. *Climax, crisis, and discovery*

- The climax occurs when Antigone goes to her death. This becomes the event that changes Creon's fate.

- The crisis, or turning point, occurs when Creon finally realizes that his attitudes and behavior toward Polynices and Antigone are contrary to important religious precepts and that, unless he can make amends, the gods will punish him. Dramatic irony makes this a powerful moment because it is too late for Creon to save anyone, including himself.

- The discovery, or recognition, occurs because of the catastrophe of Haemon's death. Creon realizes that he is a beaten man and that his own errors are responsible for Haemon's suicide. Creon's later acceptance of responsibility for the queen's death is part of the resolution, the projection of the action into a future beyond the play itself.

7. *Function of mythological allusions: Niobe, Persephone, Danaë* Antigone and the Chorus use these allusions to comfort Antigone. Niobe, Persephone, and Danaë all suffered terrible fates, but all were compensated by the gods for their sufferings.

WRITING ABOUT LITERATURE

1. *Essay evaluating Creon's leadership* Students may find it helpful to refer to their answers to **U.P.** questions 2, 4, 5, and 6 and to **A.L.T.** questions 3 and 5 above. Encourage students to consider the consistencies and inconsistencies between Creon the man—uncle, father, husband—and Creon the ruler of Thebes. **AP**

2. *Essay analyzing Creon's character in terms of the concepts of* aretē, hubris, atē, *and* nemesis You may wish to assign this as an alternate to the first **W.A.L.** assignment, to which it is closely related. This writing assignment challenges students to apply their new knowledge of the personality traits of classical characters. Students who wish a further alternative could apply these characteristics to the other major character in the play, Antigone. (See **U.P.** questions 1, 2, 4, 5, and 6 and **A.L.T.** questions 3 and 5 above.) **AP**

3. *Essay analyzing the relationship between the paradox in the "Ode to Man" (lines 376–416) and the dramatic irony of the action in* Antigone Call students' attention to the suggestions in the textbook assignment. Remind them that they should use quotations from the play to support their ideas. Antigone, Creon, and Haemon all behave in ways that reflect with dramatic irony the paradox expressed in this ode. Human beings are both wonderful and terrifying; they "[forge] on, now to destruction / now again to greatness" (lines 408–9). It is ironic that for all of their material well-being and

strength of personality, Antigone, Creon, and Haemon are unable to cope flexibly and creatively with the course of their lives.

4. *Creative writing:* Antigone *from Ismene's or Haemon's point of view* Call students' attention to the suggestions in the textbook assignment.

FURTHER READING

Aeschylus, *Seven Against Thebes*.

Anouilh, Jean, *Antigone*.

Brecht, Bertolt, *Antigone and Oedipus Rex*.

Cocteau, Jean, *The Infernal Machine*.

Eliot, T. S., *The Elder Statesman*.

Euripides, *The Suppliant Women* and *The Phoenician Women*.

Seneca, *Oedipus*.

Sophocles, *Oedipus the King* and *Oedipus at Colonus*.

Voltaire, *Oedipus*.

Though heart's hurt exhausts me always now

GAIUS VALERIUS CATULLUS

INTRODUCING THE POEM

Catullus designed this poem to function as a letter that would accompany the translations of Callimachus's poems that he was sending to a friend. The poem has a double focus: first, Catullus expresses his love for his brother who died suddenly in Troy; and second, he expresses his guilt over his delay in sending the translations to his friend. Catullus combines the theme of the loss of a loved one with the theme of guilt by explaining that his brother's death is responsible for his delay.

Catullus concludes his poem by expressing his sadness and guilt with a Homeric simile: A girl hides an apple that she secretly received from her lover; she forgets that she has hidden the apple until her mother comes in; when the girl stands up, the apple falls on the floor. The humorous nature of this simile contrasts with Catullus's elegiac lament for his dead brother, thus creating a situation in which the tone of the two themes is inconsistent. This duality may be seen either as a demonstration of the various natures of human beings, or as a means of softening the poem's impact on the reader.

Personal Literary Journal: Have you ever promised to do something for someone but then put off the task until it was too late? How did you feel? Did you do something to make up for your procrastination?

Literary Terms: allusion, apostrophe, elegy, figurative language, Homeric simile, lyric, metaphor, simile, theme, tone

COMPREHENSION QUESTIONS

1. *Why is Catullus unable to enjoy writing poetry?* His brother's death has numbed his emotions.

2. *Why is Catullus writing this poem?* to accompany the translations he is sending to his friend

UNDERSTANDING THE POEM: POSSIBLE ANSWERS

1. *Companionship of the Muses* The Muses enriched Catullus's life by inspiring his mind with ideas so he could write poetry. However, his brother's death has so shocked him that he feels unable to respond to the Muses' ideas.

2. *Effect of his brother's death* Catullus feels that his love for his brother and the sadness he feels will continue to cast a pall upon his life.

3. *The unexpected death* No one is prepared for the sudden death of a loved one. Those who grieve the loss are left reflecting on what they said or did not say and on what they did or did not do. A sudden death also reminds people of the unpredictability of life and their own mortality. Catullus's grief is intensified by these issues.

4. *Combining brother's death with the sending of the poems* Catullus is explaining that he has a legitimate reason for his inability to work on the translations: his brother's unexpected death. This "poetic letter" accompanied the poems that Catullus translated.

ANALYZING LITERARY TECHNIQUE: POSSIBLE ANSWERS

*1. *Apostrophe* By addressing someone who is not present, Catullus achieves the immediacy he would experience if that person were present. The fact that the poet is addressing his brother reveals that his brother remains alive in his memory.

*2. *Allusions* The Muses are Greek goddesses who provided poets with artistic inspiration. Catullus alludes to the Muses to convey the idea that he cannot continue with life as usual (that is, he cannot continue to write poetry because he is still traumatized by his brother's death).

   Lethe is the river of forgetfulness in the Underworld. When a deceased shade drinks from the river, the shade forgets everything about the past.

*3. *Similes* The nightingale is known for its beautiful singing, which Catullus describes as sad love songs. Catullus is like the nightingale in that his poems are his songs; and because of his brother's death, his songs, too, will be sad.

   A wind can blow a speaker's words away, making them impossible to hear. Catullus is concerned that his friend will think the words asking for a translation of Callimachus's poetry were not heard.

*4. *Homeric simile* A Homeric simile is an elaborate comparison that uses a story to convey an emotion or to describe an action. The forgotten apple, a secret gift from the girl's lover, falls in front of the girl's mother. When her secret love is revealed, the girl feels both sad and guilty.

Similarly, Catullus feels sad about his brother's death. Catullus's grief has made it difficult for him to concentrate on writing poetry. The poet feels guilty because he has neglected his friend's request for the translation of Callimachus's poems.

*5. *Verbs: "bring to birth," "hovers," "yanked," "wrung"* Without medication, giving birth to a child can be an extraordinarily difficult and painful process for a mother. Similarly, creating poetry is a difficult and painful process for the poet.

Something that hovers remains suspended above a person, an object, or a place. Catullus's mind hovers over his brother's death, which was so sudden and devastating that the poet cannot think about anything else.

To yank something is to pull it quickly, abruptly, and vigorously. Death has yanked Catullus's brother out of life, since the death was sudden and unexpected.

To wring something is to squeeze or twist it, usually to extract something from it. Just as the process of wringing can cause a person to feel pain, translating from one language into another is a painful process because a translation should not obscure the writer's meaning or the emotional, visual, or intellectual appeal of the original language.

*6. *Dual themes* The dual themes are loss of love (which relates to the unexpected death of Catullus's brother) and guilt (which relates to Catullus's delay in translating poems for his friend). The two themes are connected because the loss-of-love theme is the cause of the guilt theme.

*7. *Dual tones* The first tone of this poem is sadness, which reflects Catullus's grief over his brother's premature death. Catullus achieves this tone by describing his brother's burial and by expressing his shock, his love, and his loss.

The second tone is a humorous depiction of Catullus's guilt about his delay in sending the translations that his friend requested. Catullus achieves this tone by using a Homeric simile in which a girl attempts to hide an apple from her mother.

Evaluations of the success of using conflicting tones will differ. Some readers will appreciate the poem's realistic depiction of human nature; however, other readers will think that the internal conflict weakens the power of the poem.

*8. *Elegy and lyric* The word *elegy* is Greek in origin; it refers to a song of mourning. An elegy is a poem that expresses sorrow over someone's death. The part of this poem in which Catullus laments his brother's death is elegiac.

The word *lyric* is also Greek in origin; it refers to poetry that was recited to the accompaniment of a lyre. A lyric is a poem that expresses the thoughts and emotions of a poet or a speaker. This poem expresses Catullus's grief upon hearing of his brother's death and his guilt for not having sent the translations of Callimachus's poems to his friend.

WRITING ABOUT LITERATURE

1. *Essay analyzing Catullus's style* Call students' attention to the directions in the textbook assignment. Remind students to use quotations when discussing Catullus's conversational style and his use of allusions and figurative language. (See **A.L.T.** questions 1, 2, 3, 4, 5, 6, 7, and 8 above.) **AP**

2. *Essay analyzing the tone* Call students' attention to the directions in the textbook assignment. Each theme and its related tone should be presented in a separate paragraph. The conclusions should discuss the effect of having conflicting tones in one poem. (See **A.L.T.** questions 6 and 7 above.)

3. *Creative writing: prose or poetry expressing feelings about a loss* Call students' attention to the directions in the textbook assignment. Remind them to deal with the past, the present, and the future and to use figurative language. **(P.L.J.)**

FURTHER READING

Gaius Valerius Catullus's Complete Poetic Works (or any similar title).

Two Eclipses

SHMUEL HANAGID

INTRODUCING THE POEM

In this poem, HaNagid uses a lunar eclipse and a solar eclipse in 1044 to reflect upon God's great glory and power. He begins with the universe, and he devotes most of the poem to illustrating God's overwhelming power in the heavens and on earth. He considers God's creation of the sun, the moon, and the constellations—all of which help human beings by providing light, warmth, and guidance. He sees God's power in the eclipses of the moon and the sun, unseasonable weather, and tempests on land and sea.

HaNagid closes his poem with the idea that God has given human beings the inevitable fate of death and that he himself shares this destiny. HaNagid believes that God has given human beings the freedom to choose between good and evil. He also believes that God will hold human beings responsible for their behavior and will judge them when they die. He fears God's judgment of his own deeds. While he hopes that his righteous deeds will outweigh his evil deeds on God's scale of judgment, he counts on God's mercy if they do not.

Like the Egyptian "The Hymn to the Aton," HaNagid's poem addresses the glory, grandeur, and power of the divinity. The powerful effect of HaNagid's poem results from the figurative language that contrasts God's eternal overwhelming power with the frail mortal nature of human beings.

HaNagid's God toys with his creations. The eclipsed moon and sun are like women bereaved—the moon with a bruised face and the sun "both bruised and wounded." The poet likens God to "an angry king who brings trouble / on his lords in their own domains" or to "a king who prepared a poisonous cup / for his mistress, and then for his queen." God causes the earth to eclipse the moon as if the moon were "a bird caught in a snare," and He causes the earth to "reel like a drunkard." The earth is a shield upon which all whom God rules will be trodden. God "brings affliction into the sea / like a woman in labor," and just as an "arrow flies to its target," so God casts death (as one throws a weapon) toward all who live.

The poet's final image, the scale of divine justice, reflects God's power and connects it with the power of other divinities in ancient Mediterranean cultures. The scale was an important tool in ancient commerce; it determined the value of a quantity of goods. Therefore, it is not surprising that the principal divinities of many ancient cultures are depicted using scales to judge behavior. By calculating the balance between good and evil deeds during a person's lifetime, the divinity could determine the eternal fate of an individual. The scale of justice relates God's power to the poet's own life; it causes the poet to fear God's anger and to hope for God's mercy.

HaNagid's images are based on biblical images that were well known to his readers. The biblical context enriches HaNagid's figurative language by adding depth to the ideas that the images convey. For a complete list of these biblical references, see the chart at the end of the section.

Personal Literary Journal: What aspects of nature awaken your sense of awe (wonder and terror)? Consider what natural events cause you to wonder at their beauty or cause you to feel terror.

Literary Terms: allusion, figurative language, lyric, metaphor, personification, simile, tone, voice

COMPREHENSION QUESTIONS

1. (I) *At what time of day is the poet speaking?* late at night
2. (I) *What should the poet's friend see first?* the lunar eclipse, when the full moon becomes half dark
3. (I) *What should the poet's friend notice later?* the solar eclipse, when the sun is eclipsed by the moon
4. (III) *Who caused these events?* God
5. (II) *What two characteristics do these events reveal about their creator?* splendor and strength
6. (III) *How do these events affect the world?* With a lunar eclipse, night becomes darker because there is no moonlight. With a solar eclipse, daylight turns to dusk.
7. (IV; V) *What two attributes does the poet assign to the creator of these events?* greatness and glory
8. (V) *What do these events cause the poet to fear?* God's judgment of the poet's deeds after the poet dies
9. (V) *How should the poet lead his life?* remembering God's commandments, statutes, and law

10. (VI) *What response does the poet expect from God?* God will comfort him and tell him not to be afraid.

11. (VI) *For what two things does the poet hope?* his own righteousness and God's mercy

UNDERSTANDING THE POEM: POSSIBLE ANSWERS

1. *Response to the eclipses* The poet sees evidence of God's splendor, glory, strength, and greatness in these two natural events.

*2. *God's beneficial creative power* God created the moon, the sun, and the constellations known as Orion the Hunter and the Bear (probably the Big Dipper).

*3. *Examples of God's negative power* God causes heat in winter, winter in the middle of summer, earthquakes, typhoons and other storms at sea, and the mortality of all human beings.

*4 *The poet's day of judgment* The poet fears that his evil behavior might outweigh his righteous behavior on God's scale of judgment and that God will vent His fury and punish the poet.

*5. *The poet's ultimate consolation* The poet hopes that God will be merciful when judging him.

*6. *Comparison with Psalm 8* In "Two Eclipses" the poet emphasizes God's power over all of His creation, including over human beings. God's fearsome wielding of power causes human beings to feel a sense of awe. The poet closes the poem by worrying about his own fate. He hopes that his good deeds will outweigh his evil deeds on God's scale of judgment. If they do not, he counts on God to be merciful.

In Psalm 8, the psalmist accentuates the positive qualities of both God and human beings. Man is only a little lower than the heavenly beings, and God has given them glory, honor, and power over all of His other creation.

ANALYZING LITERARY TECHNIQUE: POSSIBLE ANSWERS

*1. *Organization* The poet begins and ends his poem with a personal immediacy that focuses on the human world, the microcosm. He begins by telling his friend to wake up and notice the moon and sun in the sky. He closes by expressing his fear that God will find him unworthy when God evaluates his life and his hope for God's mercy.

In contrast, the poet devotes the middle sections of the poem to God's role in the universe, the macrocosm. He emphasizes God's splendor, strength, greatness, and power and His influence on human life (suffering, mortality, and divine judgment).

These thoughts lead the poet to think of his own vulnerability, to fear God's judgment of his life, and to hope for God's mercy.

2. *Lyric poetry* The word *lyric* is derived from the lyre, a harplike instrument used in ancient Greece to accompany the singing of a poem. In content, lyric poems are short expressions of the thoughts and feelings of the

speaker. In style, they emphasize pictorial imagery and sound rather than drama or narrative.

*3. *Figurative language*

a) *Leopard skin stippled* In myths and legends, great heroes kill fearsome animals and then wear animal skins as trophies to celebrate their courage, strength, and skill. God is the world's greatest hero. The image of the leopard may have been chosen because it conveys the beauty and power of one of God's creations, which—despite its strength and skill—is subject to the greater power of its creator.

b) *Kettle, kiln, face of a girl, and Libyan princess* The kettle and the kiln reflect the activities (cooking and pottery making) of an ordinary person (a girl). They contrast with the crown of a Libyan princess, which resembles the halo of the sun as it is eclipsed by the moon.

c) *Reddened—as though with tears* When human beings cry, their faces become red. The poet is personifying the earth, who is tearful at the loss of its life-nurturing sun.

d) *Toys with creation* This metaphor implies that God, for His own amusement, causes the earth and those who live on it to experience pain. God has the power to bend his creations to His will, and He does so to suit his pleasure. Certainly lunar and solar eclipses—the celestial events that inspired the poet to write this poem—have no beneficial effect for the earth and those who live on it. However, they also have no harmful effect.

e) *Women bereaved* Both beacons (moon and sun) have lost their brightness and their power, so the moon and sun are personified as bereaved women. The moon is bruised in that its face is half flushed and half darkened in shadow (bruised). The sun's light has been reduced to a halo around the moon's shadow, so her face is both bruised and wounded.

f) *Two kings* Comparing God with "an angry king who brings trouble / on his lords in their own domains" and with "a king who prepared a poisonous cup / for his mistress, and then for his queen" emphasizes God's destructive powers. The poet does not reveal whether this behavior merits this royal retribution. The poet is depicting God as a divinity to be feared rather than loved.

g) *Other depictions of God* All three similes reveal the vulnerability of God's creations when faced with God's power. God is omnipotent (all-powerful)—a puppeteer pulling the strings of His puppets.

h) *A woman in labor and the arrow* Unaided by medication, a woman in labor often experiences intolerable pain. In fact, the Bible relates that God punished Eve for her disobedience in the Garden of Eden by making childbirth a painful process. The poet chooses to compare the affliction that God creates by causing storms at sea to the pain of a woman in labor. God is all-powerful, and the human condition is fraught with insurmountable difficulties.

The poet's declaration that God will "cast toward all the living—death, / as the arrow flies to its target" makes God responsible for death's being an inevitable aspect of the human condition. Death is certain, and God has determined that everything that lives will succumb to it.

*4. *Biblical sources* These biblical passages enrich the ideas that HaNagid is expressing in the following ways:

    a) *Lines 5–12* This passage connects the lunar and solar solstices witnessed by the poet with Judgment Day. It supports the poet's fear that God will judge him unworthy and will punish him.

    b) *Lines 45–46* This passage reveals that God is all-powerful, judgmental, and punitive. Those who live on the earth must behave righteously; otherwise, they will know God's punishment.

*5. *The scale of judgment* The scale was an important major economic tool in ancient commerce, where it determined how much a quantity of goods was worth. Therefore, it is not surprising that the principal divinities of many ancient cultures were depicted as using scales to judge the behavior of human beings who died. By calculating the relationship between each person's good and evil deeds during her or his lifetime, the divinity could determine the person's eternal fate.

    The poet's choice of the scale as his closing image connects the scale of justice with its ancient religious roots. The poet was aware that his readers were also familiar with this image, and therefore, this image would enhance the power of his poem.

*6. *Biblical passages revealing God's power and anger* The two eclipses remind the poet, who is steeped in biblical literature, that such unnatural events reveal God's power and His anger, so the poet chooses biblical sources that reflect these aspects of God. The poet ignores the last two lines of the biblical quotation because those aspects of God are irrelevant to him. In his poem, God's power and anger worry him, and he fears how God will judge him when he dies. If the poet were emphasizing God's goodness, mercy, and willingness to comfort human beings, he would be writing a very different poem.

*7. *Tone of "Two Eclipses" and Psalm 8* HaNagid's tone is one of awe. The poet accentuates God's terrifying power and the consequent vulnerability of human beings. In contrast, the psalmist's tone is one of adulation and praise. It is achieved by listing God's great creative acts and the creatures that human beings are to dominate. Only positive attributes are mentioned. The psalmist does not discuss death, illness, cruelty, and injustice.

    The poets are expressing different feelings. HaNagid expresses his feelings of vulnerability and fear as he observes God's dreadful use of power in the universe that He has created. HaNagid achieves his supplicatory tone by dwelling upon the idea that God toys with his creation and willfully uses the overwhelming power that He possesses. In contrast, the psalmist expresses the wonder and joy that he feels as he observes the universe that

God has created. He achieves his joyful tone by accentuating the many positive aspects of God's creations.

WRITING ABOUT LITERATURE

1. *Essay analyzing similes* Call students' attention to the directions in the textbook assignment. (See **A.L.T.** question 3 above.) **AP**

2. *Essay comparing the tone of "Two Eclipses" with the tone of Psalm 8* Call students' attention to the directions in the textbook assignment with regard to God and human beings. Remind them to use quotations from the two poems. (See **U.P.** questions 2, 3, 4, 5, and 6 and **A.L.T.** questions 1, 3, 4, 5, 6, and 7 above. See also Psalm 8: **U.P.** questions 1, 2, 4, and 6 and **A.L.T.** questions 4, 5, and 6.)

3. *Essay analyzing the effect of the biblical allusions* Call students' attention to the directions in the textbook assignment. (See **A.L.T.** questions 4 and 6 above.)

4. *Creative writing: a poem or story describing a natural event and a personal response* Call students' attention to the directions in the textbook assignment. **(P.L.J.)**

FURTHER READING

HaNagid, Shmuel, *Selected Poems of Shmuel HaNagid,* translated by Peter Cole.

NOTES COMPARING HANAGID'S LINES WITH BIBLICAL SOURCES

Poem Lines	Biblical Reference (from the *Jewish Masoritic Text*)
Line 2: Rise and wake the dawn.	*Psalm 57:9:* Awake, my glory; awake, psaltery and harp; / I will awake the dawn.
Line 4: like a leopard skin stippled above us,	*Jeremiah 13:23:* Can the Ethiopian change his skin, / Or the leopard his spots?
Lines 5–12: And see the moon where it should be full, / go dark like a kettle, or kiln, / like the face of a girl— / half of it flushed, / the other darkened in shadow. / Return and glance at the sun, / brought to the end of the month in dimness, / its halo of light on the darkness,	*Joel 3:4:* The sun shall be turned into darkness, / And the moon into blood, / Before the great and terrible day of the Lord come.
Lines 14–15: and the earth whose sun has set, / reddened—as though with tears	*Job 16:16:* (Job) "My face is reddened with weeping, / And on my eyelids is the shadow of death. . . ."

Poem Lines	Biblical Reference (from the *Jewish Masoritic Text*)
Line 19: He covered the moon with His circle of earth.	*Isaiah 40:22:* It is He that sitteth above the circle of the earth . . .
Lines 22–23: He fashioned patches of dark in the moon, / and the sun He created clear.	*Song of Songs 6:10:* Who is she that looketh forth as the dawn, / Fair as the moon, / Clear as the sun . . .
Lines 27–28: The face of the one is bruised, / the other both bruised and wounded.	*Isaiah 1:6:* (Concerning Judah and Jerusalem) From the sole of the foot even unto the head / There is no soundness in it; / But wounds, and bruises, and festering sores: / They have not been pressed, neither bound up, / Neither mollified with oil.
Lines 30–31: And the light of night darkened at evening / during the watch.	*Jeremiah 4:27–28:* For thus saith the Lord: / The whole land shall be desolate; / Yet will I not make a full end. / For this shall the earth mourn, / And the heavens above be black; / Because I have spoken it, I have purposed it, / And I have not repented, neither will I turn back from it. *Psalms 90:4:* For a thousand years in Thy sight / Are but as yesterday when it is past, / And as a watch in the night.
Lines 32–35: Like an angry king who brings trouble / on his lords in their own domains, / first He struck the brightness of night, / and afterwards blotted the daylight.	*Jeremiah 4:23:* (God) "I beheld the earth, / And, lo, it was waste and void; / And the heavens, and they had no light."
Lines 38–39: Behold what happened— look closely in wonder, / study it well, and read.	*Isaiah 63:5:* (God) "And I looked, and there was none to help, / And I beheld in astonishment, and there was none to uphold; / Therefore Mine own arm brought salvation unto Me, / And My fury, it upheld Me."

Poem Lines	Biblical Reference (from the *Jewish Masoritic Text*)
Lines 38–39: (continued)	*Jeremiah 4:24–26:* (God) "I beheld the mountains, and, lo, they trembled, / And all the hills moved to and fro. / I beheld, and, lo, there was no man, / And all the birds of the heavens were fled. / I beheld, and, lo, the fruitful field was a wilderness, / And all the cities thereof were broken down / At the presence of the Lord, / And before His fierce anger."
Line 41: who brought the light in its weight and measure	*Leviticus 19:35:* (God) "Ye shall do no unrighteousness in judgment, in meteyard, in weight, or in measure."
Line 43: like a bird caught in a snare	*Psalm 91:3:* That He will deliver thee from the snare of the fowler. *Proverbs 6:5:* Deliver thyself as a gazelle from the hand [of the hunter], / And as a bird from the hand of the fowler.
Lines 45–46: Looking onto the earth, / you'll make it reel like a drunkard.	*Isaiah 24:20:* The earth reeleth to and fro like a drunken man, / And swayeth to and fro as a lodge; / And the transgression thereof is heavy upon it, / And it shall fall, and not rise again. *Psalm 104:32:* Who looketh on the earth, and it trembleth; / He toucheth the mountains, and they smoke.
Lines 47–48: You've ordered the moth and it eats / the Bear and Orion in great constellation.	*Isaiah 50:9:* Behold, the Lord God will help me; / Who is he that shall condemn me? / Behold, they all shall wax old as a garment, / The moth shall eat them up. *Isaiah 51:8:* For the moth shall eat them up like a garment, / And the worm shall eat them like wool; / But My favour shall be for ever, / And My salvation unto all generations. *Job 9:8–9:* Who alone stretcheth out the heavens, / And treadeth upon the waves of the sea. Who maketh the Bear, Orion, and the Pleiades.

Poem Lines	Biblical Reference (from the *Jewish Masoritic Text*)
Lines 49–50: You fixed for the living among them / a place like a shield.	*Isaiah 63:6:* (God) "And I trod down the peoples in Mine anger, / And made them drunk with My fury, / And I poured out their lifeblood on the earth."
	Jeremiah 25:29: (God) "For, lo, I begin to bring evil on the city whereupon My name is called, and should ye be utterly unpunished? Ye shall not be unpunished; for I will call for a sword upon all the inhabitants of the earth, saith the Lord of hosts."
	Psalm 91:4: He will cover thee with his pinions, / And under his wings shalt thou take refuge; / His truth is a shield and a buckler.
Lines 51–52: And all when you rule will be trodden as one, / though not with a shout in a winepress.	*Isaiah 63:3:* (God) "I have trodden the winepress alone, / And of the peoples there was no man with Me; / Yea, I trod them in Mine anger, / And trampled them in My fury; / And their lifeblood is dashed against My garments, / And I have stained all My raiment."
	Jeremiah 25:30: (God, to Jeremiah) "Therefore prophesy thou against them all these words, and say unto them: / The Lord doth roar from on high, / And utter His voice from His holy habitation; / He doth mightily roar because of His fold; / He giveth a shout, as they that tread the grapes, / Against all the inhabitants of the earth."
Line 53: Yours is the glory, yours entire.	*I Chronicles 29:11:* (King David) "Thine, O Lord, is the greatness, and the power, and the glory, and the victory, and the majesty; for all that is in the heaven and in the earth is Thine; Thine is the kingdom, O Lord, and Thou art exalted as head above all."

Poem Lines	Biblical Reference (from the *Jewish Masoritic Text*)
Line 54: Every horse and chariot houghed.	*II Samuel 8:4:* And David took from him a thousand and seven hundred horsemen, and twenty thousand footmen; and David houghed all the chariot horses, but reserved of them for a hundred chariots.
Lines 58–59: who brings affliction into the sea like a woman in labor	*Isaiah 26:17–18:* Like as a woman with child, that draweth near the time of her delivery, / Is in pain and crieth out in her pangs; / So have we been at Thy presence, O Lord. / We have been with child, we have been in pain, / We have as it were brought forth wind; / We have not wrought any deliverance in the land; / Neither are the inhabitants of the world come to life. *Jeremiah 4:31:* (God) "For I have heard a voice as of a woman in travail, / The anguish as of her that bringeth forth her first child, / The voice of the daughter of Zion, that gaspeth for breath, / That spreadeth her hands: / 'Woe is me, now! for my soul fainteth / Before the murderers.'" *Zechariah 10:11:* (God) "And over the sea affliction shall pass, / And all the waves shall be smitten in the sea . . ."
Lines 60–61: You who'll cast toward all the living—death, / as the arrow flies to its target.	*Psalm 91:5:* Thou shalt not be afraid of the terror by night, / Nor of the arrow that flieth by day. . . . *Proverbs 26:18:* As a madman who casteth firebrands, / Arrows, and death . . . *Job 16:12–13:* I was at ease, and He broke me asunder; / Yea, He hath taken me by the neck, and dashed me to pieces; / He hath also set me up for His mark. / His archers compass me round about; / He cleaveth my reins asunder, and doth not spare; / He poureth out my gall upon the ground.

Poem Lines	Biblical Reference (from the *Jewish Masoritic Text*)
Lines 62–64: you on the bitter and great / and terrible day of judgment / who will wake me and judge / all	*Isaiah 26:19:* Thy dead shall live, my dead bodies shall arise— / Awake and sing, ye that dwell in the dust— / For Thy dew is as the dew of light, / And the earth shall bring to life the shades.
	Joel 3:3–4: (God) "And I will show wonders in the heavens and in the earth, / Blood, and fire, and pillars of smoke. / The sun shall be turned into darkness, / And the moon into blood, / Before the great and terrible day of the Lord come."
	Malachi 3:23: (God) "Behold, I will send you / Elijah the prophet / Before the coming / Of the great and terrible day of the Lord."
	Daniel 12:2: (Gabriel, to Daniel) "And many of them that sleep in the dust of the earth shall awake, some to everlasting life, and some to reproaches and everlasting abhorrence."
Lines 64–66: who will wake me and judge / all who've forsaken the statues, / commandments, and Law	*Deuteronomy 29:24:* (Moses) Then men shall say: "Because they forsook the covenant of the Lord, the God of their fathers, which He made with them when He brought them forth out of the land of Egypt . . ."
	Joshua 22:5: Only take diligent heed to do the commandment and the law, which Moses the servant of the Lord commanded you, to love the Lord your God, and to walk in all His ways, and to keep His commandments, and to cleave unto Him, and to serve Him with all your heart and with all your soul.
	Daniel 12:2: (Gabriel, to Daniel) "And many of them that sleep in the dust of the earth shall awake, some to everlasting life, and some to reproaches and everlasting abhorrence."

Poem Lines	Biblical Reference (from the *Jewish Masoritic Text*)
Lines 64–66: (continued)	*Nehemiah 8:14:* (Read by Ezra the scribe) "And they found written in the Law, how that the Lord had commanded by Moses, that the children of Israel should dwell . . . "
	II Chronicles 7:19–20: (God to King Solomon, son of David) "But if ye turn away, and forsake My statutes and My commandments which I have set before you, and shall go and serve other gods, and worship them; then will I pluck them up by the roots out of My land which I have given them; and this house, which I have hallowed for My name, will I cast out of My sight. . . ."
	II Chronicles 19:10: (Jehoshaphat, King of Judah) "And whensoever any controversy shall come to you from your brethren that dwell in their cities, between blood and blood, between law and commandment, statutes and ordinances, ye shall warn them, that they be not guilty towards the Lord, and so wrath come upon you and upon your brethren; thus shall ye do, and ye shall not be guilty."
Lines 69–72: On the day you lift me up from my dust / I'll turn and my spirit in fear of your wrath / will flee, and you'll say: / "Peace be upon you; be still, and do not fear."	*Judges 6:23:* And the Lord said unto him: "Peace be unto thee; fear not; thou shalt not die."
	I Samuel 16:14: Now the spirit of the Lord had departed from Saul, and an evil spirit from the Lord terrified him.
	Isaiah 7:4: And say unto him: Keep calm, and be quiet; fear not, neither let thy heart be faint, because of these two tails of smoking firebrands, for the fierce anger of Rezin and Aram, and of the son of Remaliah.

Poem Lines	Biblical Reference (from the *Jewish Masoritic Text*)
Lines 69–72: (continued)	*Isaiah 51:7–8:* Hearken unto Me, ye that know righteousness, / The people in whose heart is My law; / . . . / But My favour shall be for ever, / And My salvation unto all generations. *Joel 3:5:* (God) "And it shall come to pass, that whosoever shall call on the name of the Lord shall be delivered. . . ."

Because you know you're young in beauty yet

DANTE ALIGHIERI

INTRODUCING THE POEM

In a poem that spans the ages, Dante expresses a young man's resentment and anger toward the young woman who has rejected his offer of love. Because the poem expresses the young man's point of view, the young woman is presented as being arrogant, proud, cruel, and stonelike in her insensitivity to his feelings. So great is the young man's anguish and anger that he concludes by hoping that she will experience similar pain in love.

It is interesting to put the speaker's feelings into perspective by imagining this relationship from the woman's point of view. The young woman simply may not like the young man and may think that it is best to act honestly toward him. She may view treating him kindly as offering him false hope and thereby postponing or prolonging his pain.

It is also interesting to consider this poem in terms of the tradition of courtly love. Courtly love often involved the idealization of the loved one, the offer of pure love from the safety of distance, and the passionate expression of emotion on the part of the lover. The lover would despair if his loved one were unattainable, and he would be angry at her cruelty if she rejected his offer of love. Dante conveys the speaker's emotions so realistically, however, that the poem is meaningful to anyone who has experienced unrequited love.

Personal Literary Journal: Have you ever cared about someone who did not reciprocate your feelings? How did the experience make you feel about that person? How did it make you feel about yourself?

Literary Terms: apostrophe, courtly love, image, lyric, stanza

COMPREHENSION QUESTIONS

1. *Describe the speaker in the poem.* a young man

2. *To whom is the speaker speaking?* a young woman

3. *What has happened to the speaker?* A woman rejected his love.

4. *What does the speaker wish for?* that the woman will suffer rejection just as he has

UNDERSTANDING THE POEM: POSSIBLE ANSWERS

1. *Validity of the speaker's analysis* The speaker is most likely incorrect. He feels that the woman is playing with his affection for her and that she is enjoying his frustration and hurt. It is more likely that she simply does not like the speaker. It is natural for the speaker to blame the woman rather than to acknowledge his own part in the failure of the relationship.

2. *Speaker's continued love for the woman* The speaker is letting his passion rather than his reason control him.

3. *Speaker's state of mind* The speaker is foolish and masochistic to persist in imposing himself on someone who does not like him. His final curse is understandable but not justified. Uncontrolled passion may cause even intelligent people to behave in a way that hurts others and may be contrary to their own best interests.

4. *The woman's behavior* The woman is correct to turn down the speaker's love if she has no interest in him. While she could make an effort to put herself into the speaker's position and to be kind to him, she may feel that she would be encouraging him.

ANALYZING LITERARY TECHNIQUE: POSSIBLE ANSWERS

1. *Apostrophe* Dante uses apostrophe to achieve immediacy. It appears that the speaker is addressing a woman who is present.

2. *Central image* The central image of the poem is that of a woman who is made of stone. The image of a stone connotes such qualities as hardness, insensitivity, and the inability to feel emotion. Thus, by describing the woman as stonelike, the speaker dehumanizes her and implies that she is unnatural because she has rejected him. His closing curse reveals the depth of his anguish and anger. However, in blaming the woman for their lack of relationship, the speaker is denying his own role in the situation. Anyone who ventures to offer love takes on the risk of rejection, for romantic love requires mutuality of regard. Unrequited love is actually infatuation.

3. *Stanzas in poem* The first short stanza (lines 1–3) sets up the central image of the poem and sets the scene. The second stanza (lines 4–10) fills out the imagery and provides additional detail. The central image of the stonelike woman, her rejection of the speaker, and Love's "stonelike" rule connect the two stanzas.

WRITING ABOUT LITERATURE

1. *Essay analyzing relationship to courtly love* Call students' attention to the information about courtly love in the introductory material. If they are familiar with the well-known version of King Arthur by Sir Thomas Malory, remind them that courtly love provides the setting for the Knights of the Round Table. Students may view this poem as a courtly lover's sincere complaint about the hardship of unrequited love. Others may think that the strong emotion in the last lines reflects a courtly lover's hostility to a tradition that encourages women to be arrogant and insensitive to a lover's plight. Most important may be the universality of the human feelings being expressed. These feelings may be adolescent and excessive, but they represent a common human reaction to rejection. **(P.L.J.)**

2. *Creative writing: retell this incident from the woman's point of view* Call students' attention to the suggestions in the textbook assignment. Encourage the students who choose to write a poem to select a central image that the woman will apply to her lover. **(P.L.J.)**

FURTHER READING

Dante Alighieri, "Inferno" from the *Divine Comedy; The New Life*.

Torn Lace

EMILIA PARDO BAZÁN

INTRODUCING THE STORY

"Torn Lace" is the story of a bride, Micaelita, who leaves her betrothed, Bernardo, at the altar because his reaction to her accidental tearing of her lace bridal veil reveals a hidden and unacceptable aspect of his personality.

The story provides an example of Pardo Bazán's favorite literary techniques, which include multiple (two) female narrators, a focus on psychological realism, and the use of an epiphany—a spontaneous and superficially trivial event, such as a comment, conversation, gesture, or behavior, that enables a witness to gain a sudden and significant insight into someone's character; this insight, in turn, causes a profound change in the witness's attitude and behavior. Because one narrator is an acquaintance who did not attend the wedding and the other narrator is the bride, expectation is contrasted with reality. This double point of view creates an aura of mystery and reveals how important an epiphany can be in a person's life.

Personal Literary Journal: Recall and record an incident in which you had an epiphany—where you learned something important about another person because that person said or did something that surprised you.

Literary Terms: characterization, climax, crisis, epiphany, figurative language, foreshadowing, metaphor, point of view, resolution, simile, symbol, theme

COMPREHENSION QUESTIONS

1. *What event does the narrator refer to as the story opens?* a wedding
2. *What surprising incident occurred at that time?* The bride refused to marry the groom.
3. *Give two reasons as to why this incident was surprising.* The incident occurred among wealthy, socially conscious people, and the bride and groom had appeared to be in love with each other.
4. *What reason was given for this surprising incident?* The bride declared that she had changed her mind.
5. *How does the narrator learn the whole truth?* She meets the bride at a spa.
6. *What two things does the narrator learn?* The bride accidentally tore her wedding veil, and the groom reacted with rage, cruelty, and contempt.
7. *What is the real reason that the surprising incident occurred?* The bride did not want to marry a man who was violent, cruel, and contemptuous.
8. *Why was this reason not given at the time of the event?* The bride thought that no one would have accepted such a simple reason for her rejection of a wealthy mate.

UNDERSTANDING THE STORY: POSSIBLE ANSWERS

1. *The narrator's absence from wedding* The narrator's absence from the wedding is important because the narrator cannot imagine why Micaelita refused to marry Bernardo. What is a mystery to the narrator is a mystery to the reader as well.
2. *Details of the wedding* The details about the wedding reveal the wealth of the society in which the wedding occurred, thus confirming both the value of the lace bridal veil that Bernardo gave to his bride and the wealth that Micaelita would have acquired had she married Bernardo. The details reveal that Micaelita was losing both financial security and social prestige by rejecting this marriage. It is surprising that a bride would relinquish security and prestige without a good reason, and it is even more surprising that Micaelita made this decision so belatedly—just as the wedding was about to begin.
3. *Micaelita's love for Bernardo* Micaelita reveals that she had no confidence in her knowledge of Bernardo's character. Because other people had called him violent (though he had always been courteous to her, no matter how she had attempted to test him), she continued to be uncomfortable about her marriage to him.
4. *Bernardo's behavior* Bernardo first revealed a possible flaw in his character when he seemed to value the lace veil that he had given Micaelita more than he seemed to care about her.
5. *The epiphany* Micaelita experienced an epiphany when she observed Bernardo's reaction when she accidentally tore the lace bridal veil that he had given her as a gift. His fury and contempt provided her with a critically

important insight into his character, revealing aspects of his personality that she had never seen and that she considered unacceptable in a husband.

6. *Validity of Micaelita's reasons* Student opinion may vary. Students may point out that people had told Micaelita about Bernardo's violence, so Micaelita's response to Bernardo's fury had, in a sense, been considered before this incident occurred. Micaelita saw Bernardo's response to the torn lace as an indication of his true personality and values.

7. *Title* "Torn Lace" is an appropriate title for this story because the lace, with its inherent fragility, symbolizes Micaelita and Bernardo's relationship. Just as an accident easily tears the lace, so Bernardo's inadvertent reaction to the torn lace easily tears apart his relationship with Micaelita. Bernardo's reaction to the torn lace becomes an epiphany that enables Micaelita to discover Bernardo's true character.

8. *Themes* Possible themes:

   - People are not necessarily what they appear to be.

   - Deceptively minor incidents can reveal important aspects of a person's character.

   - The response to an epiphany can change the course of a person's life.

9. *The story's power in terms of Micaelita's response* The power of this story comes from its epiphany—the importance of Bernardo's fleeting glance, which reveals his true character and makes it impossible for Micaelita to marry Bernardo.

   Readers admire Micaelita's ability to recognize the importance of Bernardo's reaction to the torn lace and her courage in leaving him at the altar, despite his wealth and social position. If Micaelita had been blind to the significance of Bernardo's reaction or if she had been so cowardly or so ambitious to have proceeded with the wedding despite what his reaction revealed about his character, an unhappy marriage would have inevitably resulted.

ANALYZING LITERARY TECHNIQUE: POSSIBLE ANSWERS

*1. *Point of view* This story is told from two points of view. The first narrator is a woman who had been invited to the wedding; although she had not attended, she had heard about it from those who had been present. The second narrator is the bride herself.

   The first narrator relates the mystery of the situation—why the bride abandoned the groom at the altar. The second narrator, the bride, supplies the answers to the mystery, including her experience of the epiphany that motivated her change of heart. Both the mystery and the epiphany add interest, appeal, and power to the story.

2. *Revelation of Bernardo's character* Bernardo inadvertently revealed his true character through his reaction to Micaelita's accidentally torn lace.

3. *The epiphany* Pardo Bazán's use of epiphany is a most effective literary device because it reveals the nature of Bernardo's character and explains the mystery of Micaelita's refusal to marry Bernardo, both of which are surprising.

4. *Figurative language*
   a) *simile: "his eyes blazing like coals"* The comparison of Bernardo's eyes with blazing coals effectively conveys the intensity of his fury and rage over the torn lace.
   b) *metaphor: "its weave . . . captured two hearts in its tenuous mesh"* The implied comparison of love and woven mesh conveys the intertwining of two people who are in love with each other; the tenuous nature of this mesh reveals the fragility of their love.
   c) *metaphor: "something cracked and shattered into pieces inside me"* The implied comparison of love and glass conveys the brittle and fragile nature of Micaelita's love for Bernardo. The love broke into pieces when he was unable to love her more than the lace that he had given her and unable to understand and forgive the accident that had torn the lace.
   d) *metaphor: "a curtain was parted, exposing a naked soul behind it"* The implied comparison between the revelation of Bernardo's true character and the opening of a curtain conveys the hidden nature of his character. Rather than reveal his soul, Bernardo had clothed his character in socially correct attire so that, although Micaelita had heard about his violent temperament, she had been unable to discover his true personality until she accidentally tore the lace.
   e) *symbol: "the delicate design of the lace signified a promise of happiness"* The delicate design of the lace symbolizes the promise of happiness as well as the fragility of Micaelita and Bernardo's love. Once torn, the lace symbolizes the irreparable tear in their relationship.
5. *Foreshadowing* Bernardo's response to the torn lace is foreshadowed by the fact that Micaelita had heard that Bernardo possessed a violent temperament. Micaelita's foreknowledge was important because it confirmed that what Bernardo revealed in his expression when he saw the torn lace was a revelation of his true character. It enabled Micaelita to be certain that she should not marry him.
6. *Plot structure* The crisis occurred when Micaelita accidentally tore her lace. The climax occurred when Bernardo reacted to the accident with rage, cruelty, and contempt. The resolution occurred when Micaelita refused to make her wedding vows and abandoned Bernardo at the altar.

WRITING ABOUT LITERATURE

1. *Essay analyzing the importance of point of view in this story* Call students' attention to the directions in the textbook assignment with regard to the content of each of five paragraphs. (See **A.L.T.** question 1 above.) **AP**
2. *Creative writing: this story from Bernardo's point of view* Call students' attention to the directions in the textbook assignment. (See **A.L.T.** question 1 above.)
3. *Creative writing: a story involving an epiphany* Call students' attention to the directions in the textbook assignment. **(P.L.J.)**

Pardo Bazán, Emilia, *Torn Lace and Other Stories; The White Horse and Other Stories*.

War

LUIGI PIRANDELLO

INTRODUCING THE STORY

In "War," Pirandello examines war's toll. Soldiers must confront their mortality and the ideal of a heroic death. Their parents must confront the inconsolable loss of a child. The story overflows with the emotions of anger and sorrow, opening with the sorrow of a mother who can only growl wordlessly, like a wild animal that has lost its young, and closing with the sobs of a father, for whom the best intellectual reasons are powerless to stifle the cry from his heart.

Pirandello uses the stylistic device of a debate to elaborate and intensify the nature and extent of a parent's grief. The mother of the son about to leave for the front, the fathers who have sons at the front, and the father whose son was satisfied to die a hero all mourn war's devastating effect upon their children's lives and upon their own lives. The sorrowing mother is amazed to find a parent capable of stoically accepting the loss of his child, only to find that his stoicism has been a self-protective sham and that, paradoxically, his emotions are as intolerably painful as her own.

"War" illustrates Pirandello's view that reality differs from person to person. The story's paradoxical theme is that reality may be the opposite of what one perceives it to be. People who feel unbearable emotions may conceal the emotions from themselves and from others. In the story Pirandello's attention to psychological mechanisms for controlling grief is more important than the obvious theme that war causes grief.

Personal Literary Journal: How do you deal with a great disappointment or loss?

Literary Terms: characterization, climax, conflict, foreshadowing, irony, paradox, resolution, reversal, satire, theme

COMPREHENSION QUESTIONS

1. *Why is the woman in deep mourning?* Her only son is being sent to war.

2. *What is the general reaction to her sorrow?* Others believe they have greater reason to complain.

3. *What attitude does the fat man express?* Decent young men die willingly as heroes.

4. *What question does the woman ask the fat man?* "Is your son really dead?"

5. *How does the fat man react?* senses the reality of his son's death and bursts into tears

UNDERSTANDING THE STORY: POSSIBLE ANSWERS

*1. *Nameless characters* The characters' having no names makes them universal.

2. *Parent's love for child* All children receive their parents' total love, no matter how many siblings there are.

3. *"We belong to them but they never belong to us."* Parents devote their lives to the development of their children, with the goal of rearing independent, well-functioning adults. Children grow up to become independent of their parents and to lead their own lives.

*4. *Why woman asks whether man's son has really died* She cannot believe that a mourning parent can be so stoic about his loss.

*5. *Fat man/old man* The change in description registers the toll that the realization of his loss has taken on him.

6. *Patriotism and "decent boys"* Pirandello suggests that patriotism is simply a rationalization, a way of making the devastation of war acceptable. The fat man is serious when he says that "decent boys" are patriotic. However, warlike behavior is anything but "decent," so the phrase "decent boys" has a satiric and ironic tone. The fat man's eventual rejection of his own intellectual arguments demolishes the charade of rationalization.

*7. *Themes* Themes include the following: War causes irreconcilable grief; reality may be different from, and even the opposite of, what one perceives it to be; people who feel unbearable emotions may attempt to conceal the emotions from themselves.

ANALYZING LITERARY TECHNIQUES: POSSIBLE ANSWERS

1. *Hiding one's face* The description is important because hiding a face comes to symbolize hiding emotion. The woman hides her face to conceal her sorrow. The fat man covers his mouth to hide his missing teeth, just as he hides his feelings behind his arguments. The fat man's missing teeth suggest that the substance, or bite, of his arguments also is missing.

*2. *Characterization* Characters are distinguished by the particular attitudes and ideas they express and by their physical appearance. The last description of the fat man as "old" adds a new dimension to his characterization; facing reality has sapped his vitality and has aged him.

3. *Conflict and resolution* The conflict is both external and internal. The external conflict is the debate over the proper attitude of parents when their children go to war. It includes the conflict between the intellectual and the emotional responses to the death of a child killed in war. The internal conflict is the fat man's struggle to realize his loss and express his true emotions.

*4. *Climax* The climax is the woman's question ("is your son really dead?"), when she challenges the intellectual approach to a son's death. The question touches off the plot's reversal and confirms the validity of the woman's emotional response.

*5. *Reversal* The fat man's sudden switch from an intellectual to an emotional response gives the story its surprise ending and its tremendous power.

*6. *Irony* It is ironic that reality may be the opposite of what one perceives it to be. It is a psychological paradox that people who feel unbearable emotions may conceal them or even express the opposite emotions.

WRITING ABOUT LITERATURE

1. *Essay analyzing emotional impact of story* Call students' attention to the suggestions in the textbook assignment. (See **U.S.** questions 1, 4, 5, and 7 and **A.L.T.** questions 2, 4, 5, and 6 above.)

2. *Creative writing: a poem about war* Call students' attention to the suggestions and directions in the textbook assignment. Encourage them to choose a focus and then to think in terms of images that will elicit an emotional reaction in the reader. Patriotism and heroism may inspire pride and joy; destruction and carnage may arouse disgust and horror; the thought of loved ones may arouse longing and love; and the idea of self-sacrifice may elicit feelings that depend on the person's values and his or her attitude toward the particular war.

FURTHER READING

Pirandello, Luigi, collections of stories: *Better Think Twice About It; A Character in Distress; Horse in the Moo; The Medals and Other Stories;* plays: *Enrico I; Six Characters in Search of an Author.*

Lament for Ignacio Sánchez Mejías

FEDERICO GARCÍA LORCA

INTRODUCING THE POEM

"Lament for Ignacio Sánchez Mejías" is a modern masterpiece. It speaks to every reader because it is a poem about the inevitability of death and the human need to be immortal. The poem moves on two levels simultaneously. On one level is García Lorca's eulogy to his close friend in which he documents his own gradual acceptance of Ignacio's death. On another level is García Lorca's acceptance of his own mortality. The double focus on this subject is natural because the death of a dear one always becomes, in the mind of the bereaved, both a personal loss and a reminder that death is the unalterable fate of every human being. Moreover, it is the poet's personal identification with the issue of mortality that supplies the tremendous emotional power behind the poetry.

García Lorca divides the poem into four sections. Each reflects a psychological stage in the mourning process. As the poet moves from Part 1 to Part 4, he moves from denial to acceptance of Ignacio's death and from the inability to contemplate the meaning of death to the realization that he can cope with the death through writing about it. Therefore, García Lorca's acceptance and understanding of his friend's death becomes a "night journey" in which the poet comes to terms with his own mortality.

Part 1, "Cogida (Goring) and Death," depicts García Lorca's attempt to register the fact that a bull has gored Ignacio to death in a bullfight. The event has taken the poet by surprise: He has had no time to prepare himself psychologically for it. Part 1 represents the poet's shock and horror upon hearing the news. Over and over he repeats the chant that swings like a pendulum on a clock, "at five in the afternoon." Life has stopped for both the matador and the poet. The poet expresses no emotion in this section because he feels none. He is numb with shock and disbelief.

Part 2, "The Spilled Blood," depicts García Lorca's denial of reality, his adamant refusal to face Ignacio's death. While he tentatively acknowledges his dear friend's death, the death is only an abstract phenomenon. He refuses to confront the concrete physical reality of his friend's death. He refuses to visit Ignacio and watch him wage a futile struggle for life. García Lorca's emotional response reveals the extent to which his friend's death has deeply wounded him. The pain of this raw wound forces him to cry out: "I will not see it!" "I do not want to see it!" "Do not ask me to see it." Ignacio's sudden death also has deep emotional implications for García Lorca's own life. García Lorca realizes that life is unpredictable and that he cannot predict his own death.

The poet copes with death by remembering the past. He connects Ignacio Sánchez Mejías with the bullfighters in ancient Crete, who sacrificed their lives to the bull (symbol of the god Poseidon) so that Crete would prosper. Like them, Ignacio is a hero. He bravely risked death, not blanching before the bull's horns. Although he could not avoid death, he could control the manner in which he lived and died. Thus, he faced his death with dignity and fortitude.

"There was no prince in Seville / who could compare with him," the poet says, by way of introducing a section of eloquent praise that, in fact, will make Ignacio a living memory. García Lorca can handle memory and such abstractions about death as "Now the moss and the grass / open with sure fingers / the flower of his skull. / And now his blood comes out singing." Blood both sings and forms "a pool of agony." Blood connects life and death. Visualizing the abstract is emotionally easier for the poet than confronting the corpse of his friend. "I will not see it!" he concludes.

In Part 3, "The Laid Out Body," García Lorca acknowledges the finality of death. It is no longer possible to deny the fact that Ignacio is dead. Everything dies eventually, "even the sea dies." Now the poet must confront the meaning of death, and his wish to deny death takes a new direction. He wants death to be more than eternal sleep. He contrasts stone (a symbol of death) with water (a symbol of life).

He repeats the idea that "All is finished," but the emotional issue behind the end of life and the eternity of death is not finished for him. Leave the body to the moss and the grass, but let the soul free itself of straps and fly into a sweet eternity. "I want . . . , I want . . . , I want. . . ," he repeats. For García Lorca, death cannot and must not be the complete end of life. He invokes the greatest of men

("Those that break horses and dominate rivers") and the greatest of poets ("men of sonorous skeleton who sing / with a mouth full of sun and flint") to tell him how to cope with mortality, his own as well as that of his friend, and to give him the power to create a fitting elegy for Ignacio.

Finally in Part 4, "Absent Soul," García Lorca examines the meaning of death for those who are alive. He is concerned about the anonymity that death confers, both for Ignacio and, in the future, for himself. He realizes that those who have died will be remembered by the living if a poet sings about them. His refrain, "[Nobody knows] you / because you have died for ever," gives way to his solution, "But I sing of you. / For posterity I sing of your . . ." García Lorca's poetic tribute to Ignacio Sánchez Mejías will become part of García Lorca's own legacy to the world.

The last two lines of the poem reveal García Lorca's recognition and acceptance of the universal human condition. Ignacio's special qualities make his death a cause of sorrow, but death is part of life. "A sad breeze" (for the poet, a symbol of the grief in life) blows "through the olive trees" (a symbol of the sustaining powers in life). Life is beautiful but transitory, and death is the price that each person must pay for all the joys of being human.

The language that García Lorca uses to convey his thoughts and feelings is so striking that at first it overwhelms both the intellect and the emotions of the reader and becomes a barrier to understanding and enjoying the poem. Paradoxically, with study the reader comes to enjoy the poem because of the very phrases that made the initial reading difficult. Part of the difficulty is caused by the fact that most readers have little or no knowledge about bullfights, the treatment of a wounded bullfighter, and related Spanish terminology. García Lorca is a surrealist and symbolist; part of the difficulty of understanding this work is his unusual choice of images and metaphors and their juxtaposition. Readers must cope with strange comparisons and contrasts. Familiarity and analysis foster appreciation of this important poem.

Personal Literary Journal: How would you react to the death of a very good friend? What would be your initial reaction? How would your first thoughts and feelings change with the passage of time? How would the death of someone dear to you affect your own life? How would you preserve the memory of that person?

Literary Terms: allusion, apostrophe, contrast, expressionism, figurative language, Imagism, irony, metaphor, night journey, personification, repetition, setting, simile, surrealism, symbolism, theme

COMPREHENSION QUESTIONS

1. *What event caused García Lorca to write this poem?* His friend Ignacio died.

2. *What time did the event in the poem occur?* "at five in the afternoon"

3. *What was Ignacio doing prior to this event?* fighting a bull

4. *How does García Lorca first react to the event?* with horror and denial

5. *What is García Lorca's purpose in writing this poem?* to memorialize Ignacio

UNDERSTANDING THE POEM: POSSIBLE ANSWERS

*1. *Part 1:*

a) *What happened, where, and when* Ignacio Sánchez Mejías has died in a bullfight (in a bullring) at 5:00 P.M.

b) *Why speaker isn't more specific* First, García Lorca's contemporaries know who Ignacio is and what happened. Second, the poem is more about García Lorca's reaction to the event than about the event itself.

c) *Repetition of "at five in the afternoon"* Repetition reflects García Lorca's shock and horror upon hearing of Ignacio's death. Life has stopped for García Lorca as well.

d) *Relationship between speaker's attitude and the time* His shock and lack of emotion reflect the fact that he has just heard the news.

*2. *Part 2:*

a) *What speaker doesn't want to see* He doesn't want to see Ignacio's death, either the body or the place where the death occurred. He wants no proof of his friend's death, and he doesn't want to see signs of Ignacio's suffering. He wants to ignore the fact that his friend has died (denial).

b) *Connection between speaker's refusal and his eulogy of Ignacio* Ignacio was a close friend, a fine poet and dramatist, and an excellent bullfighter who was only thirty-four years old when he was killed. He was too extraordinary, too dear, and too young to die. García Lorca does not want to think of his friend as being dead (denial). If the poet can remember Ignacio as he was when he was alive, Ignacio will remain alive, if only in García Lorca's memory.

c) *Repetition of "I will not see it!"* This repetition reflects the speaker's denial of his friend's death.

d) *Relationship between speaker's attitude and the time* The speaker's denial reflects the fact that the news of his friend's death is still very new. References to the moon indicate that Part 2 may concern García Lorca's thoughts later in the evening, in the hours after Ignacio's death. Denial is typical of the early stages of grief. One purpose of a funeral (described in the last lines of the section) is to help a bereaved person accept reality.

*3. *Part 3:*

a) *Problem speaker confronts* He confronts the meaning of death for the man who has died. He wants death to be more than nothingness or eternal sleep.

b) *Meaning of "All is finished"* "All is finished" implies that death is the end of all aspects of life, that death contains nothing.

c) *Repetition of "I want . . ."* This repetition emphasizes García Lorca's great need to learn how to cope with the finality of death. He wants the greatest of men to tell him about Ignacio's future. He wants to hear that Ignacio and other great men conquer and dominate death and that a sweet afterlife exists. In the process, he begins to conceive of how he will deal with his friend's death.

d) *Relationship between speaker's attitude and the time* More time has passed since Ignacio's death. Ignacio is about to be buried, and García Lorca is looking at his corpse. It is no longer possible for García Lorca to deny that his friend is dead.

e) *Speaker's role in Ignacio's death* García Lorca wants the greatest of men to inspire him with a lament for Ignacio that will free Ignacio from the constraints of death.

*4. *Part 4:*

a) *Problem speaker examines* He examines the meaning of death for those who continue to live.

b) *Meaning of "does not know you"* Death causes the one who has died to be forgotten by those who remain alive and to be unknown to those who live at a later time. This is an emotional issue for García Lorca because it is going to be his problem when he dies, just as it is now Ignacio's problem.

c) *Speaker's solution* García Lorca will write an elegy for his friend that will recapture Ignacio's greatness and make his memory immortal. García Lorca must realize that his own poems and dramas will be his form of immortality.

d) *Relationship between speaker's attitude and the time* Enough time has passed since Ignacio's death that the poet has been able to reconcile himself to his friend's death and his own mortality. García Lorca can now proceed with his own life as a poet.

e) *Attitude toward life at end of poem* The last two lines reflect García Lorca's acceptance of death as an integral part of the universal human condition. Life can be beautiful, but it is transitory.

5. *Night journey* The focus of the poem is García Lorca's psychological response to his friend Ignacio's death. The poet moves from the denial of Ignacio's death to the acceptance of it, and, in the process, from the inability to contemplate the meaning of death to the realization that poetry provides a form of immortality. Thus, the development of García Lorca's attitude toward death is a night journey, an experience through which the poet gains important self-knowledge and the ability to accept his own mortality.

ANALYZING LITERARY TECHNIQUE: POSSIBLE ANSWERS

1. *Apostrophe* García Lorca's technique of addressing Ignacio at the end of Part 3 and in Part 4 as if he were alive makes it appear as if Ignacio were, in fact, present with the poet. This technique would be satisfying to the poet in that it brings his friend closer to him.

*2. *Allusion to the Minotaur* The bullfights in ancient Crete are believed to have had a connection to the worship of the god Poseidon, who was symbolized by a bull. The allusion enhances Ignacio's battle with the bull and his death. It gives his death a higher purpose and emphasizes his role as a hero.

In Greek mythology, the Minotaur is a monster with a bull's head and a man's body. Archaeologists believe that Minos, the king of Crete, wore the head of a bull on state religious occasions; the Minotaur was believed to be his offspring. Theseus, who killed the Minotaur, is a symbol of the Greeks' conquest of Minoan Crete (c. 1450 B.C.).

3. *References to nature* The poet's juxtaposition of human and natural images conveys the fact that human beings are an integral part of the natural world. Examples: "moss and grass / open . . . / the flower of his skull"; "even the sea dies"; and "mouth full of sun and flint."

4. *How contrast reinforces emotional content* Contrast heightens perception because it highlights differences. The poet contrasts life with death, remembering with forgetting, past with present, and reality with denial. Each of these contrasts helps convey the depth of the poet's sense of loss and the poignancy of his search for meaning beyond the finality of death.

5. *Figures of speech* Choices will vary. Examples: Part 2: "Now the moss and the grass / open with sure fingers / the flower of his skull"—the personification of nature and the image of Ignacio's skull as a flower. Part 2: "And now his blood comes out singing"—the vitality and joy of life, even as it gives way to death. Part 3: "those men of sonorous skeleton who sing / with a mouth full of sun and flint"—the poets whose words capture heaven and earth, brilliance and darkness, the range of life experience.

WRITING ABOUT LITERATURE

1. *Essay analyzing García Lorca's use of repetition in poem* Call students' attention to the directions in the textbook assignment. Remind them to use quotations to support their ideas and to show the importance of the poem's effect on them. (See **U.P.** questions 1, 2, 3, and 4 above.) **AP**

2. *Creative writing: story of Ignacio Sánchez Mejías's death from bull's point of view* Encourage students who like this assignment to consult an encyclopedia or similar source about bullfights and the bulls that fight in them. The stories of Ernest Hemingway may also be a good resource for students. (See **A.L.T.** question 2 above.)

3. *Creative writing: essay or poem eulogizing a person* Call students' attention to the directions in the textbook assignment. Remind them that making lists may help them determine whom to write about and which qualities and details to include. Remind them also that examining their use of language will significantly improve the effect of their writing.

FURTHER READING

García Lorca, Federico, *The Selected Poems of Federico García Lorca*.

Letter to My Wife

NAZIM HIKMET

INTRODUCING THE POEM

Hikmet writes this poem to his wife to allay her fear about his imminent death. He sends her the following thoughts: First, his death will not cause her to die. She will soon forget him because people in the twentieth century mourn loved ones for a year or less. Second, although the poet cannot accept death by hanging, he will feel no fear if that is his fate. His last thoughts will be of his wife and his friends. As he dies, he will regret nothing about his life except for "an unfinished song" (poem). Third, he regrets having written to her about the authorities' wishing to hang him, because he is being tried before a court and the trial has hardly begun. Finally, his thoughts return to life. He asks her to send him flannel underwear and to think positively about his situation.

Personal Literary Journal: Think of a time (or imagine a time) when someone you love became very worried about some aspect of your life. How did you respond?

Literary Terms: appositive, apostrophe, dramatic monologue, figurative language, free verse, irony, lyric, metaphor, satire, simile, theme, tone

COMPREHENSION QUESTIONS

1. *Why does the poet write this poem?* It is a response to his wife's letter.

2. *Where is the poet when he writes it?* in prison

3. *What does his wife fear will happen to him?* that the authorities will hang him

4. *Why would the authorities look into the poet's eyes?* to see his fear—but his eyes will not show fear

5. *How does the poet feel about his life?* He has no regrets.

6. *What would the poet like to finish?* his last "song"

7. *What is happening in the poet's life?* His trial has begun.

8. *What two requests does he make of his wife?* to send him flannel underwear and to think positively about his situation

UNDERSTANDING THE POEM: POSSIBLE ANSWERS

1. *Purpose for letter* Hikmet is writing this letter for two reasons: first, to cheer his wife and to help her continue to live her own life; and second, to make her feel optimistic about his situation.

2. *The effect of death* Hikmet discusses how his death would affect him to make his wife understand that he can meet his death without fear. He has loving memories of her and his friends, and he has no regrets apart from an unfinished poem.

3. *Significance of the two requests* Hikmet's two requests—for flannel underwear and for his wife to think positively about his situation—imply that his death is not imminent.

4. *Wife's response* Hikmet hopes that his letter will lead his wife to disregard the tone of his earlier letter and become more optimistic about his state of mind and his situation.

5. *The effect of writing the poem* In the process of attempting to convince his wife to become more optimistic about his situation, Hikmet convinces himself to be optimistic. He assures himself that his mental attitude is positive and that he can face death without fear. Moreover, his thoughts that this trial has just begun remind him that he may not be convicted or he may not be condemned to death. Therefore, his thoughts turn to present needs—his need for flannel underwear and his wife's need to think positively.

ANALYZING LITERARY TECHNIQUE: POSSIBLE ANSWERS

*1. *Appositives* Hikmet uses the following appositives to describe his wife: "red-haired lady of my heart" and "Good-hearted, / golden, / eyes sweeter than honey." These pictorial descriptions enable the reader to see Hikmet's wife and know her character. They also enable the reader to realize how much the poet loves his wife.

*2. *Death and its appositive* The description of Death as "a body swinging from a rope" makes the ephemeral image of death seem real. Death becomes personal and powerful.

*3. *Apostrophe* The use of apostrophe involves addressing an absent person as if the person were present. By treating his wife as if she were with him, the poet creates immediacy. He is speaking personally and informally, which is just what he would do if he were communicating directly with his wife.

4. *The hangman* Hikmet's description of the hangman creates a word picture that has an emotional impact on the reader. The hangman seems simultaneously appealing and disgusting. The phrase "some poor gypsy" engages the reader's sympathy, implying that the hangman is in such need of money that he has taken the job of hangman, no matter how horrible the job is. In contrast, the phrase "hairy black / spidery hand" repulses the reader. It makes the reader want to run from the hangman.

5. *The last morning* The poet speaks of "the twilight of my last morning." The poet's last morning will introduce his death. The last morning will not be preceded by dawn since the darkness of the eternal night of death—rather than daylight—will follow.

*6. *Free verse* Free verse involves the use of broken lines that reproduce the rhythms of conversational speech. By writing as he would speak, Hikmet makes his poem immediate, informal, and realistic. Hikmet writes as if he were speaking directly to his wife.

Examples of Hikmet's use of free verse include the following:

- "Your last letter says: / 'My head is throbbing; / my heart is stunned!'"
- "You say: / 'If they hang you, / if I lose you, / I'll die!'"
- "But / you can bet . . ."
- "Look, forget all this."

7. *Contrast* Hikmet contrasts the past and the present. As he writes this letter, he refers to his previous letter. The letter he is writing is more consoling and affirming than the last letter he sent his wife.

8. *Satire and irony* When Hikmet states that his wife's memory of him "will vanish like black smoke in the wind" and that "in the twentieth century / grief lasts / at most a year," he is attempting to reassure his wife that she will survive his death. Hikmet is satirizing people who forget the past too quickly. Ironically, Hikmet would not expect his wife, who had been loyal to him through the years of his imprisonment, to forget him.

9. *Metaphor about his wife* The metaphor "my bee" relates to the poet's description of his wife's eyes as being "sweeter than honey." Like honey, Hikmet's wife is "good-hearted" (sweet) and "golden." The metaphor reveals the character of Hikmet's wife. It enhances the feelings of love that Hikmet expresses in the poem.

10. *Similes* Hikmet uses similes to engage the mind of the reader. The following are examples:

   - "My memory will vanish like black smoke in the wind." Black smoke, unlike white smoke, does not dissipate quickly. Likewise, true love does not dissipate quickly—though it may diffuse when the loved one has been away for a long time or is dead.
   - "Pluck a man's head / like a turnip." This comparison of a man's head to a turnip dehumanizes the man and makes him seem as meaningless as a vegetable. What is striking about this image is the implication that the authorities will take Hikmet's life seriously (will not see him as a turnip) and that they will not frivolously condemn him to death.

11. *Themes* Possible themes:

   - the enduring love between a husband and his wife
   - the sustaining value of friendship and of a life well lived
   - the possibility of facing death with courage
   - the need to live with optimism—appreciating the past and having hope for the future

12. *Tone* Hikmet achieves a tone of optimism by thinking the good thoughts that he is advising his wife to think. He accentuates the positive: his love for his wife; the value of his friendships; his ability to die without fear; his comfort in the feeling that he has lived his life well; and the fact that his trial has just begun so contemplating death is premature.

1. *Essay analyzing three aspects of Hikmet's style* Call students' attention to the directions in the textbook assignment with regard to Hikmet's use of the appositive, the apostrophe, and conversation. Remind them to use quotations and to include an evaluative concluding paragraph. (See **A.L.T.** questions 1, 2, 3, and 6 above.) **AP**

2. *Essay analyzing "Letter to My Wife" as a dramatic monologue* Call students' attention to the directions in the textbook assignment. The essay should include a thesis sentence and the definition of dramatic monologue, the analysis of four quotations that reveal Hikmet's character, and a conclusion that evaluates the poem as a dramatic monologue.

   Hikmet's "Letter to My Wife" is a dramatic monologue in that it reveals the following aspects of Hikmet's character:

   - He is loving: "My one and only!" "In the twilight of my last morning / I / will see my friends and you," "My wife! / Good-hearted, / golden, / eyes sweeter than honey—my bee!"

   - He is courageous: "But / you can bet / . . . / slips a noose / around my neck, / they'll look in vain for fear / in Nazim's / blue eyes!"

   - He is satisfied with the choices that he has made during his life: "and I'll go to my grave / regretting nothing but an unfinished song . . ."

   - He is optimistic, even when faced with death: "The trial has hardly begun, / and they don't just pluck a man's head / like a turnip."

3. *Creative writing: a poem or letter of consolation* Call students' attention to the directions in the textbook assignment that refer to their use of language. **(P.L.J.)**

FURTHER READING

Hikmet, Nazim, *Human Landscapes* (a novel in verse); *Poems of Nazim Hikmet.*

The Conjurer Made Off with the Dish

NAGUIB MAHFOUZ

INTRODUCING THE STORY

On the surface, "The Conjurer Made Off with the Dish" is a simple story about a boy's unsuccessful effort to buy beans for breakfast. However, the simplicity of the tale is deceiving. The boy's errand is a kind of quest, and his travels become an odyssey. The story depicts a boy's rite of passage from childhood toward the greater maturity of adolescence.

The boy experiences a series of wondrous delights and fearful consequences. He encounters a conjurer, who later threatens him for watching the show without paying for it. He accuses the conjurer of stealing his dish, though this is a feeble excuse for his own lack of responsibility. The boy uses his replacement coin to watch a peep show that reveals the world of heroism and romance in the form of pictures of chivalry, daring deeds, and love. This storybook experience infuses him with the ideals of courage and love. He meets a young girl who awakens within him romantic feelings that are new, strange, and obscure, and he shares his first kiss with her. However, when she hurries off to get the midwife for her mother, the boy realizes that he, too, has been neglecting his mother's request, and he hastens to make amends.

The boy's final adventure with the bean seller teaches him actions may have frightening consequences. By the time the boy returns to the bean seller with the requisite money and dish, the merchant has closed his shop. What follows is the boy's discovery of evil and a series of dangerous incidents that lead to the loss of his innocence.

First, the boy's perseverance so infuriates the bean seller that the merchant attacks him verbally and then physically. The boy summons the courage of the storybook hero and throws his dish at the merchant's head and then becomes terrified that his blow has killed the bean seller. The boy learns that unchecked anger may lead to violent behavior.

Fearing his mother's beating when he returns home without the beans, the boy postpones the inevitable by searching for the young girl. While waiting for her, he spies on an encounter between a tramp and a gypsy woman. He enjoys this lesson until the tramp strangles the woman. Again, the boy learns the danger of unchecked anger.

By the time he stops running away from the tramp, the boy is completely lost. The climax occurs as the boy contemplates the ways to handle his situation and the consequences of each choice.

In just one day, the boy has experienced the adult world and become part of it. From a thoughtless, self-centered, easily distracted, irresponsible child, the boy has "come of age." His experiences have taught him that the world is not always a good, safe place. The world is filled with the surprise of the unexpected, with the wonders of magic, and with ideal human behavior that expresses the values of love, courage, and heroism. In contrast, the world is also filled with people who become the victims of passions that incite them to perform violent deeds.

The boy learns that all people need to be on guard, prepared to defend themselves from possible harm—from without and from within. He learns that it is better to think before one acts.

The reader can only speculate on what choice the boy will make at the end of the story. However, the choice is unimportant compared with his new maturity that enables him to contemplate choices and their consequences before he acts.

Personal Literary Journal: Has a particular experience or group of experiences caused you to feel that you have left childhood behind and become more mature? Have you ever had an experience that has filled you with a sense of wonder or fear? If so, describe the aspects of the situation that have caused you to respond as you did.

Literary Terms: characterization, foreshadowing, irony, point of view, setting, theme, tone

COMPREHENSION QUESTIONS

1. *What does the boy's mother tell him to do?* to buy beans
2. *What does the mother expect the boy to do on his way to the market?* to play along the way; to let the carts distract him
3. *Why are the boy's first two attempts unsuccessful?* does not know about the oil
4. *Why is the boy's third attempt unsuccessful?* cannot find the piaster (Egyptian coin) his mother gave him
5. *Why is the boy's fourth attempt unsuccessful?* does not have the necessary dish
6. *On what does the boy spend his money?* a peep show
7. *What significant person does he meet there?* a young girl, whom he finds attractive
8. *How does the boy react to merchant and the tramp?* terrified of the merchant's anger and the tramp's brutality; runs away
9. *Why does the boy react to the tramp in this way?* fears the tramp will hurt or kill him because he has witnessed the tramp's treatment of the gypsy
10. *How does the story end?* boy is lost and must find his way home

UNDERSTANDING THE STORY: POSSIBLE ANSWERS

1. *Why boy forgets* The boy has no interest in performing the errand for his mother. Her world is serious, uninteresting, and seemingly irrelevant to him. Therefore, his attention is captured by the first appealing thing that he encounters—the conjurer.
2. *What attracts the boy* The boy is attracted by the unexpected, the unusual, and the unknown. He sees a world filled with wonders, including magic tricks and romantic adventures involving chivalry, heroic deeds, and love.
3. *Why say that the conjurer made off with the dish* The boy's statement reflects his inability to accept responsibility for his actions. He does not know what he did with the dish: He may have put it down while watching the magician or dropped it while running. He knows that if he blames the conjurer, people who see him crying will feel sorry for him.
4. *Two roles of the young girl* First, the girl provides the boy with his first experience of physical attraction. Second, the girl and the boy are counterparts. The girl's mother told her to bring a midwife. However, the girl is distracted by the peep show, then by the boy. Thus, she reminds the boy of his own irresponsible behavior.
5. *Effect of the peep show* The romantic subject matter of the peep show leaves the boy with dreams of chivalry, heroic deeds, and love that he transfers to the real world. Consequently, when the boy meets the girl who stood beside him at the show, he kisses her (love). Then when the bean seller attacks

the boy, the boy's dreams of heroic valor cause him to throw his dish at the bean seller's head (a daring and courageous deed).

6. *Significance of the tramp and the gypsy* The boy's observation of the tramp and the gypsy teaches him more about physical intimacy. However, when the tramp injures or kills the woman, the experience reveals the capacity of human beings to commit evil. Again, the boy learns that actions have consequences.

7. *Connection between the bean seller and the tramp* Both the bean seller and the tramp express their angry feelings through violent actions. The boy learns that one must control anger so that it does not lead to violent and destructive behavior.

8. *Boy's choice; why* Some students will think that he overcomes his fear of strangers to gain their help. Others will think that he will make his way home because he feels self-confident that he can surmount whatever difficulties he encounters.

9. *Quest/odyssey/initiation rite* The boy's quest is to buy beans. His adventure with the conjurer (whom he accuses of making off with his dish) teaches him to be more responsible for his belongings. His look at the peep show infuses him with the ideals of courage and love. His adventure with the girl makes him aware of his romantic feelings and his irresponsibility towards his mother. His final encounter with the bean seller shows him that anger may lead to violence. His observation of the tramp and the gypsy reinforces the danger of unchecked anger.

10. *How boy feels; effect of experiences on attitudes and behavior* At the end of the story, the boy has gained an awareness of himself, his world, and his vulnerability in that world. He fears the process of finding his way home and longs to be rescued by his mother. However, the boy has also had fascinating adventures and has survived to tell the tales. Therefore, despite his fears, he gathers the self-confidence to find his way home. In addition, the boy's attitudes have become more realistic. His experiences have taught him that he must be prepared to defend himself against self-inflicted harm as well as harm inflicted by others and that he can best do this by considering his choices and their consequences before he acts.

ANALYZING LITERARY TECHNIQUE: POSSIBLE ANSWERS

1. *First line; foreshadowing* The first line of this story reveals that from the mother's point of view, the boy is not useful. This leads the reader to expect that the boy will become distracted from the task at hand. It foreshadows that he will play along the way, confirming his mother's criticism of him. The first line tells the reader what the story will be about. The remainder of the story will fill in the details and make the first line significant.

2. *Setting* Examples of local color: the piaster (Egyptian coin); a breakfast of beans and linseed oil; swearing by the Koran; the lady Zainat al-Banat; the ancient wall; minarets; and the chief cadi.

3. *Point of view* Mahfouz takes the reader into the boy's world by having the boy tell his own story. The advantage of a first-person narrator is immediacy: Nothing intrudes between the protagonist and the reader. The disadvantage is limited knowledge: The reader knows only what the narrator thinks, sees, hears, and says.

   This technique is particularly effective in this story, where the author wishes to convey the youthful nature of the boy—how diverted he is from the prosaic world and enticed into the world of heroism and romance. The immediacy of the style also enhances the boy's responses to the unexpected dangers that he meets, such as his fear of the tramp and his concern about the possible consequences of his alternatives at the end of the story.

4. *Characterization* From the choices that the boy makes, the reader learns that his mother's evaluation of his behavior is accurate. He lets anything new, interesting, or romantic divert him from the prosaic task at hand. Moreover, when he attempts to perform his task, he does not possess the knowledge necessary to be successful or keep track of the piaster or the dish that he needs to buy the beans. The boy's attitudes and behavior reveal the gap that exists between his child's world and the world of adults.

5. *Irony* Examples of Mahfouz's use of irony: the boy's ignorance of behaviors that cause his mother to criticize him; the boy's surprise that the bean seller has closed shop for the day; and the violence that erupts at the end of the tramp and the gypsy's encounter.

6. *Tone* Mahfouz creates a gently humorous tone by juxtaposing incongruous points of view. The boy's mother and the bean seller assume that the boy can (and should) function efficiently and effectively in the adult world. Meanwhile, the boy lives in a world of innocence, emotional response, and spontaneity. To him, acting responsibly means performing a task whenever he gets around to it. He is blind to the attitudes and behavior that infuriate adults.

7. *Title* The title presents the boy's excuse for not having the dish that his mother sent with him to the market. The boy does not know what happened to his dish, just as he does not know what happened to the piaster that his mother gave him to pay for the beans. He is willing to blame someone else rather than take responsibility for his behavior. The title of the story reveals the youth of the protagonist and symbolizes his attitude and behavior.

   Reference in the title to the conjurer suggests the magical world that captures the mind of the boy.

*8. *Themes* Possible themes:
   - The world has two sides, light and dark. The light side is filled with magic and ideal human behavior that expresses the values of love, courage, and heroism. The dark side reveals people whose passions incite them to perform violent deeds.
   - The world is not always a good, safe place, and all people are not well-intentioned. Therefore, people need to be on guard, prepared to defend themselves from possible harm.

- The gap between generations cannot be bridged. Children cannot understand their parents, and parents cannot understand their children.

- The world of childhood is one of wonder and terror because so much is new but the child is able to control so little. The passage from childhood to adulthood is often painful.

- The evil actions of others can make people more appreciative of behavior that is generous and kind. Being aware of the human capacity to treat one another with cruelty may help a person behave in a manner that is good.

9. *Resolution/open-ended* The point of this story is the boy's initiation into the adult world. At the outset, his immaturity is reflected in his inattention to details in the adult world, such as which oil he eats with his beans every morning, where his piaster is, and why he needs to buy the beans early in the day.

At the end of the story, the boy has become more mature. His experiences in the adult world have led him to become aware of his actions and, therefore, to become more responsible. He knows that he has choices available to him; that each choice brings its own consequences; and that he must make his choices without letting himself become distracted.

Mahfouz does not tell the reader which choice the boy makes because the boy's choice is less important than his recognition of the importance of choosing, his understanding of the consequences of each choice, and his sense of personal responsibility in making choices.

WRITING ABOUT LITERATURE

1. *Essay analyzing thematic content* Students should choose three themes from the story to analyze. Support for their analysis should include ways in which the plot reveals each of the themes. (See **A.L.T.** question 8 above.) **AP**

2. *Creative writing: experience of a sense of wonder from a character's point of view* Call students' attention to the directions in the textbook assignment. Let them know that their journals may give them some insights. **(P.L.J.)**

3. *Creative writing: a "coming of age" experience* Call students' attention to the directions in the textbook assignment. Students should make the connection between the experience and the growth of their character. **(P.L.J.)**

FURTHER READING

Mahfouz, Naguib, *The Time and the Place and Other Stories*.

1. *Several selections in this unit contain differing views of deities at work in the world. Analyze the views of deities depicted by three speakers or characters in this unit.* Akhenaton, David, and HaNagid all view their gods as divine, creative, and powerful. Akhenaton views the Aton as being a benevolent creator who provides for all of life—human, plant, and animal. David also sees God as creator and sustainer of all life; he compares the greatness of God to the fragility of humans. While HaNagid sees God as creator of all, he fears God's judgment. Like David, he notes the contrast between God's power and human's fragility, but HaNagid focuses on the fear that this difference inspires.

   The various characters in *Antigone* also view the gods as all-powerful, and they fear the wrath of the gods. Antigone wishes to honor the gods by burying her brother, risking her life in the process (lines 81–2 and 499–518). Haemon believes that wisdom comes from following the gods' laws (lines 764–65 and 841). Tiresias (lines 1131–40 and 1181–1209) and the Chorus (lines 959–62 and 1466–70) believe that the gods will avenge themselves on the prideful and the stubborn. Creon chooses to ignore the gods, putting his wishes first, until the tragedy around him becomes so great that he must pay attention (lines 316–35, 823, 825, 833–34, 875–79, and 1228–30).

2. *Sappho, Dante, Nazim Hikmet, and Catullus use the literary device of apostrophe in their poems. Analyze the effect of apostrophe in the poems of three of these writers. Use quotations from the poems to support your answer.* The literary device of apostrophe gives a sense of immediacy to a poem. It causes the reader to react as though he or she is the one being addressed. Apostrophe can produce various effects. Sappho uses apostrophe to convey her strong sense of loss in not hearing from her friend who has moved away. Catullus uses apostrophe to convey both his grief at his brother's loss and his apologies for the lateness of his work. Dante uses apostrophe to convey his anger and resentment at the woman who has jilted him. Hikmet moves from despair over his situation to forced cheerfulness for his wife's sake. In each instance, the emotions are presented more effectively than they would be if the poet had simply described them.

3. *Luigi Pirandello, Emilia Pardo Bazán, and Naguib Mahfouz reveal their characters' personalities throughout their short stories. Using quotations from the stories, analyze how the writer portrays their main characters.* Luigi Pirandello uses both vivid descriptions of the characters' physical features ("a bulky woman . . . like a shapeless bundle," "a fat, red-faced man with bloodshot eyes of the palest grey") and actions ("The woman . . . was twisting and wriggling, at times growling like a wild animal," "a shrill laugh which might well have been a sob") to portray his characters' personalities. Pardo Bazán uses the characters' actions to reveal their personalities: Micaelita is intelligent and decisive, as shown by her endeavors to discover her fiancé's personality and her decision to leave him at the altar; Bernardo has a charming façade

concealing anger and contempt, as evidenced by his fleeting reaction to the torn lace. Mahfouz also reveals his characters' personalities through their actions: the boy's mother is contemptuous, refusing to listen to her son; the young girl is irresponsible for leaving her mother writhing in pain; the boy is thoughtless and easily distracted until circumstances and a new view of the world force him to take responsibility.

4. *Many of the characters in the stories, poems, and play in this unit are responding to crises. Analyze the responses of three characters in this unit to the crises they face.* Students might choose to examine the responses of the following characters to crises: Antigone, Ismene, Haemon, and Creon in *Antigone*; Micaelita in "Torn Lace"; the boy in "The Conjurer Made Off with the Dish"; the husband and wife in "War"; and Nazim Hikmet in his poem "Letter to My Wife."

Continental Europe

59

Human Knowledge

FRIEDRICH VON SCHILLER

INTRODUCING THE STORY

In "Human Knowledge," Schiller examines the limitations of human knowledge. He calls attention to the limitations of the subjective interpretation of facts, and he questions the value of deducing the whole by examining only part. He reveals the paradox that even scientists are as ignorant as they are knowledgeable because they emphasize an exclusively rational approach to learning.

The power of the poem comes from its structure, in which the poet concludes with an ironic question that reveals the paradox inherent in his philosophical subject. In addition, the tension between elements of classicism and romanticism adds texture and depth to the poem. Schiller relates his subject objectively, which is consistent with the highly rational content and approach of classicism. At the same time, he is a romantic in that he advocates that people rely upon their intuition and accept the existence of the irrational as an important part of the meaning of the universe.

Personal Literary Journal: How do you know that what you know is correct? Do you think that it is possible to know everything that there is to know about something? What factors determine whether or not the acquisition of total knowledge is possible? What factors may change the knowledge that one has acquired?

Literary Terms: allusion, classicism, irony, metaphor, paradox, romanticism, theme, tone

COMPREHENSION QUESTIONS

1. *What do human beings read in Nature?* their own ideas
2. *What do human beings do to Nature's wonders?* arrange them into categories
3. *What do human beings do to Nature's expanses?* tie them with cords; in other words, attempt to classify them or arrange them into manageable subunits
4. *How does the astronomer explain the universe?* through reducing it to sets of constellations
5. *What part of the heavens does the astronomer see?* only its surface

UNDERSTANDING THE POEM: POSSIBLE ANSWERS

*1. *Why people think they understand Nature* People project systems and ideas onto Nature. Once those projected systems seem to become "natural," people no longer recognize that the systems reflect their own interests, biases, and limited understanding.

*2. *Why the astronomer believes he understands the universe* The astronomer, trained to see the heavens only in terms of constellations, does what he is trained to do and ends up believing that he understands the universe. However, all he really sees are the systems of constellations—the "figures" of "the swan" and "the bull"—that he has projected onto the sky.

*3. *How stanzas relate to each other* The first stanza is concerned with "Nature"—the natural principles that govern the universe; the second is concerned specifically with the heavens. In addition, the first stanza addresses the reader directly, while the second stanza uses a third-person perspective to describe the actions of the astronomer. The astronomer is just one example of the limited thinking that the poet is criticizing.

*4. *What Schiller is criticizing* Schiller is criticizing the fact that the astronomer links stars into constellations, though the stars have no real connection with one another (they are a "Sirius-distance" apart). Consequently the astronomer, like the reader in the first stanza, reads into the universe only what he himself has written there.

*5. *Themes* Possible themes:

- A little knowledge is a dangerous thing because it is incomplete and inaccurate;

- People know much less about the universe than they think they know;

- The universe contains two types of elements—those that the human mind can grasp and those that are beyond the limitations of the human mind.

ANALYZING LITERARY TECHNIQUE: POSSIBLE ANSWERS

*1. *Paradox about knowledge* The paradox in this poem is that those who think themselves wise are, in fact, ignorant of the true nature of the universe, whether they consider the earth or the heavens.

*2. *Meaning of the "spheres' mystic dance" (line 10)* Literally, the image means "how the stars move in the sky." In a broader sense, "mystic" in this metaphor refers to the knowledge that is beyond the ability of the human mind to comprehend, and "dance" implies harmonious relationships and patterns in the universe that cannot be explained by systems and scientific methods. By using a metaphor, Schiller underscores the fact that much of human understanding of how the universe works is based on analogy—on comparing the large and mysterious with the small and commonplace.

3. *Classicism vs. romanticism* The form of the poem adheres to principles of classicism in that the two stanzas complement and balance each other and the poet stands apart from the poem and presents his ideas objectively.

On the other hand, the content of the poem is more reflective of romanticism than of classicism. The poet argues against a rational approach to understanding the universe, maintaining that its meaning is mystical and therefore beyond human comprehension. It would be in keeping with romanticism to value one's emotional instincts and intuition about the nature of the universe, even if one could find no tangible confirmation of this type of knowledge.

The tension between classical and romantic elements adds complexity and interest to the poem.

*4. *Tone of poem* The tone may be described as the ironic smile of one who is observing a very serious person pursue the wrong path. Schiller achieves this by considering the approach to knowledge of the reader and the astronomer and then asking the question about the "spheres' mystic dance." The question implies that each approach is a blind alley, for neither will lead to true knowledge.

WRITING ABOUT LITERATURE

1. *Essay analyzing Schiller's technique in presenting theme* Students' responses will vary depending on which theme they choose. (See **U.P.** questions 1, 2, 3, 4, and 5 and **A.L.T.** questions 1, 2, and 4 above.) **AP**

2. *Creative writing: changing human knowledge* Encourage students to focus on one specific issue. Changing ideas about the role of heredity and environment in human development, the ability to cure certain diseases, the role of women in society, or the effects of automobile emissions on the environment are examples of possible topics. Students should try to convey what difference a developing understanding makes in how people perceive the world. **(P.L.J.)**

FURTHER READING

von Schiller, Friedrich, "Ode to Joy"; *The Maid of Orleans; William Tell; Don Carlos*.

The Shadow

HANS CHRISTIAN ANDERSEN

INTRODUCING THE STORY

"The Shadow" appeals to readers of all ages. On the surface, it is a highly imaginative story of a shadow that becomes independent of its master and lives its own life. On this level, the language is informal and often humorous, with details that children love. On a deeper level, "The Shadow" is a serious, satirical commentary on social values and the relationship of art to life; it is also a study of human psychology.

The "learned man" in the story, a dedicated scholar of "what is good and true and beautiful," cannot share his vision because society has no interest in it. Veneer rather than substance counts. The Shadow is the learned man's double, the dark counterpart of his former master. He is the learned man's doppelgänger in that he personifies everything that the learned man cannot permit himself to be, cannot acknowledge in himself, and cannot recognize in others. The learned man and the Shadow represent one complete personality that is split between them. The learned man personifies the human desire to be good, while the Shadow personifies the human desire to be free to act without controls.

Being interested only in what is evil, false, and ugly, the Shadow easily adapts to the society in which he lives, and society rewards him. Living completely without moral or ethical values, he acquires wealth, social prestige, and power through blackmail. Meanwhile the "over-sharp-sighted" Princess, who is blind to what is good, true, and beautiful, finds the Shadow to be noble. She is impressed with his appearance of wealth and cleverness, and she fails to recognize the learned man's true value.

Through the learned man, Andersen attempts to explode one of the guiding principles of romanticism—goodness cannot destroy evil; if evil is left to its own devices, it will destroy what is good. The learned man becomes the Shadow's victim because he is unwilling to see what is evil, false, and ugly and therefore cannot deal with these qualities when they confront him. Hearing the Shadow's tales of blackmail, he says, "Extraordinary!" He makes no value judgment; he voices no condemnation. He accompanies the Shadow with no perception of what the future holds for him. Although the learned man finally takes a stand, refusing to surrender his integrity and to become the Shadow's shadow, he acts too late. The Shadow has him killed. The only ray of light in this dark tale is that the Shadow's evil cannot contaminate the learned man; he dies true to the humane values by which he has lived.

Andersen's theme belongs to a tradition that remains vital to contemporary life. Human beings cannot control their capacity to hurt others unless they recognize that each person's heart is composed of two chambers, a "heart of darkness" and a heart of virtue. From the time of the ancient Greeks, the principle "Know thyself" has demanded a self-knowledge that acknowledges the totality of what it is to be human.

The story also functions as a satire on society's inability to understand and appreciate learning and art. The landlord, who represents the ordinary person, regards Poetry's music as tiresome. The learned man, who is often called a philosopher and who is a student of aesthetics (the study of the good, the true, and the beautiful), writes about Poetry yet can find no way to approach her apartment since he is an observer, not an artist. Meanwhile the Shadow claims that he has entered the antechamber of Poetry's apartment and that he has seen everything and knows everything about Poetry. His inability to be specific reveals that his words have no more substance than he himself possesses. However, society accepts and praises the Shadow because it values his pretensions. It succumbs to his blackmail and makes him a wealthy person without ever realizing that he is a fake. The Princess easily accepts the Shadow's pretensions because they are consistent with her own.

Andersen's symbolic use of light (good) versus dark (evil) and sight (truth) versus blindness (fraudulence) enriches both the moral and satiric aspects of the story. The learned man, who is good, functions in sunlight; but he does not function during the hours around noon, when the light is brightest. He sees more clearly than others but not clearly enough to recognize evil in life. In contrast, the Shadow, who is evil, is composed of darkness and operates when light is low. Society is blind to the reality of what the learned man sees (his knowledge of truth and beauty) and therefore has no interest in his writings. The Princess, who should represent the best in society, takes pride in her "over-sharp sight" and yet cannot see beneath the appearances that she values; thus, she cannot see beneath the Shadow's pretensions.

Personal Literary Journal: What makes a person human? To what extent, if any, is an evil person human? What makes a person wise? What are the most important goals in life?

Literary Terms: characterization, doppelgänger, irony, satire, theme

COMPREHENSION QUESTIONS

1. *What is important to the learned man about being human?* to be able to appreciate what is good, true, and beautiful

2. *What is important to the Shadow about being human?* to be wealthy, powerful, and accepted by high society

3. *How does the Shadow separate from the learned man?* climbs the wall across the street and disappears

4. *How does the Shadow gain wealth?* blackmails the people he spies on

5. *How does the Shadow gain prestige?* marries the Princess

6. *How does the Shadow gain power?* through blackmail, marriage, and travel with the learned man

7. *What relationship develops between the learned man and the Shadow?* The Shadow becomes the master; the learned man becomes the shadow.

8. *What happens to the Shadow at the end of the story?* marries the Princess

9. *What happens to the learned man at the end?* The Shadow has the learned man killed.

UNDERSTANDING THE STORY: POSSIBLE ANSWERS

1. *The Shadow's identity* The Shadow takes on his own identity as an independent person who is a fraud. His responses to the learned man's questions reveal his arrogance and his pretentiousness. If he possessed the knowledge of Poetry that he claims to have, he would be able to provide detailed answers. His inability to get beyond the antechamber reveals that Poetry remained inaccessible to him, just as Poetry is inaccessible to the learned man. Andersen may be implying that a true understanding of art is inaccessible to observers (the landlord and the Shadow), to students of art (philosophers like the learned man and critics), and, in fact, to anyone except the artist. The Shadow's replies to the learned man reveal the kind of person he is, and his success in society and with the Princess reveals that they share and appreciate his fake values.

2. *Who is more human?* Both the learned man and the Shadow are human, each representing an opposite side of human nature. It is the weakness of the learned man that he confuses *human* with *humane* and refuses to consider whatever in life is not "the true and the good and the beautiful." This weakness makes him vulnerable to the Shadow, for the learned man cannot deal with qualities that he cannot acknowledge.

3. *Wisdom of the learned man and the Shadow* Each possesses a different kind of wisdom. The learned man finds wisdom in books; he knows about ideas

and facts. The Shadow finds wisdom in daily life; he knows about the values and interests of most people.

4. *Why the Shadow visits the learned man* The Shadow first comes to brag about his personal success. He wants to show off to his former master. The learned man's reaction, finding him "extraordinary" rather than repulsive, leads the Shadow to sense a tolerance in the learned man that may permit the Shadow to use the learned man, just as he uses other people, for his own personal gain. With the trip to the spa, the Shadow succeeds.

   The learned man continues to allow the Shadow to visit him because his denial of evil makes it impossible for him to deal with evil. This blind spot makes the learned man vulnerable to the Shadow. The learned man's poverty and ill health make the Shadow's offer hard to resist.

5. *The learned man's acceptance of the Shadow's terms* The learned man retains his dignity and integrity by refusing the Shadow's offer. To accept would be to deny the principles by which the learned man has lived his entire life. He would not just become a shadow but the shadow of an amoral being. For the learned man, death is preferable to a life of wealth and comfort with the loss of his integrity.

6. *Triumphs of the learned man and the Shadow* The learned man triumphs in the end in that he dies without sacrificing his integrity and his belief in the principles by which he has lived. He has not demeaned himself. The Shadow has triumphed in that he has acquired the power to put the learned man to death for not agreeing to become his servant. Evil has triumphed to the extent that the Shadow has gained wealth, prestige, and power. A significant lesson for all people is that evil behavior (like the behavior of the Shadow) can and does triumph whenever good human beings (like the learned man) stand by and do nothing. People who remain true to their humane principles when confronted with the temptations of evil are models of heroic behavior.

7. *Themes* Possible themes:
   - The serious underlying theme is that evil cannot be controlled unless individuals acknowledge its existence. All human beings can better control their behavior if they recognize their capability to be callous and cruel, dishonest and disloyal.
   - Another more obvious theme is "You cannot judge a book by its cover." The Shadow, the learned man, and the Princess all have trouble both with judging others by their appearances and with being judged by their own appearances.

ANALYZING LITERARY TECHNIQUE: POSSIBLE ANSWERS

1. *Fairy-tale effect* Andersen achieves the fairy-tale effect of the story through its informality of tone. The narrator's colloquial expressions ("My word!"; "Well") and asides ("in the hot countries every window has a balcony"; "he made up his mind to say nothing about it, and that was very sensible of

him") create the feeling of listening to a storyteller, thus adding immediacy to the story.

The first clear indication that the story has a deeper meaning than a tale told for children comes when the Shadow returns. The Shadow's treatment of the learned man's new shadow reveals that the Shadow is a cruel person and foreshadows that he will mistreat his former master.

*2. *Relationship between the learned man and the Shadow* The Shadow is the learned man's double. He is also the learned man's literal and figurative doppelgänger (dark counterpart). The Shadow personifies everything that the learned man cannot permit himself to be, cannot acknowledge in himself, and cannot recognize in others. The Shadow represents the learned man's unrestrained self, the part of his nature that desires to act without any internal or external controls.

3. *Function of light imagery* Andersen uses conventional images of light in this story. On a literal level, the sun, moon, and other lights provide the scientific rationale for the Shadow's development and activities: There can be no shadow without a source of light. On a more symbolic level, images of light and dark emphasize the importance of seeing things clearly, as they really are. The Shadow sees most of the world in twilight and moonlight; even the learned man has to retire from the "full blaze of the sun."

4. *Humor* Humor adds to the fairy-tale tone of the story. It makes the tale more enjoyable and, therefore, more likely to have an impact on the audience. Examples of humor in this story include the following:

- the basic idea of a shadow assuming an independent life;
- the Shadow's repeated comment "I have seen everything and I know everything." This response to every question about specific details allows the Shadow to evade the questions. In the end, the Shadow admits that he never entered Poetry's inner rooms;
- the Shadow's comments about the need for a beard and the importance of being fat;
- many of the narrator's asides, such as the learned man's saying " 'a man's as good as his word' " and the Shadow's replying, "the only way possible, 'And so is a shadow.' "

*5. *Irony* Irony gives the story power. It keeps the reader alert to the discrepancies between appearances and reality, and it adds the element of surprise. It is the technique Andersen uses to satirize society. Examples of irony include:

- The Princess suffers from "over-sharp sight" and can "very nearly see right through" the Shadow but cannot see what kind of a person he really is.
- The Princess remarks that the Shadow has "a noble character," but the Shadow has gained wealth, social prestige, and power through blackmail, and he instigates the murder of the learned man.

- The Shadow's remark about his "innermost nature" reveals that he is a man who evades the issue of what type of man he is.
- The Shadow's remark that he deserves respect because he is independent and well informed and has good standing and excellent connections points out false values and superficial qualities valued by the Shadow and society.
- The good learned man has no worldly success, while the evil Shadow achieves fortune and fame.

The power of "The Shadow" is in its satirization of society. Each humorous and ironic example is also an example of satire. Andersen is ridiculing the characters who are making the remarks, satirizing them for being socially pretentious and for espousing inferior values. In this story, clothes literally do not make a man.

WRITING ABOUT LITERATURE

1. *Essay analyzing Andersen's view of society* Call students' attention to the directions in the textbook assignment. (See **A.L.T.** questions 2 and 5 above.) **AP**

2. *Creative writing: a fairy tale* You may want to make some collections of fairy tales available to the class to spark students' ideas. Encourage independent thinking and creativity. **(P.L.J.)**

FURTHER READING

Andersen, Hans Christian, "The Bell"; "The Drop of Water"; "The Emperor's New Clothes"; "The Fir Tree"; "The Little Match Girl"; "The Nightingale"; "The Snow Queen"; "The Story of a Mother"; "The Sweethearts"; "The Ugly Duckling."

The Heavenly Christmas Tree

FYODOR DOSTOYEVSKY

INTRODUCING THE STORY

"The Heavenly Christmas Tree" is a small gem that displays one of Dostoyevsky's major themes, society's lack of moral responsibility for the poor and downtrodden in its midst. The style is an example of psychological realism. Dostoyevsky's respect for the poor, his interest in their plight, his concern with the moral growth of society, and his decision to portray his characters realistically reflect the influence of Nicolai Gogol and Charles Dickens. However, the psychological aspect of his realism is his own creation and his unique focus.

The plot of this story describes, with chilling dramatic irony, how a six-year-old boy becomes orphaned, starves, and freezes to death on Christmas Eve while the wealthy and the middle class turn away in self-conscious discomfort. The subject and setting appeal to readers' hearts, for Christmas is associated with love, family, plentiful food, and gifts. The contrast between this festive, joyous holiday and the poor, starving orphan's isolation and abandonment makes the story a searing indictment of any society that is indifferent to those in need.

In order to convey psychological realism in his characterization of the little boy, Dostoyevsky writes in a style that seeks to imitate a young child's thought processes and language, dramatizing his emotional as well as physical experiences. Dostoyevsky focuses on what captures the child's attention and how he reacts to what he sees, expressing his thoughts and feelings in language patterns that are appropriately repetitive and rambling.

The last line of the story reminds the educated reader that some of Dostoyevsky's writing contains the roots of existentialism. By questioning the existence of heaven (and God), Dostoyevsky leaves the fate of such children and mothers as those in this story to the social conscience of his readers. The readers, as members of society, must exert themselves to help the poor and homeless, for the compensation of a better world is not certain after death.

Your students will be interested in hearing the following descriptive passage from the April 1864 issue of *Vremya* (the literary journal that Dostoyevsky and his brother founded). It reveals what is probably the source of Dostoyevsky's inspiration for this story.

> Once I remember seeing among the crowd of people in the street a little girl who could not have been more than six years old. Her clothes were in tatters. She was dirty, barefoot, and beaten black and blue. Her body, which could be seen through the holes in her clothes, was all bruised. She was walking along aimlessly, hardly knowing where she was, and without apparently being in any hurry to get anywhere. Goodness knows why she was roaming about in the crowd; perhaps she was hungry. No one paid any attention to her. But what struck me most about her was that she looked so wretched and unhappy. Such hopeless despair was written all over her face that to see that little creature already experiencing so much damnation and despair was to the highest degree unnatural and terribly painful. She kept shaking her dishevelled head from side to side, as though debating some highly important question with herself, waving her little hands about and gesticulating wildly, and then, suddenly, clapping them together and pressing them to her bosom. I went back and gave her sixpence. She seized the small silver coin, gave me a wild look of startled surprise, and suddenly began running in the opposite direction as fast as her little legs would carry her, as though terrified that I should take the money away from her.

Juxtaposed with "The Heavenly Christmas Tree," this passage reveals how Dostoyevsky transformed a particular life experience into universal art.

Personal Literary Journal: To what extent are you responsible for the welfare of other human beings? What are your obligations to others?

Literary Terms: characterization, contrast, fairy tale, folktale, dramatic irony, narrative perspective, naturalism, paradox, protagonist, psychological realism, realism, theme, tone

COMPREHENSION QUESTIONS

1. *What sends the child wandering into the street?* mother's death, hunger

2. *How is he treated?* ignored

3. *What gives him pleasure?* Christmas store windows and parties

4. *What happens to him?* dies of cold and hunger

5. *What does the author question?* heaven

UNDERSTANDING THE STORY: POSSIBLE ANSWERS

1. *Dostoyevsky's purpose in writing this tale* Dostoyevsky has a social purpose: to dramatize the plight of the poor and to motivate others to help.

2. *Boy's treatment and society* The boy's treatment reveals that (1) a great gap exists between the rich and the poor (the Christmas parties); (2) those who have the ability to be helpful ignore those in need (the policeman; the woman at the party the boy enters); and (3) the poor are friendless and helpless (the people on the street; the bigger boy).

3. *Effect of Christmas festivities on boy's life* The Christmas festivities were the highlight of the boy's day and possibly the highlight of his life. He would have died of starvation whether or not he had seen them, so it can be argued that his life was briefly cheered by his views of Christmas magic.

4. *Importance of Dostoyevsky's final comment about Christ's Christmas tree* Dostoyevsky puts the burden of the welfare of the poor and downtrodden on society, rather than on religious beliefs. He does not permit his readers to avoid their moral responsibilities by assuming the existence of heaven and compensation there for misery on earth.

ANALYZING LITERARY TECHNIQUE: POSSIBLE ANSWERS

*1. *Why protagonist is a young child* The young child is more vulnerable, more helpless, more frightened, more appealing, and less threatening to strangers who could help him, and more appealing to readers' sympathies.

*2. *Why a Christmas setting?* Christmas is the happiest time of year for many children, who receive gifts and enjoy family parties. The holiday contrasts the plight of the poor and downtrodden child with the happiness of those who receive love and care. The story shows that most people do not act upon their religious principles of love and charity.

*3. *Important human traits* Dostoyevsky most values the human traits of love, compassion, and charity. He reveals them by negative inference, in that the reader sees the consequences of their absence for the little boy.

4. *Elements reminiscent of a folktale; their contribution* The style of the story resembles a folktale in three ways: (1) repetitive sentence structure; (2) a pattern of three episodes that invite the child's attention (two parties and a window display of toys); and (3) the use of colloquial expressions. This style conveys dramatic irony in that the story reads like a folktale, but it depicts a harsh and cruel reality.

The story is the opposite of a fairy tale in the following ways: (1) it lacks magic; (2) it has no beneficent adult; (3) it lacks a happy ending. The child dies, and Dostoyevsky states that he's not certain that a paradise exists that could compensate the child for his suffering. Nothing redeems the tragic conclusion.

*5. *Psychological realism* Examples of psychological realism include: (1) the boy's focus on his fear of the dog, his enjoyment of the parties, and his fascination with the toys; (2) the boy's rambling and repetitive sentence patterns; and (3) the boy's childlike imitation of adult expressions. These combine to make the boy a real child with whom the reader can identify. When the boy dies, the reader is profoundly affected by society's role in his fate.

6. *Irony* Irony exists in: (1) the contrast between the Christmas season, which is the time of "brotherly love," and the starving, poorly clothed boy, whom no one attempts to help; (2) the nurse, who has spent her life caring for others but is now left to die alone; and (3) the contrast between the style of a folktale for children and the content that depicts a harsh reality of life.

*7. *Tone* The tone of the story is heart-wrenching and grim. Dostoyevsky achieves it by placing the center of consciousness in a vulnerable six-year-old, whose view of Christmastime is that of the deprived outsider. The technique of psychological realism emphasizes the contrast between the child's devastating situation and the world that fascinates and ignores him.

WRITING ABOUT LITERATURE

1. *Essay on realism vs. naturalism* **AP**

   a) The story is in the tradition of realism in that it attempts to achieve an accurate depiction of life. The realists focused on ordinary people, ordinary locations, and ordinary occurrences. Specific details about the appearance of objects and people were important.

   b) The story is in the tradition of naturalism in its focus on "sordid realism" and in its more subjective presentation of the subject. The technique of psychological realism would have been too subjective for the realists. The choice of a helpless, uncomprehending protagonist helps place this story in the naturalist tradition.

2. *Essay analyzing psychological realism* Call students' attention to the directions in the textbook assignment with regard to content and organization. (See **A.L.T.** questions 1, 2, 3, 5 and 7 above.) **AP**

3. *Creative writing: this story from another character's point of view* Call students' attention to the questions suggested in the textbook assignment. Remind students that some people justify their own behavior and others feel guilty. **(P.L.J.)**

FURTHER READING

Dostoyevsky, Fyodor, "The Double"; "The Gambler"; "A Gentle Spirit"; "An Honest Thief"; "Notes From the Underground"; *Crime and Punishment*.

How Much Land Does a Man Need?

LEO TOLSTOY

INTRODUCING THE STORY

"How Much Land Does a Man Need?" is one of Tolstoy's most famous short stories. It is a traditional folktale that has been transformed into a parable that teaches that "greed is the root of evil." The plot concerns a peasant who can never resist the opportunity to acquire more good land. In the course of pursuing greater wealth, Pahóm forces his son to become a laborer, falsely accuses a neighbor of chopping down his trees, mistreats and alienates the local peasants with his selfishness, and leaves his wife behind to manage one estate while his greed compels him to acquire another. He behaves as the ultimate narcissist in that he uses all other human beings to further his own ends and never considers their needs, desires, or feelings.

The tale is a superb example of Tolstoy's interest in human nature and his ability to characterize people. It examines how Pahóm behaves, the thoughts and feelings that motivate him to behave as he does, and the consequences that result from his actions. The plot is powerful for two reasons. First, the emotions that motivate Pahóm's materialism are common in varying degree to all human beings and, therefore, all readers can relate personally to the story. Second, in examining the morality of Pahóm's decisions and their effect on his personality and, indirectly, on his responsibilities to his family and his neighbors, Tolstoy leads his readers to evaluate the morality and the pragmatic wisdom of their own materialistic attitudes and behavior.

James Joyce regarded this tale as "the greatest story that the literature of the world knows." It is possible that what Joyce so admired in this tale was Tolstoy's superb fusion of content and style. The story addresses the universal and basic human question of what should be a person's goal in life, and it is told in the simple and direct style of a folktale. Every detail in the story contributes to the total design and the underlying moral content. The opening argument between the two sisters introduces the theme of the story and brings out the factors of temptation, anxiety, and loss that accompany gain (Pahóm's acquisition of land). Finally, the nature of Pahóm's sleepless night, his reaction to his prophetic dream, and every decision he makes in the course of his final quest foreshadow his fate. Tolstoy concludes with two crowning ironies: Pahóm has gained the land, but he has lost his life; and he actually needs no more land than the space his body occupies in death.

Personal Literary Journal: What do you need in order to be happy? Is it better to be satisfied with what you have or to strive to improve it?

Literary Terms: allegory, characterization, foreshadowing, irony, parable, paradox, theme

COMPREHENSION QUESTIONS

1. (I) *What does the city sister cite as advantages of city life?* good clothes, food, and entertainment

2. (I) *What does the country sister cite as advantages of country life?* freedom from anxiety, lack of temptations, ability to keep one's wealth

3. (I) *Who wants to get Pahóm into his power?* the Devil

4. (II) *What sacrifice does Pahóm make to buy land?* hires son out as laborer

5. (III) *What does Pahóm do to Simon?* falsely accuses him of chopping down his trees

6. (IV) *When Pahóm first moves beyond the Volga, how does he get more land?* rents it

7. (VI) *When Pahóm goes to the land of the Bashkírs, how much land will he be able to acquire?* as much as he can walk around from sunrise to sunset of one day, for a payment of 1,000 rubles

8. (VII) *What dream does Pahóm have?* Devil is tempting him and laughs at his death

9. (VIII) *Why does his dream become reality?* can't pass up good land

10. (IX) *How does the tale end?* Pahóm buried in land just his size

UNDERSTANDING THE STORY: POSSIBLE ANSWERS

1. *Rural setting and a peasant protagonist* Tolstoy believes that life on the land is more natural for humans, that it appeals to basic drives and needs in all people. A tale set in the country would therefore have applications for all readers.

2. *Peasant less greedy than tradesman? Why Devil knows how to treat Pahóm* Tolstoy proves that the peasant is at least as greedy as the tradesman. His point is that most human beings, regardless of their social status, spend their lives acquiring goods rather than helping others and improving their minds. The Devil knows that given the opportunity, it is human nature to be greedy, and peasants are greedy for land.

3. *Why the Devil?* The Devil was probably part of the original folktale and would make the tale more appealing to the intended audience, the peasants. The Devil's presence in the story underscores that Pahóm's choices are choices between good and evil. Thus, the Devil functions as an allegorical figure, an external symbol of an internal psychological factor.

4. *Effect of ownership of land on Pahóm's personality* Pahóm changes in that he now cares more about his land than about any human being and, therefore, becomes inhumane. He forgets what it is like to be a landless peasant, and he attempts to keep other peasants off his land by having them fined. He also falsely accuses a neighbor of chopping down his trees and then falsely accuses the judges who acquit the neighbor of having been bribed.

5. *Factors Pahóm wisely or foolishly ignores in his choices* Pahóm ignores the needs and desires of his wife and children. He does not explore other ways of leading a rewarding life. He might have used some of his wealth to help others and to improve his community. He is foolish in that, even if he had not died, he would have ended up alone. Since he cared about no one, no one would have cared about him.

*6. *Title* The title reveals the theme of the story: Should a person's goal in life be material or spiritual? How much land a person needs depends upon the individual's purpose in life; a rewarding life is not dependent on ownership of land. Thus, the title's meaning changes with the perspective.

7. *Why Bashkír chief laughs at the end* The chief, having more land than he needs, does not value it the way Pahóm does. He cannot imagine a person being so foolish as to die from the attempt to acquire more and more land.

8. *Significance of Pahóm's dream: role of fate* Pahóm's dream confirms his sole responsibility for his fate. He ignores his dream because his greed blinds him to the consequences of his behavior.

9. *Better to be satisfied or to improve* Tolstoy would probably opt for moderation, acquiring enough for material comfort and well-being, but without sacrificing humane values and relationships.

ANALYZING LITERARY TECHNIQUE: POSSIBLE ANSWERS

1. *Function of argument between two sisters* The argument involves the theme of the story, what a person's goal in life should be or what is necessary for a person to be happy, and foreshadows the plot. The points (temptation, anxiety, loss and gain) made by Pahóm's wife ironically prove to be more applicable to Pahóm (they cause his death) than to her brother-in-law.

2. *Characterization of Pahóm* Tolstoy focuses on Pahóm's very human nature. Pahóm first feels joy and satisfaction as a landowner, but these feelings prove to be very transitory because he soon becomes accustomed to whatever he has. Ownership makes Pahóm very protective of his possessions, and he becomes selfish, greedy, and cruel. Because Pahóm's feelings are common to some extent in all human beings, he seems real to Tolstoy's readers.

3. *Foreshadowing* Examples include: (1) Pahóm's sleepless night, which foreshadows his exhaustion; (2) Pahóm's dream, which foreshadows his death; (3) Pahóm's inability to reject good land, which foreshadows his overextending himself because of his greed; (4) Pahóm's removal of his shoes, which foreshadows his difficult walking; and (5) Pahóm's exhausted run at the end, which foreshadows the strain on his heart and his death.

4. *Irony* Examples of irony include: (1) the double meaning of the title; (2) the applicability of Pahóm's wife's arguments to Pahóm; (3) Pahóm's inability to appreciate what he has; and (4) Pahóm's change in personality as he acquires land. In this story, irony adds power, humor, and pathos.

*5. *Parable* A parable is a short story designed to teach moral value. Greed, one of the seven deadly sins, is the subject of the tale. The tale's lesson is that those who succumb to the temptation of greed cause their own moral and physical destruction. Pahóm's pride and greed keep him from learning from his experience. Realizing that he will die, Pahóm still is not willing to sacrifice his pride and 1,000 rubles in exchange for his life. The story moves the reader to examine his or her own life to be certain that he or she is not as foolish as Pahóm.

WRITING ABOUT LITERATURE

1. *Essay comparing Chekhov's and Tolstoy's points of view* Encourage independent points of view, and emphasize the importance of supporting details. (See **U.S.** question 6 and **A.L.T.** question 5 above.) **AP**

2. *Creative writing: a letter from Pahóm's wife to her sister* Encourage both positive and negative points of view. Remind students to attempt to characterize Pahóm's wife through her use of language. **(P.L.J.)**

FURTHER READING

Tolstoy, Leo, "The Death of Ivan Ilych"; "Master and Man"; *Anna Karenina.*

A Doll's House

HENRIK IBSEN

INTRODUCING THE PLAY

Nora, Torvald's "sweet little song-bird," is an interesting and complex character. She is a woman of her time (the 1880s); but the restrictions she faced as a woman lasted well into the 1950s, and today women are still fighting for independence and equality. In the late nineteenth century, a middle-class woman's place was in the home, and career opportunities for women who wanted or needed to work were largely limited to those of seamstress, teacher, nurse, or in some instances clerical worker or shop salesperson. A girl was reared to be a good wife and mother. She was not expected to be educated (considered a waste of money) or to have a career (considered unnecessary) but to marry well by attracting a husband who would be a good provider as well as a loving mate. Her husband would earn and manage the family finances, giving her an allowance for household expenses and personal clothing.

As *A Doll's House* opens, Nora is a young woman who, to please her husband, must conceal whatever independent actions she takes. Some actions are trivial, such as eating sweets, but one action is crucial to the development of the plot. Nora borrowed money to finance a year in Italy for Torvald's health, and she must repay the loan. As a woman, she lacks training, experience, and opportunity in financial matters—most importantly, she lacks the legal status to negotiate the loan in her own name. That she develops a secret life to negotiate and conceal the loan reveals strength of character: She possesses the imagination, conviction, and courageous initiative to sail in uncharted waters.

Nora's explanations to Mrs. Linden (Christina) in Act I make it clear that she enjoys the independence and enhanced self-image that her secret life brings her. Working at copying to earn money has been wonderfully masculine. However, she also states that she plans to continue to be Torvald's "sweet little song-bird" until "it doesn't amuse him any longer to see me skipping about, and dressing up and acting." As tasty as the fruits of independence are, as Nora sees from Mrs. Linden's experience, the task of supporting herself would be difficult. Nora is content to pretend to be "silly" and "spendthrift" until Torvald's horrified response to her well-intentioned forgery of her father's guaranty of her loan forces her to choose between her two lives.

At the close of the play, Nora courageously faces public condemnation by leaving her husband and children to discover who she really is. The fact that she and Torvald are incompatible and that she no longer loves him are sufficient reasons to leave him. The cost of leaving her children is much higher, but she believes that greater self-knowledge will be worth that cost. The message of the play is that learning who one is and becoming that person is worth any price.

Nora and Mrs. Linden have an interesting psychological relationship in the play. Mrs. Linden functions as Nora's double or doppelgänger in that she represents what Nora secretly would like to be, an autonomous woman who is free to take risks and to assume the consequences. It is a form of dramatic irony that Nora wants the freedom that Mrs. Linden has while Mrs. Linden wants the loving husband and family that Nora has.

The plot and style of A Doll's House are completely and naturally fused so that the texture of language and action is rich with layered meanings. Ibsen carefully prepares the audience for Nora's final action through his frequent use of foreshadowing and irony. A Doll's House is an unusually good vehicle for gaining an understanding of these literary techniques.

Similarly, both Torvald and Nora provide fine vehicles for the study of characterization. Whereas Nora's actions are premeditated and conscious, Torvald's are natural and instinctive. What Torvald says and how he treats Nora and the other characters reveal his consistent selfishness and his inability to tolerate any point of view but his own.

Personal Literary Journal: Which do you consider more important, your obligation to yourself or your obligation to those you love? Are these obligations equally important? To what extent are you responsible for your own life, and to what extent are others responsible for it?

Literary Terms: characterization, doppelgänger, foreshadowing, irony, naturalism, paradox, theme

COMPREHENSION QUESTIONS

1. (I) *What do Nora and Torvald argue about?* Nora spends too much money.

2. (I) *What secret does Nora tell Mrs. Linden?* Nora secretly borrowed money for the trip to Italy and is working hard to repay it.

3. (I) *What does Nora do for Mrs. Linden?* Nora gets her a job at Torvald's bank.

4. (I) *What does Krogstad ask Nora to do for him?* Nora must prevent Torvald from firing Krogstad.

5. (I) *What crime has Nora committed?* Nora forged her father's name as guarantor of her loan.

6. (II) *Who is Dr. Rank?* A friend of Torvald's who is in love with Nora; he is dying.

7. (II) *What does Krogstad intend to do with Nora's IOU?* Krogstad will keep it for blackmail.

8. (II) *What does Nora ask Torvald to promise at the end of Act II?* Nora asks Torvald to promise not to open any letters until after the dance.

9. (III) *What is the relationship between Mrs. Linden and Krogstad?* They loved each other before Christina married for financial security; they will now marry.

10. (III) *When Torvald reads Krogstad's letter, how does Nora expect him to react?* Nora expects Torvald to try to save her and to suffer for her sake.

11. (III) *How does Torvald actually react?* Torvald considers Nora a liar and a criminal; she has ruined his happiness and his future and caused him to be blackmailed by Krogstad; she is not fit to rear the children.

12. (III) *What does Krogstad do for Nora?* Krogstad returns her forged IOU.

13. (III) *How does Torvald react?* Saved from disaster, Torvald forgives Nora and returns to his old attitudes.

14. (III) *What miracle failed to happen?* Torvald didn't support Nora against Krogstad.

15. (III) *How does Nora change?* Nora realizes her husband's limitations mean that she cannot be happy with him. She decides to leave him and the children to learn about herself and life.

UNDERSTANDING THE PLAY: POSSIBLE ANSWERS

*1. (I) *Significance of Nora's lies* Torvald is so opinionated and demanding that Nora cannot afford to be truthful. Control over sweets reveals that Torvald attempts to control all aspects of Nora's life and that he treats her like a child. The lie reveals that Nora and Torvald's marriage may be in trouble.

*2. (I) *Significance of Torvald's view of Nora as an expensive little bird* Torvald views himself as being in total charge of his household. Marriage is no partnership; Nora's role is to serve and amuse her husband.

*3. (I) *Significance of Nora's description of her own behavior* Nora is consciously playing a role in her marriage, appearing to be the kind of wife that Torvald wants her to be. If she could, she would be different: more serious, more independent, and more honest about who she really is.

*4. (I) *Irony of Nora's situation at the end of Act I* The audience knows that Nora is guilty of the same crime that Krogstad committed. The audience and Nora both suspect that Torvald will not be any more forgiving of Nora than he is of Krogstad.

*5. (II) *Significance of Nora's comment about giving in to Torvald* Nora wants to feel that she makes her own decisions.

*6. (II) *Torvald's image if Nora or others influenced him* Torvald claims that he would become a "laughing-stock" and would be regarded as ineffectual. However, Torvald need not publicize Nora's influence, and consulting with others might enable him to make better decisions. Acting hastily on his own and using poor judgment should be of greater concern to Torvald.

7. (II) *Nora's miracle* Nora realizes that Torvald will inevitably find out about the money she borrowed from Krogstad. The "miracle" she hopes for is that Torvald will take all the responsibility for the forgery upon himself—that he will "bear the whole burden" of her disgrace. However, the fact that Nora describes this act as a "miracle" shows that subconsciously she knows it is unlikely to happen: She recognizes and fears Torvald's selfishness, inflexibility, and quickness to condemn moral flaws in others.

8. (III) *Incredible things; why Krogstad should leave his letter* Mrs. Linden is worried about Nora's talk of going out of her mind, of not being there any longer, and of encountering a "miracle." She feels that if Torvald knew the truth, Nora could relax and stop lying. Mrs. Linden expects that Nora and Torvald would reach an understanding that would be satisfying to both of them and that Torvald would understand Nora's motivation and appreciate her generous efforts on his behalf.

*9. (III) *Why Nora is not pleased to be Torvald's dearest treasure* Nora has been forced to leave the dance before she was ready to go, so she is annoyed at Torvald as well as worried about how soon he will read Krogstad's letter. Nora also resents Torvald's objectification of her and his appropriation of her as something belonging to him. These emotions make her unreceptive to Torvald's ill-timed attempts at romance.

At the same time, Nora still believes that the "miracle" is possible— that Torvald is capable of taking responsibility for the loan and for the forgery. Therefore, she is concerned about Torvald's misperception of her: Although he idealizes her, she knows that she is flawed.

*10. (III) *Torvald's reactions to Dr. Rank's suffering* Torvald's reactions reveal him to be a narcissistic person, someone who is interested in others only to the extent that they reflect favorably upon himself. He has no sympathy for Dr. Rank; he finds Dr. Rank's death a horrible intrusion into his own romantic plans.

*11. (III) *Nora tells Torvald that she's never understood him* Nora has been blind to the kind of man that Torvald is because she herself has been playing a role. Because she knew she was more than a doll, she assumed he knew that too. Torvald has often professed his great love for Nora and his interest in proving his devotion; this has given her reason to believe in his love.

A further reason that Nora has been blind to Torvald's true nature is the very unpleasant emotional and economic consequences of facing up to an unsatisfactory marriage.

*12. (III) *Torvald's concern about Nora's decision* Torvald is most concerned about what other people will say, especially about what they will say about him. Given his preoccupation with himself, his attitude toward Krogstad, and his fear of anything that might involve a scandal, this attitude is consistent with his personality.

*13. *Nora's problem: personality or society's values* Nora's problem is caused both by her and Torvald's personalities and by the values of the society in which they live. Their society supports dominating men rather than liberated women, a fact that makes Nora the unconventional partner in the marriage and gives Torvald little motivation to change his attitudes. On the other hand, in any society a woman would have to be very insecure and needy to be happy with a husband who cares more about what other people think of him than he cares about his wife.

At the end of the play, Nora has exchanged one set of problems for another. She has cut herself off from the traditional support of a family, and she needs to find a job so that she can be financially independent. It might be possible, in time, for her to find both emotional and financial security.

*14. *Nora's greater responsibility: herself or her family* Opinions will vary. Nora must consider how much value she will be to her children if she is miserable living with Torvald or if she continues to treat them like dolls, the way Torvald has been treating her. She could let Torvald make an effort to change, but the evidence in the play suggests that he is incapable of empathy and independent thinking.

15. *More important character* Nora is important in that she rebels against the values of the society. Torvald is important in that he epitomizes what Ibsen is criticizing in contemporary life.

*16. *Themes* Possible themes:

- A marriage based on misperceptions and inequality is not a true marriage.

- A person's primary obligation is to himself or herself; everyone else comes second.

- The most important goal for a person is to know himself or herself.

- The development of one's personality and the fulfillment of one's goals are just as important for a woman as they are for a man.

ANALYZING LITERARY TECHNIQUE: POSSIBLE ANSWERS

*1. *Foreshadowing*

a) (I) *Opening conflict* Torvald and Nora disagree about money. Torvald opposes extravagance; he is against anyone's going into debt. Nora thinks that it is all right to borrow money and have debts. She views money as the best gift because she can decide how and when to use it. This becomes a major issue when it is revealed that Nora secretly borrowed money for the sake of Torvald's health and is secretly paying back the loan.

b) (I) *Torvald's reaction to Krogstad's crime* Krogstad's crime is similar to Nora's, so it is reasonable to assume that Torvald will react to Nora as he did to Krogstad.

c) (II) *Scene between Nora and Anna* Anna left her own child to earn a living caring for Nora (and eventually for Nora's children). Anna is pragmatic about the decision she made: "When I had the chance of such a good place? A poor girl who's been in trouble must take what comes." The scene hints that Nora may leave her own children, seeking a pragmatic solution to her own troubles.

d) (II) *Krogstad's comment about having "heart"* Krogstad's statement prepares Nora and the audience for his willingess to take back his letter and for his returning Nora's IOU to her.

e) (II) *Dr. Rank's comment about Torvald's "delicate nature"* Dr. Rank is politely expressing Torvald's selfishness. Torvald does indeed shrink from Dr. Rank's illness, considering it an intrusion on his happy life. The comment also foreshadows Torvald's shrinking from Nora's confession of forgery and debt.

2. *Irony* Following are some examples that students might choose to illustrate the effect of dramatic and verbal irony in this play.

a) *Dramatic irony* (I) Nora tells Torvald: "I shouldn't think of doing what you disapprove of." Nora, who has been going against Torvald's wishes by eating sweets and spending too much money, is telling one more lie. Her words reflect her double life: one of lies to his face and another of independent actions behind his back. The problem of the promissory note determines the course of her life. This problem, too, is based on her acting contrary to Torvald's values and her deceiving Torvald.

(II) Torvald says to Nora: "Between your father and me there is all the difference in the world. Your father was not altogether unimpeachable. I am; and I hope to remain so." Torvald knows that he himself has done nothing wrong, but he is unaware of Nora's forged note and its risk to his reputation.

(II) Torvald says to Nora: "Let what will happen—when the time comes, I shall have strength and courage enough. You shall see, my shoulders are broad enough to bear the whole burden." Torvald will have no strength and no courage in any crisis that causes him to fear for himself. Given his earlier statements, the audience suspects this. Nora learns it when he is so concerned about his reputation that he refuses to support her against Krogstad.

(II) Nora tells Dr. Rank: "You know how deeply, how wonderfully Torvald loves me; he would not hesitate a moment to give his very life for my sake." Nora does not see qualities in Torvald that Dr. Rank sees, namely his hate of ugly situations, his lack of courage, and his excessive concern for public opinion.

(III) After the dance, Torvald says to Mrs. Linden: "An exit should always be effective, Mrs. Linden; but I can't get Nora to see it." Nora's dramatic exit comes at the end of the play. It never occurs to Torvald that Nora might act without his direction.

(III) Torvald says to Nora: "I often wish some danger might threaten you, that I might risk body and soul, and everything, everything, for your dear sake." Torvald doesn't know that real danger is around the corner and that it threatens him directly.

(III) After Krogstad has returned the IOU, Torvald says to Nora: "Here I can shelter you like a hunted dove, whom I have saved from the claws of the hawk." Torvald does not realize that he is the "hawk." Nora is far from being safe; Torvald's abandonment of her when she needed him has destroyed their marriage.

b) *Verbal irony* (II) After Torvald sends Krogstad's dismissal letter and refuses to retrieve it, he says, "Too late." Nora echoes him, saying, "Yes, too late." Torvald means only that it is too late to call the maid back; he is thinking only of his own affairs, of his dislike of Krogstad, and of his desire to assert his authority over Nora. Nora means that it is too late to save Torvald, the children, and herself.

(II) Speaking about the dance that she is supposed to perform, Nora says that she can't perform without rehearsing with Torvald. When he asks whether she is nervous, she responds, "Yes, dreadfully!" Torvald connects her anxiety with the coming performance, but Nora is anxious about Torvald's impending reading of Krogstad's letter.

(III) After Torvald takes Nora away from the dance, he says, "I was right after all not to let you stop longer." Nora responds, "Oh, everything you do is right." Torvald believes that everything he does is correct, and he is delighted to hear Nora acknowledge it by her reply. However, Nora's reply contradicts her own feelings.

(III) After reading Krogstad's letter, Torvald accuses Nora of rewarding him "like this" for helping her father. Nora echoes Torvald's words, "Yes—like this!" Torvald accuses Nora of having no religion, no morals, and no sense of duty, whereas Nora realizes that these very values are what motivated her to borrow the money in the first place. Torvald's words condemn; Nora repeats them with pride. It is ironic that Torvald is incapable of acting on the values that he tells Nora he has, whereas Nora really possesses these values and acts on them.

(III) When Nora returns from changing out of her dance costume into street clothes, Torvald remarks in surprise, "You have changed your dress." Nora responds, "Yes, Torvald; now I have changed my dress." Torvald expects Nora to be dressed for bed. Nora's response refers to her psychological state as well as to her clothes. She has changed into someone else, someone who is prepared to take on the outside world.

*3. *Function of minor characters*

   a) *Mrs. Linden* Mrs. Linden brings a role model of female independence into Nora's life. She supports herself and is relieved to be rid of a husband she did not love. In some respects, Mrs. Linden is a foil for Nora: Mrs. Linden, being alone, wants someone to love and nurture, while Nora has a family but wants independence.

      On a psychological level, Nora and Mrs. Linden also function as alter egos. However, Mrs. Linden is more of a doppelgänger in her relationship to Nora. Mrs. Linden represents what Nora secretly would like to be, because Mrs. Linden is an autonomous woman who is free to take risks and assume the consequences, a condition that is made possible by her ability to support herself financially.

   b) *Krogstad* Krogstad has a pivotal role in the play, both in terms of plot and of characterization. He is important to Nora as the person who knows of the loan and who can expose her; he also functions as a double for Nora, since her crime is the same as his. Krogstad is important to Torvald because he represents the kind of individual over whom Torvald wants to assert his superiority; ironically, of course, Krogstad possesses information that gives him the upper hand over Torvald. Krogstad and Mrs. Linden's story, in the subplot, acts as a commentary on the main plot. Krogstad and Mrs. Linden are able to forget old wounds and reestablish a bond, forming a partnership that will enable both of them to find greater emotional and financial security. The forgiveness and cooperation in Krogstad and Mrs. Linden's relationship throw into relief the problems in Nora and Torvald's marriage.

   c) *Dr. Rank* Dr. Rank is in love with Nora; he has been her friend and advisor, giving her the emotional support she has lacked from Torvald. There is no evidence that Nora has returned his feelings, although she does seem to have suspected them. (Her comments to Mrs. Linden about an "admirer" are therefore ironic.)

      Dr. Rank's function in the play is to make Nora aware of her true relationship with Torvald. There are three important scenes in which he heightens her awareness. In Act I, Dr. Rank's view of Krogstad as a moral "wreck" increases Nora's worry about her secret deed and confirms her sense of isolation. In Act II, the discussion of the law of retribution increases Nora's anxiety; her children will suffer for her deeds. In Act III, Dr. Rank is a model for Nora, showing her how to value each day of life, to make the most of life, and to face whatever comes with dignity. Dr. Rank's death and the resulting loss to the Helmer family foreshadow the loss of Nora.

WRITING ABOUT LITERATURE

1. *Essay tracing Nora's development* Call students' attention to the suggestions in the textbook assignment. (See **U.P.** questions 1, 3, 4, 5, 9, 11, and 16 above.)

2. *Essay evaluating Torvald's response to Krogstad's letter* Call students' attention to the directions and suggestions in the textbook assignment. (See **U.P.** questions 2, 6, 9, 10, 12, and 13 above.)

3. *Essay contrasting Nora's and Torvald's ideas of honor* Call students' attention to the pre-writing suggestions. (See **U.P.** questions 4, 6, 10, 12, and 14 and **A.L.T.** questions 1 and 3 above.) **(P.L.J.)** 🆎

4. *Creative writing: a letter to Nora from a friend* Call students' attention to the textbook assignment, which contains the four quotations that will form the basis of the letter that they are going to write. (a) "It's your [you and my father's] fault that my life has been wasted." (b) "[I'm not] fit to educate the children." (c) "I must stand quite alone to know myself and my surroundings; so I cannot stay with you." (d) "I no longer believe [that before all I am a wife and mother]. I think that before all else I am a human being." **(P.L.J.)**

5. *Creative writing: a conversation between the nurse (Anna) and the maid (Ellen) about the effect of Nora's departure on Torvald* Call students' attention to the suggested questions in the textbook assignment.

FURTHER READING

Ibsen, Henrik, *An Enemy of the People; The Wild Duck; Ghosts; Hedda Gabler; Peer Gynt.*

The Outlaws

SELMA LAGERLÖF

INTRODUCING THE STORY

"The Outlaws" has great dramatic, intellectual, and artistic appeal. On the surface, it is a tale of adventure with touches of mystery. As two outlaws hide from the death penalty, the reader wonders whether they will evade death and how.

Intellectually the tale grabs the reader's mind with a tenacious grip. The reader ponders Tord's nature, considers his motivation for betraying Berg, and marvels at the deliberate ambiguity of the story's conclusion. Many aspects of the story are open to genuinely different interpretations, all of which have foundation in the text. The ambiguity is not only acceptable, it adds depth and richness to the tale.

Tord, son of a fisherman and a "witch," is an enigmatic character whose behavior will provoke interesting discussions. Living both in the world of reality and in that of imagination, Tord is periodically driven by irrational feelings that reflect his subconscious drives and motives. Possibly because his self-image is so low, he worships the murderer Berg, who despises him. Although Tord possesses information that would change Berg's opinion of him, he is in no hurry to reveal that information. Tord's religious conversion raises many questions. He becomes obsessed with the image of God as an avenger of misdeeds rather than with the more forgiving side of Christianity represented by Christ, the Virgin Mary, and the saints who intercede on behalf of sinners. It is not clear whether Tord's instinctive choice is a psychological reaction to the sacrifice his mother exacted of him. He may murder Berg because he has become a religious fanatic, because he hopes to have a chance with Unn once Berg is dead, or because the murder of a criminal will enhance his self-esteem by bringing him pardon and social acceptance.

Early in the tale Berg is depicted as a primeval superman, a glorious human being who is nature's crowning achievement. In fact, he is more animal than human as he eludes those who would capture him. Later in the story he becomes Tord's religious teacher, imprudently substituting Christian morality and justice for Tord's pagan fatalism. Finally, having driven Tord mad with violent visions of Christian justice, Berg finds himself torn between his affection for Tord and his own instinct for self-preservation.

Tord and Berg inhabit a world in which women are perceived as dangerously nonhuman, particularly as they wield great power over men. Tord's mother is characterized by her son as a witch, someone who claims the bodies of drowned sailors. She sacrifices her son's life to preserve the life of her husband, and Tord accepts his role as scapegoat and fugitive. Unn, described as a kind of mermaid, lures males with her sex appeal and then destroys them. She encourages love, not marriage. Loved by her cousin Berg, she tells him that the white monk's nameless but accurate public insult to them both demands harsh justice. Since her father is not present, Berg knows "what he should do to make her stay." Berg kills the monk and becomes a fugitive. Once Tord sees Unn, she inhabits his dreams. To what extent she is a key motivating factor in Tord's murder of Berg is worth discussing.

Tord's world is one of terrifying visions that blur the distinction between illusion and reality. A secluded mountain pool is home to tree roots that resemble serpents or the "blackened skeletons of drowned giants." Drowned men speak to Tord and "threaten him with withered white hands." As Tord walks alone through the woods in a storm, he is chased by invisible hunters: a huge venomous snake, a monstrous starved wolf, eerie human voices, and finally "God, the great Avenger, the God of justice" and the white monk. The story is told with such artistic power that even in translation its scenes remain in the reader's imagination long after the tale has ended.

Personal Literary Journal: To what extent do you think that human beings have the ability to control their own actions? To what extent do you think that human behavior is predetermined? What factors determine human behavior?

Literary Terms: contrast, flashback, folktale, foreshadowing, Gothic, irony, setting, symbol

COMPREHENSION QUESTIONS

1. *What crime has Berg committed?* murdered a monk
2. *What crime has Tord committed?* none; took on himself his father's crime
3. *Why did Berg commit his crime?* The monk criticized Berg's relationship with Unn; Unn threatened to leave Berg.
4. *How does Tord feel about Berg?* worships him; protects him

5. *How does Berg feel about Tord?* despises him because he thinks Tord is a thief

6. *How does Berg feel about Tord once he's learned the truth?* no longer despises him; thinks he's a fool for throwing his life away

7. *How does Tord feel about Unn?* has romantic dreams about her

8. *How does Tord feel about Berg's crime?* Berg honored Unn by killing the monk.

9. *What does Berg teach Tord?* about Christianity and justice

10. *What happens because of those lessons?* Tord kills Berg because Berg murdered the monk.

UNDERSTANDING THE STORY: POSSIBLE ANSWERS

1. *Tord destined to betray Berg* It depends on the reader's attitude toward determinism and toward the role of personality in a person's destiny. Before Tord heard Berg's sermon, Tord believed in fate.

2. *Importance of Tord's family background* Tord grew up isolated from the community because his father was a thief and his mother was a witch. He took the guilt of his father upon himself, for reasons that are not precisely explained and that are not understood by Berg. Tord may have feared his mother's powers as a witch, acted out of loving obedience to his mother, or acted out of a desire to protect his father. His loneliness and isolation may explain why he forms such an attachment to Berg and why he is eventually drawn to the possibility of a union with Unn.

   In psychological terms, Tord has no self-esteem. He was betrayed when his mother asked him to sacrifice his own life for his parents' happiness. In addition, he also may have a subconscious desire to punish one or both of his parents for not loving and valuing him. Thus, Tord identifies with God the Avenger and becomes the arm of divine justice in the world he inhabits. He is not interested in Mary because of how he was treated by his own mother. He also rejects any identification with Christ, even though he, like Christ, has sacrificed himself for the sins of another (his father).

   Tord's poverty and his parents' occupations mean that he is of a lower social class than Berg. This class difference may further explain why Tord accepts the way Berg's treats him and why he serves Berg uncomplainingly.

*3. *Tord's relationships* In all of these relationships, Tord takes directions from someone whom he perceives to be powerful. He obeys his mother's request to protect his father, he works for Berg as a servant, and he obeys what he believes is God's command to avenge the murder. All these relationships suggest that Tord has doubts about his power to act on his own and to take responsibility for his own actions. Such doubts reflect a lack of self-esteem.

*4. *Berg's sermon* On the one hand, Berg despises Tord's heathenism, which has caused Tord to be amoral, irresponsible, and fatalistic. On the other hand, because Berg knows Tord committed no crime, it is possible that Berg's sermon is directed more toward himself than toward Tord.

5. *Why Tord betrays Berg* (a) Tord's love of Unn may be very important. Tord desires her, and with Berg dead, he may think that he can win her. (b) Tord's desire for wealth and social acceptance may also be important. These ambitions were not important before he met Unn, but afterwards he wonders whether social status would enable him to win her and build a life with her. (c) Tord's desire for freedom is primarily important for winning Unn. (d) Tord's belief in religious principles is possibly his most important motivation. He believes that if he acts on religious principles—especially the principle of justice—then wealth, social acceptance, freedom, and Unn would all follow. (e) Tord's personality is possibly at least as important as his religious beliefs. Tord's childhood experiences have left him deficient in self-esteem and accustomed to worshipping someone who does not value him. Once Berg begins to love and trust Tord, Tord may have a subconscious need to betray Berg to regain his contempt.

6. *Berg as villain or victim* Berg is a villain in that he is a would-be adulterer, a murderer, and a snob (in his treatment of Tord). Some students may argue that he is also victimized by Tord, who turns his teachings against him. However, there is a strong suggestion in the story that Berg teaches Tord in order to condemn himself.

7. *Berg regarding Tord's betrayal* Berg's attitudes are not necessarily inconsistent. Berg initially considers Tord foolish because he would have betrayed Tord if their situations were reversed. However, Berg's initial contempt for Tord comes from a position of security: Berg knows that Tord idolizes him and believes that Tord would not harm him. Later Berg acts out of self-preservation, the most basic drive that he has (as evidenced by the opening of the story).

*8. *Why Berg doesn't think Tord will kill him* Tord worships Berg. Also, the white monk in Tord's vision bears an axe-blow, not a knife stab. Berg killed the monk with a knife.

*9. *God of justice* Identification with a God of justice satisfies several of Tord's needs. (a) Tord has never known anyone who would intercede on behalf of a sinner; his mother demanded his life because of his father's crimes. (b) The God of justice supplants Berg as the object of Tord's worship, just as Berg once replaced Tord's mother as the object of his worship. (c) The God of justice satisfies Tord's subconscious need to avenge the treatment he received from his parents. (d) Tord gains self-esteem by siding with justice and opposing a murderer.

*10. *Berg's sermon* Tord has understood only one part of Berg's sermon, the part about God's justice. Just as important, however, are the ameliorating influences of Christ, the Virgin Mary, and the holy men and women (the saints)—all of whom Tord ignores. Berg does not expect that his lesson will be only partially understood and has no reason to believe that Tord will suddenly act on religious principles, so he sees no threat to his own life.

Before Berg's sermon, Tord is fatalistic about human behavior. He is tolerant of others rather than judgmental. He accepts Berg's murder of the monk as well as the treatment he received from his parents. After Berg's sermon, Tord has much to gain by killing Berg: freedom, social acceptance, wealth, and possibly love. Tord's identification with an avenging God also satisfies a subconscious need to avenge the way his parents' treated him.

11. *Tord's killing of Berg in self-defense: justification for the crime* Opinions will vary. Technically, self-defense justifies Tord's action. However, as a heathen, Tord would have been more accepting of Berg and would not have changed his relationship with Berg. It is interesting to consider how the heathen Tord would have treated Berg, when Berg began to love and trust him.

12. *Why Tord praises God's greatness* Tord believes he has acted as God's agent, avenging the unjust murder of the monk. In addition, because society considers his killing of Berg to be a good deed, Tord will be pardoned and rewarded. Self-defense has also removed the dishonor that would have accompanied his betrayal of Berg. Tord has lost his best friend, but he has gained the world.

ANALYZING LITERARY TECHNIQUE: POSSIBLE ANSWERS

1. *Foreshadowing* Examples of foreshadowing include the following:
   - Tord's fear of night and of the woods, which foreshadows the later storm scene;
   - Tord's visions of Berg's ancestors, which foreshadow Tord's later visions;
   - Berg's talk of motives for Tord's betrayal, which foreshadows Tord's later betrayal of Berg;
   - Tord's vision of the monk with the axe wound in his forehead, which foreshadows Tord's killing of Berg.

2. *Symbolic use of light and dark* Light symbolizes the external world, rational forces, and what is good (day, sunshine, laughter, happiness, Unn, life). Darkness symbolizes the internal world, the irrational world of Tord's psyche, and evil (night, the storm, fear, death, God's vengeance, and Hell). The contrast between light and dark dramatizes the conflict between good and evil.

3. *Irony* Ironic aspects include the following:
   - Berg despises Tord for supposedly committing a crime, though Berg is guilty of murder and Tord is actually innocent;
   - Tord's approval of Berg's crime leads Berg to disapprove of Tord's attitude and to give Tord a lecture on Christianity;
   - Berg's teaching of Christian values leads Tord to betray Berg;
   - Berg's murder of the monk in order to keep Unn leads Berg to being an outcast without Unn;
   - Tord is loyal when Berg expects Tord to betray him, but Tord betrays Berg when Berg expects him to be loyal;
   - Tord finds the vengeance in Christianity appealing, though that religion is noted for its love, compassion, and forgiveness;
   - Tord's new religion leads him to betray and kill his friend.

4. *Women's roles in story* Women in this story are perceived as being dangerous. They violate the natural order of things, especially the natural order of society. Tord's mother seems to be responsible for isolating Tord's family from the rest of society, and it is because of her pleadings that he has become an outlaw. Unn is seen as responsible for the disruption of Berg's marriage and for the death of the monk; later she seems to be responsible for Tord's betrayal of Berg, as Tord wishes to reestablish himself in society and to win her affection.

   Students who are inclined to blame Tord's mother and Unn for the negative events in the plot should be reminded that the only way the reader comes to know these two women is through either Berg or Tord. The vision of the mermaid occurs just before Unn actually appears in the story; the men, not the narrator, connect the two.

5. *Gothic* The Gothic elements in the story are the mysterious and supernatural elements, including the witch-mother, the frightening forest, and the bloody monk's ghost. The Gothic elements make the atmosphere of the story more charged and more memorable, and they tend to shift the reader's attention from the characters and their responsibility for their own actions.

WRITING ABOUT LITERATURE

1. *Essay examining justice* Call students' attention to the directions in the textbook assignment. Remind them to find support for their ideas in the story and to use quotations as well as explanations. (See **U.S.** questions 3, 4, 8, 9, and 10 above.) **(P.L.J.)**

2. *Creative writing: a continuation of "The Outlaws" after Berg's death* Call students' attention to the questions suggested in the textbook assignment. Encourage them to write a story that is consistent with Tord's personality and character.

FURTHER READING

Lagerlöf, Selma, *Missing Links* (short stories); *The Wonderful Adventures of Nils, Gosta Berling's Saga; The Further Adventures of Nils.*

The Kiss
ANTON CHEKHOV

INTRODUCING THE STORY

"The Kiss" is appealing to adolescents because of the private fantasy world created by the protagonist after he receives a kiss. The story shows how infatuation so enhances Riabovich's self-image that his personality and outlook change. From a "timid, modest, undistinguished" staff-captain, he becomes a person who is interested in the people around him. Even though reality pops the balloon of fantasy, Riabovich recognizes that ordinary men like himself have found women to love them and that another woman will, in time, make him forget his self-consciousness and his "evil fate."

Written in 1886–87, "The Kiss" exhibits Chekhov's mature style, which he described as follows to his brother: "1. Absence of lengthy verbiage of political-social economic nature; 2. Total objectivity; 3. Truthful descriptions of persons and objects; 4. Extreme brevity; 5. Audacity and originality; Flee the stereotype; 6. Compassion."

The story is typically Chekhovian in that it focuses on the feeling of an ordinary artillery officer. Chekhov contrasts Riabovich with another officer, the "setter" Lobytko—Riabovich being as socially awkward and uncomfortable as Lobytko is sophisticated and suave. Riabovich's fantasies evoke humor and pity, making him a poignant character. Readers both laugh at the poor staff-captain and sympathize with him as, in a final ironic twist, he ignores the invitation he has longed to receive. Chekhov's gift is his ability to tell a story that is true to human nature and true to life experience yet ironic.

The ability to portray the artificiality of the von Rabbeks' tea and the lack of communication between Riabovich, Lobytko, and Merzliakov is among Chekhov's great artistic gifts. As a dramatist, Chekhov characterizes the people in his short stories by their words and actions rather than through description.

The setting of the story reveals Chekhov's roots in Russian realism. Riabovich, the protagonist, is a Russian artillery officer, a common figure in contemporary Russian life. The unintrusive artistic style and the realistic plot enable Chekhov to emphasize Riabovich's thoughts and feelings and to portray life as Riabovich would have lived it.

Personal Literary Journal: Have you ever experienced a wonderful chance meeting? How did it affect your life? Did you have an opportunity to build on the experience? How did the experience end?

Literary Terms: characterization, dramatic irony, leitmotif, paradox, realism, satire, setting, tone

COMPREHENSION QUESTIONS

1. *Why is Riabovich invited to General von Rabbek's for tea?* Local etiquette requires such hospitality.

2. *How does Riabovich feel while being entertained?* socially ill at ease and awkward

3. *What surprising event occurs?* An unknown woman, expecting someone else, kisses Riabovich as he enters a dark room.

4. *How does Riabovich react to this event?* as if true love has entered his life

5. *How does Riabovich feel at the end of the story?* angry at reality, resigned to his fate, unwilling to continue his fantasy

UNDERSTANDING THE STORY: POSSIBLE ANSWERS

*1. *Effect of the kiss* Riabovich is ill at ease socially; he has never had a romantic relationship, so he exaggerates this event beyond reality.

2. *Riabovich's behavior* The Riabovich who thinks well of himself is socially at ease, warm, and friendly. His behavior toward Madame von Rabbek elicits a genuinely friendly response.

*3. *The woman's reaction* The woman's dismay and embarrassment when she kisses the wrong man contrast with Riabovich's reactions, causing him to be seen as both humorous and poignant.

*4. *Riabovich's imagination* The event would be diminished if the woman were not suitably attractive or not real.

5. *Riabovich's regret* After Riabovich relates his experience, Merzliakov says the woman must have been a lunatic. Lobytko responds by telling about a similar personal experience that appears to be more interesting than Riabovich's experience.

*6. *The second invitation* The invitation's delay has made Riabovich confront reality. His despair and self-pity lead him to take perverse pleasure in showing Fate that he will not let himself be tempted to revive the past.

*7. *The effect of the experience; the role of illusion* After the kiss, Riabovich seems to feel more at ease in social situations. He is probably better off having had the experience, because he has begun to prepare himself to deal with future social relationships. Student opinions about whether illusions are helpful may vary. Believing in oneself can foster success.

ANALYZING LITERARY TECHNIQUE: POSSIBLE ANSWERS

1. *Chekhov's primary focus* Chekhov focuses on how a single incident affects an individual physically, socially, and psychologically. The use of an omniscient narrator enables Chekhov to explore Riabovich's experience and to reveal Riabovich's feelings to the reader.

2. *Leitmotif* Chekhov turns several details into leitmotifs. Besides unifying the story, leitmotifs perform the following functions:

   • Leitmotifs mark the passage of time. For example, the spring flowers set the scene for romance; their later absence reveals a different time of year and a different situation.

   • Leitmotifs function as a shorthand. For example, Chekhov characterizes each of the artillery officers by one behavior—Riabovich is always involved in his fantasy life, Lobytko is always pursuing women, and Merzliakov is always reading his magazine.

*3. *The artillery brigade* The army becomes an active, realistic setting in which the characteristics live before, during, and after Riabovich's fantasy life is operating. This realistic world adds dimension to Chekhov's portrayal of the characters as they are seen through Riabovich's eyes.

4. *Contrast: Riabovich and Lobytko* Riabovich is as socially uncomfortable and awkward as Lobytko is sophisticated and suave.

5. *Mispronunciation of a name* The servant's mispronunciation of von Rabbek's name is true to human nature. A person's name may not be remembered if

that person seems unimportant. To the servant, General von Rabbek is simply one more general performing his social and civic duty.

6. *Tone* The tone of this story is both comic and poignant. Chekhov follows Riabovich from the time that Riabovich treats the fantasy as reality until he finally sees the incident for what it was. Riabovich's emotions move from elation and anticipation to frustration and dismay and finally to anger and chagrin. Both Riabovich's feelings toward the young woman and his emotional reaction to the collapse of his fantasy are realistic. The beauty of the story resides in Chekhov's sympathetic depiction of human attitudes and emotions.

7. *Irony* Chekhov's use of irony adds gentle humor and poignancy to the story. For example, it is ironic that Riabovich becomes so angry at himself and at von Rabbek that he ignores the invitation when it finally arrives.

8. *Chekhov's use of satire* The central target of satire in the story is the insincerity of most social interactions. The first (and probably the second) von Rabbek invitation is not sincere, the time for the event is inconvenient, and the social obligation is tedious. Madame von Rabbek's smile disappears when she is out of sight, General von Rabbek speaks with "affected joviality," the hosts pretend to be serious about topics they know little about, and Riabovich is impressed with the von Rabbek family's ability to act so graciously.

   However, the satire is gentle rather than biting. Chekhov and the soldiers understand the difficulties under which the von Rabbek family is operating; under similar circumstances, they would feel the same way. Riabovich's exaggerated response to the mistaken kiss is also treated with gentle satire.

*9. *Realism* The following aspects of this story are characteristic of realism:

   • The feelings of an ordinary person are described.

   • People and objects are described as they appear to the eye and ear, without exaggeration or artificiality.

   • The story is presented objectively, without interpretations.

   • The story focuses on a slice of life—one experience in a person's life.

WRITING ABOUT LITERATURE

1. *Essay on realism* Students who read carefully probably will defend Chekhov's use of details, recognizing that each piece of information helps to describe the setting and to increase the reader's sensitivity to Riabovich's loneliness and desire for connections. Students should recognize the contrast between Chekhov's description of life and Riabovich's fantasies. (See **U.S.** questions 1, 3, 4, 6, and 7 and **A.L.T.** questions 3 and 9 above.) **AP**

2. *Creative writing: an incident from Riabovich's point of view* Students should write about the incident as if they were Riabovich. Students may write as if the experience were happening at that every moment, or they may treat the experience as a memory that Riabovich is recalling. **(P.L.J.)**

FURTHER READING

Chekhov, Anton, *The Essential Tales of Chekhov* (note especially "Misery," "The Steppe," "The Duel," "A Woman's Kingdom," "The Lottery Ticket," "Vanka," "The Peasants," "Gooseberries," "The Lady with the Dog," "In the Ravine," "The Betrothed," and "The Darling"); *Chekhov: The Major Plays* (note especially *The Three Sisters* and *The Cherry Orchard*).

The Other Wife

COLETTE

INTRODUCING THE STORY

In "The Other Wife," Colette explores the psychological effects of the presence of an ex-wife on her ex-husband and his new wife. Paradoxically the ex-wife is simply a catalyst; the author does not name her, and the reader never knows whether she even notices Marc and Alice when they enter the hotel dining room. The sole concern of the story is the effect of her presence on the other two characters. Ironically, although the first wife is not even referred to by name, her presence turns out to have ominous implications for Marc and Alice's relatively new marriage.

From his first sight of his ex-wife, Marc is very uncomfortable, and he hopes that she will not see him and his new wife. Because the ex-wife was never satisfied with him, he feels with self-conscious certainty that he continues to be an object of scorn and that his new and somewhat plump wife would also be an object of scorn.

Once Marc confesses that his previous marriage failed because of his own inadequacy, Alice feels as if she possesses rejected inferior merchandise. She begins to doubt her happiness, and her initial pity for the ex-wife gives way to her envy of the woman's superior sophistication, taste, and judgment.

Personal Literary Journal: Have you ever changed your mind about something you had wanted? What caused your attitude to change?

Literary Terms: characterization, contrast, foreshadowing, irony, paradox, theme

COMPREHENSION QUESTIONS

1. *Why does Marc wish to sit where he does?* to avoid his ex-wife
2. *Why does Marc prefer his new wife?* She accepts him.
3. *Why did Marc's previous marriage end?* Marc could not make his wife happy.
4. *How does Alice feel at first about Marc's ex-wife?* sorry for her
5. *At the end of the story, how does Alice feel about Marc's ex-wife?* inferior to her

UNDERSTANDING THE STORY: POSSIBLE ANSWERS

*1. *Why Marc refuses to sit near his ex-wife* Marc feels self-conscious about being seen. He has a low self-image, and he is ashamed of himself and of Alice.

*2. *Why Alice laughs too loudly* Alice hopes to convey how happily married they are, thus revealing she is a better wife. She hopes to make the ex-wife jealous.

*3. *Why Marc improves posture* Marc wishes to make a good impression on his ex-wife. He wants to convey an attitude of self-assurance and convince her that he is thriving in his new marriage.

*4. *Marc's wisdom in telling Alice why marriage failed* Marc reveals his low self-esteem by blaming the failure on his inadequacy. His idealization of his ex-wife makes Alice feel inferior and causes her to view him as a castoff rather than a catch. Marc's revelation does not appear to be in his own best interests. It is also important to recognize that Alice and Marc have never had this conversation before. This suggests that their marriage lacks a strong base of honesty and mutual trust.

5. *Themes* More than one underlying idea is present in this story. One example is that the neighbor's grass is always greener ("the other wife" seems better). Another is that feelings of inferiority become self-fulfilling prophecies—someone who does not think well of himself or herself will not be highly regarded by others. (Marc's self-disparagement leads Alice to disparage him also.) Students should explain how the story supports each idea they suggest.

ANALYZING LITERARY TECHNIQUE: POSSIBLE ANSWERS

*1. *Irony in Marc's statement about their satisfaction* Marc's phrasing the statement as a question reveals his need to have Alice confirm their satisfaction. His need for Alice's confirmation reveals that he questions their happiness. Marc has just inadvertently told Alice that she has acquired a second-rate as well as a secondhand husband, making Alice question whether she is satisfied with Marc.

2. *Function of contrast* Colette uses contrast to highlight her subject. The two wives are opposites: The ex-wife is sophisticated, demanding, and impressive; the new wife is warm, loving, and accepting. Each becomes distinctive in contrast to the other. In addition, contrast accentuates the dramatic nature of Alice's change. Happy and satisfied at the beginning of the story, Alice is unhappy and dissatisfied at the end.

*3. *Point of view* This story is told by a third-person omniscient narrator. The narrator is able to provide information that enhances the reader's understanding of the dialogue and that shows the true stakes in the situation. Not only does the narrator comment on the characters' actions, motivations, and behavior, but the narrator allows the reader to know Alice's thoughts at the end of the story.

4. *Paradox* It is a paradox that people may base their attitudes and behavior on how they think they are viewed by others when in reality others may view them quite differently or may not think about them at all.

WRITING ABOUT LITERATURE

1. *Essay analyzing characterization* Students should look closely at what the two main characters reveal about themselves and at what the narrator reveals about them. The characters' basic insecurity and attempts to disguise their insecurity fuel the growing distrust in their marriage. Students probably will predict that Alice and Marc's marriage is in trouble, given Alice's thoughts at the end of the story. (See **U.S.** questions 1, 2, 3, and 4 and **A.L.T.** questions 1 and 3 above.)

2. *Creative writing: rewrite the story based on seeing Alice's ex-husband* Students' revisions of Colette's story may end at approximately the same place, but Marc would be feeling doubts about Alice's value as a wife. Much of the conflict and resolution will depend on the reasons given for the failure of Alice's previous marriage. If the new stories are based on Colette's characterizations of Marc and Alice, the characters should end up feeling mistrust of each other and self-doubt. **(P.L.J.)**

FURTHER READING

Colette, *The Collected Stories of Colette*.

At Sundown

RAINER MARIA RILKE

INTRODUCING THE POEM

In the lyric "At Sundown," Rilke explores a moment in time in which a mood in nature (twilight) evokes a similar mood (ambiguity) in the observer. Rilke re-creates the mood of twilight through personification and contrast. By using personification, he transfers the sense of mystery found in a veiled woman to an experience in nature. By using contrast, he accentuates the feelings of isolation, uncertainty, and ambivalence in the observer.

The high point of the poem is Rilke's analysis of what it is to be human. Through the images of stone and star, he conveys the physical and spiritual duality that exits within each human being. People are physically limited by the fact that they are only flesh and blood, yet they are free to lead a life of the mind that is limited only by the reach of their intelligence and imagination.

Rilke uses the technique of apostrophe to transfer the observer's experience to the reader. Readers may want to evaluate the effectiveness of the poet's use of "you" in the poem.

Personal Literary Journal: What is your favorite time of day? When you are outside at that time, do you experience particular feelings or think about particular subjects? Give examples.

Literary Terms: apostrophe, contrast, lyric, metaphor, mood, personification, simile

COMPREHENSION QUESTIONS

1. *Where is the observer when this experience occurs?* outside, looking at trees and houses

2. *What about this time of day inspires the observer's frame of mind?* its lack of clarity

3. *How does the experience make the observer feel?* isolated and frightened of the unknown, but also awed and inspired

4. *What two objects does the poet use to represent the two aspects of being human? What aspect does each object represent?* stone: the physical aspect; star: the spiritual aspect

UNDERSTANDING THE POEM: POSSIBLE ANSWERS

*1. *Evening* Evening is compared with a woman who is changing from "raiments" (the color of sunset) to "veils" (the shadows of leaves and tree branches against the twilight sky).

*2. *The speaker's sense of isolation* The speaker feels estranged and isolated because nothing looks the same as it does in daylight, yet all objects are still visible. The speaker wonders where he belongs between heaven and earth.

*3. *The speaker's sense of division within himself* The speaker feels as if he consists of two aspects, one corporeal and the other spiritual. While he is physically earthbound, his spirit is free to contemplate whatever his intelligence and imagination present.

ANALYZING LITERARY TECHNIQUE: POSSIBLE ANSWERS

1. *Apostrophe* Rilke uses apostrophe to transfer the experience from the speaker's consciousness to the reader's consciousness. Some students may find Rilke's use of "you" to be contrived or intrusive; they may resist the speaker's attempt to project his feelings onto the reader.

2. *Personification* Personification underscores the theme of the poem. By imagining evening as a woman, the poet makes the evening human and therefore comprehensible. At the same time, however, there is a feeling of mystery. The evening is a veiled woman.

*3. *Contrast* Contrast heightens the speaker's feelings of isolation and uncertainty at this time of day.

*4. *Stone and star* The stone and star convey the duality within each human being. Stone represents the body (physical matter), which is tied to earth. The star represents the mind (human intelligence and imagination), which can lead a life that is independent of the body.

*5. *Stage of life suggested by poem* The time of life suggested by the poem is late middle age. This is most obvious in the twilight imagery, but it is also present in the third stanza of the poem, where the individual's life is described as "still ripening." This is an image of near-completeness. The poet's reflections on the meaning and direction of an individual's life seem appropriate for a mature adult who is wondering what the next stage of life will bring.

WRITING ABOUT LITERATURE

1. *Essay analyzing tone* Students should be sure to examine the various images in the poem: evening's changing raiments, veils in the trees, darkness that resembles a silent house, star, and stone. Encourage students to examine the relationship between what the poet says and what is actually happening in the physical world. More-sophisticated students will also want to examine why the poem is addressed to an unknown "you." (See **U.P.** questions 1, 2, and 3 and **A.L.T.** questions 3, 4, and 5 above.)

2. *Creative writing: a poem about a time of day* Call students' attention to the suggestions in the textbook assignment. Encourage them to use the poet's ideas as a springboard for their own ideas. **(P.L.J.)**

FURTHER READING

Rilke, Rainer Maria, *Sonnets to Orpheus; Duino Elegies*.

A Country Doctor

FRANZ KAFKA

INTRODUCING THE STORY

On the surface "A Country Doctor" is a nightmare in which a doctor finds that his life is beyond his control, that he is incompetent professionally, that he is neither respected nor appreciated by those he would help, and that he is subject to all the limitations of being human. Thus, the situation in which the doctor finds himself is fraught with the Kafkaesque emotions of inadequacy, frustration, failure, anxiety, guilt, and despair. On a deeper level the story is a "night journey," in which the dreamer gains important insight into what it means to be a human being and, consequently, insight into the nature of society and into his own place in the universe.

In the nightmare the doctor, finding himself caught between his personal desires and his obligations to others, cannot resolve the conflict. He feels compelled to place the needs of a patient ahead of his own desire to remain at home to protect his household servant, Rose, from being sexually assaulted, and he never makes his peace with the fact that he left her.

His torment is intensified by the fact that the alarm is false. Although he sacrifices his responsibility to himself and to those who are "his," his sacrifice is ineffectual and unappreciated. His patient's illness first defies his best efforts to analyze it. The wound turns out to be a wound that has existed from birth, and although it is incurable, it could be far worse than it is. Meanwhile the patient himself defies the doctor's best efforts, wishing to die when the doctor would cure him and wishing to be cured as soon as the doctor realizes that the wound is incurable. In the end the patient accepts the doctor's analysis; he is not seriously ill; the alarm is false.

On his way home the doctor finds that his needless journey has sensitized him to the fragile nature of his own human condition. He is a naked (vulnerable) old man exposed to the hostile universe, both in terms of stormy winter weather and in terms of his profession. He feels betrayed by the inexorable nature of time and the fact that he cannot control important aspects of his life. Moreover, having taken this journey, he must accept the psychological results: He cannot forget the anxieties to which he has become vulnerable and the self-knowledge that he has acquired.

The nightmare is a "night journey," not because it is literally a journey that takes place at night but because of the story's symbolic content. In the words of Albert Guerard, a night journey is "an essentially solitary journey involving profound spiritual change in the voyager." The young patient's wound—"all [he] brought into the world" and his "sole endowment"—is the wound of being human. In recognizing the nature of his young patient's illness, the doctor becomes aware that all human beings (including himself) are imperfect, vulnerable, and fragile.

Moreover, a person's greatest expertise (the doctor's knowledge and experience) provides no bulwark against the inevitable ravages of time and mortality (the doctor's feelings of being naked, exposed, and betrayed). Those who are aware of their wounds are better off than those who do not accurately evaluate their wounds (the boy's wound actually "is not so bad"), for it is better to see life clearly than to live life blindly. It is better to be mindful, to know one's limitations, and to accept the nature of the human condition.

Finally, once an individual has taken a night journey (as the doctor did when he answered "a false alarm on the night bell") and gained insight into the human condition, that person can never be the same again. It will never be possible to ignore reality, to deny human limitations, or to expect an infinitely better society. To know the human condition is to become humble and to accept anxiety and terror ("it cannot be made good, not ever").

This story might be analyzed as a dream in which each character represents some aspect of the dreamer. The groom would symbolize the eternally youthful, sexual, and aggressive side of the dreamer; Rose would symbolize the dreamer as the victim of forces beyond his control; the boy would symbolize the dreamer's incurably wounded ageless self; and the doctor symbolizes the adult form of the dreamer who is trying to cope with all of these aspects of himself.

On one level "A Country Doctor" may be considered symbolic of Kafka's personal life. Kafka felt caught between his need for love and marriage and his self-imposed obligation as an artist to heal society through the creation of literature. On another level the story can be considered an allegory of the human condition, where the doctor is Everyperson, doing his best to handle conflicting needs and demands under impossible circumstances.

Kafka achieves high drama through the contrast between his style and his content. His simple and direct sentences lead readers to expect a description of commonplace experiences. Instead, they reveal a profusion of fantastic images that are presented in a narrative perspective that locks the reader into the consciousness of the narrator. Using the associative pattern of thinking that is characteristic of psychological realism, Kafka makes the dreamer's nightmare become the reader's nightmare.

Personal Literary Journal: Have you ever had a nightmare? What characteristics of a dream or a real experience cause you to label it a nightmare? What kinds of situations cause you to have nightmares?

Literary Terms: allegory, irony, narrative perspective, night journey, paradox, plot, psychological realism, setting, symbol, theme

COMPREHENSION QUESTIONS

1. *Where does the doctor need to go?* into the country to treat a seriously ill patient

2. *What two things delay his immediate departure?* a winter storm and his need for a horse

3. *Whom is he worried about leaving, and what is his relationship to this person?* Rose, his household servant

4. *What two major problems confront the doctor upon seeing the patient?* diagnosis and treatment

5. *How does the doctor feel about himself in the situation that he encounters?* overwhelmed, overburdened, unappreciated, and inadequate

UNDERSTANDING THE STORY: POSSIBLE ANSWERS

1. *The doctor's challenges* The challenges include the following:
   - reaching the boy's home
   - diagnosing the boy's illness
   - curing the boy
   - protecting Rose

*2. *Frustrations* The following frustrations accompany the challenges:
   - The storm and the lack of a horse make travel impossible.
   - The boy at first appears to be healthy.
   - The boy's wound is incurable.
   - The doctor could not both protect Rose and attend to the boy; in choosing to help the boy, the doctor left Rose to the groom.

*3. *Why a nightmare* The story might be called a nightmare because the doctor experiences a world that has no fixed reality and because the doctor has no control over his life. A series of bizarre events occur (the appearance of the horses, the groom's behavior, and boy's wound), and everything that could go wrong does go wrong. The doctor cannot cope with the expectations placed upon him. The storm, the groom, and the boy's wound are all beyond his control.

*4. *Themes* Possible themes:
   - Human beings are not in control of their lives. Circumstances beyond their control determine their behavior.

- Human beings are often torn between their responsibility to themselves and those they love and their responsibility to the society in which they live. Such conflicts have no happy resolution.
- No matter how gifted they are, human beings are all subject to time and mortality.

ANALYZING LITERARY TECHNIQUE: POSSIBLE ANSWERS

*1. *Setting* The abstract location in time and space conveys the world of the imagination or of a dream, a world that is not subject to rational laws. It is, therefore, a world in which anything can happen.

2. *Narrative perspective* Kafka's choice of a first-person narrator with limited omniscience locks the reader into the doctor's nightmare exactly as the doctor experiences it. This technique guarantees an immediate and powerful experience for the reader.

3. *Allegory* The story may be considered an allegory to the extent that the doctor is Everyperson and his experiences symbolize the universal human condition. Other characters in the story seem to represent specific aspects of an individual's life.

4. *Irony* The choice of a doctor as the main character is an ironic twist that reveals one of Kafka's themes. The healer is unable to cure the wound; he who has sacrificed his personal life for his profession is not respected or valued for his profession.

5. *Style* Kafka's simple clauses, concrete descriptions, and matter-of-fact presentation of his subject matter contrast with the fantastic nature of the events that he is describing. The simplicity heightens the drama of the plot.
   Kafka's technique of relating the entire story in one paragraph heightens the intensity of the drama by compressing the action. He relates parts of the story by stringing clauses together to avoid the pauses that would naturally occur between sentences. The story's style creates a nightmarish, surreal stream-of-consciousness effect.

6. *Importance of plot or character* Kafka's theme deals with human beings as they function in society. This is best revealed through action (plot) rather than through introspection (complex depiction of character). To the extent that the story is an allegory, each character symbolizes an idea, and these ideas are dramatically conveyed through plot.

*7. *Night journey* Rose's comment that "You never know what you're going to find in your own house" suggests that the doctor is about to begin a night journey. In this story the doctor looks within himself. Through his experiences and feelings, he acknowledges the true nature of the human condition: the ability within each human being to be both good and evil, knowledgeable and ignorant, responsible and irresponsible, powerful and weak and the inability of each human being to achieve perfection and to defeat death. Having confronted the issues of human frailty, vulnerability, imperfection, and mortality and having acknowledged that such failings are an integral part of life, the doctor is no longer able to ignore his failings.

*8. *Psychological realism* Psychological realism is accomplished by associative thinking. For the doctor, thoughts of the groom call forth thoughts of Rose, and the sight of the horses calls forth the desire to return home. The technique reinforces the nightmarish quality of the experience, in that one thought or event tumbles upon another in rapid succession based on patterns of thought rather than on an orderly progression of events.

WRITING ABOUT LITERATURE

1. *Essay analyzing "A Country Doctor" as a nightmare* Call students' attention to the directions in the textbook assignment regarding content (setting, characters, plot). Remind them of the importance of using quotations to support their ideas. (See **U.S.** questions 2, 3, and 4 and **A.L.T.** questions 1, 7, and 8 above.) **(P.L.J.)** 🅐🅟

2. *Creative writing: a nightmare* Call students' attention to the suggestions in the textbook assignment. Remind them that dreamers do not always appear as themselves in their dreams. **(P.L.J.)**

FURTHER READING

Kafka, Franz, "The Metamorphosis"; *The Trial*; "In the Penal Colony"; *The Castle*.

Voronezh

ANNA AKHMATOVA

INTRODUCING THE POEM

Akhmatova dedicates "Voronezh" to Osip Mandelstam, a personal friend and fellow poet who is currently living in exile in the city of Voronezh. With a subtlety that is probably intended to pacify government censors, Akhmatova expresses the fear that the repressive Stalinist regime has created in the Russian people. She acknowledges the support of the Russian people for the courageous poets who remember their great heritage and speak out against the tyranny of their government. Then she closes with two lines that are ambiguous. Akhmatova may be inferring that although those who are responsible for the growing reign of terror think that their power will never end, tyranny and terror will give way to a rebirth of freedom and happier times. However, it is also possible to read these lines more literally and to interpret them as meaning that this evil will remain unmitigated and that the impending terror has no redemptive feature.

To express these sentiments Akhmatova opens her lyric poem with a description of the icy scene outside her window, equating the unsteady passage of people and sleighs over ice with her own unsteadiness as a poet at a time when other outspoken poets, such as Osip Mandelstam, have been sent into exile. The exiled poets are guarded in turn by Fear, who reminds them of their vulnerability as poets, and by the Muse, who continues to inspire them with the courage to use their poetry as she is using this poem—to encourage the people to remember Russia's past with pride, to tolerate the present, and to have confidence in a bright future. Using wedding imagery, she expresses the loving support of the Russian people for their poets.

As Akhmatova continues to look out her window, she sees a "triumphant landscape" of poplar trees and St. Peter's steeple, and she remembers that the fourteenth-century battle of Kulikovo was fought and won nearby. She implies that the Russian people eventually will triumph over their barbaric Communist government just as, long ago, they were victorious over the Tartars at Kulikovo. She concludes her poem with metaphors of night and dawn. Night represents the increasingly tyrannical, repressive, and punitive present government; dawn represents a time of future freedom, which—despite the current government's arrogant and self-serving myopia—is sure to come.

A different translation of this poem, although very similar in all other respects, concludes with great pessimism: "and the night is coming on, / which has no hope of dawn." One problem with this second translation is its inconsistency. "Night" (personifying the evil Stalinist regime) would never hope for "dawn" (a new era of freedom that would destroy the regime). It is worth analyzing both translations to determine which translation is more consistent with the ideas expressed and implied in the rest of the poem.

Personal Literary Journal: Describe a situation where something you saw reminded you of something in the past. Compare your attitude and feelings about the situation with your attitude and feelings about the memory that was called forth.

Literary Terms: allusion, figurative language, lyric poem, metaphor, personification, simile, tone

COMPREHENSION QUESTIONS

1. *What season of the year is the poet describing?* winter
2. *Where is the poet at this time?* in the city of Voronezh
3. *What does the scene cause the poet to remember?* the great battle at Kulikovo against the Tartars
4. *When did the event the poet remembers occur?* in the fourteenth century
5. *What two figures guard the banished poet?* Fear and the Muse
6. *How do the Russian people regard their poets?* They love their poets.
7. *What is coming quickly at the end of the poem?* night

UNDERSTANDING THE POEM: POSSIBLE ANSWERS

*1. *Unsteady ways of poet and sleighs* The sleighs are unsteady as they travel icy roads. The poet's way is unsteady because she knows of a poet who currently resides in fear in the city of Voronezh because he has been banished by the government. Akhmatova fears that she could incur a similar punishment.

*2. *Triumphant landscape* Both the church, with its proud steeple, and the regal poplar trees are triumphant. They have survived many events that have occurred over the years. The poet may be implying that the Russian people will be triumphant as well.

*3. *Kulikovo* Akhmatova, visiting the city of Voronezh, remembers a famous fourteenth-century battle fought in nearby Kulikovo. There the Russian people triumphed against their Tartar enemy. The poet implies that the time will come when the people will triumph over the barbaric Stalinist regime, just as they were once victorious over the barbaric Tartars.

*4. *Poplars and wineglasses* Both the poplars and the raised wineglasses stand tall and assertive.

*5. *The union in the wedding simile* The union or marriage in the wedding simile unites Akhmatova with the banished poet (Mandelstam) and other like-minded Russian poets.

*6. *Assembled host* The Russian people are "the assembled host." They love the poets who give them hope and courage by speaking out against their repressive government.

*7. *Fear and the Muse* Fear guards the place where the banished poet has gone because the poet (Mandelstam) fears that the authorities will imprison and kill him because of his poetry. Meanwhile the Muse continues to inspire him with the ideas that he expresses in his poetry.

8. *Namelessness* Akhmatova does not name "the banished poet" or "the assembled host" to protect both herself and others from government retaliation. Her goal is to express antigovernment attitudes with a subtlety that will not aggravate the government's censors so that her poetry will not be banned and so that she and her friends will not be punished.

*9. *Night and dawn* "The night that comes with quickened pace" is the Stalinist government's increasing threat to the freedom of thought and action and to the personal well-being of Soviet artists and other Russian citizens. The night arrived as expected; it is known as the reign of terror or the years of terror.

   The current government is so powerful, so arrogant, and so self-confident that it cannot imagine that it ever could or would be overthrown. The poet may be implying that the dawn is some time in the future when the Stalinist government (or similar government) will be overthrown and a new government will restore the freedom of the Russian people.

*10. *Comparison* The poet implies a comparison between the Russian victory over the Tartars at Kulikovo and the eventual victory over the equally barbaric Stalinist regime under which the Russians are currently living.

   The poet may also be contrasting the current "night" with the coming "dawn" (explained in question 9).

*11. *Tone* The poet expresses pride in the past glory of Russia; fear and sadness about the present tyrannical, repressive, and punitive Stalinist regime; and possibly the optimism that a new government will come to power and restore political and artistic freedom.

The second translation concludes with a pessimistic tone, stating "and the night is coming on, / which has no hope of dawn." One problem with this translation is its inconsistency. If "night" symbolizes the evil Stalinist regime, "night" would never hope for "dawn"—that is, the Stalinist regime would not hope to be replaced by a new era of freedom. The translation in the text appears to be more consistent with the other ideas expressed in the poem: Russia's success against barbaric enemies in the past (at Kulikovo) and the support of the people for the poets (and presumably others) who are critical of the present government.

12. *Censored last four lines* The Soviet censors removed the last four lines because the first two of these lines state that a poet has been banished and that he has reason to fear the future. The final two lines deal with the ideas of night and dawn, inferring that the current government (night) either knows no better way to govern or will be replaced by a more enlightened government (dawn).

ANALYZING LITERARY TECHNIQUE: POSSIBLE ANSWERS

*1. *Ice, glass, and crystals* Ice is slippery; it causes people to walk tentatively and carefully lest they slip and fall. Glass is so fragile that it breaks easily, and crystals are crushed when something heavy lands on them. All three substances convey the vulnerability of any poet, including Akhmatova herself, who criticizes the current repressive government.

*2. *Wedding simile* The toast made by the wedding guests to the poets expresses the regard that the Russian people have for their poets. This simile encourages the Russian poets to continue to be outspoken because the poets have the support of the Russian people despite the hostility of the Russian government.

*3. *Personification of Fear and the Muse* The technique of personification breathes human life into abstract concepts. Through personification Akhmatova dramatizes the power that Fear and the Muse have over the banished poet's life. This fear was so real and so valid that the censors prohibited the publication of the two lines that refer to Mandelstam (the banished poet) because these lines would be seen as being critical of the Soviet government.

*4. *Metaphors of night and dawn* Akhmatova is using night with its darkness to allude to the current repressive government and dawn with its ever increasing light to allude to the regime that will restore freedom to Soviet Russia's citizens. Apparently the subtlety of the metaphors kept Akhmatova safe from severe punishment by the government. However, the censors obviously understood the metaphorical meaning of these two lines, and they responded to the implied criticism of the current Soviet regime by insisting that this poem be published without these lines.

WRITING ABOUT LITERATURE

1. *Essay comparing two translations:* (a) "and the night is coming on, / which has no hope of dawn"; (b) "And the night that comes with quickened pace / Is ignorant of dawn" (the translation in this text).

Call students' attention to the directions in the textbook assignment with regard to the church steeple and the poplar trees, the battle of Kulikovo, and the wedding. (See **U.P.** questions 1, 2, 3, 10, and 11 above.) **AP**

2. *Essay analyzing the poet's use of figurative language* Call students' attention to the directions in the textbook assignment. (See **U.P.** questions 4, 5, 6, 7, and 9 and **A.L.T.** questions 1, 2, 3, and 4 above.)

3. *Creative writing: a story in which a person sees something that calls to mind an earlier event* Call students' attention to the directions in the textbook assignment. **(P.L.J.)**

FURTHER READING

Akhmatova, Anna, *Poems* (Lyn Coffin, trans.); *Poems of Akhmatova* (Stanley Kunitz, trans.); *Complete Poems*.

The Wall

JEAN PAUL SARTRE

INTRODUCING THE STORY

"The Wall" is one of the classics of existentialism. It is the story of a man, Pablo Ibbieta, who is arrested and condemned to die by the Spanish Fascists (falangists) because he is active in an anarchist movement that wishes to liberate Spain from Franco and his government. Imprisoned with two other men, he must come to terms with his impending death. In time he is offered his life in exchange for revealing the location of Ramon Gris, an important fellow anarchist and his friend. Pablo knows with certainty where Ramon has been hiding but also knows that only torture could pry the truth from him. Enjoying the prospect of sending the soldiers on a frustrating and fruitless search, he names a false location. Not long thereafter he is amazed to learn that the soldiers have found and killed Ramon just where he told them to look, Ramon having left his hiding place without Pablo's knowledge.

In the ways they confront their deaths, Pablo, Tom, and Juan represent three facets of a human being. Both Tom and Juan are doubles of Pablo, representing emotional facets of him that he must bring under intellectual control if he is to take control of his life. Juan is Pablo's doppelgänger. Like Juan, Pablo is terrified of death; Pablo controls his emotions—eradicating the emotional aspect of personality—by despising Juan. Pablo has a harder time coming to terms with Tom, for Tom functions as Pablo's alter ego as well as his doppelgänger. Both Pablo and Tom are political activists; they have lived in the same environment and have had similar experiences. Tom asks the some intellectual questions about life and death that Pablo would ask if he permitted himself to do so. However, such questions arouse emotional concerns, so Pablo criticizes Tom to distance himself from the concerns that he and Tom share. Pablo consciously works to divorce his intellectual self from his emotional self, and that process involves Pablo's forcing himself to give up all relationships with other human beings.

"The Wall" is constructed on the basic existential paradox that while people act on the belief that they live in a comprehensible, predictable universe, the universe is in reality irrational and unpredictable. Pablo's manipulation of the soldiers with regard to Ramon's location and their finding Ramon there illustrates this paradox.

In addition, Pablo embodies many existential ideas and attitudes. Existentialists believe that human beings are "condemned to be free," in that the tragic human condition is the only absolute in a universe that contains neither God (according to the atheistic branch of existentialism) nor good nor evil nor hope. Instead of having been created for some divine purpose, human beings must create their own personal values, their own meaning, their own sense of purpose. They determine the course of their own lives. In an irrational world in which actions have unpredictable consequences, the process of striving is a valid end in itself, and active commitment throughout one's life will reward the individual with identity, integrity, and self-esteem. Although the human condition is tragic, freedom enables human beings to be dignified, courageous, noble, and even heroic.

Personal Literary Journal: To what extent, if any, does the existence of death give meaning to life? How would you feel about yourself and about others if you learned that you would die tomorrow?

Literary Terms: alter ego, contrast, doppelgänger, existentialism, foil, irony, limited omniscience, narrative perspective, paradox, symbol, theme

COMPREHENSION QUESTIONS

1. *As the story opens, what has happened to the narrator?* He has become a political prisoner.

2. *Why is Juan in the same situation?* His brother is an anarchist, but Juan himself is innocent.

3. *What does the Major announce?* death sentences for all three

4. *What is Pablo's goal in the story?* to accept death with dignity

5. *What bargain do the officers try to make with Pablo?* his life if he will turn in his friend Ramon Gris

6. *How does Pablo react to this opportunity?* refuses to turn Ramon in; fabricates the story that Ramon is hiding in a cemetery vault or the gravediggers' shack

7. *What happens to Juan?* is killed

8. *What happens to Pablo?* liberated from the death sentence and the military court; is sent to a civilian court

9. *What does Garcia reveal to Pablo?* Ramon was found where Pablo had sent the soldiers.

10. *What is Pablo's response?* laughs at absurdity of life

UNDERSTANDING THE STORY: POSSIBLE ANSWERS

*1. *Why Pablo criticizes comment about Saragossa* Pablo doesn't want to envision his own death.

*2. *Pablo's dislike of pity* Pity entails emotional involvement with other people. Feeling pity for someone would lead Pablo to pity himself. To face death, Pablo thinks he must disconnect from life.

*3. *Pablo's being alone and hard* Feeling alone and hard enables Pablo to prepare for his death by divesting himself of his emotions. If he can view his past life as having no meaning, it will be easier for him to face death with self-control and dignity.

*4. *Meaning of "I want to die decently"* Dying "decently" means dying with self-control, without self-pity, and with dignity. Pablo's self-assertion against fate is that although he cannot choose when to die, he can choose how he will react to death.

*5. *Changes imminent death makes in Pablo's attitude toward life* The only way that Pablo can face death is to forget the joyful and rewarding aspects of being alive. Pablo cuts himself off from all human relationships, including the woman he loves and the men who share the death sentence with him. He refuses to permit himself to feel sympathy, pity, or love for others.

*6. *Pablo's near approach to death* By accepting his death as inevitable, Pablo gains control over his life, including both his emotions and his actions. Once he has no fear of death (the greatest of fears), he fears nothing. He has power over his enemies because they no longer have power over him.

*7. *Pablo's refusal to turn in Ramon Gris* In an irrational world, people's actions define the quality of their lives. Pablo achieves pride in himself through his behavior. He is proud not to succumb to the temptations set forth by his enemies, proud to retain his chosen principles in the face of death.

*8. *Themes* The universe operates without the principle of reason governing it. Cause and effect are an irrational pairing. The only meaning in life is the meaning that people create for themselves through their conduct.

ANALYZING LITERARY TECHNIQUE

1. *Function of Tom and Juan* Both Tom and Juan serve as contrasting characters, or foils, for Pablo. Tom is Pablo's alter ego in that both men are political activists in the same environment, they have had similar experiences, and they are facing death. Tom is also Pablo's doppelgänger, in that Tom faces death more emotionally than Pablo, asking questions about the meaning of life and death that Pablo does not allow himself to consider. Pablo forces himself to be critical of Tom to distance himself from Tom's concerns because they are his own concerns as well.

   Juan's situation differs from that of Tom and Pablo and illustrates the theme in the story that life is irrational. Juan, who is not involved in politics, is innocent of the charges; it is his brother who is the politically active anarchist. Juan functions as Pablo's doppelgänger in that Juan responds with unrestrained emotion to his impending death. Pablo forces himself to disconnect completely from Juan to conquer his own terror and to face death with dignity.

2. *Function of Pablo's humor* Humor requires emotional distance. When Pablo separates himself from his situation, he is able to view the officers as insects. Pablo's final laughter is bitter. The universe is completely irrational, and illusions about oneself and reality are foolish. Ramon Gris's fate destroys whatever illusions Pablo has left.

*3. *"The Wall" as symbol and title* The wall symbolizes the barriers that separate the living from the dying. "The Wall" is an appropriate title in that Pablo constructs a barrier between his old emotional self and the intellectual self who is preparing to die. He also constructs a wall between himself and the prisoners who are confined with him. Similarly, the other two prisoners live behind their own walls. Each of the three men face death alone, neither giving support to the other two nor receiving it from them.

On a literal level, the condemned men are now separated from the world of the living by a wall (the hospital-prison), and they are placed against a wall before being shot.

4. *Why the narrative perspective is appropriate to the theme* A first-person narrator possesses limited knowledge. Pablo does not know why he has been arrested, what will happen next, or what his real future will be. His lack of knowledge permits him to speculate, and the difference between what he expects and what actually happens creates irony. Irony is at the heart of an irrational universe, where one cannot predict effects from causes.

*5. *Relationship between irony and theme* The following ironies are important to the story: Pablo escapes death because he unwittingly enables the army to find Ramon Gris; Juan is killed even though he is innocent, while his brother, the anarchist, escapes capture; and Gris never expects to be captured in the cemetery. These three ironies support the theme that the universe is irrational and unpredictable.

WRITING ABOUT LITERATURE

1. *Essay analyzing Pablo's remarks in terms of existentialism* Call students' attention to the quotation and overview of existentialism that are given in the textbook assignment. (You may wish to discuss existentialism more thoroughly with your students before giving them this assignment.) Remind them to combine quotations with their own analysis. Existentialist ideas in the quotation include the following: the idea of being alone, undergoing a struggle in solitude and isolation; the idea of having no understanding because the universe is incomprehensible and unpredictable; the importance of asserting oneself and being true to oneself. (See **U.S.** questions 1, 2, 3, 4, 5, 6, 7, and 8 and **A.L.T.** questions 3 and 5 above.) **AP**

2. *Creative writing: Pablo's diary after his release* Call students' attention to the quoted passage in the textbook. **(P.L.J.)**

FURTHER READING

Sartre, Jean Paul, *The Wall and Other Stories; The Flies* (drama).

The Guest

ALBERT CAMUS

INTRODUCING THE STORY

"The Guest" combines the appeal of an adventure story with that of a mystery story. The schoolmaster, Daru, is ordered to house a murderer overnight and then to take him to government officials in Tinguit. He despises the Arab for resorting to murder and for permitting himself to be caught, yet he considers his own role to be dishonorable and humiliating. Recognizing their common humanity, Daru treats the criminal like a guest and puzzles over how best to reconcile his respective responsibilities to the Arab, to France, and to himself. He decides to provide the Arab with the means and the knowledge necessary either to escape or to deliver himself to the proper authorities. However, the Arab's compatriots—who see Daru set off with the Arab towards Tinguit—leave Daru a message that blames him for the Arab's fate and threatens him with retribution. Daru is now vulnerable and alone.

Daru is Camus's Everyman, in love with the beauty of the universe and the pleasure of simply being alive. He struggles to remain true to the moral principles by which he lives, respecting the needs of all people to determine the course of their own lives. However, the outside world will not let him remain neutral in an escalating political struggle. Human contact forces people to commit themselves, to take risks, and to fight for their beliefs. Daru views turning in the Arab as dishonorable and therefore humiliating because the Arab's crime is neither a personal nor a political threat. Moreover, Daru does not want to be responsible for delivering the Arab to a possible death sentence, a punishment that Daru considers to be a crime against nature. In the end, Daru feels alone in a hostile world.

Personal Literary Journal: What do you need in life to be happy? What aspects of your life do you value most? What principles guide your behavior? If you are asked to do something, what determines whether or not you do it?

Literary Terms: allegory, conflict, contrast, existentialism, irony, limited omniscience, narrative perspective, setting, symbol, theme

COMPREHENSION QUESTIONS

1. *Where is Daru's school?* isolated, high on mountain plateau in Algeria
2. *What is the political situation in Algeria?* French officials fear an Arab uprising for independence.
3. *What responsibility is Daru given?* to turn the Arab murderer in to police
4. *How does Daru feel about his responsibility?* doesn't want to do it
5. *What crime did the Arab commit?* killed his cousin
6. *How does Daru treat the Arab?* feeds and houses him as if he were a guest
7. *In the middle of the story, what does Daru hope the Arab will do?* escape
8. *How does Daru resolve his problem?* gives the Arab the choice of freedom or imprisonment

9. *What does the Arab do?* walks toward the authorities

10. *What happens to Daru?* threatened by Arab activists

UNDERSTANDING THE STORY: POSSIBLE ANSWERS

1. *Relationship between Daru's surroundings and his personality* Daru lives in an isolated area where few people are involved in his life. Daru is independent and self-reliant, preferring isolation to the intrusion of society. Daru values his independence and his fidelity to moral principles. He lives in self-imposed exile because he considers human relationships to be greedy, hateful, and bloody.

*2. *Principal conflict* The principal conflict, which is internal (it occurs in Daru's mind), is whether or not to turn the Arab over to the authorities. Daru resolves the conflict by giving the Arab a choice.

3. *Balducci and Daru* Balducci views Daru's independence and moral convictions as "cracked" because these principles are idealistic and impractical. However, Balducci likes Daru (he refers to him as "son"), so he simply does his job and lets Daru act on his own. The freedom of choice that Balducci allows Daru foreshadows the freedom that Daru allows the Arab.

*4. *Why crime revolts Daru; why he treats the Arab as a guest* Daru hates murder; he sees it as unnecessary and irrevocable. He also is angry that the Arab let himself get caught, causing Daru to be saddled with the responsibility of dealing with him.

   Daru treats the Arab as a guest because he believes all people are related through their common humanity. He does not fear the Arab, since the man's crime was the result of a family squabble.

*5. *Why turning in the Arab is dishonorable and humiliating* Daru views turning in the Arab as dishonorable and humiliating because the Arab's crime is neither a personal nor a political threat. Also, the Arab's fate may be death, and Daru does not want to be responsible for a punishment he considers to be a crime against nature. Daru is caught with the paradox of detesting the Arab for his crime and being the cause of a similar crime if he turns the Arab in to the authorities.

*6. *Why Camus omits violence* Camus is interested in the plight of a human being who hates violence and who wishes to lead a moral life in a world filled with destructive actions. He concludes that one cannot lead a moral life and remain uncommitted and impartial. If one does not choose sides, society will make that choice.

*7. *Tragic end: why Daru "had loved" the landscape* Daru is a tragic figure; by trying to stay uninvolved and impartial, he offers the Arab freedom, a freedom that imperils Daru himself.

   The landscape symbolizes Daru's independence; now he will be forced to side with the French, and for his own safety he may have to move into town. His place in the universe is no longer what it was, an island separated from society by his attitudes and his location. A darker reading is that Daru will be killed to avenge the Arab's death.

8. *Title* Opinions will vary, depending on whether the Arab or Daru is viewed as more important. Both "The Guest" and "The Host" emphasize the human connection and the responsibility of one human being for the life of another.

ANALYZING LITERARY TECHNIQUE: POSSIBLE ANSWERS

1. *Function of Balducci* Balducci is a foil for Daru. Balducci performs a task he does not like because it is his job. He, too, is careful not to hurt the Arab. The freedom of choice that Balducci gives Daru foreshadows Daru's offer to the Arab.

2. *Suspense and fear* Camus uses the following details to create suspense and fear: Daru's handling of Balducci's gun; the Arab's night venture; Daru's hearing furtive steps around the schoolhouse at night and slight sounds behind him in the morning.

*3. *Relationship between political setting and plot* Balducci's talk of an imminent Arab uprising and police mobilization makes the Arab's crime and his village's agitation over his whereabouts sources of fear and uncertainty. Balducci does not think that the Arab is politically involved, but he can't be certain. In addition, the political situation forces Daru to choose between his identification with French culture and his love of the Algerian land and people.

4. *Function of Camus's narrative perspective* Camus uses the third-person limited omniscience, with the center of consciousness located in Daru's mind. As a result, the reader knows only what Daru thinks, sees, and hears. This creates suspense and immediacy.

5. *Irony* Ironic aspects include the following:
   - The French treat the Arab like a criminal when he is no apparent threat to the French colonists.
   - Daru thinks that his neutrality makes his position safe.
   - Despite Daru's rejection of the responsibility that Balducci places on him, the Arab's compatriots blame Daru for the Arab's fate.
   - Daru detests the Arab because of his crime, yet if the authorities kill the Arab, Daru will have inadvertently played a role in the Arab's death.

6. *Allegory* Daru's physical environment symbolizes Camus's universe that is clean and beautiful, even austere. The universe is not concerned with the cycle of human existence; one human being is as good as the human being that he or she replaces.

   Daru symbolizes the human condition. He is Camus's Everyman, in love with the beauty of the universe and the pleasure of simply being alive. Human contact forces people to commit themselves, to be involved, to take risks, and to fight for what they believe in. In the end, each person is alone to lead life as he or she sees best, in an uncaring universe where he or she must persevere even when misunderstood.

WRITING ABOUT LITERATURE

1. *Essay on "No man is an island . . . "* Call students' attention to the quotation and the suggestions in the textbook assignment. (See **U.S.** questions 2, 4, and 6 above.) **AP**

2. *Essay on Daru's choice* Call students' attention to the directions in the textbook assignment. (See **U.S.** questions 2, 4, 5, 6 and 7 and **A.L.T.** question 3 above.)

3. *Creative writing: "The Guest" from the Arab's point of view* Call students' attention to the questions suggested in the textbook assignment. Students should consider what code of behavior guides the Arab's actions. They should note that the Arab killed his cousin, who was a runaway thief, but the Arab does not run from the consequences of his actions. It is also possible that the Arab may turn himself into the authorities because he fears the nomads more than he fears the French. **(P.L.J.)**

FURTHER READING

Camus, Albert, *Exile and the Kingdom* (short stories); *The Stranger; The Plague.*

1. *The short stories of Albert Camus, Colette, Anton Chekhov, Fyodor Dostoyevsky, and Franz Kafka illustrate the use of paradox. Define paradox and then use quotations and examples from three of the five stories to examine what paradox contributes to the meaning of each work.* The paradox in "The Guest" is that Daru treats the Arab as a guest, though the Arab is a prisoner accused of murder. The paradox in "The Other Wife" is that Alice and Marc are preoccupied with how his ex-wife perceives them, although she may not see them or may hold a different opinion than they imagine. Riabovich's newfound happiness and self-esteem in "The Kiss" are paradoxical because they stem from a kiss meant for another man and because the woman who bestows the kiss is appalled. It is paradoxical in "How Much Land Does a Man Need?" that Pahóm and his family are less happy after they acquire new land and wealth than they were when they were poor. The main themes of "A Country Doctor" are underscored by the paradox that a man who has dedicated his life to serving others finds himself useless both to his patients and to those closest to him.

2. *Nature plays a key role in the poetry in this section—"Human Knowledge," "At Sundown," and "Voronezh." How does nature imagery function in these poems, and what does this imagery contribute to the meaning and tone of the poems? Use quotations and examples to support your points.* Nature imagery contributes to the tone and meaning of the poems by linking the authors' themes with the setting. Imagery in "Human Knowledge" includes "suns that by Sirius-distance are parted" and "the swan and . . . the horns of the bull." The cosmos, which is both mysterious and distant, mirrors the endless quest for human knowledge and people's tendency to impose human ideas on nature. The imagery in "At Sundown" includes the "distant trees" and "stone in you and star"; the tree and stars lend a serene mystical tone to this poem as it gracefully explores the meaning of being human. Akhmatova writes of "the grip of ice— / Trees, walls, snow, are as under glass," "crows, / And poplars . . . / Blurred, lackluster, in the sunny dust," and "poplars like wineglasses raised in a toast." The ice alludes to both the emotional frigidity of the Communist government and the hardship faced by people living in the Soviet Union. The poplars' toasting the poets implies that the current political situation goes against nature and that this regime will eventually be overthrown.

3. *A Doll's House and "The Guest" are both considered tragedies. What is a tragedy in literature, and why are these pieces defined as tragedies? Why is tragedy an effective way of exploring the themes of these works? Compare and contrast the ways that Henrik Ibsen and Albert Camus use the societies and personalities of their protagonists to construct these tragedies.* A Doll's House and "The Guest" are tragic because their protagonists are content in the beginning of the story and miserable by the end. Tragedy magnifies the hardships that arise

when a person's values do not coincide with the events or social conventions of their time. Tragedy is, therefore, an effective way for Ibsen and Camus to explore the themes of autonomy, values, and society that are integral to their works. The downfalls of the Helmer family and of Daru are caused in large part by the personalities and beliefs of the main characters, as well as by the circumstances in which these characters find themselves. Students should list specific incidents in each work, describe how these incidents contribute to the tragedy, and explain how each character's behavior affects the outcome of the story.

4. *In their selections in this unit, Hans Christian Andersen and Leo Tolstoy examine the influence of the darker aspects of society—such as greed and hypocrisy—on their protagonists. How does the contrast of good and evil play a role in "The Shadow" and "How Much Land Does a Man Need?" How is this contrast highlighted? What do these authors seem to be saying about human nature? Use quotations to support your points.* The contrast of good and evil and its effects on the protagonists of "The Shadow" and "How Much Land Does a Man Need?" offer profound insight into human nature. Evil is highlighted in "The Shadow" by the interplay of dark and light, by the extreme hypocrisy of the princess, and by the Shadow's methods of attaining wealth. It is contrasted by the extreme goodness of the learned man, who is incapable of seeing evil in others. Tolstoy includes the Devil as a character in his story, making it clear that evil has entered Pahóm's life and that this will have dire consequences. Pahóm's greed is shown in his dealings with neighbors and family. Students should outline how the contrast affects the setting, characterization, tone, and themes of each story.

Africa

Song for the Dead

DAHOMEY (TRADITIONAL)

INTRODUCING THE POEM

The "Song for the Dead" is a song about the value of life. In the words of the Dahomean song, "Dance all the colors of Life"—for once people have died, they can no longer enjoy life's pleasures. While the Dahomeans dance for the dead, they also dance for themselves. Recognizing that all people share an inevitable mortality, they find it important to enjoy their own lives.

The style of the Dahomean song is dynamic, expressing an important message clearly, succinctly, and energetically. Repetition is the key to the song's effect, and the closing metaphor ("all the colors of Life") is a beautiful expression of the human life experience.

Personal Literary Journal: What effect would stopping each day to reflect on the fleeting nature of life have on you?

Literary Terms: metaphor, repetition, theme

COMPREHENSION QUESTIONS

1. *What does the song say about death?* Enjoyment dies with one's death.

2. *What does the song say about wives?* Passion dies with one's death.

3. *What does the song say about food and drink?* Pleasure dies with one's death.

4. *What pleasure does smoking pipes bring?* quiet

5. *What does the song advise the living to do for the dead?* to enjoy life for them

UNDERSTANDING THE POEM: POSSIBLE ANSWERS

1. *Why dance for the dead* The dead can no longer enjoy life, so the Dahomeans enjoy life for them. Whether the dead gain vicarious enjoyment from the joys of the living is a matter of personal belief. However, celebrating life makes the living more appreciative of being alive.

2. *Attitude toward life* The theme of the poem: Enjoy each day of life to the fullest, for no enjoyment exists after death.

ANALYZING LITERARY TECHNIQUE: POSSIBLE ANSWERS

1. *Appropriateness of "all the colors of Life"* The metaphor is simple enough to be appreciated by young and old, uneducated and educated. It reveals the people's appreciation of the natural world. The range of colors in nature is wondrous, varied, and changeable. Life, too, is wondrous, varied, and changeable.

2. *Effect of repetition* Repetition of "I say to you say" gives the poem the vitality of rhythm. Repetition of the internal structure of each stanza and of the phrase "Goes with you" emphasizes the theme of the song.

*3. *Arrangement of stanzas* Like a well-organized essay, the first stanza introduces the thesis or thematic idea: "There is no enjoying beyond Death." The next four stanzas supply specific supporting examples that relate to the thematic statement. The last stanza concludes the song with practical advice on how to cope with the idea presented in the thematic statement.

WRITING ABOUT LITERATURE

1. *Essay analyzing the poem's organization* Direct students' attention to the suggested comparison in the textbook assignment. (See **A.L.T.** question 3 above.)

2. *Creative writing: an essay or poem expressing a philosophy of life* A philosophy may express any belief that can direct one's choices in life. Students should be encouraged to choose their supporting details thoughtfully and to consider the images that best express the philosophy of their choice. **(P.L.J.)**

FURTHER READING

Courlander, Harold, *A Treasury of African Folklore*.

Herskovits, Melville, and Frances Herskovits, *Dahomean Narrative*.

Mista Courifer

ADELAIDE CASELY-HAYFORD

INTRODUCING THE STORY

In "Mista Courifer" Casely-Hayford dramatizes the generation gap in an African family. The story is appealing and powerful because of the universality of its themes and the author's ability to depict with compassion the humor and irony that are inherent in the situation.

Mista Courifer, an undertaker and preacher, considers certain English customs to be symbolic of the civilized, modern, and successful Sierra Leonean and has spent his adult life emulating English ways. Instead of having pride in his native customs, he is ashamed of them. He and his family live in the European-style house that he built for them, and he dresses in the attire of an English undertaker. Mista Courifer is proud that he has chosen what he considers to be the best of both worlds, an English veneer in public and the authoritarian manner of a traditional Sierra Leonean male at home. Mista Courifer's son, Tomas, is his pride and joy. Tomas wears imported English clothes to his government job. Mista Courifer expects Tomas to rise to the top of the bureaucracy.

Suddenly Tomas rebels. He announces that he prefers to combine native African customs with English ways to suit his own values and tastes, which are contrary to his father's. He and his well-educated bride will live in a mud hut, dress in native attire, and have an English-style family life. Mista Courifer becomes frustrated and furious at the change in his son's image. Tomas remains loving but intransigent.

When Tomas and Accastasua appear in church in native costume, Mista Courifer is so shocked and ashamed that he no longer has the desire and confidence to be a preacher. A defeated man, he takes refuge in his undertaking business, which deals with the dead rather than the living.

Personal Literary Journal: How are your parents' goals for you different from your own? If you intend to pursue your own goals, how will you deal with your parents? How do you expect them to react?

Literary Terms: characterization, irony, symbol, theme, tone

COMPREHENSION QUESTIONS

1. *What is Mista Courifer's favorite occupation?* preacher
2. *What is characteristic of Mista Courifer's way of life?* emulates European housing and clothing
3. *What is Mista Courifer's goal in life?* Europeanize his son, Tomas, whom he is proud of
4. *What does Tomas do to his father?* disappoints him by returning to native clothing and a mud hut
5. *How does Mista Courifer react?* furious and too ashamed to continue preaching

UNDERSTANDING THE STORY: POSSIBLE ANSWERS

1. *Why Mista Courifer values certain English styles* Mista Courifer chooses values that will enhance well-being. Since the English rule Sierra Leone, most Sierra Leoneans who are successful in the community emulate English ways. However, since Sierra Leonean tradition elevates the father in the home, Mista Courifer perpetuates that tradition in his home. He expects Tomas to share his values, and he grooms Tomas to be successful in the community.

2. *Why Tomas opposes Mista Courifer's values* Tomas comes into his own when his initiative improves his job situation. He then begins to function as an adult rather than as a grown child. He decides against wearing the clothes he has always hated, and he plans to have the kind of marriage that suits his personal needs and values.

3. *Mista Courifer as father* Mista Courifer has been a good father in that he has loved Tomas and has done his best to train his son to succeed in the community. Tomas acquires self-esteem in part from Mista Courifer's great pride in him.

4. *Compare/contrast Tomas and Mista Courifer* Both Tomas and Mista Courifer are loving people who act in accordance with their personal convictions. Both believe in combining English and Sierra Leonean ways according to their personal tastes. They are different in that Tomas looks forward to independence—independence both from his father and from colonial rule.

5. *Why Tomas changes his mind about his job* Tomas expects that his boss, Mr. Buckmaster, will dismiss him because of his recent attitude and behavior. Tomas is amazed to hear that Mr. Buckmaster values him, and he becomes ashamed of the quality of his recent work. When Mr. Buckmaster explains he has been concerned about Tomas, Tomas explains his problems and

thereby earns self-respect, respect from Mr. Buckmaster, and increased benefits. Tomas now decides to keep his job.

6. *Why Mista Courifer gives up preaching* Tomas's new behavior contradicts Mista Courifer's values, and Mista Courifer feels that this devalues his position as a leader of the congregation. He finds it hypocritical to preach one way of living while his son chooses a different way for himself. Mista Courifer views native dress and native homes as inferior to English dress and homes. Instead of having pride in his national customs, he is ashamed of them.

7. *Author's attitude toward Mista Courifer* The author views Mista Courifer sympathetically, but it is clear from her description of his European house and clothing that she finds his English affectations inappropriate, unpatriotic, and silly.

8. *Author's attitude toward Tomas* The author's favorite characters are characters like Tomas, people who are authentic and sensible. They take the best of both cultures, but the best is determined by what enables them to be proud of who they are. Tomas will keep his job with the government, which he performs well. He will return to mud huts, which are more comfortable and airier than English houses, and he will wear traditional clothing. These decisions reflect pride in his culture. However, he will choose the English style of family life, because he believes it is better for the entire family.

9. *Title* The choice of title makes one character more important than the other. This tale begins and ends with Mista Courifer. It is he who lacks pride in the traditions of his culture, finds self-esteem in trying to be English, and leaves his preaching position because of his son's adoption of certain traditional ways.

10. *Themes* Possible themes:
    * Grown children must function as adults and make their own decisions.
    * Each person is entitled to his or her own values and style.
    * Parents cannot expect their children to be carbon copies of themselves.
    * Parents do not have to accept the values and style of their children.
    * Some people who try to balance two diverse cultures place more emphasis on assimilation, while others place more emphasis on cultural heritage.

ANALYZING LITERARY TECHNIQUE: POSSIBLE ANSWERS

1. *Connection between Mista Courifer's sermons and his life* Mista Courifer is outraged by his son's advocacy of all that he has worked so hard to discard. Thus, he responds to Tomas's return to traditional ways as Jonah and Noah responded to their sinful environment: He takes refuge inside his workshop as Jonah and Noah retreated inside the whale and the ark.

2. *Relationship between the author's attitude and the tone of story* Although the author clearly disagrees with Mista Courifer's values, she understands the

political causes of those values. Thus, she criticizes him gently, with sympathy and humor. Her sympathy and humor create the tone of the story.

3. *Function of Keren-happuch* Keren-happuch is treated with sympathy. She is a source of irony and humor because of the way her attitudes and values contrast with those of Tomas. She values Tomas's English clothes because her father doesn't give her such clothes.

*4. *Examples of humor are:*

- The contrast between Mista Courifer as a quiet husband and coffin-maker and as a wondrous religious leader (singing, praying, sermonizing);

- Mista Courifer's obstinately wishing to appear English despite the obvious disadvantages and impossibility of achieving the goal;

- The visual humor in Keren-happuch's and Tomas's wearing English clothes to church;

- Mr. Buckmaster's visit to Mista Courifer's workshop and the testimonial he writes for Tomas;

- The contrast between Mista Courifer's suggestion and Tomas's choice of vacation pursuits.

   Casely-Hayford's use of humor enables her to treat serious issues—the clash of generations, racial differences, and colonialism—in a way that brings people to a better understanding of the problems and their solutions.

*5. *Irony* Examples of irony include the following: Mista Courifer's desperate effort to appear English; Tomas's return to traditional home and dress; and Mr. Buckmaster's testimonial. All contribute humor to the story.

WRITING ABOUT LITERATURE

1. *Essay analyzing irony* Call students' attention to the directions in the textbook assignment with regard to content and organization. (See **A.L.T.** questions 4 and 5 above.) **AP**

2. *Creative writing: letter about life in the Courifer family after Tomas's marriage* Call students' attention to the questions suggested in the textbook assignment. **(P.L.J.)**

FURTHER READING

(Works by other prominent Ghanaian writers)

Armah, Ayi Kwei, *The Beautiful Ones Are Not Yet Born* (novel).

Awoonor, Kofi, *Ride Me, Memory* (poems); *This Earth, My Brother* (novel).

Kayper-Mensah, Albert, *The Drummer in Our Time* (poems).

A Drink in the Passage

ALAN PATON

INTRODUCING THE STORY

"A Drink in the Passage" conveys a sense of the tragic barrier that exists between whites and blacks in the Republic of South Africa. For many years, that nation had the policy, known as apartheid, of social segregation and economic and political discrimination against blacks and other non-European groups. Edward Simelane, an educated black man and winner of a national sculpture contest, meets Jannie van Rensburg, a white man, when they are both admiring the prize-winning sculpture. van Rensburg desperately wishes to "talk out [his] heart to" the sculptor of the work. Even though he is ignorant of Simelane's identity, he invites Simelane back to his apartment for a drink. Simelane accepts, but the encounter fails.

Although van Rensburg wishes to bridge the racial barrier, his manner of walking and his way of serving the drinks reveal an underlying discomfort. His well-meaning family does its best to converse with Simelane, but communication is obviously difficult since Simelane is a stranger and the black experience is foreign to them.

Although Simelane recognizes and appreciates van Rensburg's courage and good intentions, he makes little effort to respond to van Rensburg. Being in a white area close to curfew and breaking the liquor laws, Simelane is very anxious to return home before the police discover him. A political activist might love the opportunity van Rensburg presents; Simelane has no interest in it.

Later Simelane feels guilty for his treatment of van Rensburg, so he asks Paton to write this story, hoping that others will understand the feelings of both parties. When he asks Paton whether it is too late for the two races to relate to each other, the author, caught between hope and despair, does not respond.

The power of the story lies in the similarity of people who are separated only—but completely—by a racial barrier. Paton, with his gift for depicting attitudes and feelings, conveys the humanity of all involved and reveals the racial barrier to be a wall that the best-intentioned people can breach only with great effort.

Personal Literary Journal: Have you ever attempted to become acquainted with a stranger? How did you go about it? How successful were you? What circumstances would increase the success of such a venture?

Literary Terms: climax, exposition, foreshadowing, irony, metaphor, narrative perspective, symbol, theme

COMPREHENSION QUESTIONS

1. *What caused the nationwide sensation at the Golden Jubilee?* A black man, competing against whites, won the sculpture competition.

2. *How had this occurred?* The committee forgot to add "for whites only" to the contest rules.

3. *Why didn't Simelane attend the ceremony?* He said he wasn't feeling up to it; his attendance would have provoked a racial demonstration, and he is not politically oriented.

4. *What does Simelane observe in the bookshop window?* the exhibition of his prize-winning sculpture

5. *Whom does he meet there?* a white man who loves his sculpture

6. *Why do they drink in the passage?* Because of segregation, van Rensburg is not comfortable inviting Simelane inside.

7. *How does van Rensburg's family feel about the stranger?* wants to be friendly, but doesn't quite know how

8. *How does Simelane respond to van Rensburg and his family?* without interest

9. *At the end, what does Simelane ask Paton to do?* write this story

UNDERSTANDING THE STORY: POSSIBLE ANSWERS

*1. *Sculpture's appeal to van Rensburg* The mother-child relationship is a bond shared by all people on Earth. Simelane's rendition of this loving relationship reveals the common bond that should exist between whites and blacks but does not because of apartheid. This universal bond appeals to van Rensburg. van Rensburg feels that "God must be in the man who made it"; he thinks that Simelane has perpetuated God's values in his own work.

2. *Sculpture competition and Simelane's visit to van Rensburg's apartment reveal the structure of society* Both events reveal a society in which blacks and other non-Europeans are segregated from whites because of apartheid. Note the error in the contest rules, the curfew for blacks, the rules about blacks and whites walking together and using the same entrances to buildings, the rules about blacks being in white neighborhoods and in buildings inhabited by whites, and the rules about blacks and liquor.

3. *Simelane not a demonstrator* Simelane has no personal interest in trying to improve the political, economic, and social condition of his people. If he were interested in civil rights, he would have claimed his prize in person, hoping to further his status and the status of his people. He also might have been more interested in communicating with van Rensburg because he might have had ideas about ways in which van Rensburg could organize whites to help the black cause. As it is, he fears trouble with the police more than he wishes to respond to the gestures of friendship.

4. *Why Simelane doesn't reveal his name* Simelane does not reveal his name because he is self-conscious about being the sculptor of the winning entry, because years of segregation have trained him to keep a social distance from whites, and because he has no genuine interest in communicating with van Rensburg. Once Simelane has lied, he cannot reveal the truth.

5. *Why van Rensburg's background is important* van Rensburg's background reveals the ways in which Simelane's background is superior to his own. It also reveals areas of common interest. Had both men been of the same race,

they might have become friends. This commonality points up the significance and injustice of the racial barrier.

6. *Why van Rensburg offers Simelane a drink in the passage* Neither van Rensburg nor his family is completely comfortable with Simelane. Years of segregation have trained them to keep a social distance from blacks. Ironically this causes van Rensburg to be more comfortable drinking in the passage where they can be discovered than drinking in the apartment.

7. *Simelane thanks the woman at van Rensburg's* How Simelane thanks the woman reflects his social relationship to her. *Dankie, my nooi* and *dankie, missus* are unacceptable because these responses assume that the woman is socially superior to Simelane and he doesn't wish to act as if he were a servant. Simelane fears that *mevrou* may anger the woman with its implication of social equality, but given the choice, he decides to err on the side of appearing to be disrespectful and presumptuous. The woman is comfortable with his choice.

8. *Why the country breaks van Rensburg's heart* van Rensburg wants to be sure Simelane understands that he thinks apartheid is shameful and that he is opposed to it.

9. *How van Rensburg feels at the end* van Rensburg feels frustrated, sad, and possibly angry that genuine, mutually motivated communication did not and could not occur between him and Simelane. His best efforts could not breach the racial wall.

10. *Why Simelane's wife weeps* Simelane's wife weeps for her husband and for van Rensburg, and she weeps because the institution of apartheid has created an insurmountable wall between two men of goodwill.

11. *Why Simelane asks Paton to write his story* Simelane asks Paton to write the story because he wants to make amends for refusing to reciprocate van Rensburg's efforts to relate to him. The story he tells Paton reflects both his awareness and appreciation of van Rensburg's attitude and efforts and his own terrible fear of being caught by the police for breaking the rules of the white establishment. Paton's story may explain the feelings of the educated black toward the enlightened white so that these whites won't be unrealistically optimistic about resolving the racial problem easily or soon.

ANALYZING LITERARY TECHNIQUE: POSSIBLE ANSWERS

1. *Function of story within a story* At the beginning, the framework (a conversation between Simelane and Paton) serves as exposition, providing background information about the contest and the reactions to it, thus supplying the setting of the story. At the end, the framework supplies a commentary for the story and gives it a broader meaning. The ending adds an optimistic note, revealing Simelane's conversation with another white man—in this case, an educated and enlightened author. It also enables Paton to give his opinion on the subject of race relations.

2. *Foreshadowing* The background information about the sculpture contest foreshadows the setting in which van Rensburg's attempt at friendship with Simelane occurs, and it anticipates their difficult relationship. The fact that Simelane has no active interest in working for civil rights foreshadows that he would not be motivated to risk trouble with the police to respond to van Rensburg's gestures of friendship.

3. *Relationship of climax and theme* The climax occurs when Simelane and van Rensburg part without being able to relate in a meaningful way. The fact that the high point of the story is the lack of communication between two men of similar interests but different races—the one making a concerted effort to be kind and friendly and the other terrified of being caught by the police for breaking the rules of the white establishment—reveals the formidable wall between them. This wall is the theme of the story.

*4. *"Black man conquers white world"* This is an appropriate caption in that Simelane won the national sculpture contest in competition with the best of the white sculptors. It is ironic in that, generally speaking, the white world of the Republic of South Africa continued to ignore the rights of black people and to subject them to denigrating rules. It is Simelane's fear of breaking those rules and his lack of interest in those whom the rules benefit that prevent him from getting to know van Rensburg.

5. *Liquor as a symbol* Liquor is a social symbol in that it represents the spirit of good friendly fellowship. As a symbol of this spirit, van Rensburg invites Simelane to join him at his apartment for a drink. It is ironic, and significant of the relationship between the races, that van Rensburg serves Simelane the drink in the passage rather than inside the apartment.

Liquor is also an economic and political symbol of black inferiority. Blacks cannot afford expensive liquor and do not have it available to them. Laws limiting their drinking to specific times and places discourage the threat arising from group dynamics.

6. *van Rensburg's use of "mate"* van Rensburg's use of "mate" symbolizes the potential for friendship between him and Simelane, a friendship founded on Simelane's sculpture.

However, "mate" takes on ironic overtones as the emotional distance between the two men becomes evident. Even though van Rensburg is remarkably open to friendship with a black man, he is not comfortable walking next to Simelane and is not comfortable serving him a drink inside the apartment. Simelane is appreciative of van Rensburg's efforts but is more concerned about leaving the city before the curfew than about responding to a white man's overtures of friendship.

*7. *Metaphor* Examples of metaphor include the following: "touch me," "blinded by years in the dark," and "run a race in iron shoes." These metaphors describe the chasm between whites and blacks who cannot relate to each other because they are strangers. Years of government regulations and acceptance of the established order, combined with lack of knowledge and personal contact, have created a situation that will be difficult to change.

WRITING ABOUT LITERATURE

1. *Essay on function of sculpture* Students' essays should include a discussion of the common experiences shared by whites and blacks. You might encourage students to consider whether a real mother and child (rather than a sculpted mother and child) might have evoked the same kind of response from van Rensburg. (See **U.S.** question 1 and **A.L.T.** questions 4 and 7 above.) **AP**

2. *Creative writing: van Rensburg "talk[ed] out his heart" to Simelane* Call students' attention to the suggestions in the textbook assignment. They might lead to a discussion of the common human emotions of sorrow and anger shared by the two people. **(P.L.J.)**

FURTHER READING

Paton, Alan, *Tales from a Troubled Land; Cry, the Beloved Country.*

Prayer to Masks

LÉOPOLD SÉDAR SENGHOR

INTRODUCING THE POEM

Senghor wrote "Prayer to Masks" after World War II, when many thought the world was dead and without hope. He believed that even though European colonialism had exploited Africa, the future of both continents was still interconnected. The poem is a call to Africans to have pride in their heritage and to recognize that they have a unique contribution to make in the world. In this post–World War II period, Europe and Africa must discard the rubble of the past and build a new and better world. The poem states that the world will be better if it contains the joy of life, the optimism, and the vitality that only Africans can teach the people of other cultures.

Senghor includes principles of the Négritude literary movement in this poem. He personifies Africa as a "pitiful princess," but a princess nonetheless. To pity her is not to devalue her. By using the masks that represent ancestor veneration and worship, Senghor acknowledges and commends the role of tradition in African culture. Through simile and metaphor, he reveals Africa's connection to Europe and Africa's unique role in the future of the world. Senghor uses irony and paradox for dramatic effect, and he uses repetition for dramatic energy.

Personal Literary Journal: Much of the strength and vitality of the United States and Canada comes from each country's bringing together people from many backgrounds and cultures. What has your family heritage contributed to the United States or Canada?

Literary Terms: figurative language, irony, metaphor, Négritude, paradox, personification, repetition, simile, theme

COMPREHENSION QUESTIONS

1. *What do the masks represent to the speaker?* his ancestors
2. *How does the speaker describe Africa?* "a pitiful princess"
3. *How does the speaker describe Africa's relationship to Europe?* "joined by the navel"
4. *What does the speaker want the African people to do?* take part in the rebirth of the world
5. *Name two contributions that the speaker sees Africans giving to the world.* joy; memory of life and hope; the vitality of rhythm

UNDERSTANDING THE POEM: POSSIBLE ANSWERS

1. *Why speaker calls on masks* The speaker asks for the cooperation of his ancestors, whom the masks represent, in the great tasks he thinks Africans must do for the creation of a new and better world.
2. *Traditional relationship between the living and the dead* Spirits of the dead remain a part of the lives of the living. The spirits are worshiped; and in ceremonies, masked figures speak for them.
*3. *Implication of "Who give away their lives like the poor their last clothes" (line 14)* The speaker implies that the Africans can not afford to sacrifice their lives for their European colonizers and that they should not have been so generous as to fight in a war that had no impact on their own lives.
*4. *Themes* Africans have a necessary and unique contribution to make in the creation of a more harmonious world. While modern Africa may be pitiful compared with Africa of the past, the continent still possesses dignity, self-respect, strength, joy of life, and creativity.

ANALYZING LITERARY TECHNIQUE: POSSIBLE ANSWERS

1. *"Masks of unmasked faces" (line 8)* The ancestor masks represent the essential qualities of the personality and values of the ancestor, not physical appearance, physical condition, or age.
*2. *Personification of Africa* Like a princess, Africa has stature and value, even when she is living through unfortunate circumstances.
3. *Africa and Europe "joined by the navel" (line 12)* As European colonies, the African countries were linked economically and politically to Europe. The image, however, is ambivalent: Is Europe (the economically and politically stronger culture) or Africa (the older culture) the mother alluded to by the umbilical-cord image?
*4. *Yeast and white flour (line 16)* "Yeast" refers to the Africans, and "white flour" refers to the Europeans and the people of other primarily "white" continents. The resulting bread would be a reformed social order in which the Africans contribute their unique talents to the cultures of the white continents.

    The key components in the "yeast" that enable "white flour" to become bread are the African abilities to enjoy life, to be optimistic (hope), and to have creative energy (rhythm).

*5. *"Men of coffee cotton oil"* (line 20) Europeans do not view the Africans as human beings but rather as the producers of valuable commodities. Africans are important only to the extent that they satisfy the Europeans' needs.

6. *Repetition* Repetition infuses the poem with rhythm and, therefore, dramatic energy. Repetition of the word "masks" reinforces the speaker's command for the masks' attention. Repetition of "who would" and "they call us" builds to the climax at the end of the poem.

7. *Irony* It is ironic that Africa is undervalued; Africans fought beside Europeans and contributed their equal fighting skills. In the view of the speaker, it is also ironic that those who are treated like slaves hold in their hands the key to the future well-being of the world.

*8. *Paradox* It is paradoxical that Africa, although pitiful, is a princess (worthy of respect and admiration). It is paradoxical that Africans, who are ordered about like slaves, have the ability to contribute qualities to the world that will make it a better place to live. It is paradoxical that Africans are called "men of death," when they are really people of life who are able to communicate their joy of living, their vitality, and their creativity to the rest of the world.

WRITING ABOUT LITERATURE

1. *Essay analyzing Senghor's techniques that instill pride* Call students' attention to the directions in the textbook assignment. (For a discussion of figurative language and paradox, see **U.P.** questions 3 and 4 and **A.L.T.** questions 2, 4, 5, and 8 above.)

2. *Creative writing: a poem expressing pride in one's cultural heritage* Call students' attention to the suggestions in the textbook assignment. **(P.L.J.)**

FURTHER READING

Senghor, Léopold Sédar, *Selected Poems; Prose and Poetry.*

Dry Your Tears, Africa!

BERNARD DADIÉ

INTRODUCING THE POEM

"Dry Your Tears, Africa!" may be interpreted as a return from a journey that is either real or symbolic. The speaker may be speaking for all Africans who are returning home from war on the European continent. Given the poem's publication in the 1950s, Dadié's phrases "storm and squalls of fruitless journeys" and "the springs / of ill fortune / and of glory" may refer to the participation of African troops in World War II, and to the prejudice and discrimination that they experienced as they fought on the French side. Their experience later caused some within the Négritude movement to question whether World War II had been a cause that Africans should have fought for.

On a symbolic level, Africa's returning children may refer to the many Africans whom the French assimilated by educating them in French African schools, where they were taught French language, culture, and values. As a result, many Africans became more French than African. Some received their university education in Paris and continued to live there. It was the goal of the Négritude movement to bring these Africans back into African culture by showing them the unique and appealing aspects of their own traditions and values that would make them proud to be African.

Dadié's poem reflects the values of the Négritude movement in its personification of Africa as the loving mother and of those who have left Africa as her children. His emphasis on Africa's natural beauty and the love that Africans have for their native land are common themes in Négritude poetry. His use of repetition emphasizes the return of Africans to their homeland and the abiding beauty of their native land.

Personal Literary Journal: Under what circumstances would you ever want to leave your native country? Where would you choose to go? Do you think that you would want to remain there or return to your homeland? If you returned, what do you think you would find most appealing about your homeland?

Literary Terms: contrast, figurative language, metaphor, Négritude, personification, repetition, theme

COMPREHENSION QUESTIONS

1. *Why has Africa been crying?* Africa's children have left.
2. *Why should Africa stop crying?* The children are returning.
3. *What did the Africans find on their journeys?* ill fortune and glory; storms and squalls
4. *What do Africans admire about Africa?* its natural beauty
5. *What do Africans bring back to Africa?* playthings, love, dreams, and hopes

UNDERSTANDING THE POEM: POSSIBLE ANSWERS

*1. *Africans better off if they had never left Africa?* "The neighbor's grass is always greener." The returning Africans may well be more satisfied in Africa when they return from foreign cultures than they would have been if they had never experienced the foreign cultures. Learning who they were not was probably an important factor in learning who they were.

2. *"Playthings"* The returning Africans probably bring home items that were not currently available in their native land, such as typewriters and electrical appliances. Dadié calls these "playthings" because they bring pleasure and ease, but they are not necessary for a happy and fulfilling life.

ANALYZING LITERARY TECHNIQUE: POSSIBLE ANSWERS

1. *Water imagery* "squalls" (lines 3, 10): storms at sea, difficult and uncomfortable experiences; "crest of the wave" (line 4): Africans have traveled

far from Africa, crossing the sea to other continents; "drunk / From all the springs / of ill fortune / and of glory" (lines 12–15): sources of fresh water that quench one's thirst, the Africans have experimented and experienced a new life; "the charm of your waters" (line 19): part of the natural beauty of Africa that brings the Africans back, with pride, to their native land.

*2. *Personification* Dadié depicts Africa as a loving mother who weeps over the loss of her children who have gone to other lands and learned other cultures. The speaker is one of the returning Africans who now appreciates Africa's unique qualities. Like the other previously assimilated Africans, he is choosing to forego his adopted culture, returning lovingly to Mother Africa with his dreams and hopes. Personification humanizes abstract concepts, making it easy for readers to understand and identify with these concepts.

3. *Contrast* Dadié contrasts foreign with native, new with traditional, disappointment with hope, and the past with the future. Africans who were educated to value European culture and who traveled to France to live and to fight in World War II are returning to Africa disillusioned with foreign culture and interested in renewing their ties to their native heritage. They now look to their homeland to fulfill their hopes and dreams.

4. *Repetition and theme* "Dry Your Tears, Africa!" expresses Dadié's theme in the poem. The peoples of Africa have not deserted their native land and their native heritage for other lands and cultures. Having experimented with European culture, they joyfully return home, appreciative of Africa's beauty and excited about their future there. Repetition of the title reinforces the theme. By repeating the words that introduce each of Africa's attributes, Dadié emphasizes each aspect of Africa's beauty.

WRITING ABOUT LITERATURE

1. *Essay analyzing the nature of the journey* Remind students to use quotations from the poem to support their argument that the journey is literal or symbolic. (See **U.P.** question 1 above.)

2. *Creative writing: poem or description of thoughts about being away from home* Remind students of the questions suggested in the textbook assignment. Encourage them to use striking images and details to make their writing more vivid. **(P.L.J.)**

FURTHER READING

Dadié, Bernard, *Climbié* (autobiographical novel).

A Sunrise on the Veld

DORIS LESSING

INTRODUCING THE STORY

"A Sunrise on the Veld" is a powerful rite-of-passage story, an initiation journey consummately related by an author who is both a master storyteller and a master stylist. The adolescent protagonist leaves home at dawn on a hunting expedition, feeling exuberantly omnipotent. His euphoria is shattered when he discovers an injured buck in the process of being eaten to the bone by a horde of voracious ants. The sight functions as a Joycean epiphany. Suddenly the boy realizes that death is an inherent part of life and that the circumstances of his own mortality, like the fate of the buck, are beyond his ability to predict or control. He remembers times when he has injured a wild animal and left it to fate so he could be home in time for breakfast, and he suddenly feels the guilt of having acted selfishly and irresponsibly. He knows that this incident, with its accompanying insights, has irrevocably changed the course of his life, and he plans to ponder its significance. He crosses the threshold into adulthood reluctantly, nostalgic for his lost innocence and not quite ready for the pain, loss, and guilt that are part of the adult world.

The extraordinary power of the story emanates from two major themes involving the nature of the universe and the relationship of human beings to that universe. The first theme involves the issue of control over one's life. The extent to which one's fate is unpredictable and inescapable is a serious subject for every human being. Lessing's third-person limited omniscient narrative perspective dramatizes the contrast between the boy's feelings before and after seeing the dying buck. His feelings of control and power in a benign universe give way to feelings of fatalism in a cruel and uncaring universe.

The second theme involves a different but equally important conception of the universe and the relationship of human beings to it. In Lessing's hands, nature becomes a living entity that is the essence of the universe. Both animals and humans are part of the totality of the universe; they are neither more nor less. The boy's feelings and perceptions are described in figurative and sensory language that enables the reader to experience the environment as if he or she were accompanying the boy on his journey and to feel involved in the crucial issues of the story.

Personal Literary Journal: It is said that it is not what happens to you but what you make of it that counts. Look back over your life and find the point at which you left childhood behind. What happened? To what extent, if any, was the change caused by a specific incident or by a series of events? What effect did the experience have on you? What did you learn from it?

Literary Terms: connotative language, contrast, epiphany, figurative language, irony, limited omniscience, narrative perspective, realism, setting, symbol, theme.

COMPREHENSION QUESTIONS

1. *Why does the boy awaken so early?* to go hunting
2. *What is his attitude toward life?* He feels he is omnipotent.

3. *What sight shocks him?* a buck being devoured by ants

4. *What does the sight mean to him?* Life is unpredictable, and it ends in death.

5. *What does he want to think about?* his responsibility to other living things and his own fate

UNDERSTANDING THE STORY: POSSIBLE ANSWERS

1. *Importance of the boy's age* The boy is at a transitional age, moving from childhood to adulthood. This makes his reaction to the dying buck appropriate. If he were younger, he would not have made the connection between the buck's fate and his own life; if he were older, he would have already lost his innocence.

2. *Importance of the boy's being alone* If the boy had not been alone, his reaction probably would have been affected by his companions' responses. His friends might have made light of the dying buck to hide their feelings from their peers. His father's reaction, influenced by the father's own experiences, might have prevented the boy from being introspective.

3. *Quotation concerning the boy's past and future* The boy's past is his childhood—all that he had been until this moment in time. His future is the person he becomes once he has experienced the death of the buck. This story is about a rite of passage or initiation into adulthood, an event that recognizes the boy's being mature enough to acknowledge and understand the complexities of life.

4. *The buck as "a figure from a dream"* On the surface, the buck is a dreamlike figure distorted beyond recognition and imagination. On a deeper level, the buck, like a dream, is the symbol of an aspect of reality—in this instance, of the dark aspect of the life experience (illness, death, and the boy's lack of control over the environment and fate).

5. *Quotation about refusing to accept responsibility* The boy is reluctant to understand the buck as a symbol of an important aspect of his own life. He does not want to admit the darker aspects of life into his own life. He does not want his understanding of this experience to change his life. However, he realizes that the experience must affect his attitude, not only toward himself and his place in the universe but more specifically toward his hunting animals, an activity that he enjoys.

*6. *Will the boy think about the buck tomorrow?* Student responses will vary. If the boy is introspective, he will consciously think about the buck. If he is not comfortable with his thoughts about the experience, he will become busy enough to avoid thinking about it consciously, but he may dream about it.

7. *Themes* Possible themes:
   - All living things die, and no living thing can avoid its fate.
   - One cannot remain an innocent child forever; sooner or later a life experience that introduces one to the dark side of life becomes a rite of passage into adulthood.
   - Life contains both beauty and cruelty, both creation and death.

ANALYZING LITERARY TECHNIQUE: POSSIBLE ANSWERS

1. *Contrast* Lessing contrasts the boy's thoughts and feelings about himself and the universe before and after he sees the death of the injured buck. The difference in his thoughts and feelings reflects his emotional growth and confirms the experience as a rite of passage or an initiation into adulthood.

2. *Nature* Nature functions as a living part of the universe: Plants, fowl, animals, and the boy are all alive and joyful. With the death of the buck, the boy realizes that ants, too, are part of nature and part of life and that in nature one living thing lives off another. Thus, nature is both cruel and joyful. The boy himself, as a part of nature, will also experience the cruelty and the joy of life.

3. *Epiphany* The epiphany is the death of the injured buck, which reveals the nature of life to the boy. For the first time he contemplates death as a personal reality, the inescapable fate of every living thing.

4. *Symbolism of the buck* The buck symbolizes the boy and every living thing. Making the buck symbolic of the boy increases the importance and power of the experience, both for the boy and for the reader. The symbolic aspect of the story gives universal significance to the story.

5. *Narrative perspective* Third-person limited omniscience permits the author to use realistic language to reveal the boy's thoughts as he watches the death of the buck and to use sensory and figurative language to describe the death process. A first-person narrator would have expressed these thoughts and provided these descriptions more directly. For the reader, the experience would have been more intense but less philosophical and less pictorial.

*6. *Connotative and figurative language and nature* Lessing views nature as a living entity that humans, animals, and plants are all an integral part of. The living aspects of nature capture her interest. Her figurative and sensory language gives the reader a visual and aural picture of the African veld that is like watching a motion picture or a videotape. Examples are:

- "Alert as an animal he crept,"
- "Now he felt the chilled dust,"
- "the bush stood trembling,"
- "the grass stood . . . and the trees were showering,"
- "the first bird woke," "the bush woke into song,"
- "the patches of rawness were disappearing,"
- "nothing but one bird singing,"
- "big black ugly insects . . . standing and gazing . . . with small glittering eyes."

7. *Paradox* The story contains the following paradoxes: Life is both beautiful and cruel; it contains both creation and death. These paradoxes are the theme of the story. They are the lessons that the boy learns in his rite of passage.

WRITING ABOUT LITERATURE

1. *Essay analyzing Lessing's treatment of nature through connotative and figurative language* Call students' attention to the questions suggested in the textbook assignment. (See **A.L.T.** question 6 above.)

2. *Creative writing: the boy's thoughts about the death of the buck* Call students' attention to the questions suggested in the textbook assignment. (**P.L.J.**)

FURTHER READING

Lessing, Doris, *African Stories*.

Good Climate, Friendly Inhabitants

NADINE GORDIMER

INTRODUCING THE STORY

"Good Climate, Friendly Inhabitants" is the deftly told story of an aging white bookkeeper who is afraid of dying a lonely death. The story derives its power from this woman's relationship with two men. Out of the depths of her loneliness and against her better judgment, she finds herself attracted to a good-looking, ne'er-do-well white male, young enough to be her son, who conveniently lives off her as long as he can. Meanwhile she confides in Jack, a black man who has worked with her at a garage for years. Jack is a good friend to her: listening, advising, caring, and protecting. Tragically, however, she cannot breach the color barrier to find value and comfort in his friendship.

Gordimer tells the story from the woman's point of view, seeing and evaluating the two males and the woman herself through the woman's eyes. The technique of first-person limited narration adds irony, mystery, and the question of reliability to the story, for the woman often presents herself and others as she subconsciously chooses to see herself and others.

Personal Literary Journal: This is a common saying about people: We never see ourselves as we are; to know ourselves, we need to see ourselves as others see us. Think of someone you know who sees himself or herself in ways that are inconsistent with the ways that others view this person. Give examples both of what this person thinks about himself or herself and what others think about him or her. Explain why you think this person has distorted views of himself or herself.

Literary Terms: characterization, climax, interior monologue, irony, limited omniscience, narrative perspective, setting, theme, tone

COMPREHENSION QUESTIONS

1. *Whom is this story about?* an unmarried woman who works in the office of an automobile service station

2. *How does she view herself?* unusually well-preserved for her age

3. *With what two groups of people does she work?* blacks at the gas pumps; white mechanics

4. *How does she feel about them?* She thinks she has nothing in common with either group.

5. *What two men take a prominent role in the story?* Jack, a black; and the Rhodesian, a white

6. *How does the woman react to these two men?* confides in Jack but doesn't consider him a friend because he is black; is both attracted to and repelled by the Rhodesian

7. *What happens at the end of the story?* Jack gets rid of the Rhodesian for the narrator.

UNDERSTANDING THE STORY: POSSIBLE ANSWERS

*1. *Narrator's appearance* The narrator is 49, but she is trying to look 25. Her hair has been bleached and permed too many times, and her face shows her age. However, she prides herself on her figure, and she wears uniforms made for girls, not women. She fools herself, but no one else.

*2. *Narrator's friends* When the narrator boasts of friends among garage customers and those who pass by with their dogs, she is revealing her loneliness. Actually she has only one friend, with whom she goes to the movies on Fridays. She has Sunday lunch whenever she chooses with an old couple who feels sorry for her. It is ironic that she cannot value Jack—whom she should consider a good friend—because of his race.

*3. *Narrator's relationship with her daughter* The narrator's relationship with her daughter increases her social isolation. She disapproved of her daughter's marriage and implies that she disapproves of her grandchildren. She has seen her daughter's family only once in what might be ten years.

*4. *Narrator's attitude and behavior toward blacks, including Jack* The narrator views blacks as children; she calls them "boys" regardless of their ages. When she wants to assert her superiority, she sends them on personal errands. As much as she longs for a friend, she could never consider relating as a friend to a black. She complains that she works in absolute social isolation. When Jack befriends her, she cannot recognize his friendship.

*5. *Rhodesian's character* Adjectives that describe the Rhodesian include self-serving, selfish, and manipulative. For example, he lies to get housing, money, and sexual favors. His numerous lies include that he needs to change his money, that his watch is gold, that he needs a hotel room, that he has driven down from Rhodesia, that he is 37, that his scars are from old wounds, and that his car is being repaired or sold.

*6. *Narrator's relationship with the Rhodesian* The narrator is drawn to the Rhodesian because he is young, blond, suntanned, and clean-cut. His appeals for her financial aid encourage her to reach out to him. Given her loneliness, she needs whatever relationship he offers her, and she does her best to interpret his behavior as that of a person who is having a run of bad luck.

The narrator comes to fear the Rhodesian because he is unscrupulous. She believes he may steal from her or even kill her. She is equally afraid of her own inability to resist him, her loneliness having made her needy and vulnerable.

*7. *Safety in confiding about the Rhodesian* Confiding in someone would enable the narrator's body to be found soon if she was murdered. The person might also help her get rid of the Rhodesian. Her need to confide is a symbol of the magnitude of her fear.

*8. *Why Jack gets rid of the Rhodesian* Jack feels free to get rid of the Rhodesian after the narrator gives him her address so that he can have someone check on her if she does not come to work. Her request makes Jack aware of her fear of the Rhodesian.

*9. *Importance of "know thyself"* The narrator states, "To myself I admit everything," but she cannot face the reason for her attraction to the Rhodesian and her willingness to let him take advantage of her. If she could have acknowledged her great loneliness and her fear of dying alone, she could have made a concerted effort to make genuine friends. She also would have been able to recognize the Rhodesian for the kind of person he was and could have resisted his efforts to take advantage of her. If she could have acknowledged and revised her attitude toward blacks, she would have been able to recognize, accept, and appreciate Jack as her friend.

ANALYZING LITERARY TECHNIQUE: POSSIBLE ANSWERS

1. *Relationship of setting to character and plot* The narrator would not be so lonely and might accept Jack's friendship if it were not for the restrictions of apartheid.

*2. *Function of Jack* With an unreliable first-person narrator, a character like Jack is necessary. Jack is an objective witness who helps the reader evaluate the narrator's responses.

3. *Why the narrator and the Rhodesian have no names* With first-person narration, either the narrator must reveal her own name or someone else must call her by name. Jack cannot call her by name because of his lower social status. (Jack calls her "missus" occasionally, but usually he calls her nothing.) The Rhodesian has no interest in the narrator's name. He never reveals his own name, and the term "the Rhodesian" associates him with the spurious circumstances of his arrival.

4. *Tone* The tone is disturbing, projecting a sense of sadness both in the narrator's lack of control over her life and in her inability to value Jack's heart beneath his blackness. The first-person narration, with its distorted view of self and others, makes the narrator's fragility and vulnerability apparent to the reader.

*5. *Climax* The climax, or moment of highest emotional intensity, may be different for different students. For some, it may be the moment when Jack tells the narrator "he was here"; these words emphasize that the narrator is terrified of the Rhodesian's presence in her life. For others, it may be the moment when Jack tells her "I told him you're gone"; this statement proves that Jack is the narrator's true friend even though he is black. For still others, it may be the narrator's last words about having no one to speak to and living in a town filled with "people you can't trust"; her words show that she disregards Jack's concern for her and his actions on her behalf and that she cannot view him as her friend.

*6. *Relationship between last sentence and title* The relationship is ironic in that it reflects the difference between reality and the narrator's interpretation of reality. The narrator reveals herself to be a pitiful woman whose situation is made more difficult and more poignant by the society in which she lives. If it were not for the attitude toward blacks fostered by her country's apartheid policies, she would be able to accept Jack as her friend. However, because Jack is a member of the race she fears, she is unable to recognize him as a valued person in her life, and ironically she mistakenly concludes that "this whole town is full of people you can't trust." It is also ironic that the narrator contributes to her own loneliness by choosing to isolate herself from Jack and the other blacks who work in the garage. Finally, it is ironic that the narrator's attitudes and behavior toward blacks actually cause her to be an unfriendly inhabitant.

*7. *Narrative perspective* Gordimer creates immediacy and power by letting the reader enter the narrator's mind. The reader views the world as the narrator sees it, with her prejudices and her vulnerability. The narrator's spoken and unspoken thoughts ironically conflict with reality, as revealed by the words and deeds of Jack and the Rhodesian. Specific examples include the narrator's and the Rhodesian's contrasting attitudes toward the narrator's age, the narrator's comments about friends in contrast with her relationship with Jack, and the narrator's view of the Rhodesian in contrast with his treatment of her.

WRITING ABOUT LITERATURE

1. *Essay analyzing the function of narrative perspective* Call students' attention to the directions in the textbook assignment. (See **U.S.** questions 1, 2, 3, 4, 6, 7, and 9 and **A.L.T.** questions 5, 6, and 7 above.) **AP**

2. *Character sketch of Rhodesian* Call students' attention to the directions in the textbook assignment and remind them of the importance of using quotations. (See **U.S.** questions 5, 6, 7, and 8 and **A.L.T.** question 2 above.)

3. *Creative writing: retell story from different point of view* Call students' attention to the choice of topics and to the ideas suggested in the textbook assignment. **(P.L.J.)**

FURTHER READING

Gordimer, Nadine, *Selected Stories*.

Marriage Is a Private Affair

CHINUA ACHEBE

INTRODUCING THE STORY

"Marriage Is a Private Affair" explores a common theme of African literature: the conflict between tradition and contemporary behavior. It is the poignant story of the pain involved when children mature and make decisions that their parents do not approve of. Although Achebe sets his story in Nigeria, the pain engendered by the conflicting values of the older and the younger generations is present in all families when the younger generation adopts new ways.

Okeke has reared his son Nnaemeka to respect the values of the Ibo tribe. However, once Nnaemeka moves to the city (Lagos), he adopts modern attitudes, including the idea that he should be free to choose his own mate. When Nnaemeka tells his father about his decision to marry Nene, a woman from a different Nigerian tribe, Okeke believes that such a marriage will be a disaster. But Nnaemeka's choice is a good one, and his marriage prospers. Eight years pass, during which Okeke cannot reconcile himself to Nnaemeka's marriage. Finally Nene's letter imploring Okeke to let his two grandsons meet him breaks through Okeke's wall of emotional resistance. Okeke belatedly realizes how foolish he has been to let his commitment to the tribal traditions deprive him of a loving family, and he hopes that he does not die before the family can recover the joys that have been lost.

The key to the story's tone is the attitude of the three characters toward one another. Okeke remains true to the only principles that he feels can sustain him; however, Nnaemeka and Nene continue to treat Okeke with respect. They realize that Okeke is a good man whose Ibo culture does not permit him to accept their marriage.

Personal Literary Journal: How would you feel if your older brother or sister, who was also your close friend, married a person of a different race or religion? Would your parents be likely to object to such a marriage? If your parents object, what do you think the young couple should do?

Literary Terms: characterization, conflict, contrast, foreshadowing, irony, realism, setting, theme, tone

COMPREHENSION QUESTIONS

1. *What does Nnaemeka need to tell his father?* that he is engaged to Nene
2. *What plans does Okeke have for Nnaemeka?* an arranged marriage
3. *How does Okeke react to Nnaemeka's news?* He will have nothing to do with Nnaemeka and Nene.
4. *How long does Okeke refuse to see his son and daughter-in-law?* eight years
5. *How does the story end?* Okeke relents when he learns that his grandsons want to meet him.

UNDERSTANDING THE STORY: POSSIBLE ANSWERS

*1. *Okeke's objections* Okeke objects to Nnaemeka's marriage for the following reasons:

- Ibo custom dictates that parents arrange a child's marriage.

- Nene is from a different tribe. Marriage works best when partners share common bonds; different tribes means different values and different cultural heritages.

- Okeke feels that he has failed in rearing Nnaemeka because he thinks that Nnaemeka's independent behavior means that Nnaemeka no longer respects the traditions of the tribe and the values of the family.

*2. *Broken relationship with Okeke* Nnaemeka is to blame for the broken relationship with his father because he knows what effect his decision will have on his father. Nnaemeka's choice is to please himself or to please Okeke; no compromise is possible. Nnaemeka tries to help Okeke adjust to the new values that accompany city life, but he is unsuccessful.

3. *Nnaemeka's attitude toward Okeke* Nnaemeka loves, respects, and understands Okeke. He believes that Okeke has the ability to be flexible and that in time Okeke will support the marriage.

*4. *Okeke's reaction to calling a native doctor* Okeke holds some independent views. He does not share the superstitions of his neighbors, and he does not trust native doctors. This fact supports Nnaemeka's evaluation of Okeke and reveals Okeke's potential to free himself from traditional tribal constraints.

5. *Nene's letter* Okeke is pleased that his grandsons wish to know him. He is probably amazed that Nene has responded to his hostility with kindness and understanding. He finally realizes that his attitude has cut him off from love and family life.

*6. *Attitude implied in the title* The title conveys Achebe's attitude that young people are living in a new age and that they must be free to make their own decisions. Good parents should feel confident in their child's ability to choose wisely.

7. *Effect of the last sentence* The last sentence puts the events of the preceding years into perspective. Time and life are priceless. Humans die; life is short; death is often unexpected. Love and life experiences lost through estrangement are not recovered. People should look beyond their present irritations to the future; they should preserve flexible attitudes. Okeke's realization of his mortality enhances his value of life. He realizes the tragic loss of eight years, and his response makes him a more sympathetic character.

8. *Themes* Possible themes:

- New ways are not necessarily bad.

- Family relationships are more important than tradition.

- Live each day as if it were your last.

ANALYZING LITERARY TECHNIQUE: POSSIBLE ANSWERS

*1. *Contrast* Contrasts include: tribe and city, old age and youth, tradition and innovation.

2. *Foreshadowing* Nnaemeka's reaction to the suggestion that he should write to his father about his marriage foreshadows the effect the marriage will have on Okeke.

3. *Tone* The tone is poignant. It is achieved through the universal nature of the conflict, the inevitable pain and compromise that are necessary, and the fact that the three major characters are basically good human beings.

4. *Character and fate* Students' answers will vary. "Fate determines character" when external events impinge on a person's life and force that person to react in a certain way. "Character determines fate" when personality determines a person's response to a situation.

   Okeke's situation is an example of the relationship between the two views. When Nnaemeka's marriage conflicts with Okeke's tribal values, Okeke's response determines his fate. He can be true to his value system, or he can adapt his value system to the new circumstances. His initial hostile reaction creates a chasm in his family.

5. *Irony* It is ironic that Okeke can be flexible about native doctors and inflexible about relating to Nnaemeka and Nene, when both issues are important to Nnaemeka's well-being. It is also ironic that the tribal values, which were intended to be supportive, can become destructive.

WRITING ABOUT LITERATURE

1. *Essay analyzing how contrasts enhance the theme* Call students' attention to the directions in the textbook assignment with regard to content and organization. (See **U.S.** questions 1, 2, 4, and 6 and **A.L.T.** question 1 above.) **AP**

2. *Creative writing: letter from Okeke to Nene after the visit* Call students' attention to the questions suggested in the textbook assignment. **(P.L.J.)**

FURTHER READING

Achebe, Chinua, *Things Fall Apart; Arrow of God; Girls at War and Other Stories*.

The Rain Came
GRACE OGOT

INTRODUCING THE STORY

Ogot weaves many strands of meaning into "The Rain Came." Some give it romantic appeal, while others give it intellectual power. The story's romantic appeal is based on its satisfying conclusion, where love conquers adversity. Stories of beautiful maidens in distress (such as Oganda) who are rescued by handsome and courageous young men (such as Osinda) are the subject of many folktales and myths. Because the story ends with the feeling (though not the actuality) of "happily ever after," the story satisfies the human need for love, security, and justice.

The story gains intellectual appeal from its examination of the role of tradition in society. "The Rain Came" contains elements of a fertility myth, where the sacrifice of a valued and beautiful young virgin is necessary so rain will come for the crops. Ogot dramatizes the intense emotion with which individuals respond to the traditional demands of their society under circumstances where "love it or leave it" are the only options. Labong'o experiences heartrending conflict between his responsibility to his people and his responsibility to his family; as chief, however, he does not have the freedom to choose between his responsibilities. Oganda experiences anguish and terror at being the sacrificial victim. She would prefer a normal life to eternal fame; as princess, however, she does not have the freedom to choose the course of her life. Meanwhile, the villagers celebrate because, with the exception of Osinda, they have everything to gain and nothing personal to lose from the sacrifice of Oganda. Fortunately for Oganda, Osinda has both the motivation and the freedom to choose the course of his life. Valuing Oganda more than family, friends, and conformity, he leaves the village and rescues the woman he loves.

The fact that it rains despite Oganda's rescue means different things to different people. The villagers presumably are unaware of Oganda's fate, so they remain committed to their traditions. Oganda and Osinda realize that they do not have to feel guilty about achieving personal happiness and freedom since the ancestors do not punish the community for their rebellion.

The conflict between personal desires and responsibility to society and the conflict between tradition and innovation have universal application. People in every society are called upon to sacrifice their personal desires for the needs of their community, particularly in time of war. Moreover, as young people become young adults, they often find that new circumstances cause them to question traditional patterns of behavior.

Personal Literary Journal: If the well-being of you and your family is threatened, would your first responsibility be to yourself or to your family? Why? If the well-being of a country is threatened (for example, by war), how should citizens balance their responsibility to their own families with their responsibility to their country?

Literary Terms: characterization, climax, folktale, foreshadowing, irony, myth, narrative perspective, omniscient narrator, short story

COMPREHENSION QUESTIONS

1. *What does Labong'o learn from the medicine man?* He must sacrifice his daughter so that rain will fall.

2. *How does he react?* He is sad but compliant.

3. *Why do the villagers react as they do?* Survival of their village is more important to them than Oganda's life.

4. *What good luck do the villagers sing about?* Oganda's name will be remembered.

5. *What happens to Oganda?* She is rescued by Osinda.

UNDERSTANDING THE STORY: POSSIBLE ANSWERS

1. *Why Oganda must be sacrificed* The chief's only daughter is the most acceptable sacrifice. She is appealing to the lake monster and acceptable to the villagers. The chief and his wives are the only others that might be considered for the sacrifice, but they are unacceptable for many reasons: Fertility sacrifices require young healthy specimens; the political safety of the village depends on the chief; and if the chief's wives are young enough, they can bear other children.

2. *Villagers' attitude toward human sacrifice* The villagers accept wholeheartedly the necessity of human sacrifice because they believe that such sacrifice will motivate the forces of nature to sustain the village. Only Oganda, her parents, and Osinda are grieved. The other villagers are relieved that they will not be sacrificed.

3. *Labong'o's choice* Labong'o has no choice with regard to Oganda's sacrifice. As the chief of his people, he must place the well-being of the community before the well-being of his family and himself. If he and his family leave the community, they would have to find a community that would accept them. However, Labong'o would also have to accept himself, and finding self-respect could be much more difficult.

4. *Oganda's choice* Without Osinda's support, Oganda has no viable choice with regard to being sacrificed. If she runs away, she would sacrifice every source of emotional support. She would be alone in the world, presumably with no neighboring community willing to befriend her.

5. *Special protective coats* Osinda's special coats will camouflage Oganda and Osinda so that the ancestors will not easily discover them as they walk through the forest.

6. *Significance of the rain's arrival* To many readers, the fact that it rains despite Oganda's rescue reveals the futility of the practice of human sacrifice. Others may believe that the Ancestors rewarded Oganda's willingness to sacrifice herself for the good of her village.

7. *Osinda: hero or villain?* Ogot presents Osinda as the hero who rescues Oganda. Certainly Oganda views him as a hero. Even if it did not rain, Labong'o's love for Oganda would probably also lead him to view Osinda as a hero. Labong'o would probably admire Osinda's courage, and he would be thankful that his daughter would have a full life. Most of the villagers, however, would probably view Osinda as a traitor. People who conform to the demands of society often resent those who do not. From the point of view of the conformists, Osinda's actions would threaten the solidarity of the community and would undermine the certainty that adherence to tradition contributes to daily life. Many villagers would fear that Osinda's behavior would motivate others to place their own needs before the needs of their community.

8. *Oganda's heroism* Oganda is heroic in that she places the welfare of her community before her own personal welfare and accepts with dignity the burden that is placed upon her. Even when she is no longer in public view, she courageously travels through the sacred land and faces her destiny with fortitude.

9. *Villagers' view of Oganda's escape* The conformists in the village would probably regard Oganda, like Osinda, as a traitor. She would be viewed as a bad influence in the community, a threat to its solidarity and to its future welfare.

10. *Role of tradition* This story commends both those who are willing to make personal sacrifices for the good of their community (like Oganda) and those who have the courage to break with tradition in order to achieve personal happiness (like Osinda).

ANALYZING LITERARY TECHNIQUE: POSSIBLE ANSWERS

1. *Chief's characterization* The chief's sorrow over the fate of his daughter and his role in her death make him a very human figure. His situation reveals how difficult it can be for people to reconcile their personal feelings with their responsibility to their community. As the chief of the tribe, he has no choice but to sacrifice the welfare of his family for the welfare of his village.

2. *Significance of title* The title points to the climax of the story—the rain's occurring in spite of Oganda's escape—thereby directing the reader's attention to the events leading up to the rain, the irony involved, and the inhumanity of human sacrifice.

3. *Irony* The last line gives the story its power. The fact that it rains even though Oganda has escaped suggests that Oganda's sacrifice was not necessary. It is ironic that the villagers' ignorance of Oganda's escape prevents them from questioning the necessity of human sacrifice, so they probably will perpetuate this religious tradition. Until Oganda's escape, the story reads like a myth that explains the relationship between the world of mortals and the world of the divine. Her escape changes the genre and function of the story.

4. *Narrative perspective* The third-person omniscient narrative perspective, traditionally used in a tale, permits the narrator to know everything about every character and to reveal just as much as is necessary to create the desired effect. Its use permits Osinda's rescue of Oganda to be a surprise.

5. *Figurative language* Figurative language should be consistent with the time and location of the story in which it occurs. The simile "like a mouse cornered by a hungry cat" is appropriate since it reflects animals the people may know in their village life. The images of Oganda and her parents being "like three cooking-stones, sharing their burdens" and of her parents being left like "two useless stones which would not hold a cooking-pot" are superb because the cooking stones are an integral part of village life.

WRITING ABOUT LITERATURE

1. *Essay on myth and short story* Call students' attention to the directions in the textbook assignment. Remind them to use quotations to support their ideas. **AP**

2. *Creative writing: continuation of the story* Call students' attention to the end of the story and to the directions and the questions suggested in the textbook assignment. Point out that Osinda's rescue of Oganda does not automatically ensure that the couple will live "happily ever after." Encourage students to make their own stories consistent with Ogot's characterizations and setting. **(P.L.J.)**

FURTHER READING

Ogot, Grace, *Land Without Thunder; The Promised Land; The Graduate; The Island of Tears.*

The Trials of Brother Jero
WOLE SOYINKA

INTRODUCING THE STORY

The Trials of Brother Jero displays Soyinka's versatility as a writer, for he writes comic satire as well as he writes serious drama and poetry. In this farce, Soyinka exposes human weaknesses as every character tries to cope with ordinary problems of life. Brother Jero is a self-proclaimed prophet, a charlatan who cares more about himself than about anyone else. He takes advantage of people, but he causes no serious harm. He enjoys self-importance, and he is proud of the ingenuity he uses to manipulate and deceive others.

The play is both visually and verbally funny. In the comic heart of the play, Soyinka achieves humor through the dramatic technique of unrevealed identities and the growing threat of their discovery. Dramatic and verbal ironies abound in the plot. In addition, the repetitious conversational style of the major characters adds an important comic element. Surrounding the central action of the play, numerous scenes are comic gems. Among them are those in which Brother Jero escapes through a window, works hard not to lust after women, changes his name, and makes a follower of a member of parliament; Amope ceaselessly badgers Chume; Chume preaches a successful sermon; and a woman who is being chased by Brother Jero chases a drummer.

Personal Literary Journal: What is the difference between human frailties that are serious and those that are humorous? Among your relatives and friends, which traits do you find amusing? Which traits irritate you? Which traits of yours do others find amusing? Which traits of yours disturb others?

Literary Terms: allusion, characterization, comedy, discovery, farce, irony, plot, repetition, reversal, satire, tone

COMPREHENSION QUESTIONS

1. *What does Amope want from Brother Jero?* the money Jero owes her for a robe he purchased

2. *What self-sacrifice does Brother Jero demand of himself?* to ignore temptation of women

3. *What sacrifice does Brother Jero demand of Chume?* to refrain from beating his wife

4. *What leads Brother Jero to permit Chume to treat Amope as he wishes?* Jero discovers that Chume's wife is the woman he owes money to.

5. *What leads Chume to become estranged from Brother Jero?* Chume discovers that Jero is a hyprocrite and a liar and that Jero wants him to beat Amope because of Jero's relationship with her.

UNDERSTANDING THE PLAY: POSSIBLE ANSWERS

1. *Jero's character* Jero is clever, entertaining, and psychologically astute. However, since he is a charlatan, he is not admirable. He is self-serving and manipulative, taking advantage of the human weaknesses in others. The best one can say about his behavior is that he does not seriously harm anyone.

2. *Chume's character* Chume's goodwill and honesty are appealing. However, his gullibility is not admirable. He sees people as either good or evil. He blindly follows Jero when he sees Jero as the Prophet, but he rejects him completely when he sees Jero's faults.

3. *Amope's character* Amope is an unpleasant human being who nags everyone. Although Amope's behavior is counterproductive, she is perceptive in that she sees the true nature of both Chume and Jero. She is also an energetic business woman.

*4. *Realistic characterizations* Jero, Amope, and Chume are all portrayed as realistic, psychologically complex individuals. Their failings are exaggerated to make them humorous, but the fact that each possesses a combination of psychological strengths and weaknesses enables readers and audiences to relate to them and sympathize with them.

   People exist in our society who manipulate others as Jero does. Among them are certain television evangelists, advertisers, salespeople, and politicians.

5. *Source of humor in the unrevealed identities of Jero and Amope* The humor comes from the characters' attitudes as they learn the identity of the other characters. For example, Jero's attitude toward Chume's wife changes once Jero knows that Chume's wife is the woman he owes money to; Chume's attitude toward Jero changes once Chume knows about Jero's debt and about the lies Jero has told.

6. *Chume committed to asylum* It is not likely that Chume will be put into an asylum for the following reasons: The authorities will realize that Jero is at fault; Chume will no longer try to kill Jero once Chume realizes that Jero

is not romantically involved with Amope; committing Chume is too serious for the light-hearted humor of this play.

*7. *Jero's trials* The nature of Jero's trials (lust, creditors, a threatening disciple) makes them humorous. His trials are ironic in that he brings them all upon himself; he is not like the prophets in the Bible who were tested by God.

*8. *Serious subjects of this comedy* The responsibility that religious leaders owe members of their congregation and others with whom they deal; the need for mutual respect between marriage partners; and the need for politicians to be responsible to their constituents.

*9. *Soyinka's goal* Soyinka is commenting on human relationships. His farce is like a sugar-coated pill. Beneath his highly entertaining comedy are oblique but serious criticisms of certain kinds of relationships. In the ideal world, politicians and religious leaders are ethical people who are responsible to their constituents and congregations, and husbands and wives respect and help each other. Soyinka intends to remind people that human beings should acknowledge the dignity of others and treat others with respect.

ANALYZING LITERARY TECHNIQUE: POSSIBLE ANSWERS

*1. *Language as characterization* Speech patterns and vocabulary reflect social class, sophistication, and sincerity. Jero's refined speech is unnatural; it is cultivated with the intent to deceive. Chume's unrefined speech is natural, heartfelt, and sincere.

*2. *Dramatic irony* One important example of dramatic irony at the end of Scene III occurs when Brother Jero realizes that Amope is Chume's wife. Chume thinks that he is being granted permission to beat his wife because wife-beating is spiritually necessary; the audience knows that Jero wants to take revenge on Amope.

Another example of dramatic irony comes toward the end of the play when Jero is chased offstage by Chume while the Member of Parliament is praying, causing the Member to think that Jero has been transmuted.

In both examples, the dramatic irony drives the plot of the play and contributes to the humor.

*3. *Discovery* Examples: Jero's saying "So that is your wife" unifies the plot by connecting Amope, Chume, and Jero; Chume's saying "Did I hear you say Prophet Jeroboam?" reveals that Chume is beginning to understand the situation. These humorous surprises lead to humorous reversals.

*4. *Plot versus characterization* Plot is more important than characterization in this play because the plot is the vehicle for the humor. However, Soyinka's complex characterization enhances the quality of the play, making it both more humorous and more serious.

*5. *Satire* This play is a satire in that it ridicules the vices and foolishness of the characters in the play. Soyinka is criticizing human behaviors: hypocrisy, selfishness, dishonesty, disrespect.

*6. *Farce* This play is a farce in that it is a comedy with satiric overtones. It has an improbable, contrived plot and contains elements of slapstick humor (for example, Jero's sneaking out the window and the chase scene).

However, a farce usually has a happy ending. This play ends before the comic misunderstandings are resolved, possibly suggesting that Soyinka intends the play's satiric element—his criticism of society—to stand out more vividly than the play's purely comedic element.

WRITING ABOUT LITERATURE

1. *Essay analyzing how Soyinka criticizes forms of behavior* Students probably will find this a challenging assignment. The goal is for students to write a persuasive essay based on an analysis of one aspect of this play. Encourage students to focus on one thematic strand instead of trying to combine two or more elements of the play. Depending on the aspect of behavior that students choose to focus on, they may or may not find that Soyinka suggests a solution or way to reform the behavior. Encourage students to analyze whether this strengthens Soyinka's critique of society or detracts from it. Some students may want to research further the goals of satire. (See **U.P.** questions 4, 7, 8, and 9 and **A.L.T.** questions 5 and 6 above.)

2. *Essay analyzing how Soyinka creates humor* Remind students to choose two or three of the five techniques. (See **A.L.T.** questions 1, 2, 3, and 4 above.) **AP**

3. *Creative writing: dialogue resolving conflicts between Brother Jero, Amope, and Chume* Call students' attention to the questions suggested in the textbook assignment. **(P.L.J.)**

FURTHER READING

Soyinka, Wole, *Jero's Metamorphosis*; *Opera Wonyosi*; *A Shuttle in the Crypt*; *The Devil and the King's Horseman*; *Aké: The Years of Childhood*; *Ìsarà*.

The Lovers
BESSIE HEAD

INTRODUCING THE STORY

"The Lovers" is a brilliantly conceived and executed story that is satisfying on many levels. On the surface, it is the tale of Keaja and Tselane, a romantic love story that is reminiscent of the tale of Romeo and Juliet but without the lovers' tragic deaths. On a deeper level, "The Lovers" is the tragic story of a tribal society that is emotionally crippled by its devotion to traditions that control human behavior. The tribal rules are based on male jealousy and on the fear of female sexuality. The rules control relations between the sexes, requiring individuals to direct their feelings in ways that the community finds to be socially acceptable.

The narrator states:

> A delicate balance had to be preserved between a woman's reproductive cycle and the safety of the community; at almost every stage of her life a woman was a potential source of danger to the community. . . . Failure to observe the taboos could bring harm to animal life, crops and the community.

Males and females lead separate lives except for arranged marriages in which procreation is the only common interest and shared goal. Sexual taboos include communal abstinence from sexual relations from the time immediately prior to the harvest until the thanksgiving ritual. Fear of bringing disaster into the community subjugates the will of the individual to the dictates of the tribe, and all nonconformists are punished with ostracism, banishment, and death.

The power of "The Lovers" emanates from the heroism of three characters who have the courage to defy the dictates of their social, political, and religious environment. Both history and current events offer ample testimony to the fact that such human beings exist outside fiction. There are members of every society who question the inevitability of social structures—and some who have the courage to take a public stand on issues they believe in. Keaja and Tselane, motivated both by their convictions and their passions, are willing to risk death to lead more meaningful lives.

Mma-Monosi is the most interesting character in the story. Her nature, attitudes, and behavior reflect the profound psychological effect of an earlier terrifying experience. She once watched in horrified silence as the tribe killed a young man who would not agree to marry the girl his parents had chosen for him. (It is possible that Mma-Monosi herself loved the young man, though this is not explicit in the text.) As a result of this experience, Mma-Monosi has become a divided personality: She is strong and independent yet so concerned about public approval that she cannot tolerate criticism. Her bitter lesson has taught her that safety lies in accepting the established order.

Tselane's predicament forces Mma-Monosi to relive her own horrible experience, and she welcomes the opportunity to save Tselane from a similar experience. Not only does Mma-Monosi attend to "the last details of the departure," but she is the only person who watches the couple as they leave the village. Thus, Mma-Monosi is in a position to convince the tribe that the lovers are gone from the world. She is the most heroic of the three characters, because she risks her life to protect the young couple. In the end, she owes her life to a powerful ally, superstition—a perennially active and enduring force in her tribe.

At the end of "The Lovers," Head explains how Tselane and Keaja's story has become a legend. Her direct narrative style is characteristic of legends; she focuses on plot rather than character. Her subtle psychological characterization of Mma-Monosi gives an unusual dimension to the tale by adding mystery and suspense.

Personal Literary Journal: Have you (or anyone you know) ever been forced to choose between rules and values that your family has established and those that you feel are more appropriate? How did you handle this conflict?

Literary Terms: antagonist, characterization, climax, conflict, folktale, foreshadowing, irony, legend, narrative perspective, protagonist, romance, setting, short story, theme

COMPREHENSION QUESTIONS

1. *How does the love affair begin?* Two people find refuge from the rain in a cave.
2. *What has fostered Keaja's attitude toward marriage?* his father's unhappy marriage to his mother
3. *Why does Tselane take Keaja's views seriously?* her similar experiences and her attitude toward other young men
4. *In what way is Tselane closer to Mma-Monosi than to Mma-Tselane?* Mma-Monosi is a close friend; Mma-Tselane is a loving but stern parent.
5. *What is Mma-Monosi's attitude toward marriage?* She accepts the traditions.
6. *What causes Keaja to propose to Tselane?* the prospect of his own arranged marriage
7. *Why does Tselane become ill?* her conflict between her love for Keaja and the tribal traditions
8. *What causes Tselane and Keaja to reveal their engagement?* Tselane's pregnancy
9. *How is the issue resolved?* Keaja and Tselane leave the tribe for a few days so that the community's anger can die down.
10. *What permits the story to have a happy ending?* Mma-Monosi tells the villagers she has seen how Keaja and Tselane were swallowed up by the rocks, causing the villagers to call off the search.

UNDERSTANDING THE STORY: POSSIBLE ANSWERS

1. *Accepting tribal regulations and taboos* Superstition about environmental retaliation (drought, disease, and death), fear of loss of social status, and fear of tribal punishment combine to motivate the villagers to conform to tradition. Men and women adapt to the regulations by finding status and friendship among members of their own sex.
2. *Ignoring individual initiative* The tribal elders have a vested interest in preserving life as it is. Tribal rules and taboos are sacrifices to the gods to ensure community prosperity and safety. Individual initiative might create changes that would threaten the authority and power of the elders. Therefore, the tribal elders ignore the possibility that individuals could deviate from community rules.
3. *Rra-Tselane's reply to Rra-Keaja* Rra-Tselane is more interested in maintaining his position in the tribe than in preserving Tselane's life; as a father, he has spent little time with Tselane. Rra-Keaja has developed a close relationship with his son and loves his son above all else.
4. *Why Mma-Tselane acts* Mma-Tselane realizes that she must make an effort to prevent Tselane's death. She knows that she risks losing social status,

but she loves her daughter enough to assume the risks. She gains a new self-esteem because she knows that she has done her best for her daughter.

*5. *Mma-Monosi's story* The horrible story about the young man who was killed may be Mma-Monosi's own story. The evidence for this interpretation includes her willingness to give in to tribal customs, her initial refusal to tell the story, her enthusiasm for Tselane's love, and her willingness to die on Tselane's behalf.

6. *Why Keaja and Tselane don't return* Keaja and Tselane may have chosen to live with a different tribe. Keaja had "heard stories about . . . other hospitable tribes who lived distances away and whose customs differed from theirs." Not only do Keaja and Tselane wish to marry whom they choose, but they probably do not want their children to live under their tribe's social regulations and taboos.

7. *Factors affecting the legend* The villagers accept Mma-Monosi's story because they believe that sinister forces always lie in wait, ready to destroy life, and that those who question life upset the natural order and invite these forces to bring death and disaster into the village. A more optimistic worldview would have had the lovers rewarded by the gods, who would have taken the spirits of the young lovers up to the heavens, where the couple would live in eternal bliss.

8. *Themes* Love is stronger than tradition. Necessity is the mother of invention. Superstition blinds the mind.

ANALYZING LITERARY TECHNIQUE: POSSIBLE ANSWERS

1. *Relationship between setting and plot* The setting is the tribal village. The unity of setting and plot creates a tightly knit structure for the story.

2. *Antagonist* The tribe, with its values and taboos, is the antagonist. The tribe is in conflict with the lovers (the protagonists). Society, having overwhelming authority, is a formidable adversary.

*3. *Mma-Monosi's characterization* Mma-Monosi's characterization adds mystery and suspense without detracting from the narrative emphasis of the tale. Mma-Monosi's story about the young man who is killed by the tribe provides a counterpoint for Tselane and Keaja's unfolding story.

4. *Climax* The climax is Mma-Monosi's report of the lovers' end. It gives an added dimension to the story, causing the reader to analyze Mma-Monosi's character and to question the validity of her report.

5. *Foreshadowing* Tselane's willingness to face trouble and death foreshadows the risks Tselane and Keaja take at the end. Mma-Monosi's story and her initial refusal to reveal it, the two sides of her personality ("sane and balanced" yet "very precariously unbalanced"), and her declaration that she will die if necessary to keep Tselane safe all foreshadow Mma-Monosi's decision to support Tselane.

*6. *Narrative perspective* The third-person omniscient narrator, the storyteller, is traditional in folktales and legends. This approach permits the reader to learn background material and to know the thoughts and actions of all the characters. What is lost is immediacy—the reader's emotional involvement with the plot. Student opinion will vary as whether a third-person narrator is preferable to a first-person narrator.

7. *Folktale, legend, or romance* "The Lovers" is a folktale, a tale from oral tradition about common people. It is a legend because the story was said to have actually occurred. It is a romance because it is an adventure story with an internal mystery and a miraculous ending.

WRITING ABOUT LITERATURE

1. *Essay analyzing narrative perspective* Call students' attention to the directions in the textbook assignment with regard to content and organization. (See **A.L.T.** question 6 above.) **AP**

2. *Creative writing: "The Lovers" from Mma-Monosi's point of view* Call students' attention to the directions and suggested questions in the textbook assignment. **(P.L.J.)**

FURTHER READING

Head, Bessie, *The Collector of Treasures and Other Botswana Village Tales.*

1. *In several selections in this unit, the main characters defy their families' wishes—and sometimes society's wishes too. Using examples, describe three characters' struggles to live within the bounds of the family or the regulations of society and the characters' eventual decisions to follow their own course. In your answer, consider the effects of their decisions on the family or society left behind.* Students may use Tomas in "Mista Courifer," Nnaemeka in "Marriage Is a Private Affair," Oganda (and Osinda) in "The Rain Came," and Tselane and Keaja in "The Lovers" as examples. Tomas in "Mista Courifer" submits to his father's whims with growing resentment. His first attempt to break away by burning his clothes is foiled by his sister; his second attempt to live his own life is successful when he finds a sympathetic listener in his boss, Mr. Buckmaster. Tomas's new way of life makes him very happy; however, it breaks his father's spirit. Nnaemeka in "Marriage Is a Private Affair" moves away from home to escape his father's influence. When Nnaemeka chooses his own wife, his father is furious and practically disowns him. While Nnaemeka is distressed over his father's attitude, he is happy with his decision. Ultimately, Nnaemeka's father realizes what he has been missing. Oganda submits to the wishes of her father and her tribe, sacrificing herself for the good of the people in "The Rain Came." Only when Osinda appears does she question the decision, and even then she struggles with her desire to save her people. Even though she saves herself, the rain comes and saves her people. Tselane and Keaja realize they are defying the wishes of their tribe and families by deciding to marry, but they have thought their decision through carefully. Their future happiness means more than abiding by the rules. Their decision causes the madness of Mma-Monosi and the death of Mma-Tselane, as well as the eventual move of the whole tribe.

2. *Race has long been an issue in African society. Two of the writers in this section touch on this difficult topic in their short stories. Analyze the writers' messages about race in "A Drink in the Passage" and "Good Climate, Friendly Inhabitants." How effective do you think these two stories are in helping readers acknowledge the issue of race?* In "A Drink in the Passage," Paton shows how good-hearted people can be trapped by the issue of race. In a culture where racial divisions are institutionalized, attempts to bridge the divide cause fear and uncertainty. Paton's story can inspire people to come up with better solutions to similar situations. In "Good Climate, Friendly Inhabitants," the racist narrator is blind to the true value of the other characters. In her eyes, the white man, although he is threatening and intimidating, is good because he is white. The black man, although he watches out for her, can never be anything but black. Gordimer's portrayal of the narrator's narrow view of people might help others recognize their own attitudes in dealing with people of different races.

3. *Discuss the use of humor and irony in* Brother Jero *and "Mista Courifer." How do Wole Soyinka and Adelaide Casely-Hayford use humor and irony to treat serious issues in these selections? Would their messages be more or less effective without the use of humor?* Soyinka and Casely-Hayford use humor and irony to deal with serious issues. Soyinka deals with such issues as marital abuse, hypocrisy, greed, and lust. By drawing his characters with such broad and humorous lines, he is able to call attention to these issues without seeming preachy. Likewise, Caseley-Hayford is able to poke fun of Mista Courifer and other characters because she exaggerates their personalities and preferences. In so doing, she subtly sets up her message about taking what is good from both cultures.

4. *Several of the writers in this unit focus on the beauty of the African land. Write an essay in which you describe how one's perception of the landscape affects one's feelings about one's homeland. Use quotations from these selections to support your points.* Dadié writes in the tradition of Négritude, which, as part of its goal of inspiring pride in Africa, emphasizes the natural beauty of Africa. In his poem "Dry Your Tears, Africa!" Dadié stresses how the beauty of Africa—"the peaks of the proud mountains / and the grasslands drenched with light"—calls her people to return. In Paton's "A Drink in the Passage," van Rensburg sees Africa as beautiful, so beautiful that what goes on culturally breaks his heart. He hopes that the beauty of their shared land will help him reach across the racial divide to connect with Simelane, but the divide is too wide. In Lessing's "A Sunrise on the Veld," the boy is strongly connected with the veld in his early morning jaunts, noticing the beauty and feeling the freedom of such a vast landscape. The veld plays an important part in his coming of age. As he watches a young injured buck being devoured by ants, he realizes that nature is indifferent.

5. *The Dahomey and Léopold Sédar Senghor find hope and life in the traditions of their people. Using examples from "Song of the Dead" and "Prayer to Masks," show how these traditions inspire Senghor and the Dahomey.* In "Song of the Dead," the Dahomey celebrate the pleasures of life. In their tradition, the pleasures that one experiences while alive go with one in death. They dance the traditional dance of the dead to celebrate the traditions and joys of life. Senghor, in "Prayer to Masks," addresses the spirits of the ancestors to ask for their help in guiding Africa. Senghor takes comfort from the traditions of the ancestors watching over Africans and draws "new strength pounding the hardened earth" in the traditional dances.

Asia and the South Pacific

Fighting South of
the Ramparts

LI PO

INTRODUCING THE POEM

"Fighting South of the Ramparts" cautions against war by emphasizing the carnage that affects both the aggressor and the defender and both the officer and the common soldier. Li Po based his poem on an old Han dynasty folk song (first century A.D.) that honors soldiers who die serving their prince. Li Po changed the point of view from that of the prince to that of the soldier, creating an attitude of protest in place of the folk song's attitude of adulation. He subtly criticizes the expansionist policies of the T'ang dynasty (627–650) by his treatment of the comparable situation under the Han.

The poem reflects Li Po's interest in Taoist philosophy, particularly Chapter 31 of the *Tao-te Ching*, "Quelling War." The poem concludes with a paraphrase of the Taoist principle that nations should wage war only under duress. Only a few years later Li Po saw China's border armies rebel; the civil war that ensued destroyed the China that he had known. Both events were tangible proof of the Taoist principle that rulers who cause the slaughter of their subjects will encourage revolution.

Li Po's use of detail vividly conveys war's carnage. He contrasts the aggressive Han dynasty with the preceding, more defense-oriented Ch'in dynasty and the bloodthirsty Huns and Tartars with the more civilized Chinese. He depicts the ravages of war in searing connotative language.

Personal Literary Journal: To what extent do you think that soldiers should be responsible for their own behavior in battle? To what extent do you think that soldiers should obey orders regardless of the nature of those orders?

Literary Terms: connotative language, contrast, figurative language, first-person narrator, irony, narrative perspective, theme

COMPREHENSION QUESTIONS

1. *How long have the emperor's armies been fighting?* long enough to have grown old and gray

2. *What is the nature of the enemy troops?* barbaric; war is their only occupation

3. *What attitude toward war was held by the House of Ch'in?* defensive; built Great Wall

4. *What attitude toward war is held by the House of Han?* Its expansionist policies encourage war.

5. *What has happened to Han armies?* Death and devastation have come to soldiers and captains alike.

UNDERSTANDING THE POEM: POSSIBLE ANSWERS

1. *Purpose of specific battle locations* These locations, familiar to Li Po's audience, testify to the great range and number of frontiers on which border wars were being fought. This knowledge, in turn, supports Li Po's antiwar attitude.

2. *Importance of the Huns* Li Po contrasts the barbaric, warlike Huns with the civilized, usually peaceful Chinese. The Chinese prefer farming to fighting, whereas war is the way of life for the Huns.

3. *House of Ch'in vs. House of Han* In contrast to the aggressive and territorially acquisitive House of Han (206 B.C.–A.D. 220), the House of Ch'in (third century B.C.) was interested in preserving peace in China and built the Great Wall to keep out potential invaders. The two dynasties represent opposite political philosophies. Li Po implies that the Ch'in dynasty was a better period for China. However, he is living in the T'ang dynasty, at a time when T'ang leaders have been operating with the same political attitudes and actions as the House of Han.

4. *Meaning of "The general schemed in vain"* This line puts the blame on the commander and shows the futility of his plans: His own men were destroyed in the battles. The line also supports Li Po's Taoist theme, which is stated in the last two lines of the poem.

5. *Risks in speaker's point of view* The speaker's point of view is that of a common soldier who views the border wars as disastrous for all of China. If enough soldiers share his view, they might desert or revolt. If military leaders share his view, they might lead their troops against the government.

ANALYZING LITERARY TECHNIQUE: POSSIBLE ANSWERS

*1. *Speaker's point of view* Li Po chooses the perspective of a common soldier because it is the soldiers who provide the power behind the emperor's policies of territorial expansion. They are the most likely to oppose the border wars because they have the least to gain and the most to lose from the wars. As peasants, they are treated like objects by their social superiors. Under imperial orders they are required to leave their families forever, to spend their lives living on one border or another, farming and defending the land against barbarian tribes. Whether they win or lose a particular battle, they have sacrificed their lives and their families to their emperor's lust for power.

*2. *Function of contrast* Li Po uses contrast to reveal better alternatives to the Han (and T'ang) imperial policy of territorial expansion. Examples include the following:

- The contrast between the Huns and the Chinese reveals differences in lifestyle and values. The Huns lack the civilized values and interests of the Chinese. They have little learning and few possessions, and they value nothing but accomplishments in war. They are nomadic desert tribes, not farmers.

- The contrast between the House of Han and the House of Ch'in reveals differences in political values. The Ch'in dynasty was oriented toward peace; it built a huge and extensive defensive wall to protect the country from aggressive neighbors. In contrast, the Han dynasty is ambitious and aggressive, accepting constant war as the price for acquiring more land.

*3. *Use of irony* Li Po stresses the irony that war can be equally devastating to the aggressor and the defender, to the winner and the loser, and to the officer and the common soldier. No one "wins" a war.

*4. *Relation of connotative language to theme* Li Po's connotative language vividly conveys the devastation that occurs as a consequence of war. Examples are:

- The Huns live on desert lands where "white bones lie among yellow sands."
- "The horses of the conquered neigh piteously to Heaven."
- Birds "peck for human guts, / Carry them in their beaks and hang them on the branches of withered trees."
- "Captains and soldiers are smeared on the bushes and grass."

War in this poem is not glorious; instead, it is a cursed event to be waged only when a nation finds itself faced with dire necessity.

*5. *Function of last two lines* The last two lines, paraphrased from the *Tao-te Ching*, express the theme of the poem. Structurally they form the culmination of Li Po's examples of war's disasters. The poem moves from the range and duration of the border wars to the responsibility of the Han dynasty for the wars, to the devastation caused by war, and finally to the conclusion that war should be an option only when no peaceful alternative exists.

WRITING ABOUT LITERATURE

1. *Essay analyzing treatment of theme* See **A.L.T.** questions 1, 2, 3, 4, and 5 above. Students should analyze two or three techniques from questions 1–4. The theme is referred to in question 5. Call students' attention to directions in the textbook assignment with regard to examples, quotations, and analysis. **AP**

2. *Essay analyzing Taoism in poem* The theme of the poem, that war is disastrous to everyone in the warring nations, leads to the implications that any leader who enjoys conquest has caused the death of many and that those who oppose the leader's policy will unite and render that leader powerless.

   Students who wish to learn more about Taoism may be directed to various references, including most encyclopedias and *Sources of Chinese Tradition*, Second Edition, Volume 1, by De Bary, Bloom, and Adler (Columbia University Press). (See **A.L.T.** question 5 above.)

3. *Creative writing: a war poem* Call students' attention to suggestions in the textbook assignment with regard to content, use of language, and possible procedure. Remind them that they may adopt any narrative persona. Points of view may be for or against war. **(P.L.J.)**

FURTHER READING

Birch, Cyril and Donald Keene, eds., *Anthology of Chinese Literature from Early Times to the Fourteenth Century*.

Prince Huo's Daughter

JIANG FANG

INTRODUCING THE STORY

Because it is a well-told story of a love gone awry, "Prince Huo's Daughter" has a timeless appeal. Jade, a beautiful young woman from a lower social caste, becomes fatally heartsick when the famous poet Li Yi breaks his marriage vows to her to marry the woman that his mother finds socially desirable. Before Jade dies, she tells Li that her spirit will haunt those he loves in the future, and her curse becomes a reality.

The story is appealing on three levels. First, it is a love story that reads with the simplicity and familiarity of a folktale. Second, it is a morally satisfying tale of good and evil in which goodness ultimately triumphs and evil is punished. Finally, buried in this old tale is a modern psychological study of the effect of cruel behavior on the mind of the perpetrator. Jade's curse becomes a self-fulfilling prophecy for Li. It is the external manifestation of Li's guilt. Because of his unfaithfulness to Jade, Li imagines that each of his successive loves is unfaithful to him. His doubts (in psychological terms, his projection and paranoia) destroy his relationships and his happiness, creating an appropriate lifelong self-punishment for his heartless treatment of Jade.

Personal Literary Journal: Have you ever broken a promise? What caused you to do so? How did your feel? What did you do about it?

Literary Terms: catharsis, characterization, climax, folktale, foreshadowing, irony, melodrama, narrative perspective, plot, resolution, setting, theme, tragedy

COMPREHENSION QUESTIONS

1. *What is Li's reputation?* He is a great scholar and poet.
2. *How does Li meet Jade?* through a matchmaker
3. *Why does Li leave Jade?* He was given an official post because he "came first in his examination."
4. *What promise did Jade ask of Li?* that he would love her for eight years, until he reached the age of marriage
5. *What conflict occurs?* Li's mother chooses a wife for him.
6. *What happens to Jade when Li does not return?* She becomes very ill.
7. *Why doesn't Li attempt to see Jade?* He is ashamed of his broken promise.
8. *Who brings Li to Jade?* a young nobleman in a yellow shirt
9. *How does Jade react to Li's visit?* She curses him for his mistreatment of her, and she vows to seek revenge through the women Li will love.
10. *What happens in the end?* The curse works—Li becomes a jealous husband and lover.

UNDERSTANDING THE STORY: POSSIBLE ANSWERS

1. *The title* The story focuses on Jade's effect on Li's life. The title emphasizes the appropriately narrow focus of the short story.

*2. *Li* Li is a self-centered man, with social and economic ambitions. He is a traditionalist, bound to the marriage his mother arranged for him, even though he could have avoided the marriage by not raising the betrothal money. Li is also a sensitive artist; in the end, his guilt destroys him.

*3. *Why Li avoids telling Jade the truth* Li appears to be unable to handle confrontations. He does not argue with his mother about the arranged marriage, and he does not discuss this situation with Jade. He solves his problems with as little conflict and effort as possible.

*4. *Jade's illness* Although the author and Li's contemporaries blame Li, some students may argue that Jade is equally to blame for her illness. Realizing the difference between her social position and Li's, Jade acknowledges that Li will eventually marry someone else. Making herself ill is an illogical response to Li's unfaithfulness.

*5. *Li's shame* Li's shame is not an excuse for his behavior. In fact, his callous behavior should increase his shame. Li's shame is a rationalization for his unwillingness to tell Jade the truth. Li is living his life in the way he wishes to live it.

*6. *Significance of Jade's dream and her curse* As in folktales and myths, Jade's dream prophesies the future. Jade interprets her dream as a prophecy of a reunion and a separation, and the dream comes to pass. Jiang Fang's relating of the dream *after* the prophesized events have occurred undercuts some of the dream's supernatural power.

*7. *Li's attitude toward women after Jade's death* The ostensible cause of Li's attitude is Jade's curse. However, a modern reader may see guilt as the real cause of Li's attitude. Subconsciously Li knows how cruel he was to Jade, and he cannot forgive himself. Thus, he punishes himself by depriving himself of marital happiness. He convinces himself that women are treating him the way that he treated Jade. In psychological terms, he projects his own attitudes and behavior onto women, and he suffers from paranoia.

8. *Life in China during the T'ang dynasty* Parents were authoritarian figures who arranged marriages for their children. Women did not have the social mobility or freedom that men had. Education was highly prized and very competitive. Social status was important, and it was enhanced by wealth, education, and fame.

9. *Importance of intelligence and moral character* In the story, moral character is more important than intelligence, although it would be best to have both traits. Moral character is why even those who admire Li's accomplishments sympathize with Jade and why Li cannot forgive himself for his treatment of Jade.

10. *Themes* Possible themes:

- People reap what they sow; cruel behavior destroys the perpetrator as well as the victim.
- Love is often destroyed by ambition.
- It is better to love wisely than too well.

ANALYZING LITERARY TECHNIQUE: POSSIBLE ANSWERS

1. *Tragedy* The story is tragic in that Li's behavior helps cause Jade's death. The reader pities Jade but not Li. Unlike the great tragic heroes, Li does not outwardly acknowledge his immoral behavior, and he gains no insight into his own personality. He punishes himself without understanding that he is doing so.

   The plot is melodramatic in that it deals with strong passions: "true love," deceit, a death-curse, and an avenging spirit. Like characters in a melodrama, Li and Jade are not psychologically complex. Li is not torn between his love for Jade and his commitment to someone else. Jade is loyal beyond all reason. Li and Jade suffer melodramatic (dire) fates. Jade dies, and Li destroys his marriages by tormenting his wives. On the other hand, most melodramas have happy endings, whereas this story does not. Although Jade is able to exact retribution for Li's unconscionable behavior, Jade is dead and Li is miserable.

2. *Narrative perspective* The traditional third-person omniscient narrative style is appropriate to this short story because the story is a type of folktale. Folktales are part of the oral tradition of a culture. Oral tales keep listeners' attention by being simple in structure, characterization, detail, and language and by adhering to familiar and predictable plot patterns.

3. *Setting and plot* The setting affects the plot in that both Li's and Jade's social fates are determined by the social customs of their society. Thus, Li's mother arranges a proper marriage for Li, and Jade cannot compete because of her low social position.

4. *Li's contemporaries* Li's contemporaries function as a Greek chorus; their attitudes reveal how the reader should view Li's behavior.

5. *Foreshadowing* Jade's repeated concern about losing Li's love and Li's related protestations of his own fidelity foreshadow Li's infidelity.

6. *Catharsis* The climax of this story is Jade's confrontation with Li, in which she complains about his treatment of her, explains the effect his desertion has had on her life, and announces her curse. Until this point, both Jade and the reader have had to accept Li's behavior. Such a situation creates tension that needs to be resolved. Finally Jade is able to confront Li with his disgraceful behavior. As a result, both she and the reader are relieved—catharsis is achieved.

7. *Resolution* Li's subsequent unsuccessful relationships with other women, whether attributed to Jade's curse or to Li's psyche, are the plot's resolution.

Because Li deserves punishment for his treatment of Jade, the resolution gives the story a sense of completeness and the readers a sense of satisfaction.

WRITING ABOUT LITERATURE

1. *Essay analyzing characters* Li's values offend his friends and the reader. Li deserves to be punished, and his punishment is appropriate for his misbehavior. Jade wins the affection of all through her loyal devotion to Li. Readers identify with Jade. They hope that Li will be punished, and they are satisfied by Li's fate and Jade's role in that fate. (See **U.S.** questions 2, 3, 4, 5, 6, and 7 above.)

2. *Creative writing: the story from Li's point of view* The challenge is to find justifiable reasons for Li's behavior. Li might state that Jade knew from the beginning that their relationship was temporary. He might point out that it was his duty to accept the marriage that his mother arranged for him. Li probably would blame his wives for his suspicions and jealousies. **(P.L.J.)**

FURTHER READING

Yang Xianyi and Gladys Yang, trans., *T'ang Dynasty Stories*.

Wuling chun

LI QINGZHAO

INTRODUCING THE POEM

Li Qingzhao is considered one of the masters of the poetry form *ci*, in which the poet sets new words to song melodies. The irregular line lengths and the rhyme scheme are patterned on the original song. The poem's title usually is the title of the original song rather than a reference to the content of the poem itself. While many considered the *ci* a diversion, Li Qingzhao took its form seriously, writing six volumes of *ci* as well as an essay on its form.

"Wuling chun" is an excellent example of *ci*. The emotions expressed in the poem are both lyrical and immediate. Through the imagery of a boat sinking under the weight of grief and a woman too tired to dress her hair, the reader gains a realistic picture of the speaker's sorrow. The speaker contrasts herself with the rest of the world to show her heightened sense of loss and separation. While the rest of the world is enjoying spring, the speaker sees fallen petals. While the world sees her lover's possessions, she sees only that his things remain without him. Although we know the speaker's loved one has been gone six years, the grief and longing are as fresh as if he had left the week before.

Personal Literary Journal: Have you ever felt an emotion that overwhelmed you? If so, what images could you use to describe how it felt?

Literary Terms: contrast, imagery, tone

COMPREHENSION QUESTIONS

1. *What emotion is the speaker feeling? Why?* The speaker is sad because her loved one is gone (line 3).

2. *What prevents the speaker from enjoying spring at Twin Creek?* The speaker would like to enjoy spring in a boat on the creek, but she is afraid that her grief will (figuratively) swamp the boat.

UNDERSTANDING THE POEM: POSSIBLE ANSWERS

1. *Why the speaker is "too tired"* Weighed down by grief, the speaker feels she cannot exert the energy to make herself beautiful for someone who is no longer here.

2. *"Things remain but he is gone"* "Things remain" may be referring to the physical possessions that the speaker and her loved one owned together. These possessions are still around, though the loved one is not. The speaker may be surprised that physical objects remain when something so significant—her loved one—is missing. Even though "things remain," possessions no longer have meaning because of her loved one's absence.

3. *What the speaker wishes she could do* The speaker wishes she could enjoy the spring by taking a boat out on the creek. In so doing she would be joining people who are enjoying life.

ANALYZING LITERARY TECHNIQUE: POSSIBLE ANSWERS

*1. *Images* The "dust" and the "fallen petals" in line 1 convey a sense of death and decay. The image of a woman "too tired" to comb her hair (line 2) conveys the sense of weight and loss. The image of a small boat floating on a creek (line 6) conveys a sense of peace and tranquility, ideas that are in opposition to the weight and exhaustion expressed in the first stanza. The image of a "frail grasshopper boat / [unable to] carry this load of grief" (lines 7–8) shows how heavy and overwhelming the speaker's sorrow is.

2. *Tone* The tone of the poem is one of overwhelming grief and longing. While the speaker wishes to rejoin the world of people who enjoy life, she cannot move past her sorrow.

3. *Contrast* The contrast between the possessions that remain and the loved one who is gone (line 3) shows the contrast between the superficiality of possessions and the emotional attachment to a human being. The contrast between the fallen petals (line 1) seen by the speaker and the signs of spring seen by the rest of the world (line 5) demonstrates how the speaker can only see decay, even when nature is springing into bloom. The contrast between the "frail grasshopper boat" (line 7) and the "load of grief" (line 8) shows the difference between contrasting emotions—the joy of floating on a creek and the weight of sorrow and longing.

WRITING ABOUT LITERATURE

1. *Essay analyzing the use of imagery* Remind students to use quotations from the poem to support their ideas. (See **A.L.T.** question 1.)

2. *Creative writing: poem to the tune of a popular song* Students may use the melody of a popular song, whether it has a regular or irregular rhythm. Students should use concrete images to convey the emotions they are expressing. **(P.L.J.)**

FURTHER READING

Rexroth, Kenneth, and Chung Ling, eds., *Li Ching-Chao: Complete Poems.*

Wang Jiaosheng, *The Complete Ci-poems of Li Qingzhao: A New English Translation.*

Say Who I Am
JALAL AD-DIN AR-RUMI

INTRODUCING THE POEM

Rumi's "Say Who I Am" captures the spirituality and grace of the speaker's beliefs in intriguing imagery. The clarity of Rumi's voice has made him a beloved poet around the world, most notably in the Islamic world where the *Masnavi* is sometimes referred to as the "Persian Koran." In "Say Who I Am," Rumi explores the nature of the cosmos as having an encompassing scope that moves between nature and invention and between the galaxy and the metaphysical world. This range invites various interpretations of the poem and of Rumi's view of the cosmos.

The range of imagery illustrates Rumi's conviction in God's omniscience and links the universe into a symbiotic whole. This imagery is deceptively simple. In such descriptions as dust floating in the sunlight, Rumi captures moments that are both commonplace and lovely, illustrating that beauty can be found in unexpected places. However, these images are interwoven in such a way that they form layers of meaning. As he passes from small scale to grand scale and moves between civilization and nature, the reader sees the scope of the poem reaching beyond the ideas that are mentioned.

"Say Who I Am" is a good introduction to the poetry of Rumi, illuminating some of the themes that run throughout Rumi's works: self, the world, and spirituality and the relation of these concepts to one another. In "Say Who I Am," these facets of life meld together into a whole that is the cosmos. God is the center and the creator of all things; therefore God understands all things best. The world and all things in it are related because God made everything.

Personal Literary Journal: How do you view the world around you? Is it exciting, boring, soothing, spiritual, or beautiful? Describe a place, object, or event that encapsulates your thoughts about the world.

Literary Terms: apostrophe, contrast, imagery, theme, tone

COMPREHENSION QUESTIONS

1. *What is lost in the fragrance of the rose?* a nightingale

2. *What do "silence, thought, and voice" describe?* a parrot in a tree

3. *What is the meaning of "Say I / am you"?* Rumi believes that the universe is intertwined with everything in it. Therefore, he is a part of everything, including the dust, sunlight, trees, and circling galaxies.

UNDERSTANDING THE POEM: POSSIBLE ANSWERS

1. *Speaker's audience* The speaker is addressing the cosmos. He believes that the universe is connected with everything in it and that he is therefore a part of the universe.

2. *What the speaker says to the dust and the sun* The speaker might tell the dust to stay because dust is a concrete part of the world. The speaker might tell the sun to keep moving because its movement is essential for life on earth.

3. *Meaning of "Mast . . . founder on"* The speaker believes that he is a part of everything that surrounds him—therefore he is not only part of human technology, such as ships, but he is also present in nature. He is in the inventions that make humans powerful, and he is in parts of nature that can destroy these inventions. For example, he sees himself in a coral reef that can destroy a ship.

4. *Evolutionary intelligence* Evolutionary intelligence is human intelligence that has developed over centuries as civilizations have evolved, religions have formed, and people have learned more about the workings of the world around them. From a modern perspective, evolutionary intelligence can also be seen as the intelligence that has developed in various plants, animal species, and life forms over millions of years.

5. *Theme* Possible themes: A common spirit runs through all creation, inextricably tying together all aspects of creation. One aspect of the world cannot be separated from other aspects—everything is needed for the earth to function.

ANALYZING LITERARY TECHNIQUE: POSSIBLE ANSWERS

1. *Tone* The tone of the poem is one of reverence and wonderment. The speaker, who is in awe of the many facets of life and the universe, shows respect for all creation. The tone is also imploring—the speaker longs for a clearer understanding of his relationship with the cosmos and his place within it.

2. *Apostrophe* The use of apostrophe lends the poem an air of thoughtful contemplation. The speaker is addressing the cosmos with his thoughts on the nature of divinity. Instead of mulling over these ideas alone, the speaker is sharing these ideas with whomever is listening—nature, the galaxy, or humanity. The speaker believes that the cosmos is within him and, therefore, that the cosmos knows his true self. The speaker also believes that he is an integral part of his environment; he is not just a person—he is also the dust and wind that surround him. Apostrophe allows the speaker to illustrate what he believes about his relationship with the cosmos.

Without apostrophe, the poem may feel less personal. By speaking directly to the universe, Rumi illustrates that his relationship with his surroundings is one of closeness and respectful understanding.

3. *Contrast* Contrast functions in the poem by showing the duality of nature and the need for diversity and understanding in the world. The candle and the moth are not merely two sides of a common occurrence; both are essential parts of the world. By highlighting the relationship between opposites, Rumi shows the complexity of the world.

WRITING ABOUT LITERATURE

1. *Essay analying the use of imagery* Students should use quotations from the poem to illustrate their themes. **AP**

2. *Essay analyzing a quotation in relation to the poem* Call students' attention to the directions in the text.

3. *Creative writing: poem* Call students' attention to the directions for the poem. Remind students that their personal belief does not need to focus on religion; they can explore politics, nature, or culture. **(P.L.J.)**

FURTHER READING

Rumi, Jalal ad-Din, *Birdsong; The Illuminated Rumi.*
Barks, Coleman, trans., *The Essential Rumi; The Soul of Rumi.*

Not all the sum of earthly happiness

HAFIZ

INTRODUCING THE POEM

Hafiz's "Not all the sum of earthly happiness" examines a question that is as relevant to students today as it was to Hafiz's contemporaries who turned to him for religious and spiritual guidance: Do material possessions and riches equal a life of happiness? As Hafiz moves through his poem, his descriptions of life brim with truth and rich imagery. He weighs both sides of his argument, highlighting the hardships of poverty and questioning the value of material objects. In the end, he concludes that true riches include the "Land where [his] Lady dwells," "a loyal heart," and a "tranquil breast."

The majority of Hafiz's poems are written in the *ghazal* form, which originated in Persia. Although its origin is unknown, some scholars believe it stemmed from early Iranian folk poetry; others claim it is an integration of Persian lyric poetry with earlier Arabic poetry. A *ghazal* poem has a single meter and rhyme running throughout it. Each verse is divided into two halves, with the second half balancing the theme of the first and repeating its rhythm. Each verse is complete in itself.

Hafiz begins his poem by stating that "Not all the sum of earthly happiness / Is worth the bowed head of a moment's pain." The simplicity of this statement characterizes the poem and foreshadows that the speaker will weigh the things he values in life against the things he feels are superfluous to true happiness. He draws his readers into the poem by using an example that is universal: the "bowed head of . . . pain." He then moves throughout a series of images, evaluating his tattered clothes, his love for his Lady and the land they share, his carpet, the way in which he is treated, and the price of power and wealth. His examination of varied facets of life lends the poem an all-encompassing tone that strengthens his argument. The poem embraces so much of "the sum of earthly happiness" that it is clear the speaker's concern has been well thought out and analyzed. The beauty of Hafiz's imagery is striking. It shows that he finds happiness in the simple joys of life—from the sea to the skin of a grape.

Personal Literary Journal: What makes you happy? What things or beliefs do you have that will lead you to have a happy life? Why?

Literary Terms figurative language, imagery, metaphor, personification, repetition, stanza, theme

COMPREHENSION QUESTIONS

1. *What holds the speaker "enchained"?* the land where his Lady lives

2. *Who is the enemy that "heaped scorn" on the speaker?* The enemy is a person more prosperous than the speaker (who is a beggar). The enemy sees the speaker as a nuisance.

3. *What is not worth "the Conqueror's reward"?* the trials and possible death faced by the Conqueror's armies

4. *Where does the speaker say to store "a mind at rest"?* "in the treasury of Ease"

UNDERSTANDING THE POEM: POSSIBLE ANSWERS

1. *Value of wine* One interpretation is that the wine may literally cost more than the clothes the speaker wears, since he lives in poverty. A second interpretation is that since wine is the product of grapes—which are produced by the earth—it is a part of an earthly happiness that cannot be duplicated by man-made possessions.

2. *"Pledge of piety"* The speaker believes that his pledge of piety is brave because a life of poverty is harder than a life of wealth. Poverty brings with it hunger, scorn, and inadequate clothing and shelter.

3. *"Sorrow of the sea"* "The sorrow of the sea" refers to the idea that the treasures of the sea are stolen by greedy people. Pearls (the "hope of gain") are not worth the destruction of their sea habitat.

4. *Value of Sultan's crown* The crown of the Sultan, though worth a great sum of money, comes at the risk of ridicule and death. No matter how wealthy the Sultan is, he may still be criticized—or even killed—by those who do not approve of his reign. The Sultan's wealth cannot protect him from

"constant dread." Conversely, no one is jealous of the speaker's poverty, and no one will threaten the speaker because of it.

5. *Meaning of "Thy soul's disgrace"* The speaker believes that greed is the soul's disgrace. When people are willing to steal, kill, and focus their happiness on material possessions, their souls are disgraced by the loss of spirituality and tranquility.

ANALYZING LITERARY TECHNIQUE: POSSIBLE ANSWERS

1. *Repetition* The repetition of the phrase "not worth" functions as a way for the speaker to question the values people place on various facets of life. Each statement beginning with "not worth" ends differently. When speaking of journeying over land and sea, the speaker exclaims "Not worth the toil!"; when questioning his treatment by his enemy, he asks "Not worth the dust?" These phrases encompass a range of feelings from indignation to poignancy to resolution, illustrating that our choices in life are the result of many emotions.

*2. *Significance of the grape's purple garment* The color purple signifies regality or high rank; therefore, "Where word and deed alike one colour bear / The grape's fair purple garment shall outshine" can be interpreted to mean that the grape fulfills both its "word and deed." The grape is regal in color, and it produces food and drink that are also regal. The grape's garment can be easily interpreted. However, a person wearing "many-coloured rags and tattered gear" may not live up to his or her appearance. Someone who looks like a beggar may be rich in life and spirit; but not everyone dressed in beggar's clothes is spiritual.

*3. *Personification* The two examples of personification in the poem—the land that holds the speaker "enchained" and "the sorrow of the sea"—illustrate that Hafiz considers the entire world involved in "the sum of earthly happiness." It is not the Lady herself who holds the speaker "enchained," it is the land they share that enchains him. The land—water, air, and dirt—is a separate entity from the relationship between the speaker and the Lady, but it is something they have in common. The sea suffers when its riches are stolen from it in "hope of gain," just as people suffer when their riches are stolen.

4. *Treasure of a mind at ease* The speaker may mean that a person who stops longing for riches gains a mind at ease and finds earthly happiness in "a loyal heart" or "a tranquil breast." People can live more fulfilling lives if they accept what they have and let their minds stop worrying about what they do not have. The word "treasure" plays on the idea of what a treasure is and what it signifies for different people. For Hafiz, spirituality is a treasure; but wealth and power are the Sultan's treasure.

5. *The function of other people in the poem* The speaker mentions the Lady, the enemy, and the Sultan as devices for weighing what is important to him against what he believes is important to others. The Lady illustrates that love and companionship are riches that are greater than the wealth that can be gained through travel and acquisition. The enemy, who would rather

kick the beggar off his stoop than show compassion, demonstrates the value the enemy places on dominance. The Sultan is an example of the extreme wealth and power that a person can attain; yet even power and wealth do not guarantee the Sultan earthly happiness. Finally, Hafiz mentions himself to reiterate his own stance and to encourage others to live more like him and less like his enemy or the Sultan.

WRITING ABOUT LITERATURE

1. *Essay analyzing a stanza* Remind students to answer each question thoroughly. Point out that they can highlight imagery or figurative language that stands out to them (**A.L.T.** questions 2 and 3.)

2. *Essay on wealth and happiness* Encourage students to explain their ideas clearly and thoroughly. Point out that students need not agree with Hafiz's ideas; they can feel free to examine their own thoughts. (**P.L.J.**) **AP**

3. *Creative writing: letter to a friend* Remind students that they will be able to evoke the same ecstatic tone that Hafiz writes with if they focus on something they are passionate about. Students should provide examples of how something has affected their lives, and they should use one or two literary techniques.

FURTHER READING

Hafiz, *The Divan-I-Hafiz*; *The Gift: Poems by Hafiz*; *The Green Sea of Heaven: Fifty Ghazals from the Diwan of Hafiz*; *The Hafez Poems of Gertrude Bell*.

The Rich Eat Three Full Meals

NGUYEN BINH KHIEM

INTRODUCING THE STORY

Nguyen Binh Khiem was a scholar, a statesman, and a poet, and his poetry reflects elements of all three aspects of his working life. As a scholar, he enjoyed the intricacies of *nôm* poetry, in which various Chinese characters are combined to form distinctly Vietnamese words. As a statesman, he acknowledged the problems of society. But as a poet, he celebrates the simple joys of country living and encourages a return to nature.

In "The Rich Eat Three Full Meals," Nguyen Binh Khiem the statesman notes the disparity between rich and poor, as the rich have plenty to eat while the poor have a minimal amount. But more important than the distribution of wealth is peace. Indeed, Nguyen Binh Khiem the poet seems to be urging others to enjoy the gifts of nature as a means to end strife. The contentment and pleasures that nature brings are more than enough to allow him to enjoy life, and he has no need to accumulate material possessions to make him happy. His "damask," or his bedding, is the grass. His art is the beautiful mountains and rivers, which are both free and ever changing; they afford him a constant supply of delight. But most of all, he has found peace in his simple life, which allows him to "rest easy, / . . . awake with the sun / And [enjoy] Heaven's heaped-up favors."

Personal Literary Journal: Think about what makes you happy. Is it a place? A person or people? An accomplishment? Describe that feeling and the people, places, or things that lead to that feeling.

Literary Terms: contrast, imagery, metaphor

COMPREHENSION QUESTIONS

1. *What does the speaker do to take care of his needs?* If he's thirsty, he drinks tea; if he's warm, he lies down in the shade and feels the breeze. In other words, he turns to nature to supply his needs.

2. *According to the speaker, what matters most?* peace

UNDERSTANDING THE POEM: POSSIBLE ANSWERS

1. *Societal problems* The speaker acknowledges hunger and the division between rich and poor.

2. *The speaker's pleasure* The speaker takes pleasure in nature.

3. *"Heaven's heaped-up favors"* Heaven's favors are peace and easy rest.

ANALYZING LITERARY TECHNIQUE: POSSIBLE ANSWERS

1. *Contrast* The speaker contrasts the rich with the poor—those who have plenty to eat with those who make do with a minimal amount.

*2. *Metaphors* The speaker's paintings are mountains and rivers, while his damask—his bedding—is the grass (lines 5–6). The poet is criticizing the reliance of the rich on material possessions; they should be focusing on peace and contentment.

*3. *Imagery* The use of images from nature—such as "breeze," "mountains," "grass," and "sun"—all lead to the poet's point that he is "enjoying Heaven's heaped-up favors." He does not need material possessions or even three fancy meals a day to enjoy life and be at peace.

WRITING ABOUT LITERATURE

1. *Essay analyzing the poet's use of metaphors and imagery* Direct students to follow the directions in the textbook. (See **A.L.T.** questions 2 and 3.) **AP**

2. *Creative writing: poem about contentment* Suggest that students visualize themselves in a place where they feel happiest. Ask them to use images and metaphors to convey their feelings about that place. **(P.L.J.)**

FURTHER READING

Nguyen Ngoc Bich, ed., *A Thousand Years of Vietnamese Poetry.*

The Post Office

RABINDRANATH TAGORE

INTRODUCING THE PLAY

On the surface *The Post Office* is a simple story about how a little boy named Amal, housebound because of an illness, passes the time of day and eventually dies. However, the simplicity of the story is deceiving.

Amal finds all of life fascinating, and he wants to "see everything." Although he cannot go outside, he enriches the lives of those who pass by his window by questioning them about their daily activities. Amal's ability to appreciate the wonder and beauty of life helps others appreciate their own ordinary lives. His desire to experience life as they experience it leads them to see their ordinary lives through his eyes, and they become happy about who they are and what they do. Amal converses with a parade of people. This play is, in fact, a window that permits the audience or reader to look at the real world and see its variety.

Amal brings joy to Madhav Dutta, the uncle who has adopted him, and to other passersby; however, the family doctor and the Headman cannot be influenced by Amal's attitude toward life. The doctor is well-meaning but he takes Hindu scripture literally and cites verses that would deny Amal everything that makes his life worth living. The Headman is a self-centered misanthrope.

When the Watchman shows Amal the new post office, the little boy decides that he wants to become a royal messenger so that he can deliver the Raja's messages from door to door and country to country—and thus see everything. The Watchman also suggests that the Raja may send Amal a letter through this post office, since the Raja writes letters to children. Amal becomes absorbed with the idea that the Raja will write to him, and he discusses this eventuality with the Headman and others.

As Amal's disease progresses, Thakurda returns to amuse the boy with tales of fantasy. Meanwhile the Headman taunts Amal and his uncle with a fake letter in which the Raja declares that he will visit Amal. Contrary to what the Headman expects, the Raja sends his royal physician to Amal, as well as his herald, who announces that the Raja will visit Amal in the dead of night. Amal, who is now dying, soon falls into a death-like sleep, but he expects to awaken when the Raja calls to him. At that time, however, his soul will arise and go with the Raja, who will show him "all things." According to Tagore, "that which is 'death' to the world of hoarded wealth and certified creeds brings [Amal] awakening in the world of spiritual freedom."

The play ends when Shudha, the flower-seller's daughter, arrives with flowers for Amal. She tells the Raja's physician to whisper in the boy's ear that she has not forgotten him. According to Tagore, "The only thing that accompanies him in his awakening is the flower of love given to him by Shudha."

Shudha speaks for everyone who has known Amal. Because of his personality and the way he chose to live his life, Amal leaves an indelible mark on all who knew him. Amal achieves what many believe is the only immortality that is available to human beings: His attitudes and values will live on in the lives of others. Through the ages, achieving immortality has been one of the greatest concerns of human beings as they come to terms with their inevitable mortality.

Personal Literary Journal: What is your attitude toward life? What aspects of life do you value most? To what extent, if any, do other people—both those you know, and those whom you do not know—interest you? What do you want people to remember you for after you die?

Consider the people who bring out the best in you. What about them inspires you? How do you connect those aspects of their lives to your own life?

Literary Terms: characterization, foreshadowing, irony, protagonist, setting, theme, tone

COMPREHENSION QUESTIONS

1. *What does the doctor advise Madhav Dutta to do with the boy?* keep the boy indoors

2. *Why does Madhav Dutta fear Thakurda?* Thakurda has a reputation for .playing outside with children.

3. *How many books has Amal read?* none

4. *What does Amal want to do with his life?* "see everything"

5. *How does Amal disobey Madhav Dutta?* Amal talks with strangers.

6. *Why does the Curdseller give Amal a gift?* Amal has shown him the joy in being a Curdseller.

7. *What building does the Watchman talk about?* the new post office

8. *What does Amal want from the Raja? Why?* a letter from the Raja and an invitation to be a royal messenger so he can see everything as he delivers the Raja's letters

9. *What does Amal give away?* his toys

10. *Who tells Amal about imaginary faraway places? Give his real name.* Thakurda

11. *What does the doctor blame for Amal's declining health?* Amal's exposure to the outside air

12. *What wish of Amal's is finally granted?* He receives a letter from the Raja.

13. *What is unusual about the letter the Headman reads to Amal?* The Headman and Thakurda "read" a blank sheet, but the events told in the letter will actually happen.

14. *According to the Raja's physician, who will visit Amal in the dead of night?* the Raja

15. *Who is the last person to visit Amal?* Shudha, the flower-seller's daughter

UNDERSTANDING THE PLAY: POSSIBLE ANSWERS

1. *Illiterate protagonist* Amal learns though experience rather than through books. His ability to learn by talking with people reveals that books are not the only source of knowledge about life—nor are they necessarily the best.

2. *Suffering and happiness* The doctor tells Madhav Dutta that "the greater the suffering, the happier the outcome." Illness does not prevent Amal from having a fulfilling life because he enjoys talking with people who pass by his window. They respond by giving Amal companionship and gifts, such as curds and flowers. However, Amal might have been happier if he could have gone outdoors to play or to travel to the faraway hills that engage his imagination.

3. *Hills: invitation vs. barrier* Amal would love to cross over the faraway hills. He has the attitude of an adventurer. Life on earth calls to him. He questions it and seeks its answers. In contrast, Madhav's eyes and mind are confined by self-imposed blinders. He is most comfortable with what he already knows and people who prefer to be authorities, though Amal's disease has made him hungry for knowledge that would cure Amal.

4. *Watchman's job* The Watchman views his job as important because he marks the passage of time throughout the day and night, helping people to do things and to arrive at places on time. He reminds all who hear his gong that time does not stand still. Because of his conversation with Amal, the Watchman may also feel that his gong reminds human beings of their inevitable mortality.

5. *Watchman's doctor* The Watchman's Great Doctor is a divine spirit that frees those who are sick. The Watchman tells Amal that no one should wish for the doctor to come because it is wrong to wish for one's own death.

6. *Significance of the post office* The Raja's post office becomes the focus in Amal's life. Because Amal wants to be able to see everything, he wants to become a royal messenger so he can go from door to door and country to country. Waiting for the Raja's letter enables Amal to entertain himself by imagining when and how the letter will arrive.

7. *Thakurda as a fakir* Thakurda is known for his ability to play with children. He can entertain Amal with his fabulous tales, since fakirs are reputed to have had marvelous experiences. His tales delight Amal, who intends to become the fakir's disciple and travel with him as soon as he is well. Madhav's view of the fakir's words as "crazy talk" is correct because Thakurda is creating these experiences out of his imagination. However, Thakurda's ability to help Amal forget the world of disease, discomfort, and confinement is common sense, rather than nonsense.

8. *Headman's letter* The Headman tells Amal he has brought a letter from the Raja; however, the letter is blank. The Headman laughs as he reads because he is fabricating the contents. He reads what he does because he is genuinely mean-spirited and enjoys ridiculing Amal and Madhav. He has every reason to believe that what he is reading could never happen.

   Thakurda sees a different message on the sheet. Since the sheet is blank, he reads the message that he creates. The fact that the Raja's herald and physician do come gives a magical touch to the final scene.

9. *Headman and Herald* The Headman's reaction to the arrival of the Raja's herald ("Disaster!") indicates that he realizes that his plot against Madhav has failed and that the Raja may be aware that he wrote the anonymous letter condemning Madhav and Amal.

10. *Royal physician and Headman* The royal physician's comment "That man should not be permitted here" acknowledges the extent of the Headman's infamous reputation and confirms the appropriateness of the Headman's reaction ("Disaster!") to the arrival of the herald.

11. *Royal physician's demands* The royal physician demands that the windows and doors be opened and that Amal's room be cleaned and filled with flowers. He says these are preparations for the Raja. However, they are also preparations for Amal's death.

12. *Amal's final request* Madhav regards Amal's request (that the Raja make him a royal messenger) as childish and romantic. He asks Amal to beg the Raja "to give us something."

13. *Madhav's final questions; Thakurda's response* Madhav's final questions (Why has the room been darkened? What use is starlight?) reveal that he is denying Amal's death. Thakurda criticizes Madhav for asking questions when it is more appropriate to appreciate the mystery of life.

14. *Last line* Tagore chooses to end this play on an optimistic note. Not only has Shudha not forgotten Amal, but no one who has ever known Amal will forget him. Moreover, once an audience or reader has spent time with Amal, his attitudes and values will make their way into an ever-increasing number of human hearts.

15. *Magical events* Even before the Headman arrives with the letter, Thakurda assures Amal that the letter will arrive, and that it will arrive that day since he himself has talked with the Raja about Amal.

    The letter is blank because the Raja did not send Amal a letter. The Headman brought in a blank sheet, claiming it was a letter from the Raja to Amal. The Headman and Thakurda "read" different messages because the blank sheet enables them to create whatever words they wish to read. The hostile and ridiculing nature of the Headman's laughter reveals that he is fabricating what he reads. However, when the Raja's herald and physician arrive, they fulfill what the Headman has "read" in the letter, down to the request for a meal of puffed rice and parched paddy with molasses.

    It is clear that the Raja did not write the letter to Amal. However, the Raja acts upon his conversation with Thakurda and proceeds to send his herald and his physician to visit Amal while the little boy yet lives. It is possible that the Raja will actually arrive later that night, and it is also possible that Amal still has enough life within him to respond to the Raja's call before he dies.

    An alternative reading of the deathbed scene is that Thakurda has contrived it to comfort Amal. In this interpretation, Thakurda has two friends who pretend to be the Raja's herald and the Raja's doctor. This interpretation is possible since Thakurda has already demonstrated that he is willing to "lie" in order to comfort Amal, as he did in "reading" the Raja's letter.

Yet another reading of this scene is that it is magical and allegorical. The appearance of the Raja's herald and doctor is magical. The idea of the Raja's midnight arrival is allegorical because it symbolizes Amal's death and the arrival of the benign divine spirit. This interpretation is possible since the Raja presumably could have decided to appear.

ANALYZING LITERARY TECHNIQUE: POSSIBLE ANSWERS

1. *Setting* Examples that reveal the story's location include the following:

   - Characters' names: Madhav Dutta (Amal's uncle); Thakurda (the fakir); Shudha (the flower-seller's daughter); Shashi (Shudha's mother); Meni (Shudha's cat); Panchanan Morhal (the Headman); Jatai (the old witch); Badal and Sharat (the Raja's messengers); and Chakradhar Dutta (one of the doctor's authorities)

   - People: the Raja (the ruler) or maharaja (great raja); the fakir; the *Daiwallah* (Curdseller); *didi* (elder sister); sepoy

   - Locations: the Panchmura Hills, the Shamli River, and Kalmipara

   - Hindu texts: the *Ayurveda* (the ancient system of medicine recorded in the *Vedas*, the earliest and most sacred Hindu texts), which Amal's doctor quotes as scripture; and the *Ramavana* (one of the two ancient Indian epics), which Amal's aunt reads

   - Mantras: Hindu hymns or portions of a text, especially from the *Vedas*, that are chanted as a prayer or incantation. (The fakir recited texts that are related to travel.)

   - Local color: women who carry pitchers on their heads and wear red saris; banyan trees; *champak* flowers (magnolias); *bene-bou* (clay doll)

2. *Irony* Examples of Tagore's use of irony include the following:

   - (I) Amal is confined to his house, but he is able to learn about the world by questioning the people who pass by.

   - (II) The Watchman tells Amal that the Raja may send Amal a letter some day because the Raja has built his post office outside Amal's window. The Raja actually sends his herald and doctor.

   - (II and III) The Headman sarcastically tells Amal that the Raja will write to Amal because the Raja is Amal's dear friend and he is sad that he has not seen Amal lately. Later, the Headman appears with what he claims is the Raja's letter. He laughingly "reads" that the Raja will be visiting Amal soon and wants to eat a meal of puffed rice and parched paddy with molasses. This comes to pass when the Raja's herald and doctor arrive.

   - (II and III) The Headman says he will inform the Raja about Amal. He thinks that Amal talks about the Raja because Amal's uncle, Madhav Dutta, has been name-dropping. The Headman believes that Madhav's arrogance will anger the Raja. However, when the Raja's physician arrives to attend to Amal, the physician expresses his anger toward the Headman, not Madhav.

- (III) Amal can see that the Headman's letter is a blank sheet. Both the Headman and Thakurda fabricate the contents of the letter; however, the events that both read about actually occur.

3. *Tone* Tagore creates an optimistic tone both in the human world and in the divine world. Amal lives in a world in which most people are good. Although Amal is a child who will experience an untimely death, he does more for humanity in his short life than many people who live into old age. Death—while not to be wished for—is not to be feared. The divine world welcomes the soul of the deceased. The governing spirit, first represented as the Great Doctor and later as the Raja, is an eternal companion who frees the soul from its mortality, offers compassion and a sense of well-being, and encourages adventure and discovery.

4. *Passage of time* The passage of time in the play follows the course of Amal's illness. In Act I, the doctor confines Amal to the inside of his house. In Act II, the Watchman notices that Amal's face is pale, that dark rings lie below his eyes, and that the veins stick out of his arms. In Act III, Amal is in bed because the doctor has forbidden him to sit near the window. Amal tells the Raja's physician that his pain and illness have departed, and the physician announces that Amal's sleep is coming.

The passage of time is also marked by the time of day: Act I takes place in the morning; Act II moves from morning to late afternoon; and much of Act III occurs in the evening.

Finally, time is marked by the striking of the Watchman's gong.

*5. *Foreshadowing* Foreshadowing is a great unifying factor in this play. Note the following examples:

- Madhav Dutta opens the play by questioning the doctor as to whether Amal will die, and the play closes with Amal's death.

- The Watchman tells Amal that some day he may receive a letter from the Raja because the Raja does send letters to children. That letter, of course, plays a significant role in this play.

- The Watchman tells Amal that the Headman's job is to make trouble for everyone, and the Headman later does his best to make the Raja angry with Madhav and Amal.

- The Headman tells Amal that a letter from the Raja will arrive soon, and he later brings what he declares is that letter.

- Both the Headman and Thakurda "read" in the Raja's letter that the Raja will soon visit Amal, and the reader can assume that he does.

- Shudha promises Amal that she will not forget him and that she will return at the end of the day with a flower for him. She returns in the final moments of the play.

*6. *Repetition: theme and variation* Repetition unifies a work. The idea of divine spirit leading the soul of a person is repeated as a variation on the theme of life after death. First the Watchman discusses it, and then the Raja's physician asks Amal whether he will rise and go with the Raja when he arrives in the dead of night.

   The Raja's letter also unifies the play because Amal learns about the possibility from the Watchman and then discusses it with the Headman, the boys, and Thakurda. The arrival of the letter, as well as its contents, are significant to the plot.

*7. *Themes* Possible themes:

   • People can motivate others to be kinder, happier, and more helpful.

   • Life is a journey, rather than a destination, and its delights can be found along the way.

   • Each day is a blessing because it brings the opportunity to enrich the lives of others.

   • Life is full of variety.

   • Searching is more important than finding answers.

WRITING ABOUT LITERATURE

1. *Essay analyzing Tagore's techniques for unifying the action (theme and variation, repetition, foreshadowing)* Call students' attention to the directions in the textbook assignment with regard to choosing three literary techniques and analyzing them. (See **A.L.T.** questions 5 and 6.) **AP**

2. *Essay analyzing thematic content* Call students' attention to the directions in the textbook assignment with regard to choosing three themes and analyzing them. (See **A.L.T.** question 7.)

3. *Essay characterizing Amal* Students should use quotations as their examples and explain what each quotation reveals about the character they have chosen. For example, if their character is Amal, they should consider some or all of the following: Amal's wishes; his treatment of the Curdseller; his attitude toward the Watchman; his conversation with Shudha, the flower-seller's daughter; his conversation with the boys; his treatment of Chidam, the beggar; and, finally, his treatment of the Headman. If their character is the Headman, they should consider some or all of the following: what the Watchman tells Amal about him; what the Headman says to Amal; what the Headman says to himself; what the Headman later says to Madhav Dutta; what he then says about Amal and the Raja; how the Doctor reacts to the Headman's arrival at Madhav's house; and, finally, how the Raja's physician reacts to the Headman's presence in Amal's room.

4. *Creative writing: portrait of one who leads a life that inspires others* Call students' attention to the directions in the textbook assignment. **(P.L.J.)**

FURTHER READING

Tagore, Rabindranath, *An Anthology; A Tagore Reader; Collected Poems and Plays.*

The Fly

KATHERINE MANSFIELD

INTRODUCING THE STORY

"The Fly" is a fine example of how an apparently minor incident can illuminate a character's fundamental personality. The story is a character sketch of a man known only as "the boss." He is visited by an old friend and associate, Mr. Woodifield, who refers to their sons, both of whom were killed six years earlier in World War I. Later, in coping with memories of his son, the boss tortures a fly to death, revealing his basic personality and confirming earlier hints that he is more complex than he appears.

Every word in this story sounds casual but proves to have far-reaching significance. Mr. Woodifield's thought that "we cling to our last pleasures as the tree clings to its last leaves" provides one of the story's themes; the description of the photograph of the boss's son introduces the question of his son's personality; and Mr. Woodifield's memory lapse foreshadows the boss's memory lapse.

Jung defines the Shadow as "a living part of the personality" that "personifies everything that the subject refuses to acknowledge about himself and yet is always thrusting itself upon him directly or indirectly." Just as a bully conceals a Shadow that is a coward, the boss conceals a Shadow that is a wimp. The boss in "The Fly" always feels compelled to overcompensate for his weak Shadow-self by taking total control of himself and others. His fear of weakness makes him intolerant of weakness in others—Mr. Woodifield, his son, and the fly.

The boss handles weakness in others by giving them challenges. He encourages Mr. Woodifield to drink straight whiskey, and he dares the fly to overcome the ink blots. Unfortunately the boss's fear of weakness is so strong that the challenges he creates for others may be too great for them. Although he recognizes that the fly's efforts have become timid and weak, he is compelled to give the fly the challenge that kills it. Thus, the boss's behavior is both sadistic and tragic.

The power of the story resides in what the boss's treatment of the fly and his reaction to the fly's death reveal about him and his son. James Joyce would call this incident an epiphany, a sudden moment of illumination that reveals the boss's true character and destroys the veil that has concealed the private man beneath the public image. Memories of his enjoyment of his son's success in learning the family business lead the boss to challenge the fly; in the process, he unconsciously re-creates the pattern of his son's life and death. As the fly copes with its challenges, the boss enjoys its successes with the same pleasure that he watched the success of his son. When the fly dies, the boss's "grinding feeling of wretchedness" frightens him into disconnecting his emotion from his memory.

The boss does not usually permit himself to think about his son's death because the memory destroys the principle that has governed his life: Those who are strong enough can overcome any adversity, even death. His torture of the fly is an experiment which, on a symbolic level, re-creates his son's life and death. When the fly's death confirms the destruction of the principle that has been crucial to his life, the boss finds that he must forget the fly and his emotional response to it.

On a different level, "The Fly" presents two ways of handling the death of a loved one. Mr. Woodifield mourns the loss of his son but proceeds to live life as meaningfully as his poor health will permit. In contrast, the boss lives as a mechanical being after his son dies,. Health, financial success, and family mean nothing to him. The son was an extension of the boss, and the son's death killed the boss's interest in life.

Personal Literary Journal: Have you ever had a goal that you could not achieve because of circumstances beyond your control? How did you react? To what extent, if any, did you come to accept the situation?

Literary Terms: characterization, epiphany, foreshadowing, narrative perspective, paradox, psychological realism, Shadow, theme, tone

COMPREHENSION QUESTIONS

1. *What important topic does Mr. Woodifield mention?* the grave of the boss's son
2. *How does the boss react?* He appears not to care. But later when he asks to be left alone, he can't cry.
3. *What happens to the fly?* The boss tortures it to death.
4. *Name two characters who lack proper names.* the boss and his son

UNDERSTANDING THE STORY: POSSIBLE ANSWERS

*1. *The Boss's lack of a proper name* The constant use of the boss's title, rather than his name, reveals who the boss is and how he functions in interpersonal relationships. The need to be "the boss" reveals his fear of weakness in himself and his inability to tolerate weakness in others.

   The boss's behavior, consistent with his title, reflects his overwhelming need to control not only others but also himself. This is demonstrated in his response to Woodifield in the opening scene, his thoughts about his son and his son's death, and his treatment of the fly in the closing scene.

*2. *Why the boss keeps the photo* The boss may keep this photo on his desk, even though he doesn't like it, because it makes a good public impression. The boss can be proud to have had a son who died a heroic death. This effort to make a good impression is consistent with the boss's interest in redecorating his office and his determination to maintain absolute control over his emotions in public. Maintaining appearances is second only to exercising control; in fact, maintaining appearances is a way of exercising control.

*3. *Why the boss never uses his son's name* Calling his son "the boy" creates an emotional distance almost as if the boy were not the boss's son. Distance relieves the pain. Memories of his son call forth memories of his son's death. His son's death reminds him that he had no control over his son's death and he will have no control over his own death, even though control is the most important factor in his life.

*4. *Why the boss has not seen his son's grave* The boss has the financial ability but not the motivation to see the grave. His decision reflects a form of denial, his inability to deal with the reality of his son's death and the effect that loss has on his own life. His son's death is a reminder of his inability to control mortality, including his own.

*5. *Why the boss can't cry* With time, the boss has been able to bury his emotions in an area of his psyche where he can no longer feel them. However, although he cannot summon them, they still exist, and they erupt when the fly dies. Part of a person's reaction to something is a response to the questions "How does this affect my life? What will happen to me?" The boss's tears reflect his response to these questions. The death of his son (who was an extension of himself) was an excruciatingly personal loss. That death also contradicted the principle by which the boss lived: strength can overcome all adversity.

*6. *Why the boss tortures the fly to death* The experience provides an acceptable outlet for great anger and frustration: anger at his son's death and the loss of his own dreams and frustration at his inability to control what was most important to him in life (his son's life). His method of killing the fly enables him to examine the process of life and death.

The boss admires the fly's heroic efforts, but he is unaware that his challenges are torturing the fly to death. However, when it dies, he feels wretched because he subconsciously realizes that his treatment of the fly has reproduced the pattern of his son's life and death and that his own life and death will follow the same pattern. The boss has constructed his life on the principle that those who are strong enough can overcome any adversity, even death. The fly's death reinforces the message of his son's death—no one can control all aspects of life.

7. *Themes* Possible themes: A person's actions reveal aspects of that person's character. People who feel unbearable emotions may conceal them from themselves and others.

ANALYZING LITERARY TECHNIQUE: POSSIBLE ANSWERS

1. *Function of Woodifield* Woodifield's major function is to evoke the boss's memories of his son. Woodifield also acts as a contrast to the boss. Woodifield accepts his lack of control over life, while the boss cannot tolerate lack of control. Woodifield accepts the death of his son and continues to appreciate all the good in life; the boss died with his son, whom he viewed as an extension of himself.

*2. *The photo of boss's son as a symbol* The photo is a symbol of reality. The difference between the son's photograph and the boss's memory of his son reveals the difference between reality (the photo) and illusion (the boss's memories). The "grave-looking" photo of a "cold, even stern-looking" youth depicts the real son as a young adult, possibly unhappy and possibly a victim of his father's need to control everything and everyone. To be sure that his son became strong, the boss may have given his son overwhelming challenges just as he did with the fly. The boss cannot acknowledge the true nature of either his son or himself. He lives with the illusions that he has created to satisfy his own needs.

*3. *The fly as a symbol* The fly symbolizes the boss's life experience. Like the fly, the boss is subject to forces beyond his control. (He had no power to control his son's death.)

The fly also symbolizes the boss's son. The boss challenges the fly to be successful, enjoys its success, and then finds that its ability cannot prevent it from being killed by forces beyond its control. The boss challenges both to be as strong as they can because the boss's fear of his own inner weakness makes him intolerant of weakness in others. The boss's torture of the fly is a re-creation of his son's life and death. The fly's death confirms what his son's death taught him about life, and the boss is so distressed and frightened by this knowledge that he does not permit himself to remember it.

*4. *Role of memory* The boss has chosen to forget the emotionally unpleasant subject of his son's death in World War I. The death contradicted the principle by which the boss lives. He cannot permit himself to remember anything that causes him to question the validity of this principle.

5. *Psychological realism* Mansfield creates a limited but effective form of psychological realism. By using the narrative perspective of a third-person narrator, the boss becomes the center of consciousness. This technique enables the reader to enter the boss's mind and gain access to his thoughts and feelings without forcing the author to sacrifice objective descriptions that the boss would not use.

*6. *Epiphany* The scene in which the boss tortures the fly to death is an epiphany in that, in Joycean terms, it is an insignificant event that suddenly reveals the boss's essential nature. He has lived his life according to the principle that those who are strong enough can overcome any adversity, even death. His torture of the fly is an experiment which, on a symbolic level, re-creates his son's life and death. The fly's death, like the death of the boss's son, confirms the faulty nature of the boss's guiding principle. In response, the boss is at first distressed, but then his fear of weakness causes him to "forget" the incident.

7. *Paradox* Paradoxes found in the story: People act as if they live in a universe that is comprehensible and predictable; whereas in reality the universe may be irrational and unpredictable; the most powerful human being is unable to control many aspects of his or her own life.

WRITING ABOUT LITERATURE

1. *Essay analyzing appropriateness of the name "boss" for main character* Call students' attention to the directions in the textbook assignment. Remind them to use quotations to support their ideas. (See **U.S.** question 1 above.) **(P.L.J.)**

2. *Essay applying Woodifield's thought about our pleasures to a theme* Call students' attention to the directions in the textbook assignment with regard to content. Remind them of the importance of using quotations to support their ideas. (See **U.S.** questions 2, 3, 4, 5, and 6 and **A.L.T.** questions 2, 3, 4, and 6 above.)

3. *Creative writing: point of view of the boss's son* Call students' attention to the choices suggested in the textbook assignment. **(P.L.J.)**

FURTHER READING

Mansfield, Katherine, *Bliss; The Dove's Nest; The Garden Party; Something Childish.*

The New Year's Sacrifice

LU HSÜN

INTRODUCING THE STORY

"The New Year's Sacrifice" is a poignant and powerful story of hypocrisy that reaches from the old China into cultures of all times and places. The story revolves around the celebration of the Chinese New Year, a time when families participate in an elaborate religious ceremony, called "the sacrifice," to welcome the God of Fortune and to ask for a blessed life during the coming year.

Against this setting, the narrator relates the sad tale of a family servant, Hsiang Lin's Wife, who works for Fourth Uncle and Fourth Aunt at two different times. Fourth Uncle's and Fourth Aunt's character flaws, apparent during Hsiang Lin's Wife's first employment, intensify during her second sojourn in their house. Fearing that their servant's catastrophic life experiences will contaminate their own well-being, Fourth Uncle and Fourth Aunt refuse to let Hsiang Lin's Wife participate in any of the many rituals that are connected with the New Year's festival. Their refusal to accept her worthiness, even after she has used her year's wages to purchase a threshold in the temple of the Tutelary God (guardian god of the village), destroys her spirit and eventually destroys her life. She commits suicide in spite of her fear of the afterlife.

Lu Hsün leaves the reader with a sense of the hypocrisy that is pervasive in the society that he is satirizing and that can be found in all cultures. The attitudes of Fourth Uncle and Fourth Aunt are typical of the attitudes in their community, where people feel certain they will secure divine blessings as long as they pay scrupulous attention to the old customs. Attuned only to their own lives, they remain insensitive to the needs of others. However, the power of the story resides in the story's universal truths. People are hypocrites whenever they espouse liberal and righteous principles and then act in a way that negates those principles.

The life of Hsiang Lin's Wife is presented as a collection of personal disasters because, for Lu Hsün, social commentary was as important as literary artistry. In order to depict the deplorable social attitudes and behavior that were common in the rural China in his day, Lu Hsün had to include situations where society typically responsed insensitively. The short story genre, with its brevity and its unity of focus, made it necessary for him to create one character who would become the victim of many catastrophes, and Hsiang Lin's Wife is the result.

Personal Literary Journal: What principles of behavior govern your own life? To what extent do you find it difficult to remain true to principles that are important to you? What factors create difficulties? Do you know any well-meaning people who act in ways that contradict the principles that they believe govern their lives?

Literary Terms: characterization, flashback, irony, paradox, satire, setting, symbol, theme

COMPREHENSION QUESTIONS

1. *What is the purpose of the New Year's sacrifice?* a ceremony to invite a year of good fortune

2. *What social position do Fourth Uncle and his family have in Luchen?* upper middle class; highly educated

3. *What is the relationship between Hsiang Lin's Wife and Fourth Uncle's family?* She is their servant.

4. *Name two catastrophes that occurred in Hsiang Lin's Wife's life.* Her first husband died; her second husband died; a wolf carried off her son and ate him.

5. *In the end, how is Hsiang Lin's Wife treated by Fourth Uncle and Fourth Aunt?* treated as if contaminated by the catastrophes in her family

6. *What kind of life is Hsiang Lin's Wife living when the narrator meets her at the beginning of the story?* She is a beggar.

7. *What does Hsiang Lin's Wife do that bothers the narrator?* She asks him three difficult questions about death.

8. *What finally happens to Hsiang Lin's Wife?* She commits suicide.

9. *What is Lu Hsün's attitude toward Fourth Uncle and Fourth Aunt?* They are religious people who are callous and cruel without cause.

UNDERSTANDING THE STORY: POSSIBLE ANSWERS

*1. *Lu Hsün's definition of a good person* A good person's attitudes and actions would be sensitive to the needs and feelings of others, regardless of their social or economic status. A person's secular life and religious life should be harmonious; daily life should be lived according to religious principles.

2. *Hsiang Lin's Wife's three questions* Hsiang Lin's Wife wants to know whether she's going to be punished in the lower world by being cut in two and divided between her two husbands, as Liu Ma has told her she will be.

Being a modern intellectual, the narrator feels estranged from the values of the old China, yet he feels helpless in terms of changing the society to which they all belong. Consequently he does not feel comfortable about relating to Hsiang Lin's Wife, and he does not ask what is behind the questions that she asks him. Their meeting continues to bother him. Later he fears that his responses confirmed her fears about the lower world and her fate after death and that somehow his words led to her suicide.

*3. *Why Fourth Uncle thinks Hsiang Lin's Wife is "a bad character"* Hsiang Lin's Wife decides to commit suicide at a time when everyone is praying for blessings in the coming year. Her death interferes with Fourth Uncle's ability to concentrate on convincing the gods that he deserves to be blessed. In addition, Fourth Uncle may subconsciously realize that he has some responsibility for Hsiang Lin's Wife's death and that her action threatens the blessing he desires. He distances himself from the darker aspects of his own character by blaming her.

*4. *Why Hsiang Lin's Wife dies at this time* Hsiang Lin's Wife feels sinful, worthless, and ostracized by society. Even her contribution to the temple did not change anyone's response to her, and she expects that the gods will be even more censuring than the townspeople. She may have chosen to sacrifice herself to the gods during the New Year's festival to obtain their blessings in her afterlife in the lower world. Sacrificing oneself is more meaningful than sacrificing animals, and Hsiang Lin's Wife has tried everything else in her power to atone for the sins that the townspeople and her employers have made her feel that she has committed in her life. Hsiang Lin's Wife may also have committed suicide because she felt particularly depressed at a time of year when everyone else was celebrating good fortune.

*5. *Why Fourth Uncle won't let Hsiang Lin's Wife participate in New Year's rites* The catastrophes that have occurred in Hsiang Lin's Wife's life lead Fourth Uncle to think that the gods are punishing her for improper behavior. Therefore, when he is trying his best to prepare for asking the gods to bless him and his family, he fears that Hsiang Lin's Wife's participation in the preparations will pollute his efforts and bring the gods' anger rather than their blessing.

*6. *Why people in Luchen view Hsiang Lin's Wife with contempt* At first Hsiang Lin's Wife's catastrophes remind the people of Luchen of their own good fortune, so they enjoy listening to her complaints. Later her problems make them feel guilty about their own good lives and their lack of effort to help her. Her problems also remind the people of Luchen that good fortune may leave unpredictably. Therefore, they fear and despise Hsiang Lin's Wife because her presence reminds them of something that they would like to forget. In their minds, if her behavior caused her problems, they can avoid such problems by controlling their behavior.

*7. *Lu Hsün critical of Fourth Uncle and household* Lu Hsün is critical of all hypocrites. He expects people to treat one another with respect, kindness, and generosity. Fourth Uncle and Fourth Aunt think only of themselves. Lu Hsün is also critical of a religion that encourages people to please the gods and earn blessings by making animal sacrifices instead of requiring them to base their human relationships on moral behavior.

8. *Social attitudes in rural China* Hsiang Lin's Wife's life experiences reveal that men have a privileged place in society and in religious practices (Fourth Uncle and the New Year's sacrifice), parents dominate their grown children and their children-in-law, a woman may be sold in marriage so that her labor may be exploited by her husband's family (as in Hsiang Lin's Wife's first marriage), and a woman may be treated like a slave (as in Hsiang Lin's Wife's second marriage).

*9. *Title and theme* Both "The New Year's Sacrifice" and "Benediction" reflect the irony that the people of Luchen expect to be blessed on the basis of the quality of their performance of religious rites rather than on the quality of their treatment of other human beings. "The New Year's Sacrifice" has an additional meaning in that it can also refer to Hsiang Lin's Wife's sacrifice of her own life. Both titles relate to the theme that sacrifice and benediction should focus on the moral actions of human beings and emphasize respectful, kind, and generous relations between people.

ANALYZING LITERARY TECHNIQUE: POSSIBLE ANSWERS

1. *Why Lu Hsün begins and ends with the current New Year's holiday* The current holiday establishes the religious framework within which Hsiang Lin's Wife's story occurs, and it emphasizes the townspeople's hypocrisy—the gap between their beliefs and actions. The story within the story (Hsiang Lin's Wife's story) emphasizes the inhumanity of these people. The contrast between the people's religious sentiment and their treatment of Hsiang Lin's Wife gives the story its great power.

2. *Flashback* The structure of a flashback permits Lu Hsün to select the memories that the narrator recalls. His thoughts are all focused on the part of Hsiang Lin's Wife's life that relates to her mistreatment by her family, her employers, and fate. Extraneous detail, although interesting, would weaken the power of the story by diluting the story.

*3. *Depiction of Fourth Uncle and Fourth Aunt* Both Fourth Uncle and Fourth Aunt think only of their own welfare. Both are insensitive to the needs of Hsiang Lin's Wife. Their callous behavior, which destroys Hsiang Lin's Wife's life, illuminates the hypocrisy of their religious practices. The attitudes and behavior of the aunt and uncle are the major sources of irony and satire. Fourth Uncle and Fourth Aunt give the story its power.

*4. *Elements of satire* The story is a bitter satire in that it ridicules vices that cause human tragedy. (Compare satire to folly, which provokes humorous, gentle criticism.) The story reveals the hypocrisy of people who value meticulous ritual more than moral behavior. Lu Hsün finds the idea of pleasing divinities with animal sacrifices instead of treating people humanely to be morally unacceptable.

In addition to the actions of the mother-in-law and brother-in-law, the arrogant attitudes and cruel behavior of Fourth Uncle, Fourth Aunt, and Liu Ma ruin Hsiang Lin's Wife's life. During her first employment, Fourth Uncle and Fourth Aunt underpay her and treat her like a slave. They hand her and her wages over to her mother-in-law upon demand, pitying only themselves. During Hsiang Lin's Wife's second employment, Fourth Uncle views her misfortunes as a sign of divine displeasure, and he and his wife treat Hsiang Lin's Wife as a pariah. They break her spirit, making her useless as a servant; then they fire her, leaving her to become a beggar.

*5. *Irony* Irony is the source of the satire and the power of the story. Liu Ma, "a devout woman who abstained from meat [and] did not kill living things," terrifies Hsiang Lin's Wife with convictions about Hsiang Lin's Wife's sinful life and about her consequent treatment in the lower world. When Liu Ma tells Hsiang Lin's Wife that she should have killed herself, Liu Ma is being as harmful and unjust as everyone else. Liu Ma appears to be more worried about the lives of domestic animals than about the lives of humans.

The final paragraph reveals that the people of Luchen consider themselves to be good people whose prayers and offerings will reward them with the favor and blessings of "the saints of heaven and earth." They do not consider their treatment of Hsiang Lin's Wife and others to be relevant to the gods' treatment of them. The most disturbing irony in this story is that bad things happen to good people and that good things happen to bad people. The people of Luchen may continue to be "blessed," in that they will not be punished for their callous and cruel behavior.

*6. *Paradox* It is paradoxical that basically good people, through ignorance of their prejudices, can be cruel to others.

WRITING ABOUT LITERATURE

1. *Essay analyzing use of satire* Call students' attention to the directions in the textbook assignment with regard to content and organization. (See **U.S.** questions 1, 3, 4, 5, 6, 7, and 9 and **A.L.T.** questions 3, 4, 5, and 6.) **AP**

2. *Creative writing: a contemporary version of Lu Hsün's story* Direct students to suggestions in the textbook assignment. Actions involving hypocrisy and injustice can result from religious, economic, political, social, or gender issues. **(P.L.J.)**

FURTHER READING

Lu Hsün, *Selected Stories of Lu Hsün*.

In a Grove
RYŪNOSUKE AKUTAGAWA

INTRODUCING THE STORY

"In a Grove" is a first-class mystery story, a "whodunit" without an obvious solution. A robber confronts a married couple and rapes the wife. Then the husband is murdered. Each of the principal characters, to enhance his or her self-esteem and public image, confesses to the crime—creating an elaborate rationalization of his or her behavior and leaving the reader with a fascinating intellectual puzzle.

Akutagawa tells the story from six points of view. His portraits of the three principal characters reveal the psychological complexity of human nature and the bias that is inherent in any individual's point of view. Each has important personal and public reasons for claiming to have done the stabbing. The thief may take pride in his self-image and in his reputation. Once he is caught, he justifies his actions by declaring affection for the wife and by describing the relations between the husband and wife. The wife, shamed by the rape's effect on her own self-image and reputation and resentful of her husband's attitude toward her, may confess to the crime so she will be punished, thus relieving her shame and guilt. The husband may claim to have committed suicide to relieve his private and public shame about his wife's rape and to die the honorable death of a warrior.

Through the use of a multiple narrative perspective, Akutagawa reveals that the human mind is complex, objective truth is elusive, and ambiguity is an inherent part of life. In the culture he is depicting, one's public image determines one's self-esteem. People act—and depict their actions—in whatever way will lead others to accept and admire them. However, in any culture, the egoism that is an inherent part of human nature makes it difficult to learn the objective truth about an event, even from participants and witnesses. When events involve the elemental human passions of love, hate, and jealousy, the human psyche blurs the line between reality and illusion, often making it impossible to distinguish objective truth from subjective fiction.

Personal Literary Journal: Which is more important to you: how you feel about yourself, or how others feel about you? To what extent is your self-esteem determined by how others evaluate your behavior?

Literary Terms: characterization, irony, limited omniscience, narrative perspective, plot, setting, theme, unreliable narrator

COMPREHENSION QUESTIONS

1. *Why is the police commissioner questioning people?* A man was murdered.
2. *What position does the robber Tajomaru take?* confesses to murder
3. *What position does the wife take?* confesses to her husband's murder
4. *What position does the husband take?* confesses suicide
5. *How does the reader learn the husband's views?* through a medium

UNDERSTANDING THE STORY: POSSIBLE ANSWERS

*1. *Why husband, wife, and thief all confess* Through confessing to the crime and explaining the motive, each gains self-esteem and public approval.

*2. *Characters' testimony*

   a) *The thief* The thief's declaration of affection for the wife makes his motive for rape more acceptable in his own eyes. His statement that everyone is greedy makes his motive similar to the motives of others. His statement that the wife made him kill the husband and that he fought the husband fairly exonerates him. The thief has little to lose by confessing. Circumstantial evidence (the husband's property in the thief's possession) and the thief's reputation will convict him. His goal is to die with honor.

One would expect the thief to deny responsibility for the crime in hope of saving his own life, even though he most likely killed the husband to prevent the husband's revenge for the rape.

b) *The wife* The wife hopes that her confession of murder will result in punishment, thus relieving her sense of shame and her guilt about having been raped and having run away.

The wife risks imprisonment or loss of life, but she believes that a life filled with shame and guilt is not worth living.

One would expect the wife to be the innocent, ravaged victim. Only self-serving males (both the thief and her husband) would insinuate that she would have found the thief attractive or appealing. In these circumstances, it is more likely that she would have killed herself than killed her husband.

c) *The husband* The husband confesses because it is more honorable to commit suicide than to be murdered by his wife or by the thief. Even if it were true, the husband would not believe his wife's view that his facial expressions revealed that her rape disgusted him and that he despised her for it. He gains self-esteem and honor at the expense of his wife's reputation, but he cares more about himself than about his wife. His attitude toward her testimony lends credence to his wife's view that he despised her because of the rape. His testimony reveals him to be cruel and despicable.

Being already dead, the husband has nothing to lose except a relationship with his wife after her death.

One would expect the husband to act like the victim of a vicious crime. His likely response would have been to accuse the thief of the murder and to be sympathetic toward his wife.

3. *Themes* Possible themes:

- Objective truth is elusive.

- Ambiguity is an inherent part of life.

- The human psyche interprets experience in a way that is compatible with the need for self-esteem and public approval.

ANALYZING LITERARY TECHNIQUE: POSSIBLE ANSWERS

1. *Choice of narrative perspective* Telling one story from various points of view reveals how the individual psyche interprets experience to its own advantage. The human mind is complex, objective truth is elusive, and ambiguity is an inherent part of life.

2. *Why unsolved mystery?* Dramatically, the technique creates suspense and involves readers in the story; it challenges their intelligence. Psychologically,

the technique reveals a truth about life: Objective truth is elusive, and ambiguity is inherent in human experience.

3. *Irony* It is ironic that three characters confess to the stabbing, when two of the three risk their lives by doing so. This irony creates the dramatic surprise, and it reveals the complexity of the human psyche.

*4. *Testimony of minor characters* The testimonies of the minor characters are at best only partly reliable. Their inaccuracies lead the reader to assume that the testimonies of the participants will be accurate; ironically, however, no one's testimony is reliable.

- The woodcutter accurately reveals basic facts but makes a conjecture about a battle.

- The priest adds facts but then makes a conjecture that the two people he saw were husband and wife.

- The policeman reveals facts about the thief when he describes the arrest but shows his prejudice because of the thief's reputation.

- The old woman's testimony reveals her views of her daughter and son-in-law. Although she claims to recognize her son-in-law, she calls him Takehiko instead of Takejiro.

WRITING ABOUT LITERATURE

1. *Essay analyzing the reliability of confession of the thief, the wife, or the husband* (See **U.S.** questions 1 and 2 above.) **(P.L.J.)**

2. *Creative writing: an objective version of the story* Use of a hidden observer is possible; however, students should be aware of the bias of eyewitnesses. (Even film director Kurosawa's woodcutter is unreliable.) The objective version should be consistent with the indisputable facts. (See **A.L.T.** question 4 above.)

FURTHER READING

Akutagawa, Ryūnosuke, *Rashomon and Other Stories*; "The Nose"; "The Spider's Thread"; *Kappa*; "The Hell Screen."

The Grasshopper and the Bell Cricket
YASUNARI KAWABATA

INTRODUCING THE STORY

"The Grasshopper and the Bell Cricket" captures a special moment in time. In the process of hunting for insects, a boy (Fujio) offers a girl (Kiyoko) the insect that he has caught and wants to give her. When Kiyoko accepts the insect, she discovers that it is not a common grasshopper but a rare bell cricket. In the process, only the narrator notices that the light from Kiyoko's lantern casts the reflection of her name on Fujio's waist and that the light from Fujio's lantern casts his name on Kiyoko's breast, suggesting a relationship that the children themselves are unaware of.

The narrator uses the grasshopper and the bell cricket on two levels, the real and the symbolic. They symbolize what is ordinary and what is rare. For the narrator, the exchange of reflected names symbolizes all that is mysterious in life, the extra dimension of human experience that is often unrecognized and beyond comprehension. Being male, Kawabata identifies with Fujio, dividing females into "grasshoppers" and "bell crickets." He pities Fujio for being unaware of the larger mysterious reality of this moment because if Fujio could react more completely to the experience, this ability would sustain him through times of skepticism and loss of faith, times when he might so doubt the existence of what is rare and beautiful that he would be incapable of recognizing its presence in his life.

Kawabata has written a type of haiku in prose. The significant moment that he preserves functions on two levels. On the surface level, it is a moment that is pictorially beautiful and emotionally satisfying. On the symbolic level, it is an epiphany, a moment of sudden revelation in which the deeper meaning in this ordinary event flashes into the narrator's mind.

The symbolic meaning of the moment not only enriches the narrator's life but has universal significance. Moments of pure beauty are rare and fleeting, but like the bell cricket, they can be found and captured in a world that is filled with ordinary grasshoppers. It is important for each person to remain open to the discovery of these moments so that the rare and beautiful can be recognized when it is present. Kawabata ironically mentions that a person is as likely to consider the ordinary to be rare as to consider the rare to be ordinary. However, he is rightfully more concerned with a person's inability to recognize beauty than with a person's inability to recognize the rarity of beauty.

Personal Literary Journal: Have you ever witnessed a very special and private moment, one in which you were, in effect, an invisible outsider who was looking into someone else's world? For example, have you ever come upon animals in their natural setting or observed a child alone at play? If so, did you stop and observe, or did you continue on your way? To what extent, if any, did the moment affect your life?

Literary Terms: apostrophe, connotative language, epiphany, irony, narrative perspective, repetition, setting, symbol, Symbolist, theme, tone

COMPREHENSION QUESTIONS

1. *Where does the narrator observe this story?* at the base of a slope near a school playground
2. *What is happening?* Children are hunting insects.
3. *What are the children using to help them?* handmade paper lanterns
4. *What does Fujio give Kiyoko?* a bell cricket that he thinks is a grasshopper
5. *What does the narrator see that most impresses him?* Kiyoko's name reflected on Fujio's waist and Fujio's name reflected on Kiyoko's breast

UNDERSTANDING THE STORY: POSSIBLE ANSWERS

1. *Role of surprise* The two surprises (the bobbing lanterns and the reflection of the names) act as flags to direct the reader's attention to the special significance of the event that the narrator is about to describe. The surprises create climaxes out of these important scenes. They enhance the story by adding vitality, though the scenes would be just as effective without the markers.

2. *Children* The story is about being able to appreciate wonder and beauty in life. Children are usually more sensitive than adults to the wonder of small things. The world is still new to children, and they often experience the joy of discovery. In contrast, adults often think that they have discovered it all and no longer look at the world outside themselves. Most adults would not choose to go on an insect hunt, and they would not take time to create beautiful lanterns.

3. *Children's attitude toward the lanterns* Their attitude reveals their desire to have something that is beautiful and to be creative. Kawabata prizes these qualities.

4. *Significance of Fujio's repeated question* Fujio's repeated offer, despite numerous acceptances, reveals his desire to give his insect to Kiyoko. Fujio's persistence is the first personal touch to the story. The story now concerns particular children rather than a group.

5. *Fujio's feelings about the bell cricket* Fujio is probably embarrassed that he kept calling an insect by the wrong name. However, he was less interested in the insect than in using it to gain Kiyoko's attention. Fujio is probably interested in the insect only to the extent that Kiyoko is pleased by it.

*6. *Uses of light*

   a) Bobbing: The colorful moving lanterns create a beautiful visual atmosphere.

   b) Illuminating: When Fujio uses his lantern to illuminate Kiyoko's face, he reveals his purpose in rejecting so many offers to take the grasshopper. Illuminating Kiyoko's face makes the reader interested in Kiyoko's character.

   c) Reflecting: The reflection of the names of Fujio and Kiyoko on each other's bodies gives the event a mysterious and symbolic dimension that emanates from the event itself but extends beyond it.

7. *Contribution of narrator's point of view* The narrator's ideas add the philosophical content of the story. The narrator gives the story a symbolic dimension. It is important that each person recognize the beauty in life, regardless of what life may look like.

ANALYZING LITERARY TECHNIQUE: POSSIBLE ANSWERS

*1. *Relationship of setting and tone* The colorful bobbing lanterns create a visual picture of a special idyllic moment.

*2. *Relationship of narrative perspective and tone* The narrative perspective of a third-person omniscient author permits the narrator to philosophize about the story's symbolic significance. An omniscient narrator knows more than the characters, and the narrator uses his or her special knowledge to think about the characters. This adds a serious quality to the idyllic tone.

*3. *Relationship of apostrophe and tone* When the narrator speaks directly to Fujio, he is creating a personal connection between Fujio and himself. This technique adds a personal aspect and a level of importance to the tone of the story.

*4. *Irony* It is ironic that the children, like most adults, are unaware of the beauty and wonder that fill their lives. This lack of awareness adds a sad and wistful aspect to the tone of the story.

5. *Relationship of symbols and theme* The grasshopper symbolizes what is ordinary and common in life; in contrast, the bell cricket symbolizes what is rare and special. Kawabata's principal themes include the following: A person must be aware of the bell crickets in life, even when they look like grasshoppers, so one does not miss what is rare and beautiful. A person's attitude makes an experience common or beautiful; grasshoppers can be turned into bell crickets, or bell crickets into grasshoppers.

   Advertently or inadvertently, Kawabata has achieved the major goal of the Symbolists with this story. By recapturing and reproducing the experience that originally inspired particular thoughts and emotions within himself, Kawabata succeeds in re-creating these feelings in the reader. Thus, the story becomes the symbol of the reactions that it inspires.

6. *Function of repetition* Examples of repetition:

   - The growing number of children emphasizes the cumulative process.

   - Fujio's repeated question reveals his interest in Kiyoko.

   - The children's repeated comment "It's a bell cricket!" emphasizes the value of that insect.

   - The reflected names emphasize the epiphany, the symbolic significance of the event.

WRITING ABOUT LITERATURE

1. *Essay analyzing Kawabata's use of light* Call students' attention to the types of light suggested in the textbook assignment. Remind them of the importance of quotations. (See **U.S.** question 6 above.)

2. *Essay analyzing how Kawabata achieves tone* Call students' attention to the techniques suggested in the textbook assignment. Remind them that quotations must support their ideas. (See **A.L.T.** questions 1, 2, 3, and 4 above.) **AP**

3. *Creative writing: a real or imagined special moment in time* Call students' attention to suggestions in the textbook assignment. Remind them to aim for details that will create a sense of immediacy for their readers. **(P.L.J.)**

FURTHER READING

Kawabata, Yasunari, *Palm-of-the-Hand Stories;* "Of Birds and Beasts"; *The Sound of the Mountain;* "One Arm."

Life

SHEN CONGWEN

INTRODUCING THE STORY

"Life" is a magnificent story because of its plot, its structure, and the relationship between the plot and structure. The stylistic aspects of this deceptively simple story are so interwoven that readers uncover the point of the story regardless of how they analyze the plot's construction. The linchpin in the story is the surprising set of facts that the author reserves for the final two paragraphs: The puppeteer has created a puppet show that reenacts a personal tragedy, the death of his son in a wrestling match that occurred ten years before the story opens. Although the puppeteer has been performing this show all over Peking for ten years, he is unaware that the victor of that match has been dead for five years.

The show involves two puppets that wrestle with each other until the white-faced puppet wins. The puppeteer always speaks aloud to the white-faced puppet, treating it as his son. His secret is that the white-faced puppet (Wang Jiu) is symbolic of his son and the black-faced puppet (Zhao Si) is symbolic of his son's opponent, the man who killed him.

The reader discovers that the puppeteer is tormented by feelings of guilt over his son's death—possibly because he has survived his son or possibly because he feels somehow responsible for his son's tragedy. The author reveals why the puppeteer acts as he does but provides no window into the puppeteer's mind and heart. To gain some respite from the guilt that tortures him, the puppeteer performs a drama that is a fantasy version of his son's fatal wrestling match. He manipulates the fight so that the white-faced puppet always possesses the skill to win the match. The tragedy is that the psychological relief that the puppeteer achieves lasts only as long as the performance. He has, therefore, been repeating the drama day after day, month after month, and year after year for ten years.

Just as it is a tragic irony that the two puppets and their wrestling match symbolize real people and a real event, it is also a tragic irony that the puppeteer feels compelled to perform his show even though his son's opponent has been dead for five years. The author implies that the puppeteer is ignorant of the victor's death. The reader is left to imagine how this knowledge might have affected the puppeteer. Part of the complexity of the structure of the story is the belated revelation of the puppeteer's double dimension. Climax, foreshadowing, irony, and tone are all tightly interwoven with characterization and theme. Until the omniscient author reveals the puppeteer's secret, the puppeteer seems to be an ordinary poor man with enough talent to make people laugh by wrestling with himself in a creative way. He is optimistic that an audience will arrive once he begins his act, and he is self-confident about his ability to entertain the audience. He appears to accept the reality that he must put on his show, come rain or shine, to collect money for his next meager meal. With amazingly good cheer, he puts on his exhausting performance in weather that is so hot that someone nearby collapses from heat stroke. However, once the author reveals the puppeteer's secret, readers see the puppeteer in a different light.

The puppeteer is not simply an old man working for a few coins. He is a psychologically complex person who is struggling with pain and guilt. The story becomes a feat of ingenuity and skill.

The omniscient author approaches the story as if the event were being recorded with a motion picture camera. Characters are described by an aspect of their physical appearance. Every detail in the story has a specific purpose. For example, the author prepares for the arrival of the puppeteer by describing a toy vendor working in the same location. This scene sets a carefree tone as the vendor's toy airplane attracts an audience of curious people who, having nothing better to do, enjoy being entertained. The puppeteer's show is a variant of this scene, but the carefree tone is shattered in the story's final two paragraphs. Another example of detail is the frequent reference to the day's heat. When someone collapses from heat stroke, the puppeteer's psychological need—as well as his economic need—to perform his show is reinforced.

The descriptions of two members of the audience reveal the additional psychological complexity of human beings. First, a young army officer leaves the scene with a frown on his face after tossing a handful of coins on the ground. The puppeteer's need to beg for money to pay the concession fee obviously makes the officer uncomfortable. The officer donates money but forces the puppeteer to demean himself by picking up the coins from the ground. Second, the pock-faced policeman leaves the show with a smirk on his face, murmuring "Wang Jiu, Wang Jiu." The policeman is ridiculing the puppeteer, who had earlier criticized the policeman by saying to Wang Jiu "He knows very well that we can't afford a simple wheatcake to fill our stomachs."

Finally, the author's use of detail enables this story to reveal many realistic facets of human experience. For example, the puppeteer symbolizes human beings who cope with life but suffer silently beneath their smiles. The audience behaves like real people who are fascinated by awful spectacles. On the other hand, as the toy airplane scene reveals, the audience also shows that every adult is capable of finding great joy in simple pleasures.

Note: To produce the most accurate translation (one that ignores the later "politically correct" revisions), the translator worked with both the pre-Communist version and the revised version that appears in Shen Congwen's collected works. Consequently you will read this story as Shen Congwen would have wanted you to read it.

Personal Literary Journal: Imagine the life of a person who has experienced a tragedy. How does that person attempt to cope with what happened? To what extent, if any, would you expect to find connection between what happened and how that person is leading her or his life? What would such a connection accomplish?

Literary Terms: characterization, climax, foreshadowing, irony, point of view, theme, tone

COMPREHENSION QUESTIONS

1. *Where is this story set?* in a landfill in Peking where people dump stove ashes

2. *What does the main character do for a living?* He is a puppeteer.

3. *Describe the show.* Two puppets wrestle until the white-faced puppet wins.

4. *Who is present when the main character arrives?* no one

5. *Why does the main character expect people to arrive?* He sees empty lotus pods, so he knows people are eating lotus fruits in the area.

6. *How does the main character treat the white-faced puppet?* as human

7. *How does the show always end?* The white-faced puppet (Wang Jiu) defeats the black-faced puppet (Zhao Si).

8. *Who arrives and disturbs the main character? Why?* A policeman arrives to collect a sideshow concession fee.

9. *Who solves the main character's problem? How?* A young army officer tosses him a handful of coins.

10. *Why do the outsiders leave?* Something else arouses their curiosity.

11. *What surprises the main character?* The second policeman does not ask for a fee.

12. *What is the main character's secret?* He had a son named Wang Jiu who died ten years before in a fight with a man named Zhao Si.

13. *How does this secret relate to the main character's activity?* In the puppet show, the puppet that represents the puppeteer's son always defeats the puppet that represents the son's opponent.

14. *How long has the main character been doing what he does?* ten years

15. *What does the final sentence in the story reveal?* The son's opponent has been dead for five years.

UNDERSTANDING THE STORY: POSSIBLE ANSWERS

*1. *Characterization of the puppeteer* The puppeteer has a down-to-earth honesty in that he has no pretenses about himself. He accepts his situation, including his poverty, and he deals respectfully with his audience. He is probably unaware of his subconscious need to repeat the fantasy version of his son's fatal wrestling match to gain some respite from the guilt that tortures him.

The puppeteer is determined to put on his show so he can earn the money he needs for food. He is confident that as long as he performs well, his audience will pay him and will tell others about his show. He has the inherent ability to bolster his self-confidence by talking encouragingly to

Wang Jiu, the white-faced puppet. Finally, the puppeteer has the pride to keep his son's death a secret from everyone so that the audience will have no additional reason to pity him and so that he can resist the pain of self-pity.

2. *Role of puppets* The puppeteer speaks to the white-faced puppet as devotedly as a father speaks to his son. In fact, that puppet bears his son's name and symbolizes his son. The puppets and the drama represent real people and a real wrestling match that concluded with the death of the puppeteer's son. The puppeteer has created a fantasy in which his son defeats the opponent. For the duration of the puppet show, the puppeteer gains some respite from the guilt that tortures him.

3. *Final paragraph* The final paragraph turns the poor but optimistic puppeteer into a poignant human being who is continually compelled to act out a fantasy version of his son's fatal fight.

4. *Final sentence* With the words "as to the real Zhao Si," the author indicates that the puppeteer is unaware of the real Zhao Si's death.

5. *Title* "Life" is an appropriate title because the story reveals many realistic facets of human experience. The puppeteer is a realistic human being who is coping well on the surface while suffering silently beneath his smile. Moreover, his traumatic experience has profoundly affected his behavior. The people in the audiences also behave like real people. They are curious about adversities, and they find joy in simple pleasures, such as playing with toy airplanes.

6. *Themes* Possible themes:

   • "You can't judge a book by the cover"; people are more complex than they appear to be.

   • People are inherently curious. They are drawn to awful spectacles, such as accidents, fires, and traumas.

   • Every adult is a child at heart, capable of finding great joy in simple pleasures.

   • A person's traumatic experience may profoundly affect her or his behavior.

ANALYZING LITERARY TECHNIQUE: POSSIBLE ANSWERS

1. *Toy vendor* The author begins with the toy vendor to set the scene for the puppeteer. The toy vendor is working in the same location. An audience of curious people are entertained by his toy airplane. They are willing to pay a few cents for their experience, and the vendor is happy with the meager amount of money that he earns. The scene involving the puppeteer is a variant of the scene with the toy vendor. However, the toy vendor scene sets a deceptively carefree tone for the story.

*2. *Point of view* The story is told from the point of view of an omniscient narrator who knows everything about everyone and can reveal whatever he chooses.

If the story were told from the puppeteer's point of view, it would be limited to the puppeteer's perception of himself and the world in which he lives. Readers would know no more than the puppeteer knows; specifically, they would not learn that the puppet show is a fantasy, would not realize the significance of the puppet show, and would not know that the victor of the real wrestling match died years ago. The advantage of having the puppeteer's point of view would be to gain insight into the puppeteer's view of the world and his feelings about his son's death. If the story were told from the point of view of a member of his audience, readers would know only what that person knows. That observer would know only what the audience sees and hears and would not realize whom the puppets symbolize or what event is being dramatized.

3. *Details*

  - The description of the toy vendor's airplanes adds realism to the story by enabling readers to imagine the scene.

  - The significance of the person's collapsing from heat stroke supports the information that the puppeteer is compelled to perform his show regardless of the weather.

  - The detailed depiction of the young army officer who tosses coins at the edge of the crowd and leaves with a frown on his face and the pock-faced policeman who leaves with a smirk on his face reveal how other people may respond to the puppeteer.

4. *Climax* The climax of the story is the omniscient author's revelation that the puppeteer did not want people to know that he had had a son named Wang Jiu who had died in a fight with Zhao Si.

*5. *Foreshadowing* Part of the superb construction of this story is that the puppeteer is continually speaking to the white-faced puppet as if it were his son, yet the reader does not imagine the connection between the puppet Wang Jiu and the son Wang Jiu until the author reveals the connection, in the form of a climax at the end of the story. The remarks that the puppeteer makes to his puppet/son have greater depth and sense of psychological realism once the climax reveals the symbolic nature of the puppets and their fight. The foreshadowing of this relationship greatly enriches the character of the puppeteer and enhances the psychological dimension of the story.

6. *Irony* It is a tragic irony that the two puppets and their wrestling match symbolize real people and a real fight. This irony changes the character of the puppeteer and the tone of the story. The puppeteer becomes a poignant figure who has a double dimension. On the surface, he appears to cope well with his poverty and to have an optimistic attitude toward life. Beneath the surface, however, he is a sad human being who is compelled to repeat the fantasy version of his son's fatal wrestling match to gain some respite from the guilt that tortures him. The irony changes the tone of the story from an optimistic tale of a poor entertainer who copes with life to a tragic tale

of a poor entertainer who compulsively performs a puppet show to cope with his personal tragedy.

It is also a tragic irony that the puppeteer has been compelled to perform his fantasy version of his son's fatal fight even after his son's opponent has been dead for five years. The author implies that the puppeteer is ignorant of the victor's death. How that knowledge would have affected the puppeteer depends upon the nature of the puppeteer's guilt. If he feels guilty because he has survived his son, then the knowledge of the victor's death would not have relieved his torment, and his psyche will probably condemn him to reenact his fantasy for the remainder of his active life. However, if his guilt is caused by feelings of responsibility for his son's death, then the victor's death might have alleviated that guilt.

7. *Tone* The most striking aspect of the story is its change in tone from one of determined optimism despite adversity to one of tragic pessimism. The author achieves this through his revelations in the final two paragraphs of the story, which come as a complete surprise despite the author's foreshadowing the father-son relationship of the puppeteer and the white-faced puppet. Once the author reveals the connection between the puppets and the puppeteer's personal tragedy, the puppeteer becomes a poignant figure who has a double dimension.

WRITING ABOUT LITERATURE

1. *Essay analyzing point of view* Call students' attention to the directions in the textbook assignment with regard to content and paragraphing. (See **A.L.T.** question 2 above.) **AP**

2. *Essay analyzing foreshadowing* Call students' attention to the direction in the textbook assignment with regard to content, quotations, and paragraphing. (See **A.L.T.** question 5 above.)

3. *Essay analyzing the puppeteer's character* Call students' attention to the directions in the textbook assignment with regard to content, quotations, and paragraphing. (See **U.S.** question 1 above.)

4. *Creative writing: a story about coping with personal tragedy* Call students' attention to the directions in the textbook assignment. **(P.L.J.)**

FURTHER READING

Shen Congwen, *Imperfect Paradise*.

Lau, Joseph S. and Ou-Fan Leo Lee, ed., *Modern Chinese Stories and Novellas 1919–1949*.

Chih-Tsing Hsia, ed., *Twentieth-Century Chinese Stories*.

A Certain Night

TING LING

INTRODUCING THE STORY

"A Certain Night" conveys the atmosphere in which a group of Chinese communists are executed by their political enemies, the nationalists. The communists' hatred for their oppressors gives way to hope for their cause as their final thoughts move away from themselves and toward the ideals for which they are sacrificing their lives. Ting Ling concludes with snow falling on dark corpses and the question "When will it be light?" "Light" implies more than the dawn of the next day. It refers to the dawn of a new political day, one in which the Chinese people will work together to create a better environment for the common people—the peasants and the workers. For the men in the story, political slogans dispel the darkness and give meaning to their deaths. For them and for Ting Ling, the new communist state is a brilliant source of light.

Ting Ling effectively creates the mood of the situation by her repeated attention to the weather. She has created a physical environment that reflects the atmosphere of the political execution, as if nature abhors the actions of the nationalists. The execution occurs on a black night; it is carried out by people who operate in secret. A ferocious wind lashes faces as rifle butts smash chests and gunshots lacerate bodies. Ting Ling's use of color and sound creates lasting images in the mind of the reader.

Note: Anglo-Saxon obscenities suggested in the translation have been omitted without damage to the meaning of the story.

Personal Literary Journal: If someone dear to you died, how would you honor that person's name?

Literary Terms: connotative language, figurative language, metaphor, realism, repetition, setting, symbol, theme, tone

COMPREHENSION QUESTIONS

1. *Whose feet are tramping?* the feet of the nationalist soldiers who will shoot the communist activists

2. *Who is the main character?* a young poet condemned to death for his communist activities

3. *Describe the weather* a stormy winter night

4. *What do the prisoners do just before the end?* shout communist slogans and sing a socialist song

5. *What happens to the prisoners in the end?* They are executed by nationalist soldiers.

UNDERSTANDING THE STORY: POSSIBLE ANSWERS

*1. *Author's attitude toward prisoners* It is clear from the way the author describes the two political groups that she sympathizes with the prisoners.

Her closing question about light refers to the new communist age in China. Her description of the poet as loyal and hardworking depicts him as an innocent victim of nationalist oppressors.

*2. *Nationalists versus communists* Ting Ling describes the nationalist soldier who sentences the communist prisoner as having a "cunning face, malicious and smug, . . . with a revolting moustache of the sort imperialists wear." Later she writes that the face of the chief executioner "seemed to symbolize the cruelty of all the rulers to the oppressed." She refers to communists as "dispelling the darkness" and welcomes the "brilliance of a new state being founded."

*3. *The nationalist attitude toward the condemned prisoners* The nationalists consider the prisoners to be criminals, traitors to their country who deserve death. The nationalists know that the goal of communism is to take over the government of China.

*4. *Change in the poet's attitude toward death* At first the poet is angry at being deprived of a trial and being sentenced to death; however, being with his comrades comforts him. In the end he dies happily for his cause, which he believes is greater and more important than any individual.

*5. *Purpose of the story* The story honors Ting Ling's husband for being a political martyr and communism for saving China from imperialist domination.

6. *Themes* Possible themes:

- Power tends to corrupt, and absolute power corrupts absolutely.
- A person whose life has been devoted to a great cause may find death easier to bear.
- For some people, sacrificing their lives for a cause is worthwhile.

ANALYZING LITERARY TECHNIQUE: POSSIBLE ANSWERS

1. *Tone* The tone is depressing, but there is a vision of hope. Despite the depressing subject of a political execution, the story leaves the reader with the real possibility of a better future. The prisoners believe that they are sacrificing their lives for a just cause that is about to become a reality through the efforts of courageous people like themselves. The men and women consider themselves martyrs rather than victims, and they take comfort in their shared values and goals and in their accomplishments. Ting Ling describes both the cruelty of their imprisonment and murder (which is dark in tone) and their optimism (which is hopeful in tone). The optimism is evident in one comrade's ability to inspire courage and in another's reminder to celebrate the founding of a brilliant new state.

2. *Setting and tone* The stormy setting complements the dark tone of the current political situation. A black stormy night forms the backdrop for the horror of a political execution.

3. *Symbolism* The primary symbols in the story are light and the storm. Ting Ling uses light to symbolize communism. Communist slogans dispel the darkness and reveal the brilliance of the new communist state that is being

founded. Ting Ling's closing question about light means "When will China become communist?"

The storm symbolizes nature's abhorrence of the foul secret deeds of the nationalists by reflecting the turbulence in the political world in the natural world. It also symbolizes the darkness of the tunnel that one must traverse before reaching the light at the end.

4. *Connotation of trampling feet* Trampling feet connote the force, intent, power, and feeling of victory of the huge escort of nationalist soldiers. The image is repeated to emphasize the presence of the soldiers and their contribution to the dark tone of this part of the story.

WRITING ABOUT LITERATURE

1. *Essay analyzing the propagandistic elements in this story* Call students' attention to the textbook assignment, reminding them to include an evaluative conclusion and to support their ideas with quotations. (See **U.S.** questions 1, 2, 3, 4, and 5 above.) **AP**

2. *Creative writing: the story from a nationalist soldier's viewpoint* Remind students that nationalists have their own political and social bias.

FURTHER READING

Ting Ling, *Miss Sophie's Diary and Other Stories; I Myself Am a Woman: Selected Writings of Ding Ling.*

Downtown
FUMIKO HAYASHI

INTRODUCING THE STORY

Set in Tokyo shortly after the end of World War II, "Downtown" is a story about the will to survive. It shows that human relationships can make life worth living even amid destruction and poverty.

Having received no word about her soldier-husband for six years, Ryo takes her young son to Tokyo to start a new life. A woman from the country, she is unaccustomed to being independent and to being solely responsible for herself and her son. Her friendship with Tsuruishi enables her to come to terms with the past and to move ahead with her new life.

The story is a poignant tale of the cost of war to the wives who remain behind. Tsuruishi's wife loses faith in her husband's return and takes up with another man. His sister supports herself and her two children by making clothes. Ryo survives by peddling tea door to door.

The role of luck in life, both good and bad, permeates the story. Life or death, kindness or callousness, success or failure in selling tea are all a matter of serendipity. Yet in spite of the trials and losses that are part of living, the good people whom

Ryo meets—those who are kind, sympathetic, and caring—bolster her with the courage to continue and the comfort that she is not alone in her plight.

Personal Literary Journal: Imagine what your life would be like if you survived a war or a natural disaster in which you and your family were directly affected. What problems would you anticipate? How would you attempt to cope with these problems? What aspects of life would sustain and comfort you?

Literary Terms: characterization, irony, setting, theme, tone

COMPREHENSION QUESTIONS

1. *Why has Ryo come to Tokyo?* to earn a living so she can support herself and her son

2. *How does Ryo earn a living?* sells tea from door to door

3. *Where is Ryo's husband?* He is a prisoner of war in Siberia; he may be dead.

4. *Who is Tsuruishi?* a man who becomes Ryo's friend

5. *How do other women like Ryo earn a living?* by sewing

UNDERSTANDING THE STORY: POSSIBLE ANSWERS

*1. *Ryo's world* Ryo's postwar world is one in which survival is primary. Order and predictability no longer exist. Ryo's husband may or may not return; Ryo may or may not be successful selling tea.

   "Downtown" is universal in its application. Catastrophes force those who are victims to be flexible and to adapt to new circumstances. War always causes death and destruction, leaving widows and fatherless children.

*2. *Remaining values* Humane values continue to exist in this postwar world: love, friendship, and empathy.

*3. *Why Ryo's husband is an embarrassment* The imprisonment of Ryo's husband reminds people of the unpleasant fact that Japan lost "the war" (World War II).

*4. *Why Ryo remains after Tsuruishi dies* Ryo has learned that she can survive in Tokyo. She will be able to earn a living, and she will be able to meet good people who will become her friends.

*5. *Tsuruishi: better or worse for Ryo* Student opinions will differ. Some will agree that "'Tis better to have loved and lost / Than never to have loved at all." Ryo's feelings for Tsuruishi make her realize that she can love someone other than her husband if he does not return. Also, since Tsuruishi has recently returned, meeting him gives her hope that her own husband will still return. Others may think that under these circumstances it would have been better not to have loved, since loving creates a greater sense of loss; it will also create a great sense of guilt if Ryo's husband returns.

*6. *Ryo a sympathetic character* Hayashi presents Ryo very sympathetically. She is a wife in limbo; she has not heard from her husband for six years and does not know whether he is alive. She attempts to earn a living in a decent manner, enabling both herself and her young son to survive. Ryo is a good human being: generous and caring but also very lonely.

7. *Role of luck or fate* Luck or fate reflects the unpredictability of life and an absurd universe. Ryo may or may not be successful selling tea each day. Tsuruishi dies while on a journey that was unnecessary. Ryo's husband may or may not be alive to return home.

8. *Attitude toward war* War brings loneliness, pain, poverty, and death into the lives of innocent people. Hayashi deals with war by examining its effect on individuals who are also representative of larger groups. Hayashi's characters do not preoccupy themselves with the philosophical, political, religious, and economic causes of war.

9. *Themes* Possible themes:
   - Live each day to the fullest, for tomorrow is a mystery.
   - War destroys the lives of both those who fight and those who remain behind.
   - It is possible to remain kind and loving in spite of great adversity.

ANALYZING LITERARY TECHNIQUE: POSSIBLE ANSWERS

*1. *Relation of setting to plot* This story, set in postwar Japan, concerns Ryo's survival without her husband. He has not returned because he is a prisoner of war who may or may not be alive. Ryo is compelled to find a way to earn enough money to support her young son and herself. All of the other characters in the story are also suffering from the effects of war on their lives.

2. *Tsuruishi's function* Tsuruishi's life teaches Ryo that her husband may return, that she can live and find love even if he does not return, that life continues, and that good people continue to exist. Tsuruishi's death teaches Ryo that nothing is predictable in life and that one can only do one's best to make the most of each day.

3. *Irony* It is ironic that Tsuruishi survives the war and imprisonment only to be killed in a freak accident in the course of an unnecessary journey. It is also ironic that Tsuruishi encourages Ryo to become involved with him after losing his own wife to another man. Irony reinforces a major theme of the story: Life is unpredictable and people need to create their own meaning in an absurd universe.

4. *Tone* The tone is compassionate and poignant. It is created by the facts of Ryo's life and by the way that Ryo reacts to adversity. Ryo never loses her determination and ability to work hard and to care about others.

5. *Title* "Downtown" is general, whereas "Ryo" is specific and individual. Hayashi views Ryo not as a particular individual but as an individual who is symbolic of thousands of poor widows who must struggle to survive in postwar Japan.

WRITING ABOUT LITERATURE

1. *Sympathetic character sketch of Ryo* Ryo is determined, courageous, friendly, kind, and optimistic. Remind students to use quotations to describe their choice of supporting incidents. Students should relate Ryo's character to conditions in postwar Tokyo and consider the plight of single women in Japanese urban society. (See **U.S.** questions 1, 2, 3, 4, 5, and 6 and **A.L.T.** question 1.)

2. *Creative writing: a sequel to this story* Remind students that suggested questions in the textbook assignment may be helpful. **(P.L.J.)**

FURTHER READING

Hayashi, Fumiko, "Late Chrysanthemum"; *Drifting Clouds*.

Forty-Five a Month

R. K. NARAYAN

INTRODUCING THE STORY

"Forty-Five a Month" is the story of Venkat Rao, a bookkeeper, who works under a workaholic boss. Venkat Rao devotes long hours to tedious tasks for which he receives low pay. Because he feels guilty about having little time to spend with his family, he promises to take his daughter, Shanta, to the movies. When he realizes that he is going to have to break his promise, he writes a letter of resignation, but he retracts it when he is offered a small raise in salary. In the end, he is caught in a life of quiet desperation. He will still earn too little to provide the life he wishes for his family, yet he lacks the courage to quit his job and take a chance on the future.

The story has universal appeal in that many people around the world work long hours at jobs they do not like. Venkat Rao's attitudes and behavior lead readers to examine the importance of career, financial success, and family responsibilities and pleasures in their own lives.

Narayan uses an interesting narrative technique to convey Venkat Rao's personality. First an omniscient narrator introduces the reader to Shanta. Then the narrator tells the story from Venkat Rao's point of view, revealing his world to the reader as he reacts to events. The double point of view gives the reader a partial reality check on Venkat Rao's attitudes and reveals him to be his own worst enemy. Lacking the courage of his convictions, he is a sorrier figure than his wife and daughter because he is a willing pawn in his manager's game.

Personal Literary Journal: Do you value yourself more highly or less highly than others value you? How does your self-worth affect your life? To what extent do you aim higher or lower because of how you view yourself? How do you view those people whose opinions of you differ from your own self-evaluation?

Literary Terms: characterization, conflict, foreshadowing, irony, narrative perspective, omniscient narrator, paradox, theme, third-person limited omniscience, unreliable narrator

COMPREHENSION QUESTIONS

1. *Why is Shanta anxious to leave school?* She has a movie date with her father.
2. *How does Venkat Rao view Shanta?* neglected, ignored, deprived
3. *What does Venkat Rao plan to do about his job?* resign
4. *Why doesn't Venkat Rao carry out his plan?* He is offered small raise.
5. *How does Venkat Rao feel in the end?* torn between job and family

UNDERSTANDING THE STORY: POSSIBLE ANSWERS

*1. *Why Venkat Rao makes a date with Shanta* Venkat Rao agrees to the date to feel in control of his life. He is asserting his independence from his job.

*2. *Accuracy of Venkat Rao's view of Shanta* Venkat Rao's view of Shanta appears to be inaccurate. The omniscient author presents Shanta as happy at school, describing her as having friends and an understanding teacher. At home, her mother also is understanding. Shanta has a choice of clothes to wear, including warm ones, and she is adequately cared for.

*3. *Why Venkat Rao neither quits nor demands more money* Venkat Rao accepts the terms of his employment because he lacks the courage to risk what he has to improve his circumstances.

*4. *How Venkat Rao's personality contributes to his problems* Venkat Rao is his own worst enemy. He is dissatisfied with many aspects of his job and with his contribution to family life, yet his attitude at the office is so meek and accepting that his boss is able to work him beyond reason. Venkat Rao lives with constant inner conflict that he is unable to resolve.

*5. *Role of the family in Venkat Rao's decision to take a lower-paid job* Students' opinions will vary; discussion will reveal students' values.

6. *Themes* Possible themes: To be happy, people must have the courage of their convictions. People who do not value themselves will not be valued by others.

ANALYZING LITERARY TECHNIQUE: POSSIBLE ANSWERS

*1. *Focusing on Shanta* By beginning with the omniscient narrator, the author gives the reader an objective reality that can be compared to Venkat Rao's distorted point of view.

*2. *Narrative perspective* First the omniscient narrator reveals Shanta to be a happy, contented child. Then the narrator tells the story from Venkat Rao's point of view, revealing his inner conflicts and torments and his inability to take control of his life. Venkat Rao feels sorry for his family and himself; he complains about many aspects of his job but does nothing to improve life for anyone except his boss.

3. *Foreshadowing* Venkat Rao's description of his work habits indicates that he will have to break his promise. When Venkat Rao's wife admonishes him about making false promises, the reader expects that his promise is indeed false. Both incidents prepare the reader for what follows, and they make the plot internally consistent.

*4. *Irony* It is ironic that Venkat Rao complains so much about his job, but when he is given the opportunity to do something about it, he fails to act. If Venkat Rao were as unhappy about his job and his time with his family as he professes to be, the reader would expect him to have the courage to take a necessary risk to improve his life.

5. *Tone* The tone is mildly ironic and sweetly sad. Narayan achieves the balance by presenting the mother and child as satisfied with their lives. Their lack of complaint makes Venkat Rao's inability to resign less important. He is the most unhappy member of his family, and he is a principal cause of his own unhappiness.

WRITING ABOUT LITERATURE

1. *Essay analyzing "pattern of existence" versus moment in time* Students probably will argue that Narayan portrays Venkat Rao's character in such a way that the reader sees a pattern of existence rather than a moment in time. Venkat Rao lets a significant moment pass him by when he breaks his promise to Shanta. He does not resolve his crisis; he simply perpetuates it. (See **U.S.** questions 1, 2, 3, 4, and 5 and **A.L.T.** questions 1, 2, and 4 above.) **(P.L.J.)**

2. *Creative writing: retelling story from point of view of Shanta's mother* Students may choose various points of view:

   - Venkat Rao's wife appears to be satisfied with her life, which is filled with her friends and her daughter.

   - Venkat Rao's wife is dissatisfied with her life. She resents the demands of Venkat Rao's job. She wishes that Venkat Rao were more assertive, and she would like him to be more involved with his family.

FURTHER READING

Narayan, R. K., *Under the Banyan Tree* (short stories); *The Ramayana* (epic); *The Guide* (novel); *Malgudi Days* (short stories); *Gods, Demons, and Others* (legends).

Pineapple Cake

ANITA DESAI

INTRODUCING THE STORY

"Pineapple Cake" is a story of social anxiety—the anxiety of Victor Fernandez and the anxiety of his mother as they attend the Bombay wedding of Carmen Maria Braganza and George de Mello. Victor, a little boy who is dragged along to a boring wedding, worries he will inadvertently misbehave. He knows that if he does, his mother will deprive him of the reward that she has promised him— pineapple cake. Mrs. Fernandez worries about what others think of her and whether Victor will exhibit some behavior that will reflect negatively upon her (for example, sweating in church or wetting his pants). She reveals her concern for social niceties by primly wiping her mouth after she eats dessert.

The characters are Hispanics living in Bombay, India. A social and economic hierarchy exists within their social group, just as it exists within Indian society. Social status confers self-esteem and makes social occasions more pleasant. The groom's family is hosting the wedding reception at Green's and has cabs ready and waiting to take the wedding party to the reception—so the family must be relatively wealthy. In contrast, those of lower social position must catch-as-catch-can. Mrs. Fernandez must look for a cab, which she is forced to share with two other passengers, and then she must look for a seat at the reception.

The story's crisis occurs at the reception when the man who shared the cab with Victor and his mother suffers a fatal heart attack. There follows a scene replete with satire and black humor as the mother of the bride bemoans the selfishness of the man who has spoiled her daughter's wedding reception by choosing to die at this time and the waiters come forth with dessert just as the corpse is carried away. Victor's mind has fastened on the impending arrival of the hearse. The story's climax occurs when Victor shows no interest in the pineapple cake. Humor and irony rule as Victor's mother, who appears to be totally impervious to the man's death, impatiently moves Victor's piece of cake to her own plate, quickly eats it, primly wipes her mouth, and efficiently prepares to leave the reception.

Desai is considered an imagist because she uses details to make each scene come alive—both visually and aurally—for her readers. Her photographic descriptions— images highlighted by fabric and color, unusual verbs and adjectives, and creative similes and metaphors—sharpen the focus of the scene as a whole. These details combine to make the readers experience the sights and sounds of the wedding celebration (the macrocosm) as if they were among the invited guests.

In contrast, Mrs. Fernandez and Victor reflect two divergent microcosms. While the cinematographer's camera is recording highlights of the social setting, each character's stream of interior monologue reveals relevant aspects of their mother-son relationship as well as thoughts about the social event. The story reflects Desai's sympathy for her characters. Victor's thoughts are typical of a child his age, and his mother's anxieties are understandable. The result is a deftly told story.

Personal Literary Journal: Describe a real or imaginary situation that you know as an insider but can observe with the objectivity of an outsider. Use language as a camera. Jot down words and phrases that will enable readers to visualize the situation that you are describing.

Literary Terms: antagonist, black humor, characterization, climax, crisis, figurative language, humor, imagist, interior monologue, irony, limited omniscience, metaphor, narrative perspective, point of view, protagonist, resolution, satire, setting, simile, tone

COMPREHENSION QUESTIONS

1. *What are Victor and his mother doing at the beginning of the story?* attending a wedding ceremony

2. *What motivates Victor's behavior?* the reward of pineapple cake

3. *What do Victor and his mother do after the wedding ceremony?* take a cab to the wedding reception

4. *Describe the people who travel with them.* a tall, thin man and his short, fat wife

5. *What unusual event occurs?* The man who shared the cab suddenly dies.

6. *What happens to Victor's pineapple cake at the end of the story?* His mother eats it.

UNDERSTANDING THE STORY: POSSIBLE ANSWERS

1. *Opening sentence* The story's opening—"Victor was a nervous rather than rebellious child"—foreshadows the nonantagonistic relationship that exists between Victor and his mother.

2. *Success and satisfaction* Mrs. Fernandez is not satisfied with success because she sees life as a series of stressful events, and she makes no connection between the success of past events and the success of future events. For example, Victor's good behavior at the church does not assure Mrs. Fernandez that Victor will behave properly during the cab ride and at the wedding reception. Each event of the day—procuring a cab, handling the payment (or nonpayment) of the cab driver, and finding a seat at the wedding reception—is stressful for Mrs. Fernandez.

3. *Characterization of Mrs. Fernandez* Mrs. Fernandez feels insecure in this social environment. She is impressed by signs of wealth, appears to have no friends, and seems to feel she is on the fringe of society. As a result, she is nervous about Victor's behavior, and she constantly strives to impress others with her manners.

4. *Victor as "man"* Mrs. Fernandez addresses Victor as "man" to motivate him to behave like a boy who is older than he is.

5. *Response of the bride's mother to the crisis* The "Why Me?" response of the bride's mother to the guest's death is a realistic thought. However, voicing such a response is so socially inappropriate that it becomes an example of black humor.

6. *Role of the pineapple cake* Pineapple cake takes center stage in this story because it is the carrot that Mrs. Fernandez holds before Victor as he copes with the boring events of the day. In the end, Victor is unable to eat his well-earned piece of cake because the death of a wedding guest has aroused his interest and destroyed his appetite. Once Victor refuses the cake, it becomes Mrs. Fernandez's reward for tolerating the stresses of the wedding.

7. *Characterization of Victor* The following scenes characterize Victor:
   - In church, Victor behaves like all other boys his age who have been "threatened or bribed into docility."
   - After the church service, Victor fantasizes about escaping from his mother's grasp and speed skating to the reception ahead of the others. However, he realizes the foolishness of his thoughts.
   - When Victor leaves the cab, he is tempted by the wonders of the Bombay harbor; however, Victor curbs his childish thoughts by exerting a mature sense of responsibility. (The fact that Mrs. Fernandez worries that Victor will wet his pants reveals that he is probably about four years old.)
   - Victor finds the man's death to be both frightening and fascinating. Although he cannot muster the appetite to enjoy his pineapple cake, he is fascinated by how the corpse is carried away, and he eagerly watches for the arrival of the hearse.

8. *Desai's favorite character* Desai reveals great sympathy for both characters. Student opinion will vary about her preference.

ANALYZING LITERARY TECHNIQUE: POSSIBLE ANSWERS

1. *Significance of the opening sentence* The opening sentence prepares the reader for the lack of a protagonist/antagonist conflict in the story. Mrs. Fernandez, although worried about her son's behavior, encourages and praises Victor. When Victor fantasizes about escaping from his mother, he thinks about being independent only for a brief time.

2. *The settings* Desai's intent is to enable her readers to visualize the social scenes in which Victor and his mother find themselves. Therefore, Desai makes language function as a camera lens, enabling readers to see the humor, satire, and black humor that are present.

3. *Narrative style* Desai alternates between the objectivity of a photographer and the subjectivity of an author who has limited omniscience. As a photographer, she records the visual and aural details. As an author with limited omniscience, she uses interior monologue to express the thoughts and feelings of the characters.

*4. *Imagist writer* Desai uses concrete images rather than abstractions to sharpen her focus on a variety of subjects. The details clarify the whole picture.
   a) *Similes*
      - When the boys shut their eyes, it was "as if half the candles in church had gone out."

- Victor was "like some underground creature, an infant mole, trying to make out what went on outside its burrow."
- The mother's gloves were "like fresh bandages."
- The sound was "as of a choked drain being forced."
- The head was hanging "as though dangling at the end of a rope."
- Head and shoes were "dangling like stuffed paper bags."
- Victor stared "as though it [the pastry dish] were the corpse on the red rexine sofa."

b) *Metaphors*

- The eyes of the little boys at the wedding "were the eyes of prisoners."
- The wedding guests were a "lake of breathless witnesses."
- Victor and his mother "were streaming out with the tide."
- For Victor's mother, "the party atmosphere began quickly to dissolve in the acid of bad temper."
- "The frog in his throat [that is, the adam's apple of the man in the cab] gurgled to itself."
- "Vases marched up the centres of the tables, sprouting [flowers]."
- "The knot of guests . . . loosened and came apart."

c) *Colors*

- Victor's "purple velvet shorts"
- "frocks like crêpe-paper bells of pink and orange"
- "the grey padre in his faded purple [robe]"
- "a silver basket full of [pink paper flowers]"
- "the purple net frock"
- "purple hands"
- "pink and silver gauzes" (mother-of-the-bride's dress)
- "the red rexine sofa"

d) *Adjectives and nouns*

- "loud breathing *bottled* inside his chest"
- "what made his shoes so *vicious*"
- "face gleamed with *fanatic* self-importance"
- "the *acid* of bad temper"
- "dreadfully *new* ones [gloves] of *crackling* nylon lace"
- "*slippery-smooth* waiter"
- "head hanging . . . in a curiously *unhinged* way"
- "a long, *ripping* groan"
- "her mouth gave an *impatient* twitch"

e) *Verbs and adverbs*
  - "new shoes that *bit* his toes"
  - "*crepitating* [crackling] with excited little girls"
  - "silence *straining in their chests, soundlessly clamouring*"
  - "*swiveled* his head about on the top of it [his neck]"
  - guests "*rustled* about"
  - "wiping her mouth *primly*"

5. *Plot development*
  - *Crisis* Mrs. Fernandez experiences a series of crises, each of which is tolerably resolved: Victor's behavior in church, the acquisition of the cab and the payment for it, and the seating arrangement at the reception.
  - *Climax* The climax of the story occurs when Victor finds that, because of the guest's death, he does not want his hard-earned prize of pineapple cake.
  - *Resolution* The issue is resolved when Mrs. Fernandez eats the cake for him.

6. *Significance of the title* "Pineapple Cake" is an appropriate title because the anticipation of the pineapple cake is what motivates Victor to please his mother. Throughout the day Mrs. Fernandez encourages Victor by reminding him that the time for his prize is approaching. Therefore, it is ironic that when the cake is finally set before Victor, the man's death has taken away Victor's appetite. Mrs. Fernandez's choosing to eat the cake herself is a fitting conclusion to a humorous story.

*7. *Humor and satire* Examples of humor and satire include the following:
  a) *Satire:*
    - the unwillingness of the adults to pay for the taxi ride
    - Mrs. Fernandez's determination that Victor's pineapple cake should not go to waste
  b) *Humor:*
    - Mrs. Fernandez's annoyed expression as she observes Victor's perspiration
    - Victor's fantasy of escaping from his mother's hold, "breaking into a toy shop for skates and speeding ahead of the whole caravan on a magic pair, to arrive at Green's before the bride, losing his mother on the way"
    - the taxi ride, with descriptions of the shake of the woman's bottom and the man's adam's apple
    - the three adults who try "to be polite and yet not pay the taxi"
    - Mrs. Fernandez as she forks Victor's pineapple cake onto her own plate, eats it quickly, and wipes her mouth primly

c) *Black humor:*

- The mother of the bride groans, "Oh, why did it have to happen *today?* Couldn't he have gone into another day?"
- The reception schedule continues as if no tragedy has occurred. The waiters bring the wedding dessert just as the corpse of the wedding guest is carried from the room.

WRITING ABOUT LITERATURE

1. *Essay analyzing tone* Call students' attention to the directions in the textbook assignment with regard to (a) humor; (b) satire; and (c) black humor. (See **A.L.T.** question 7 above.) **AP**

2. *Essay analyzing images* Call students' attention to the directions in the textbook assignment with regard to similes, metaphors, colors, adjectives, and verbs. (See **A.L.T.** question 4 above.) **AP**

3. *Creative writing: a social function* Call students' attention to the directions in the textbook assignment with regard to the use of figurative language, adjectives, and verbs that convey the atmosphere of the scene. **(P.L.J.)**

FURTHER READING

Desai, Anita, *Games at Twilight and Other Stories; The Village by the Sea; Clear Light of Day.*

A Way of Talking

PATRICIA GRACE

INTRODUCING THE STORY

The subject of "A Way of Talking" is the power of language. Throughout the story, the remarks that people make—either intentionally or unintentionally—communicate their attitudes and values. Depending on the particular circumstances, their use of language either celebrates their commonality or highlights their differences. It either draws the others in and gives them verbal hugs, or it pushes them away and gives them a verbal cold shoulder. Language expresses a person's mind and heart, both in this story and in the real world.

"A Way of Talking" demonstrates how groups of people develop ways of expressing themselves that connect and bind them to each other, such as by using jokes that remind each of them of notable experiences that they have shared. These experiences may be painful, embarrassing, amusing, or comforting. Often these remarks create a line between those who are members of their particular group (the insiders) and those who are not (the outsiders), as outsiders are often unaware of how other groups use the language that everyone shares. Outsiders may not understand the vocabulary, or they may understand it but not recognize what is funny. In fact, outsiders are in a foreign environment, and they are listening to a foreign language.

In "A Way of Talking," Rose has returned from college to visit her family, and the reader watches her function in two worlds, the world of the Pakeha and her own world of the Maori. Both at home and away, Rose is a Maori in a predominantly Pakeha environment. However, at her college, the Maori students have become conscious of their own nationality. They may have organized themselves and have staged marches and demonstrations on campus in order to protest their unequal treatment by Pakeha administrators and teachers. The Maori want the Pakeha majority to respect them and to appreciate both the humanity that both groups share and the diversity that provides an enriching contrast. It has become fashionable for a Pakeha to have a friend who is Maori, but Rose and her classmates view the current fashion as merely decorative clothing and Pakeha taste as certainly fickle.

Rose, like the other members of her family, has been deeply hurt by the barbs of the Pakeha—their slurs, their stereotyping, and the social, economic, and political barriers that they have erected. However, whereas Rose's family has been afraid to say or do anything that might call negative attention to themselves and provoke members of the Pakeha to treat them in an even more unfair and hurtful way, Rose has always used her tongue—her only weapon—in order to fight back.

Pakeha comments about the Maori people anger Hera, Rose's older sister, as well as Rose. However, Rose's imprudent responses to such provocative comments have always embarrassed Hera. Rose behaves true to form when a Pakeha dressmaker refers to Maori workmen in a manner that leaves them nameless.

However, later, Hera suddenly realizes that Rose speaks out because the way that Pakehas treat Maori people hurts her. Once Hera understands Rose's behavior, she becomes determined to support Rose verbally—even though she is shy and inarticulate in English.

Personal Literary Journal: Have you ever experienced prejudice because of your gender, race, religion, nationality, or economic class? If so, how has this prejudice expressed itself? How have you felt about it? How have you dealt with it?

How do you, your family, and your friends use language to affirm your close relationship? Of what common experiences do you remind each other in order to share your laughter? What jokes affirm your commonality?

To what extent, if any, do you refer to outsiders by ethnic names or tell jokes about people of a different background? Give examples. When do you do this? What purpose(s) does it serve?

Literary Terms: characterization, foreshadowing, irony, metaphor, point of view, setting, theme, tone

COMPREHENSION QUESTIONS

1. *Of what group of people are Hera and her family members?* Maori
2. *Where does Rose usually spend her time?* college
3. *Where is she when this story takes place?* at home

4. *Where do Hera and Rose go together, and why?* to Mrs. Frazer's, the dress-maker, to fit a dress for Hera's wedding

5. *What problem arises there?* Mrs. Frazer does not know the names of her husband's Maori workmen/scrubcutters.

6. *Who speaks out about it, and why?* Rose is hurt by Pakeha insensitivity to Maori feelings.

7. *Why will this not become a serious problem?* fashionable for a Pakeha to have a Maori as a friend

8. *Give one example of how the narrator's family treats the Pakeha as the Pakeha treat the narrator's people.* Hera's family says "Pakeha doctor" and "the Pakeha at the post office" instead of knowing and using their given names.

9. *List two qualities that the Pakeha in the story value in the narrator's people.* friendly; natural; clean

10. *Of what in the Pakeha's family is the narrator critical?* Mrs. Frazer permits her children to jump up and down on the family's sofa.

11. *Choose two adjectives that describe the relationships in the narrator's family.* loving/caring; fun-loving

12. *What change occurs at the end of the story?* Hera decides to support Rose and the Maori people in their relationships with Pakehas and to let Rose know that she will do so.

UNDERSTANDING THE STORY: POSSIBLE ANSWERS

1. *Effect of Rose's college experiences* Rose's college experiences may involve participating in marches and demonstrations designed to call attention to the lack of equality experienced by the Maori, who are native New Zealanders but a minority among the Pakeha. Historically, Rose has always been smart and sassy in her relationships with Pakehas. However, college has made her more sophisticated about the inequality of the Maori-Pakeha situation and more of an activist in her attitudes and behavior.

2. *Significance of scrubcutters* Mrs. Frazer does not know the name of the scrubcutters who work for her husband because they are workmen and are not social friends or businessmen of equal social or economic status. Rose thinks that it is because they are Maori, but the Frazers would probably regard Pakeha scrubcutters in the same way and for the same reasons.

   In our country today—and in other countries, as well—this difference is revealed in the use of first and last names. Employers and teachers often call their respective employees and students by their first names while those employees and students are expected, out of respect for their superiors, to call their employers and teachers by their last names. This social pattern is based on the assumption that older, more knowledgeable, wealthier, and/or more powerful people deserve more respect than those who are younger, less competent, poorer, and/or weaker. This convention is based upon an aristocratic view of these relationships. In contrast, a democratic view emphasizes the basic equality of all who are human and considers all human beings entitled to respect unless they speak and/or act in a way that destroys their entitlement.

3. *Rose's response to Mrs. Frazer* Rose tells Mrs. Frazer exactly what she thinks because she wants to make Mrs. Frazer aware that the Maori people are not inferior to Pakehas and are entitled to the same sensitivity and respect.

   Not only does Rose feel better when she addresses Mrs. Frazer's insult to her people, but she also has nothing to lose by embarrassing Mrs. Frazer. Rose knows that Mrs. Frazer is pleased that the Maori people value the fact that she does something (dressmaking) better than they could do it themselves. Rose also knows that, in Mrs. Frazer's group, it is fashionable to have a Maori for a friend. Therefore, the relationship between Mrs. Frazer and Rose's family will continue, unharmed by Rose's outspoken remarks.

4. *Fashion and Pakeha stereotyping of Maori* Fashion is fickle in that what is in fashion is here today and gone tomorrow. Therefore, if it is fashionable for a Pakeha to have a Maori for a friend, this friendship is not a sincere, permanent, reciprocal relationship. It is based upon what other Pakehas currently value rather than upon an individual Pakeha's independent judgment, and the relationship is totally from the Pakeha point of view.

   To stereotype an individual is to view that person as being identical to everyone else in that person's particular group (that particular group's being distinguished by its gender, age, nationality, religion, race, social or economic class, or political way of thinking).

   To stereotype a group is to view everyone in that group as being identical to everyone else in that group in terms of attitudes, values, and behavior.

   According to Rose, Pakehas who have a Maori friend characterize all Maori as "lovely people," "so *friendly*" and "so *natural*" and all their homes as "absolutely *spotless*." This is a positive stereotype; however, these Pakeha attitudes also reveal a negative stereotypical view of the Maori in that they imply that most Pakehas view the Maori people as dirty, unintelligent natives who are silent and withdrawn—at least when they are not at home.

5. *Hera's self-consciousness* Rose's way of saying what she thinks to the Pakehas embarrasses Hera because it makes Hera feel self-conscious of the fact that she is a Maori and, therefore, considered inferior to a Pakeha. Since the Pakeha consider the Maori to be of a lower social and economic class, Hera feels that Rose is delivering a blow to her (Hera's) self-esteem.

   Hera is also self-conscious about the fact that many among the Maori people are prejudiced toward Pakehas.

6. *Maori attitudes toward Pakehas* Rose denies that the Maori people and the Pakeha are prejudiced against each other. She tells Hera that only the older Maori generation, which has grown up with such prejudice, and Maori children, who are too young to know better, are prejudiced against Pakehas. She declares that, in contrast, the attitudes of their own age group are more tolerant.

Students may wonder whether Rose, being a Maori, is putting a better face on Maori attitudes toward Pakehas than is actually the situation.

7. *Hera's sulking* Hera's sulking is her way of reacting with an angry silence to situations that demean her and her people. Because she feels unable to respond with intelligence and wit to situations that reveal the Pakeha prejudice against the Maori, and she feels unable to cope with the response of the Pakeha should she call attention to their prejudice, she says nothing at all.

8. *Hera's change of mind* Hera changes her mind about how to deal with the Pakehas' prejudice once she realizes that Rose's confrontational words hide the deep injury that their prejudice has inflicted upon her. Moreover, because she is in a politically, socially, and economically powerless position, Rose's tongue is the only weapon she has with which to strike back.

    Hera also realizes that her silence and that of her family have left Rose to stand alone and attempt to deal with a problem that, in fact, their entire family shares but has been too frightened to confront. Therefore, they have all been very unfair to Rose when they have permitted her to carry such a burden alone.

9. *Hera's difficulty in changing* Hera thinks that she will find it difficult to change because she has never learned to defend herself. Such behavior has been unnecessary within her own loving family, and, in the world of the Pakeha, it has been viewed as inappropriate and dangerous in that it would invite unpleasant and harmful consequences.

    Moreover, unlike Rose, Hera also is not comfortable and clever with the English language. Therefore, in the world of the Pakeha, she is shy and inarticulate.

10. *Prejudice* This story reveals subtle forms of prejudice against the Maori people, often in the form of attitudes and behavior that are so accepted in the Pakeha world that Pakehas do not recognize them as prejudicial.

    Other forms of prejudice include those against particular races, religions, nationalities, social or economic classes, and groups categorized by gender or by age.

ANALYZING LITERARY TECHNIQUE: POSSIBLE ANSWERS

1. *First paragraph; foreshadowing* The first paragraph foreshadows that Rose's intelligent but inappropriate responses will be the subject of this story. Rose's sister describes her as always being outspoken ("talks all the time flat out") and as "the hard-case one" and "the kamakama one" in the family.

    The fact that members of Rose's family call her by a different name (Rohe, instead of Rose) foreshadows the possibility of prejudice against a group in which English is a second language.

2. *Setting* Grace reveals the story's setting by providing many examples of "local color" that reveal the story's location. Because the title and subject

of the story is the importance of language, the examples of local color all involve the use of language.

a) Characters' names are Maori: Rohe, Matiu, and Heke, and members of Hera's family usually speak in their native language, which is not English, or in their own version of the English language. For example, Hera explains: "That's the lovely way she has of talking, Nanny, when she speaks in English."

b) Certain words are Maori: *kamakama; hoha; Pakeha* and *Pakehafied; E ta.*

c) Certain expressions are a Maori form of English: Dad to Hera: "You'll stand on your lip." Nanny: "The mouths steal the time of the eyes." A teacher: ". . . how and when to say your minds." Heke: "Be the day."

d) The Maori way of saying something negative as a compliment when they actually mean the opposite: "The bread's terrible . . ." "How awful the corn [is]."

e) The Maori way of saying the opposite of what is true as a form of humor: "Let your hardworking father and your two hardworking brothers starve. Eat up." "Come on, my fat Rohe. Move over and make room for your daddy."

3. *Point of view* Grace takes the reader into the Maori world by relating this story from the point of view of a Maori young woman. The reader joins her and her sister as they converse with one another as well as when they are with their family and with the Pakeha dressmaker. Through them, the reader gains insight into some of their attitudes and values—toward each other, toward their family, and toward the larger, Pakeha world in which they live.

   This technique is successful because Pakehas do not view the Maori and themselves as the Maori view themselves and the Pakehas. Therefore, the only way to discover the Maori world is to view it through the eyes and ears of a Maori.

4. *Characterization* Grace enables her readers to know something about what it is like to be a Maori through her characters' attitudes, values, and decisions as well as by how Pakehas respond to them. It is clear that Grace's characters are loving, fun-loving, intelligent people to whom family is very important.

   It is also clear that the Maori and the Pakeha are not well integrated in New Zealand society. Rose and Hera are angry that they are victims of the hurtful arrows of Pakeha prejudice. They are proud of their own people and are critical of the Pakeha, who have stereotypical views of them.

   Pakehas appear to respond to the Maori in one of two ways. Some Pakehas are prejudiced against the Maori, viewing all of them as dirty, unintelligent, taciturn natives. Other Pakehas consider themselves to be liberal and conform to the fashion in liberal circles of choosing to have a Pakeha as a friend. These Pakehas view their Maori friends with an equally stereotypical and therefore unrealistic view—that the Maori are all friendly, natural, intelligent, and clean.

5. *Irony*

a) It is ironic that Mrs. Frazer is not aware that her attitude toward people's names, such as not knowing the names of her husband's Maori workers, humiliates the Maori people. However, while Rose interprets this as an anti-Maori prejudice, it could just as easily reflect broader class differences that are reflected in traditional modes of behavior. For example, even if her husband's employees were Pakeha, Mrs. Frazer probably would not know their names. Moreover, among the Pakeha, employers usually call their employees by their first names, whereas employees are often expected to call their employers by their surnames. This is actually another subtle form of prejudice because it assumes that employers are entitled to more respect than that to which their employees are entitled.

b) It is ironic to a Pakeha that Rose's family—through which Grace probably typifies Maori attitudes and behavior—appreciates by condemning. Ironic sarcasm condemns by appreciating in such a way that the underlying condemnation is clear to the listener. However, here, the situation is the opposite. Rose's family declares how much they like something by deriding it, and the worse they profess it to be, the better they actually think it is. Similarly, Rose's father calls her fat, although she is thin, and his baby although she is a young adult. The Maori would not find this practice ironic since they are accustomed to it and accept it as reflecting harmonious and lighthearted family relationships. It is only ironic to those who are unfamiliar with it and who might, at first, take their words literally and be amazed at the apparent rudeness of one Maori family member to one another.

6. *Tone* Grace achieves a rainbow of tones in this story—hostile, embarrassed, proud, loving, and humorous—all through the different uses of words. Rose is hostile to the point of being borderline belligerent about the way the Pakeha automatically view and treat members of the Maori people. Yet, among members of her own close-knit family, she easily returns to the comfortable and loving give-and-take of family humor. Hera is embarrassed about Rose's attitudes and behavior toward the Pakeha until she finally understands them. Both sisters are proud to be members of the Maori people. However, until the end of the story, it is Rose alone who asserts this pride when she is among the Pakeha.

*7. *Significance of the title* The title, "A Way of Talking," expresses the subject of the story—the power of language. Throughout the story, the remarks that people make—either consciously or unintentionally—communicate their attitudes and values. Depending on the particular circumstances, their use of language either celebrates their commonality or highlights their differences. It either draws the others in and gives them verbal hugs, or it pushes them away and gives them a verbal cold shoulder. Language expresses a person's mind and heart, both in this story and in the real world.

"A Way of Talking" demonstrates how groups of people develop ways of expressing themselves that connect and bind them to each other, such as by using jokes that remind each of them of notable experiences that they have shared. These experiences may be painful, embarrassing, amusing, or comforting. Often these remarks create a line between those who are members of their particular group (the insiders) and those who are not part of their group (the outsiders). Outsiders are often unaware of how other groups, among themselves, use the language that everyone shares. Therefore, should outsiders hear insiders' speaking to one another, they (outsiders) will not understand their (insiders') use of language. Outsiders may not understand the vocabulary, or they may understand it but not recognize what is funny. In fact, outsiders are in a foreign environment, and they are listening to a foreign language.

8. *Themes* Possible themes:
   - Many prejudices are socially accepted ways of treating other people.
   - Prejudice can be so subtle that people are not aware of their own prejudice.
   - Prejudice is passed along from one generation to another without necessarily being taught.
   - Language both brings people together and separates them.
   - Understanding why people behave as they do can enable others to change their own attitudes and behavior.
   - Social relationships create insiders and outsiders, based on such divisions as family, nationality, race, religion, economic class, and social class.
   - Most people feel more comfortable with people with whom they have important attitudes and values in common.

9. *Resolution of issues* Grace resolves one issue set forth in this story, that of Hera's silence. Once Hera realizes that Rose copes with her own hurt feelings by responding in a forthright and assertive manner to Pakehas who reveal their anti-Maori prejudices, Hera determines to support her sister by expressing herself as well.

   However, the issue of anti-Maori prejudice is not resolved. Grace hopes that writing stories about the Maori people in English for a Pakeha audience will introduce readers to the Maori, make this audience feel more comfortable with them, and therefore come to accept them. This is a valuable form of education, and it is very important. Once people recognize shared attitudes and values, they have a greater respect for each other and can build friendships on a firm foundation.

WRITING ABOUT LITERATURE

1. *Essay analyzing the significance of the title* Call students' attention to the directions in the textbook assignment with regard to the multiple uses of language, the use of quotations, and related significance. (See **A.L.T.** question 7 above.)

2. *Creative writing: a story in which a character is both an insider and an outsider*
   Call students' attention to the directions in the textbook assignment.
   (P.L.J.)

FURTHER READING

Grace, Patricia, (short stories) *Waiariki and Other Stories; The Dream Sleepers and Other Stories; Electric City and Other Stories; Selected Stories; The Sky People;* (novels) *Mutuwhenua: The Moon Sleeps; Potiki; Cousins; Baby No-Eyes; Dogside Story.*

1. *Grief manifests itself in various ways, as evidenced by many of the selections in this unit. Describe the way grief plays out in the actions of the speakers or main characters in three selections in this unit. Use quotations from each selection to support your ideas.* In the poem "Wuling chun," the speaker's loss of interest in life and inability to move past her pain show her grief. Grief in this poem is heavy and tangible—the speaker does not even have the energy to comb her hair. In "Prince Huo's Daughter," grief is manifest in Jade's melodramatic reaction when Li breaks his pact with her. She refuses to leave her house, makes herself sick, and finally dies at his feet. In "Downtown," grief has a positive outcome in that it renews Ryo's commitment to "make it" in Tokyo and to provide for herself and Ryukichi. The Boss in "The Fly" deals with his grief over his son's death in World War I by denying that he feels any grief and by exhibiting an underlying cruelty that leads him first to test Woodifield by making him drink and then to test the fly by challenging it with ink. The communists' grief when facing their deaths in "A Certain Night" leads to greater resolve and commitment to communism. They die singing a political song to demonstrate this resolve to the nationalists.

2. *Various philosophies of life are expressed in selections such as "Say Who I Am," "Not all the sum of earthly happiness," "The Rich Eat Three Full Meals," and* The Post Office. *Describe the philosophies of life expressed in three of these selections. How are these beliefs conveyed? Are the speakers in these selections simply expressing their own beliefs, or are they trying to persuade the reader to their way of thinking?* The speaker in "Say Who I Am" views himself as an integral part of the universe, united with his surroundings. He believes that both positive and negative aspects of life are essential and that a common spirit runs through everything. The speaker of "Not all the sum of earthly happiness" lives by the philosophy that wealth does not equal happiness and that living in harmony as a beggar is better than living in fear or with greed. Peace is the main philosophy of "The Rich Eat Three Full Meals." The speaker, while noting the great disparity between the rich and the poor, concludes that peace is the essential element in life. The philosophy of *The Post Office* is manifest in Amal, who appreciates the minutiae of daily life and longs to do tasks that other people find menial or boring. He brings happiness to his friends by pointing out that joy can be found in simple things.

3. *In "Fighting South of the Ramparts" and "A Certain Night," Li Po and Ting Ling respond to political situations in their country. Discuss the effectiveness of taking on political questions in literature. What are the advantages and the disadvantages of this approach?* A country's political climate often has great impact on the lives of its citizens. Literature is a powerful medium for expressing political concerns, and it has proved to be an effective one. Many great works have influenced government (*The Communist Manifesto*),

social reform (*Cry, the Beloved Country*), discrimination (*Native Son*), and sexism (*The Second Sex*). Chinese politics at the times of Li Po and Ting Ling were extremely controversial. In "Fighting South of the Ramparts," Li Po expresses his anger at the T'ang government for having more interest in expanding Chinese borders than in providing for the well-being and happiness of its citizens. The poem explores the effect of the Han war policy on Chinese peasants and their families, which Li Po wants his readers to correlate to the policy of the T'ang dynasty. Ting Ling envisions her husband's death in "A Certain Night," a death she believes was for a noble political purpose. The story's premise that the political movement takes precedence over the good of the individual is effective political propaganda.

4. *The point of view of the narrator of a story affects the reader's perception of the action in the story. Discuss how the narrator's perspective influences the way the reader perceives the story lines of three of the following short stories: "In a Grove," "A Way of Talking," "Pineapple Cake," and "The Grasshopper and the Bell Cricket."* The plot of "In a Grove" relies on the points of view of witnesses at a trial, and their versions of the same event vary dramatically. The mystery and intrigue of Akutagawa's story stems from this multiplicity. Hera, who narrates "A Way of Talking," relates how she finally came to understand her sister, Rose. Hera's point of view is essential to the story because it lets the reader understand what Hera thinks of Rose, what shocks her about Rose, and why she responds emotionally to Rose's outspokenness. The third-person omniscient narration of "Pineapple Cake" allows the reader to know both Victor's and Mrs. Fernandez's thoughts, envision the setting of the wedding and Green's, and see the guests' reactions to the death. The broad focus is ideal for relating this story because a first-person narration would have allowed for the thoughts of only one character. The third-person point of view of "The Grasshopper and the Bell Cricket" allows the narrator to observe Fujio's wish to give Kiyoko the insect, the play of light on Fujio's and Kiyoko's kimonos, and the excitement of the children. A child narrator would not be sophisticated enough to appreciate the feelings and symbolism of the events.

South and Central America

219

Vicarious Love

SOR JUANA INÉS DE LA CRUZ

INTRODUCING THE POEM

In "Vicarious Love," Sor Juana Inés de la Cruz contrasts infatuation with true love. She begins by exposing the shallowness of those who are looking for worship and admiration. They "covet" admiration, they "protest to Fortune" if not enough admirers come along, and they feel "cheated" if they don't get enough attention. By contrast, the speaker wants to be loved and valued for herself, by "one who feels [her love] cannot be replaced," rather than worshiped as "a deity." She wants love that will grow over time rather than admiration that will fade as age sets in. And the moderation that she prizes is reflected in her statement that "one pinch too much or little spoils love's taste."

The sonnet is an excellent structure for a contrast of this type. An Italian, or Petrarchan, sonnet contains two ideas, with a change in attitude (the volta) between the octave and the sestet. In the first eight lines, Sor Juana describes what women usually want. In the last six lines, she reveals what she wants, which is in direct contrast to what others want. The shift in tone and the figurative language mimic her message.

Personal Literary Journal: Do you agree with the speaker of the poem that "Love's delicacy consists in being loved; / one pinch too much or little spoils love's taste"? Think about whether you'd prefer many admirers or just one and explain why.

Literary Terms: apostrophe, contrast, metaphor, sonnet, tone

COMPREHENSION QUESTIONS

1. *What do the "pretty women" want?* every man to worship them
2. *What does the speaker have no use for?* "throngs of suitors"
3. *What does the speaker want?* one man who loves and values her

UNDERSTANDING THE POEM: POSSIBLE ANSWERS

1. *Pretty women feel cheated* when only one man admires them
2. *"Being a deity"* being entreated by many suitors rather than one true love
3. *What the speaker values* moderation
4. *"Love's increase"* True love grows over time; it is contrasted with infatuation, which is shallow.
5. *Title* Sor Juana is a nun, and so she is not able to be in a romantic relationship. Thus, the conversation with Fabio about love is purely theoretical.

ANALYZING LITERARY TECHNIQUE: POSSIBLE ANSWERS

*1. *Structure of the sonnet* It is a Petrarchan, or Italian, sonnet. The sonnet has an octet and a sestet.

*2. *Tone* The tone at the beginning of the sonnet is ironic and mildly disdainful. The tone at the end is earnest and slightly wistful. The shift in tone relates to the poem's structure as a sonnet; the tone in a Petrarchan sonnet changes between the octet and the sestet.

3. *Metaphors* The poet uses religious metaphors to describe what "pretty women" want. These women want "worship" from all men. They are unhappy unless their "altars" are overloaded with the men who worship them. The pretty women see themselves as deities.

4. *Contrast* The speaker notes that while the other women want many suitors, she wants only one man who will love and appreciate her. While the other women want altars groaning with "the weight of victims," the speaker refers to "Love's delicacy." The other women want to be entreated and worshiped, while the speaker wants to be loved.

5. *Apostrophe* The function of the absent Fabio, to whom the poem is addressed, is to give the poem immediacy and intimacy. The reader feels that he or she is listening in on a conversation in which the speaker is pouring out her heart to a friend.

WRITING ABOUT LITERATURE

1. *Essay analyzing the structure of the sonnet* Remind students of the directions in the textbook assignment. Encourage them to use quotations from the sonnet to illustrate their points. (See **A.L.T.** questions 1 and 2 above.)

2. *Creative writing: sonnet or poem about preferences for being loved* Remind students of the directions in the textbook assignment. Suggest that students imagine that they are in the midst of a conversation with a friend. Ask them to make sure to respond to Sor Juana's point that "Love's delicacy consists in being loved; / one pinch too much or little spoils love's taste" (lines 13–14). **(P.L.J.)**

Serene Words

GABRIELA MISTRAL

INTRODUCING THE POEM

The appeal of "Serene Words" is its comforting tone, its emphasis on the beauty of the natural world, and its use of language. The beauty of nature reminds Mistral that life, despite its problems, is a good experience. Nature, like a mother and God, is a source of joy and comfort in the face of pain, sorrow, and death.

The source of "Serene Words," the collection *Desolation* (1922, with significant revisions in the 1923 and 1926 editions), includes some of Mistral's finest early work. Three of the book's four sections draw a picture of life as a lonely, sorrowful experience, a picture that has much in common with existentialism. However, Mistral's existentialism is softened both by her feelings (especially feelings of love and desire) and by her strong belief in Christianity. The final section of *Desolation* is filled with striking images of cold and deserted landscapes. These images often identify the landscape, or the world, with women. Most of the poems in the collection follow a similar structure: A series of items are compared in each stanza, with the final stanza unifying all of the images. Mistral's poetic language is intentionally simple and close to the spoken word.

Personal Literary Journal: What do you value most in life? Why? What decisions have your values affected? Who or what gives you comfort when you need it (for example, a person, a pet, a book, an exercise, or a piece of music)?

Literary Terms: connotative language, contrast, figurative language, lyric

COMPREHENSION QUESTIONS

1. *How old is the speaker in this poem?* middle-aged
2. *What does the speaker compare life to?* nature
3. *What is the speaker's attitude toward life?* positive: beauty and love compensate for pain and death

UNDERSTANDING THE POEM: POSSIBLE ANSWERS

1. *Attitude toward good and evil* The speaker sets life's advantages and disadvantages side-by-side and decides that love and the beauty of nature can make one forget fatigue, sadness, pain, and death. The power of love and of nature's great beauty makes life good. Faith and love protect people from harm, and they temper death's sting.

2. *Experiences; sources of emotional support* The poem suggests that many experiences, especially those related to nature, shape people's ideas and values. Possibilities include a field of wheat (line 3), blooming violets (lines 7–8), a lily (line 12), a brook (line 14), and a skylark's song (lines 15–16). Sources of support include love (lines 4, 18), a mother's care (line 19), and God (line 20).

3. *Connection between age and attitudes* A child or a senior citizen might be more likely to emphasize either the positive or the negative in life. The child lives in the present and has limited experience. The senior citizen, who may be in declining health, has a lifetime of memories.

ANALYZING LITERARY TECHNIQUE: POSSIBLE ANSWERS

*1. *Function of contrast* Mistral juxtaposes words that are connected with life (nature, farming) with those that are connected with death (war, sadness). Her choice of language changes what could be a complex philosophical discussion into an experience that all people can understand. The juxtaposition of opposites enhances the examples of love and nature as powerful positive experiences. Responses will vary as to which contrasts are most effective, such as thirst and the twisting hillside versus the lily (lines 11–12), or the skylark's song versus death (lines 15–16). In the last stanza, lack of contrast creates a mood that is unconditionally positive. Love brings peace, and death is simply a form of sleep.

*2. *Connotative language* Mistral's word choices convey the joy of life. Examples include "a flower's freshness" (line 2), "a smiling verse" (line 5), "heavenly violets" (line 7), "the man who breaks into song" (line 10), "a skylark's song bursting heavenward" (line 15), and "God is putting me to sleep" (line 20).

*3. *Figurative language* Mistral's use of metaphor and personification conveys the beauty of life through the beauty of nature. Examples include "I glean / this truth . . . : / life is the gold and sweetness of wheat" (lines 1–3), "the wind blows a honeyed breath" (line 8), and "a lily can ensnare our gaze" (line 12).

4. *Lyric poem* "Serene Words" is a lyric poem in that it expresses the personal mood of the speaker. It also emphasizes pictorial detail rather than a story.

WRITING ABOUT LITERATURE

1. *Essay analyzing contrast* Call students' attention to the directions and suggestions in the textbook assignment with regard to content and organization. Remind them of the importance of using quotations. (See **A.L.T.** questions 1, 2, and 3 above.) **AP**

2. *Creative writing: a poem about comfort* Call students' attention to the directions in the textbook assignment. Remind them of the importance of detail. **(P.L.J.)**

FURTHER READING

Mistral, Gabriela, *Selected Poems of Gabriela Mistral.*

The Tree

MARÍA LUISA BOMBAL

INTRODUCING THE STORY

"The Tree" is a story of life without love. It describes a young woman's thoughts about her younger self and her past marriage as she listens to a piano recital. Brígida's fantasy life responds to the various musical passages; it culminates, with the end of the concert, in greater self-knowledge. Bombal uses a combination of psychological and poetic devices to create this complex portrait of a young adult whose experience with criticism devastated her youth and adolescence and led her into a disastrous marriage.

Bombal tells Brígida's story by using a third-person narrator who enters Brígida's mind for most of the story. Bombal's choice of narrative perspective permits her to combine her interest in psychological realism with visually and symbolically textured settings.

The characteristics of each piece of music suggest the direction of Brígida's thoughts: Mozart's capricious spirit suggests thoughts of her own youth; Beethoven's rhythms evoke the development of frustration and disappointment in her marriage; and Chopin's sadness provokes her to dwell on her melancholy acceptance of her sterile married life.

Accompanying each musical selection is an appropriate symbol of water. Mozart's youthful vitality suggests the happy and youthful image of singing water in tall fountains. Beethoven's rhythms suggest the ebb and flow of the sea, which envelops and controls Brígida just as her marriage does. Finally Chopin's melancholy strains evoke the sadness and agitation of rain and symbolize Brígida's futile efforts to adjust to her marriage.

Once Brígida is involved with thoughts of her marriage, the tree outside her dressing-room window becomes the symbol of the fantasy life that made it possible for her to survive the sterility of her marriage. When the tree is suddenly removed, nothing can shield Brígida from the reality of her life. Paradoxically all her physical comforts do not bring happiness. She courageously confronts her emotional starvation and divorces Luis.

Bombal is considered a surrealist writer because of her interest in the human psyche, her use of unusual symbolism, and her striking use of language. One of Bombal's most striking images is Luis's description of Brígida as "a necklace of birds," which is doubly symbolic in that the birds reflect Brígida's personality and the necklace reflects her relationship to Luis.

Personal Literary Journal: What is your attitude toward failure? Do you prefer to aim high and risk not achieving your goals, or do you prefer to aim only for what you are certain that you can accomplish? What do you gain by the attempt? What do you lose by the failure? Which is better?

Literary Terms: characterization, connotative language, figurative language, irony, metaphor, narrative perspective, paradox, psychological realism, setting, surrealism, symbol

COMPREHENSION QUESTIONS

1. *Where does this story take place?* at a piano concert

2. *What is the first part of the story about?* Brígida's youth

3. *Describe Brígida's husband.* her father's friend; a workaholic businessperson

4. *Describe Brígida's marriage.* sterile; unloving

5. *What happens to Brígida's great source of comfort?* The tree is cut down.

UNDERSTANDING THE STORY: POSSIBLE ANSWERS

1. *Effect of the father's view of Brígida* Brígida's father gave her the impression that she was incapable of doing what others could do and that he expected no accomplishments from her. His view became a self-fulfilling prophecy. Brígida was happy not to worry about failing to meet the demands of others, though this meant she was considered stupid. At eighteen she is happy to be "a necklace of birds": silly, playful, and lazy.

   Brígida operates on the mistaken belief that she won't fail if she doesn't try. (It is mistaken because her lack of effort guarantees her failure.) She accepts the fact that others think that she is stupid, believing that they will not expect anything from her and that they will not be disappointed in her. The acceptance comes at great personal cost: Brígida leads a boring life, and she has no friends.

2. *"To be intelligent you should begin from childhood"* Brígida is correct to the extent that it is easier to begin when one is young, but motivation and effort can accomplish miracles. Also, since Brígida's insights into herself and Luis reveal that she is intelligent rather than "retarded," the comment reflects Brígida's low self-esteem.

3. *Why Brígida conceals her anger from Luis* Brígida fears confrontation because she risks criticism and the loss of Luis's acceptance. She responds like a child by taking refuge in the safety of sleep and silence. In this way Brígida inadvertently leads Luis to think that she no longer loves him, and she lays the foundation for the dissolution of their marriage.

4. *Brígida's problem with Luis* Brígida's problem is that Luis treats her like a child or an object rather than an adult. She wants to feel that he loves her and that her love is important to him. His question implies that he needs her love; however, his immediate acceptance of a loveless marriage destroys that possibility.

5. *"Always" and "never"* "Always": Life will always be irremediably mediocre. Luis will always ignore her needs. "Never": Life will never contain love, excitement, and joy. Luis will never love her.

6. *Brígida's philosophy about happiness* Brígida adopts this philosophy as a way of accepting the sterility of her marriage. However, when the tree is destroyed, Brígida confronts the quality of her life and rejects this philosophical rationalization. She divorces Luis and tries to create a more satisfying life for herself.

ANALYZING LITERARY TECHNIQUE: POSSIBLE ANSWERS

1. *Connection between setting and structure* The setting is a concert hall, and the nature of each musical selection determines the path of Brígida's thoughts. Bombal weaves the setting and structure so closely together that a stream of consciousness (a complex type of associative thinking) results as one thought leads to another.

2. *Narrative perspective* The third-person narrator spends most of her time in Brígida's mind, giving the reader an intimate insight into Brígida's personality. However, because the narrator is separate from Brígida, the narrator is also able to provide striking descriptive passages that give the story added depth and texture.

3. *Irony* It is ironic that Brígida is far more intelligent than she thinks she is. Her insights into people's lives, the condition of happiness, and her own needs are very sophisticated. She is sensitive and creative, as evidenced by her imaginative responses to the music and to the tree.

*4. *Music as symbol* Mozart's felicitous and capricious music evokes Brígida's memories of her youth and adolescence, when she was felicitous and capricious, lacking responsibility and devoting her energy to silly playfulness. Beethoven's undulating rhythms evoke Brígida's thoughts of her early marriage to Luis, when she searched for a love that Luis was incapable of giving her. Chopin's melancholy tonalities evoke Brígida's thoughts about the final period of her marriage, when she tried to resign herself to the sterility of her life but was driven to escape into a world of fantasy.

*5. *Water as a symbol*

- During the concert, various associations with the three composers are made: Mozart—singing water in tall fountains symbolizes the tone of Mozart's music and the prevailing tone of Brígida's youth; Beethoven—the currents of the sea symbolize the rhythms of Beethoven's music and the ebb and flow of married life that Brígida encounters as she searches for love and emotional satisfaction; Chopin—the melancholy agitation of the rain and the hidden waterfall symbolize the tone of Chopin's *Études* and Brígida's melancholy and agitated search for a way to accept the sterility of her married life.

- Brígida compares her dressing room to "a world submerged in an aquarium." In this image of water, the dressing room is both a magical escape and a place of artificiality and imprisonment. Brígida has found an escape from her father's house and a retreat from her unsatisfactory marriage, but she is still within Luis's house. Her lack of control is made apparent when the tree, which provides this green retreat, is cut down.

- Water as rain is also symbolic. The storm comes after Luis has violently left the house. The storm both reflects the mood of the marriage and prevents Brígida from taking action. She chooses not to leave Luis because she wants to listen to the rain in the tree.

*6. *Tree as symbol* The tree symbolizes Brígida's emotional life; it is as fertile as Brígida's day-to-day life is sterile. It provides her with a refuge from reality, offering her a fantasy world in which she finds emotional solace. With the tree's removal, she finds herself forced to face reality, and she divorces Luis.

The title, "The Tree," emphasizes the tree's role as the symbol of Brígida's emotional life.

*7. *"Necklace of birds"* Birds symbolize Brígida—both birds and Brígida chirp happily and flit from one pursuit to another. A necklace also symbolizes Brígida—as a child, she hugged Luis by putting her arms around his neck; as Luis's wife, she is a decorative object that he wears or puts aside as he wishes.

*8. *Mirrors and the window* The mirrors in Brígida's dressing room function as intensifiers, magnifying whatever they reflect: the earlier, magical world of green forests, mist, and firefly-like lamps; and the later, harsh reality of apartment windows and automobiles. The window serves as a way for Brígida to let light and life into her sterile world.

It is important that Brígida is not seen looking into the mirrors (which would be self-reflective or self-centered) but is seen looking out the window (which connects her with other living things).

WRITING ABOUT LITERATURE

1. *Essay analyzing Bombal's use of symbolism* Call students' attention to the directions in the textbook assignment with regard to content and organization.

Remind them of the importance of using quotations to support their ideas. (See **A.L.T.** questions 4, 5, 6, 7, and 8 above.) 🆎

2. *Creative writing: sequel describing Brígida's life after her divorce* Call students' attention to the suggestions in the textbook assignment. **(P.L.J.)**

3. *Creative writing: this story from Luis's point of view* Call students' attention to the questions suggested in the textbook assignment.

FURTHER READING

Bombal, María Luisa, *"New Islands" and Other Stories; House of Mist and The Shrouded Woman*.

The Story from Rosendo Juárez

JORGE LUIS BORGES

INTRODUCING THE STORY

On the surface, "The Story from Rosendo Juárez" is an action-packed story about the life of a tough in the old days in Argentina. Below that surface, it is the thought-provoking story of the narrator's psychological development from a youth who lets himself be manipulated by others to an adult who is self-confident and independent regardless of the cost to his reputation. In the process, Rosendo learns about life's fragility and its value, and, in the end, he discards his old life for a life he has greater control over.

Written late in Borges's life, "The Story from Rosendo Juárez" was created to be the companion piece to "Streetcorner Man," one of Borges' earliest short stories. "Streetcorner Man" tells the same story, but it is told by a narrator who views Rosendo as a coward. In a commentary about "The Story from Rosendo Juárez," Borges says that the later version depicts a "character who sees through the romantic nonsense and childish vanity of dueling, and finally attains manhood and sanity."

In "The Story from Rosendo Juárez," the antagonist (the Yardmaster) functions as Rosendo's double. The Yardmaster is Rosendo's mirror image; almost identical to Rosendo in appearance. The Yardmaster is also the image of Rosendo's insecure and aggressive inner side, an aspect of the double known as the doppelgänger.

Paradoxically the character in this story who appears to be the coward is actually the one who is brave. Rosendo has the courage to think for himself and to act with independence and good judgment. Those present are amazed when he ignores the Yardmaster's challenge to his reputation. However, the onlookers are unaware that the behavior and death of Luis Irala, Rosendo's valued friend and alter ego, has laid the foundation for Rosendo's decision to ignore the challenge. Borges, in his comments on "The Story from Rosendo Juárez," considers Rosendo's decision to be the mark of maturity and sanity.

Personal Literary Journal: To what extent, if any, do you let the opinions of others influence your attitudes and behavior? What factors determine whom you choose to follow and whom you choose to ignore?

Literary Terms: allusion, alter ego, characterization, doppelgänger, exposition, flashback, foreshadowing, irony, limited omniscience, narrative perspective, paradox, symbol, theme

COMPREHENSION QUESTIONS

1. *Why does Rosendo talk with the author?* to give him the correct version of an incident the author has written about

2. *How did Rosendo learn to handle a knife?* As a child, he used charred sticks as knives in mock duels.

3. *How did Rosendo happen to kill Garmendia?* Garmendia challenged Rosendo to a knife duel and lost.

4. *What was the advantage for Rosendo in signing a confession?* Rosendo was freed from prison in a few days.

5. *What was Rosendo's next job?* He became a party tough who got out the vote.

6. *Why did Irala fight?* He didn't want to be called a coward by people who knew his girlfriend had left him for another man.

7. *What advice did Rosendo give Irala?* Ignore other people's views and forget an unloving woman.

8. *What happened to Irala?* He was killed in knife duel.

9. *What did Rosendo notice about the Yardmaster?* The Yardmaster looked and acted like Rosendo.

10. *What decisions did Rosendo make at the end of the story?* He refused to fight the Yardmaster, and he left to begin a new life.

UNDERSTANDING THE STORY: POSSIBLE ANSWERS

1. *Effect of passage of time on understanding the past* With the passage of time, a person can become less emotionally involved and more able to analyze an event. Experience can also be a great teacher. Seeing oneself in others and seeing a pattern in one's experiences can lead to insights.

*2. *Effect on Rosendo of his experience with Garmendia* Rosendo's experience with Garmendia taught Rosendo that it is easy to kill or to be killed, for no worthwhile reason.

3. *Rosendo's attitudes toward providence and toward Garmendia's death* Rosendo's attitude toward Garmendia's death reveals the unpredictable nature of a duel: it happened "almost without thinking"; "there was a second when anything could've happened." In contrast, Rosendo's remark about providence implies the existence of a divine plan underlying human behavior. In this instance, both the serendipitous outcome of the duel and its providential effect on Rosendo's future have worked in Rosendo's favor.

*4. *Effect of Luis Irala's death on Rosendo's attitudes and behavior* Irala's death reinforced what Rosendo had learned from killing Garmendia: It is easy to kill or to get killed, for no worthwhile reason.

*5. *Why the Yardmaster made Rosendo feel ashamed* The Yardmaster's behavior was adolescent and foolish, motivated only by the Yardmaster's need to prove his superiority and his skill with a knife. Seeing that attitude in the Yardmaster made Rosendo ashamed that he had once felt and acted the same way.

*6. *Why Rosendo decides to lead a new life* Rosendo had grown old enough to value being alive. Gratuitous violence no longer excited him. He learned from his own experiences and from those of Luis Irala that it is all too easy to die for unimportant reasons. He knew he had courage and skill. Since he no longer needed to prove anything to anyone, these insights about life and death motivated him to create a new life for himself.

*7. *Rosendo's psychological development* As a youth, Rosendo went along with the games of his peers, including mock knife fights. He exhibited no independent thinking. His goal was to acquire the skills respected by his peers. As an adolescent, Rosendo chose gaucho outlaws as his role models. This involved accepting any and all challenges, risking his life, and proving his skill. He exhibited no independent thinking. His goal was to win the respect and admiration of others in any way possible. As an adult, Rosendo exhibited independent thinking. He decided that he valued life too much to risk death needlessly, and he had the self-esteem to disregard what others thought of his behavior.

*8. *Themes* Possible themes:

- People who have the courage to live by their own convictions live satisfying lives.

- People who let the opinions of others determine their behavior can never be at peace.

- Experience teaches valuable lessons to those who are observant and willing to reevaluate their attitudes.

*9. *Appeal of knife fighters* Knife fighters appealed to Borges because they were people making decisions that involved life and death; they were living at the crux of life. How they chose to act revealed their values. In the end, Rosendo's behavior affirmed the value of life.

ANALYZING LITERARY TECHNIQUE: POSSIBLE ANSWERS

1. *Exposition* The exposition relates this story to an earlier version of the story. It explains the new point of view and indicates that the story will be an argument against the earlier point of view.

2. *Flashback* The flashback permits Rosendo to present his story selectively, with attention only to the details he now finds important. It also permits him to interpret his earlier behavior in light of hindsight.

3. *Foreshadowing* Both Rosendo's attitude toward the cockfight and his advice to Luis Irala predict how he is likely to react to the Yardmaster's challenge. Foreshadowing makes Rosendo's behavior at the end of the story consistent, plausible, and courageous.

4. *Irony* It is ironic that Rosendo gives Luis Irala advice that he himself did not follow in his own life, even though Irala has greater reason to fight than Rosendo did. The advice reveals Rosendo's new emotional maturity. It is also ironic that Rosendo doesn't understand the behavior of the cocks when he lives among people who behave as mindlessly as the cocks and when he himself has behaved that way. This also reveals Rosendo's new emotional maturity.

*5. *The Yardmaster as Rosendo's mirror image and doppelgänger* The concepts of the mirror image and the doppelgänger refer to the Yardmaster's relationship to Rosendo. The Yardmaster functions both as a mirror image of Rosendo's public self (one aspect of the double) and as the worst side of Rosendo (the aspect of the double that is known as the doppelgänger). When Rosendo sees the Yardmaster—who shares Rosendo's appearance and reputation— Rosendo recognizes his old needlessly aggressive adolescent self in the Yardmaster, and he feels ashamed.

*6. *Symbolism of the cockfight* The cockfight symbolizes the senseless, merciless dueling of the gaucho outlaws and the other toughs in that society. Subconsciously it becomes connected in Rosendo's mind with the challenges one knife fighter hurls at another to prove his courage and skill.

7. *Narrative perspective* The first-person narrator is reliable (in contrast with the view of another narrator in the earlier version of the story). The author, who introduces the tale, lets Rosendo tell his own story, and the lessons that he learns from his experiences attest to the reliability of his explanation.

*8. *Paradox* It is paradoxical that a courageous person can appear to be a coward in the eyes of the group by choosing independent behavior in preference to the actions that the group advocates.

WRITING ABOUT LITERATURE

1. *Essay applying quotations from Borges's "Streetcorner Man" to "The Story from Rosendo Juárez"* Call students' attention to the quotations and directions in the textbook assignment. Pertinent quotations from "The Story from Rosendo Juárez" include the following: "I jumped him, almost without thinking." "There was a second when anything could've happened." "I learned that night that it isn't hard to kill a man, or get killed yourself." "Either you kill him and you get sent off to stir, or he kills you and you get sent off to Chacarita." "You mean you're going to stake your peace of mind . . ." "He went off to get killed and he got himself killed, right honorably." (See **U.S.** question 8 above.) 🅐🅟

2. *Character sketch of Rosendo's emotional development* Call students' attention to the suggestions in the textbook assignment. Rosendo changes from being dependent on the opinions of others (being manipulated into acting

against his own self-interest) to being self-confident (giving advice to Luis Irala) to finally being self-directed and self-sufficient (ignoring the Yardmaster's challenge and beginning a new life). (See **U.S.** questions 2, 4, 5, 6, 7, 8, and 9 and **A.L.T.** questions 5, 6, and 8 above.)

3. *Creative writing: a dialogue about whether Rosendo is a coward* (See **U.S.** questions 2, 4, 5, 6, 7, 8, and 9 and **A.L.T.** questions 5, 6, and 8 above.) **(P.L.J.)**

FURTHER READING

Borges, Jorge Luis, *The Aleph and Other Stories; Ficciones; Labyrinths; Dreamtigers; A Personal Anthology; Borges: A Reader.*

The Word

PABLO NERUDA

INTRODUCING THE POEM

Neruda's "The Word" is a tribute to language. From the opening image of "born in the blood," Neruda values language as an inherent and integral part of life itself. He moves from a poetic description of its birth (stanza 1) to its ancient history and development (stanza 2) to its value as a means of communication with peoples past, present, and future (stanza 3). He then returns to the first word (stanza 4), which sets a powerful chain reaction of sound into motion. He moves beyond nouns to verbs because verbs "blended existence with essence" (stanza 5). Neruda considers communication to be the essence of life and its absence to be the death of the human spirit: "not to speak is to die" (stanza 6). He believes that language defines a human being and proves a person's existence: "I utter and I am" (stanza 7). He concludes with a toast to language, for language gives "life to life itself" (stanza 8).

"The Word" is also a tribute to metaphor, for Neruda conveys the nature and power of language through his striking use of figurative language. Images tumble forth like jewels from a treasure chest: for example, "lands that had returned to stone"; "pain took to the roads"; "dressed up in / terror and sighing"; "the electricity of its beauty"; and "hereditary goblet." Even in translation, the poem's beauty and power impress themselves on the mind of the reader.

Personal Literary Journal: How important is language to you? If you could speak but not read and write, what would you lose? What would be lost if your language was not a written language?

Literary Terms: allusion, figurative language, irony, metaphor

COMPREHENSION QUESTIONS

1. *According to the poem, what is the function of words?* to communicate

2. *According to the poem, what is the value of words?* communication in the present; connection with the past and the future

3. *According to the poem, what part of speech is most important?* the verb

4. *What word associated with birth and life opens and closes the poem?* blood

5. *At the end of the poem, what great ability do words have?* They give life to life.

UNDERSTANDING THE POEM: POSSIBLE ANSWERS

1. *What motivated the first word* The first word was motivated by terror (fear of danger and death; need to protect self and others) and by sighing (desire to express love, wishes, and concerns).

2. *"Inheritance" of words* Words connect readers with the thoughts, feelings, and experiences of others across time and through space. Words give pleasure and instruction, and literature enriches the experience of living. Prior knowledge is often the building material of new knowledge.

3. *Verbs* Some verbs are intransitive, expressing being and existence. Other verbs are transitive, expressing action. Together the two types of verbs comprise all aspects of living.

4. *"Not to speak is to die"* Neruda's hyperbole emphasizes the importance of written and oral language to human beings. He is exaggerating to make a point.

5. *Themes* Possible themes:

   - Language is critical to human life: "not to speak is to die" (line 45).

   - Language defines what it is to be human: "I utter and I am" (line 53).

   - Language gives form to life experiences: "words give . . . life to life itself" (lines 67–68).

ANALYZING LITERARY TECHNIQUES: POSSIBLE ANSWERS

*1. *Metaphor in stanza 1* Flight and the beating of wings suggest a bird whose travels are described at the beginning of Stanza 2.

*2. *Metaphors in stanza 2* (a) "Lands that had returned to stone" (line 8) refers to the changes in weather that caused severe drought, turned arable land into deserts, and forced people to leave their homelands in search of a more hospitable and nurturing environment. (b) "When pain took to the roads" (line 10) refers to the mental and physical condition of those who were forced to relocate. It implies food shortages, inadequate clothing, difficult travel conditions, and danger from animals and hostile people. (c) "New lands and water reunited / to sow their word anew" (lines 12–13) refers to the place of relocation, which had lakes or rivers and rainfall so that the environment could provide food for animals and human beings.

   People planted farmland for physical sustenance, and they planted their language for both physical and intellectual sustenance. They used the language they had brought with them, and they added words that evolved from their new experiences and their contact with new peoples. Metaphor functions as a type of shorthand or shortcut by suggesting detail through the use of a few suggestive words, by appealing to the senses and the imagination, and by enriching abstract ideas through reference to concrete objects.

3. *Stanza 7: allusion to Descartes* The statement "I think; therefore, I am" affirms that humans' ability to think proves that the humans exist. Neruda alludes to

this statement with the paraphrase "I utter and I am," implying that speech is what distinguishes human beings from all other forms of life and from all objects. Neruda elevates human speech to the position of the prime human quality. Since language is the verbal and written expression of thought, a natural connection exists between Descartes's statement and Neruda's statement.

*4. *Metaphor of the cup* Words contain meaning as cups contain liquid, so words are cups of meaning. The hereditary goblet refers to language that is inherited from one's parents and one's culture.

*5. *Metaphor of blood* According to the poem, words possess the life force of blood. When Neruda says that words are "born in the blood" (lines 1–2), he is connecting words with human beings. Words are an inherent part of being human; they are latent in infants, and they develop along with the human being. At the end of the poem, the verb is "blood" because it is both the source and vitality of life (lines 63–68).

*6. *Metaphor of water* Water possesses the qualities of movement, flexibility, fluidity, continuity, and variations in mass. Thus, water is a good metaphor for language, which also develops, changes, and increases across time and space. In stanza 4, "the first / word uttered" was only a drop or a ripple that became a great cataract (lines 26–30).

WRITING ABOUT LITERATURE

1. *Essay analyzing Neruda's use of metaphor* Call student's attention to the directions in the textbook assignment with regard to content and organization. Possible metaphors include water, blood, cup, and wine. (See questions **A.L.T.** 1, 2, 4, 5, and 6 above.) **AP**

2. *Creative writing: a poem that gives the history of a verb and provides synonyms of the verb* Call students' attention to the directions in the textbook assignment with regard to procedure, content, and style. Possible verbs include walk, talk, eat, work, and play. **(P.L.J.)**

FURTHER READING

Neruda, Pablo, *Twenty Love Poems and a Song of Despair;* "The Heights of Macchu Picchu," in *Selected Poems;* "The Word," in *Memoirs.*

The Third Bank of the River

JOÃO GUIMARÃES ROSA

INTRODUCING THE STORY

"The Third Bank of the River" is the poignant story of a son (the narrator) whose dutiful and orderly father leaves his wife and young children without explanation to live the remainder of his life floating in a boat in the middle of the nearby river. The son respects and admires his father. The greater part of a lifetime passes while the father in his boat and the son on the shore continue to renounce the joy of human relationships.

The son lives only for his father, who remains silent. Although the son describes his father's actions, neither the narrator nor the reader knows the father's thoughts or emotions. It is possible that the father devotes his life to asserting, by his actions, the lack of meaning in the universe and that he lives for the day when his son will take his place and perpetuate his philosophy. However, other reasons may govern the father's actions, including his psychological need to exist as an independent person and his feeling that he must separate himself from his family to achieve autonomy. It is consistent with Rosa's philosophy of life to interpret the father's behavior either as having no explanation or as having a multitude of explanations, any one of which may or may not be correct. Rosa's decision to have the father remain mute and to tell the story from the point of view of the son, whose knowledge is limited, reflects this view of life.

To Rosa, life is an enigma. It is a natural phenomenon that, like the river, is constantly moving and changing. Part of life is rational; part is irrational. Reality has a variety of faces that may be completely visible, partly visible, or invisible. The "third bank of the river" symbolizes the irrational dimension of reality, and the narrator speaks for the author when he states: "Nobody is crazy. Or maybe everybody."

Although the son thinks he is like his father, the father and son learn that they are not identical. The son offers to take his father's place, but when his father accepts that offer, the son is unable to continue his father's silent protest against a world devoid of meaning, and he lacks his father's courage to divorce himself irrevocably from life. The father can survive (and possibly can only survive) in an emotional desert, absorbed by and locked into his autonomous solitude, but the son cannot survive in an emotional desert. Although the son has sacrificed most of his life for his father, the son's failure to relinquish the rest of life destroys him.

The reader who accepts the son's remarks about his family and himself as those of a reliable narrator can find a psychological basis for the behavior of both the father and the son. The story includes the following details: (1) The mother appears to rule the submissive father and the children. (2) The father deserts his family but remains within their sight. (3) The son states that he feels anxious, bad, and guilty, and he juxtaposes these feelings with thoughts of his father's desertion. (4) The son is the only family member who chooses not to marry and who remains at home so that he can devote his life to his father, even though he views his father as an impediment. (5) In the end, when the son cannot adopt his father's way of life, he feels that he is "what never should have been."

These details suggest that the father has no viable masculine identity as long as he is a passive male in a home dominated by his wife. He asserts himself by leaving home. He remains within sight so that his family will see that he continues to exist. With these actions, he suddenly achieves both independence and importance. It is important to realize that the behavior of both the father and the narrator can symbolize the relationships of real people. Real individuals may find family life intolerable for a variety of reasons—including the need to retreat emotionally from their families because they have never resolved their own questions of identity and autonomy as they grew up. They may become workaholics, with their work providing both personal satisfaction and success as well as a socially acceptable excuse for a their lack of emotional involvement with their families. They may also retreat in front of television screens or behind housework.

The narrator's self-knowledge is limited to recognizing his feelings without understanding them. Those who wish to analyze his psyche may examine the possible effect that his parents had on him as a little boy. They may consider his conscious and subconscious feelings about his mother, his father, and his developing male identity. They may consider his need for a male role model and the role that his father's behavior, both off and on the river, plays in his life. Finally they may evaluate the closing paragraph, in which the narrator questions his masculinity because he cannot choose to live his father's kind of life.

The narrator and his father appear to have an instinctive mutual understanding. Until the climax, when the narrator breaks his promise, he views his father as his alter ego, or second self. Afterward the narrator's reaction to his own behavior suggests the concept of the Shadow, or dual personality, in which the subconscious fundamental self is quite different from the conscious social self.

All young children make choices to acquire and keep the love and approval of their parents. Like the narrator, children who must cope with particular psychological idiosyncrasies in their parents may have to choose between identifying with their parents and being independent. The need to remain connected with a parent may force them to sacrifice an independent life; however, independence may cause them to lose their connection with their parent. Inevitably such a choice is sad and unsatisfactory.

Personal Literary Journal: How do you react to people whose behavior you do not understand? To what extent are you comfortable being different from members of your family? How do you react when they make you feel as if you are disappointing them by not conforming to their expectations?

Literary Terms: alter ego, characterization, climax, limited omniscience, narrative perspective, point of view, realism, setting, Shadow, symbolism, theme

COMPREHENSION QUESTIONS

1. *What action does the narrator's father take?* He leaves his family and lives on a river nearby.
2. *How do members of the narrator's family react?* They move away, and they move on with their lives. They act as if the father were dead.
3. *How does the narrator react?* He remains nearby to care for his father.
4. *What offer does the narrator make?* to take father's place
5. *What finally happens?* The father accepts the offer, but the son lacks the courage to fulfill this commitment.

UNDERSTANDING THE STORY: POSSIBLE ANSWERS

1. *Description of the father* The contrast between the father's behavior at the beginning of the story and his desertion of his family reflects Rosa's premise that human behavior can be irrational.

2. *Why the father abandons the family* There are several plausible explanations.

- The father cannot handle the responsibility of a wife and children.
- The father hates his wife because she controls his life. He belatedly compensates for his passivity in his marriage and acts upon his emotional need to assert his autonomy and his masculine identity. He feels that he can only do this by leaving home. By removing himself from his family, he can be the master of his own life.
- The father believes that life (the universe and human behavior) is absurd, and he has the courage to live according to his convictions. His living in the boat is his public statement (in the form of a silent protest) that all of life is pretense and illusion.
- The father has become insane, and his actions are irrational.
- The father's physical separation symbolizes the emotional separation that fathers and mothers may make in real life when circumstances remind them of their unresolved issues of identity and independence.

3. *Why the father remains visible to the family* Possible responses include the following:

- The father wants to retain some connection, tenuous as it is, with his family.
- The father acts as he does to feel as if he is a separate and important person; having someone in his family sympathize with him and be attentive to his physical needs reinforces the success of his desertion.
- Although the father feels compelled to act strangely, he wants to provide a good masculine model for the narrator by proving that he is an autonomous, independent male.
- The father's public statement of his autonomy has meaning only for people who know him; strangers would think that he was insane.
- The father's actions reflect his insanity.

4. *How the father could return home* The father could return home only if he felt that his autonomy would be assured. If his presence was important to the family, the family would have to respect his needs, and the power structure within the family would have to change.

5. *The father's right* Opinions will vary as to whether the father's primary responsibility is to himself or to his family. Many people who need autonomy remain at home but keep a psychological distance from their families.

6. *Narrator's affection and respect for his father* The narrator admires his father for having the courage to leave his domineering wife and to assert his masculinity and independence. He admires his father for having the courage to act upon his convictions, even though the idea that life lacks any meaning is frightening. The narrator's fears about his father mask his fears about himself; the narrator's affection and respect for his father mask the negative feelings that he has about his father, feelings that the narrator cannot accept.

7. *Why the narrator attributes his own behavior to his father* All children need to have wonderful parents. Those who don't have good parents may fabricate them. The narrator creates the father he wishes he had. That father is psychologically true in that the narrator believes, with part of his mind, that the ideal father exists. However, part of the narrator recognizes reality and realizes that he is lying to himself.

8. *Why the narrator never marries and remains determined to stay near father* The narrator feels responsible for his father because he loves and respects his father; he believes that his father would not be able to survive without him.

   The fact that the narrator never marries reflects the psychological damage the father has caused by being a passive husband and father and by abandoning his family.

   The father's need for the narrator is partly a rationalization, because the father could have accepted help from another family member. However, the narrator needs a father-figure with whom to identify psychologically as a male, and so he remains near his father.

9. *Significance of "Nobody is crazy. Or maybe everybody."* The narrator's statement reflects Rosa's view that human behavior can be irrational as well as rational and that any behavior can have many interpretations.

*10. *Why the narrator volunteers to change places* The narrator may love and admire his father and wish to ease his father's old age by taking over for him, just as a child may take over a parent's business. Alternatively, the narrator may feel responsible for his father's welfare, or he may feel that he needs to be like his father to confirm his own masculinity.

   The father accepts the son's offer because the offer implies that the son has accepted his father's right to be autonomous. Then the father no longer needs to assert his independence. However, the narrator is terrified by the possibility of changing places with his father; he cannot face the personal consequences of acting on his words. The narrator may not need to assert his autonomy. He may lack the courage or the madness to live in his father's world. He may realize that he does not share his father's view that life is devoid of meaning or that he cannot face the possibility of cutting himself off from society.

11. *Meaning of the narrator's concluding remarks* By the end of the story, the narrator is quite psychologically disturbed. He views his life as a catastrophic failure. Not only has he disappointed his father and thus severed his one remaining relationship, but he has lost confidence in himself because of his failure to be like his role model.

12. *Responsibility for the narrator's life* The narrator, his father, and his mother are all responsible for the narrator's life. As a child, his reactions were determined by many factors: his own psychological and chemical framework; his parents' personalities; and his parents' relationship to each other, to his siblings, and to him. It may have been better for the narrator if his father had been more assertive at home. However, the adult narrator is

responsible for his own life. If he feels psychologically damaged, he must make an effort to repair the damage.

ANALYZING LITERARY TECHNIQUE: POSSIBLE ANSWERS

1. *Relationship between setting and plot* Rosa set the story by a river because of the symbolic connection between a river and human life. Both are natural phenomena that change as they continuously move from their origin to their end.

   Many in the field of psychology consider water to symbolize the human unconscious. The narrator fears the loss of his masculinity when he cannot act like his father. At the end, he incoherently loses himself in the river, which is a symbol of his father ("between the long shores") and of the mother's womb ("inside the river").

2. *Narrative perspective* By using a first-person narrator, with his limited omniscience and unreliability, Rosa forces the reader to experience everything through the narrator's perceptions. The father's motivations, thoughts, and feelings remain open to individual interpretation, since the father is silent. An omniscient author or an informed third-person narrator would be able to understand the motivations, thoughts, feelings, and behavior of every character. The choice of narrator is consistent with Rosa's view that no one can really know and understand someone else (or even know and understand oneself).

3. *Realism* The realism with which Rosa tells the story contrasts with the bizarre content of the story. Rosa's style portrays the extraordinary as ordinary.

*4. *Climax* The climax occurs when the narrator cannot keep his word and take his father's place. It is critical to both the philosophical and psychological aspects of the story. The narrator cannot actively adopt his father's view that life is devoid of meaning, and he cannot cut himself off from society. The narrator's reaction to his failure provides a clue to his psyche and an explanation for all of his actions and emotions—as he has described them. His concern about his masculinity reveals that he is functioning psychologically like a little boy who can identify himself as a male only by being just like his father. Concern about his masculinity also ties in with the narrator's self-imposed obligation to his father, his refusal to marry, his description of his mother in his childhood home, and his feelings of anxiety, guilt, and pain.

5. *River as symbol* The river itself symbolizes human life. Both the river and life are fluid, flexible, and constantly changing. Since a river has only two banks, the "third bank" symbolizes the irrational and mysterious aspect of life.

WRITING ABOUT LITERATURE

1. *Essay justifying or criticizing the narrator's change of mind* Call students' attention to the directions, the questions, and the suggestions in the textbook assignment with regard to content. The narrator can be condemned or justified, depending on what a person believes the son owes the father,

what he owes himself, and which obligation is the more important of the two. (See **U.S.** question 10 and **A.L.T.** question 4 above.) **(P.L.J.)**

2. *Creative writing: story from the father's point of view* Call students' attention to the questions suggested in the textbook assignment.

FURTHER READING

Rosa, João Guimarães, *The Third Bank of the River and Other Stories.*

End of the Game

JULIO CORTÁZAR

INTRODUCING THE STORY

"End of the Game" is a story about three girls—Letitia, Holanda, and the narrator—who come of age while playing their favorite game. The girls amuse themselves by entertaining passengers on passing trains with their performance of Statues and Attitudes. A boy named Ariel becomes involved in the game by sending the girls notes. In time he reveals that he is interested in Letitia, whom he considers to be the prettiest of the three. Limited by his view from the train window, he does not realize that Letitia is partially paralyzed. Letitia, however, is well aware that her affliction affects others, so she decides not to play the game on the day that Ariel plans to meet the girls. Instead she arranges for Holanda to give him a sealed letter. The next day Letitia appears as a regal statue, and that turns out to be the end of the game. When Holanda and the narrator watch the train on the following day they do not see Ariel.

Cortázar creates an atmosphere of ambiguity by placing the story in the hands of a narrator who is one of the trio. Because the narrator tells the story from her point of view, she is ignorant of facts that readers would like to know. What does Letitia tell Ariel in her letter? Why will she no longer play the game? Why does Ariel stop watching the girls from the train window? Readers know what the narrator sees and what the girls say to each other. However, the narrator is not omniscient and cannot read Letitia's mind. Cortázar allows readers to unravel the mystery.

In the process all the girls come of age. They learn the difference between fantasy and reality. Once Ariel contacts them, the real world makes an ever-widening wedge into their play world. Whereas Letitia's paralysis is probably of little importance to other girls, the trio learns that it separates Letitia from other girls in the male world. Ariel apparently flees from Letitia—despite her beauty—because of her handicap. This world of teenage fantasy and reality give the story universal appeal.

Personal Literary Journal: Relate an experience you have had that caused you to learn that fantasy differs from reality. To what extent was it a painful lesson? How did this experience change your life?

Literary Terms: allusion, figurative language, foreshadowing, hyperbole, irony, limited omniscience, metaphor, narrator, personification, point of view, simile, theme

COMPREHENSION QUESTIONS

1. *Who plays the game?* three girls—Letitia, Holanda, and the narrator
2. *Where do they play the game?* by the railroad tracks
3. *How is the game played?* Wearing ornaments as a costume, one girl stands beside the railroad tracks as a Statue or an Attitude.
4. *Who is the leader of the game?* Letitia
5. *What makes Letitia different from the other characters?* She is partially paralyzed.
6. *How does Letitia react to Ariel's note?* She decides not to go to the tracks that day, but sends Ariel a note.
7. *How does the game end?* Letitia performs one last Statue for Ariel.
8. *What does Ariel do at the end of the story?* Ariel sits on the other side of the train.

UNDERSTANDING THE STORY: POSSIBLE ANSWERS

1. *The real game* The real game the girls play is attracting the attention of people, particularly males, on the train. If Mama and Aunt Ruth knew about the game, they would prohibit the girls from making exhibitions of themselves.

2. *Letitia's Attitudes and Statues* Letitia chooses to perform Attitudes that represent Generosity, Piety, Sacrifice, and Renunciation; as a Statue, she imitates the *Venus de Milo* (from ancient Greece). Her choices are consistent with her circumstances. She compensates for her paralysis by making an effort to be generous and good. Knowing that she has a pretty face, she feels comfortable imitating one of the most beautiful statues in Western tradition.

3. *Feelings toward Letitia* Letitia is the object of love and resentment, pity and envy. The girls love her because she is a good person; however, they resent her for the special treatment she receives because of her handicap. They pity her for her paralysis and her limitations; however, they envy her pretty face and her intelligence. The girls realize that Letitia's handicap is a burden that will cause her disappointment and sorrow.

4. *Ariel* Ariel's presence adds an intensity to the game. His preference for Letitia makes the girls jealous of Letitia. They long for Ariel to realize that Letitia is partially paralyzed. However, the girls feel guilty about their jealousy, so they encourage Letitia to meet Ariel.

*5. *Letitia's reaction to Ariel's interest* Letitia feels ambivalent about Ariel's interest in her. She is delighted that her pretty face has captivated him; however, she believes that her handicap will frighten him away. To avoid confronting him with her paralysis, Letitia decides not to meet him. Although no one knows what Letitia tells Ariel in her letter, both her behavior and his response lead the reader to conclude that she tells him that she is partially paralyzed and that she will perform for him one last time. Unfortunately Ariel's reaction to her letter confirms Letitia's worst fears.

*6. *Letitia's final performance* Letitia wants to be the actress on the last day because she has probably promised Ariel that she will give a final performance. Letitia chooses to be a regal statue to reveal her self-esteem and her pride. However, she keeps her eyes closed so she will not spoil her act by watching for Ariel's response. She chooses to return home alone so she will have the privacy to experience the joy of Ariel's appreciation and the sorrow of his anticipated rejection.

7. *Ariel's departure* After seeing Letitia's last Statue, Ariel no longer looks for the girls because Letitia has probably told him she is partially paralyzed and that she will no longer play the game. Letitia probably chooses to stop playing the game because she assumes that Ariel will no longer be interested in her.

*8. *End of the game* The game ends because the fantasy has ended. Holanda has probably guessed what Letitia wrote to Ariel. Holanda is aware that the game's fantasy has given way to reality.

9. *Title* "End of the Game" is an appropriate title because it applies to the story in two ways. It highlights the climax of the story (Letitia's revelation and Ariel's response) which brings about the end of the game. It also highlights the end of the illusion or fantasy that the game has represented.

10. *Intelligence* References to intelligence and education include the following:

- allusions to the burning of Troy (a classical story), G-flat (a music term), and Ponce de Terrail (a French author)
- allusion to *Venus de Milo* (a second century B.C. Greek statue)
- Letitia's presiding over both the girls' game and their kingdom because she is "quicker at saying things"
- the girls' need to impress Ariel because they have only been through grade school, where they studied just home economics and learned how to do raised needlework
- the girls' disappointment that Ariel attends the Industrial High School, not an English high school
- the girls' disappointment in his manner of expressing himself and his handwriting

These references to intelligence and education are significant because of their insignificance. The girls in this story are typical teenage girls, just as Ariel is a typical teenage boy. This gives the story universal appeal.

*11. *Coming of age* Coming of age involves recognizing the disparity between illusion and reality. At some point, most people experience a rite of passage—an event that teaches something so important about the real world that they must leave behind the world of childhood innocence. The girls' experience with Ariel teaches them that a world of difference exists between what they depict on their stage and what happens in real life. Letitia can look beautiful and act gracefully, but the reality of her paralysis casts a blight on her life.

ANALYZING LITERARY TECHNIQUE: POSSIBLE ANSWERS

*1. *Point of view* Cortázar tells this story from the point of view one of the three girls. As a first-person narrator, she does not know what anyone else is thinking or feeling unless that person reveals information to her. If Cortázar told the story himself, he could function as an omniscient author, revealing the thoughts and feelings of everyone in the story. If Letitia were the narrator, she could reveal her thoughts and feelings; this would make the story less ambiguous. Cortázar choose to use the limited-omniscience point of view to achieve a sense of mystery and ambiguity.

2. *Figurative language*

   a) *Allusion:* The allusion to the burning of Troy conveys the sort of confusion that could release the girls from their tasks, leaving them free to do what they choose.

   b) *Personification:* The personification of "freedom, which took us by the hands" enhances freedom's importance in the girls' lives.

   c) *Metaphor:* The metaphor that compares the play area to a kingdom conveys the idea that the girls control the play area, in contrast to their home, which is controlled by their mother and aunt.

   d) *Simile:* The simile of a folded-up ironing board, with the wide part leaning closed upon the wall, describes the stiffness of Letitia's back and her inability to move her head from side to side.

   e) *Hyperbole:* The hyperbole "lunch lasted for days" conveys how long the lunch seemed to be, given how anxious the girls are to be free of household chores so they can welcome Ariel.

3. *Foreshadowing* Foreshadowing prepares readers for the end of the game.

   • To avoid meeting Ariel, Letitia writes him a letter. Readers can assume that Letitia reveals her affliction.

   • The narrator says Letitia shouldn't be afraid to meet Ariel because true affection knows no barriers. However, both Letitia and the reader know that Ariel can have no true affection, because he has never actually met Letitia.

   • The narrator's repeating that she does not know what Letitia told Ariel in the letter reminds readers of the letter's probable contents and Ariel's probable response.

   • Holanda's remark to the narrator that "the game's finished from tomorrow on" foreshadows that the end of the game is in sight.

   • Letitia's standing "still with her eyes closed and enormous tears all down her face" foreshadows that the game is over.

4. *Irony*

   a) The narrator resents being called upon to perform household tasks that Letitia is not asked to do. She describes Letitia as free to "laze away the day reading." Irony is implicit in the narrator's point of view because Letitia would rather perform the tasks that the narrator dislikes than endure her paralysis and discomfort.

b) The narrator's "gushy" remark that "true affection knows no barriers" is ironic because Letitia's fear is justified. When Ariel learns about Letitia's paralysis (which she probably reveals in her letter), he loses interest in Letitia. The irony is that the distaste for Letitia's paralysis prevents Ariel—and probably many other boys—from getting to know Letitia and, therefore, from developing an affection for her.

WRITING ABOUT LITERATURE

1. *Essay analyzing point of view* Call students' attention to the directions in the textbook assignment with regard to the content of the five paragraphs. (See **A.L.T.** question 1 above.) **AP**

2. *Creative writing: write a story in which a character comes of age by discovering that fantasy is different from reality.* **(P.L.J.)**

3. *Creative writing: retell this story from Letitia's point of view.* (See **U.S.** questions 5, 6, 8, and 11 and **A.L.T.** question 1 above.)

FURTHER READING

Cortázar, Julio (Short story collections) *Blow-Up and Other Stories* (originally *End of the Game*); *All Fires the Fire*; *We Love Glenda So Much*; *A Change of Light*. (Novels) *Hopscotch*; *The Winners*; *62: A Model Kit*.

Two Bodies

OCTAVIO PAZ

INTRODUCING THE POEM

In "Two Bodies," Paz describes the relationship between two people, probably lovers, and their relationship to the world in which they live. Using metaphor as a form of shorthand, the poet describes five aspects of their relationship, each accompanied by a different relationship to the universe. The poem moves through the following stages: The two are synchronized with each other and in harmony with the universe (stanza 1). The two are together, but each is preoccupied with self in a universe that ignores them (stanza 2). The two are intertwined in a universe where they must nourish and sustain each other (stanza 3). The two are confrontational or hostile in a universe that provokes friction between them (stanza 4). The two are mortal in a universe that is devoid of intrinsic meaning (stanza 5).

The last stanza functions as the climax of the poem; it provides the pessimistic backdrop against which human relationships achieve significance. Because of the inevitable mortality of human beings and (in Paz's view) the lack of inherent meaning in the universe, human relationships are vitally important. Despite the limitations of an intimate relationship, love and friendship enrich lives that are fragile and brief, and they provide the only meaning and soul-satisfying values that are possible in the universe.

Personal Literary Journal: Think about the people you know. To what extent, if any, do your relationships with different people differ? List the kinds of relationships that you have. Do you know anyone with whom your relationship varies from time to time? If so, list the variations.

Literary Terms: existentialism, figurative language, metaphor, surrealism, symbol

COMPREHENSION QUESTIONS

1. *How does the poet describe the position of the two bodies?* "face to face"

2. *What objects are the bodies compared to?* waves (line 2), stones (line 5), roots (line 8), knives (line 11), stars (line 14)

3. *How does the poet describe the sky at the end of the poem?* empty

UNDERSTANDING THE POEM: POSSIBLE ANSWERS

1. *Why "face to face"* "Face to face" implies the possibility of relationship and communication.

2. *Why at night* Night is the time of the greatest intimacy between lovers. It is the time when distractions of the day have ceased and people are more aware of the emotional realities of their lives. Thoughts and feelings that have been pushed aside during the day reappear at night.

3. *Significance of "at times"* "At times" signifies change, and Paz describes five aspects of a human relationship. He omits the phrase from the last stanza to emphasize the inevitable mortality of human life.

4. *Human beings and the universe* Human relationships are imperfect, subject to change, and finite. Moreover, they exist in a universe that is devoid of any meaning other than the meaning that people bring to it. Because of the nature of human life and the nature of the universe, relationships are to be valued in spite of their many limitations. At best, they provide meaning and value where no other meaning or value exists. At worst, they are little better than nothing.

ANALYZING LITERARY TECHNIQUE: POSSIBLE ANSWERS

*1. *Night as symbol* Night is the time when it is difficult to be distracted from the basic realities of life. These realities may appear in symbolic form in dreams. They may include the mortal nature of human existence and the place of human beings in a meaningless universe. Paz gives the poem a universal dimension by relating night to water (stanza 1), earth (stanzas 2 and 3), fire (stanza 4), and air (stanza 5)—the four elements once thought to make up the physical world.

*2. *Metaphors and human relationships*

- The metaphor of waves in an ocean (stanza 1) suggests that the pair of human beings moves together in synchronization and in harmony with the universe, propelled by life forces and by activities in the environment.

- The metaphor of two stones in the desert (stanza 2) suggests that the two human beings are separate—physically together yet each withdrawn into his and her own self—and that they exist in a universe that ignores them.

- The metaphor of two roots (stanza 3) suggests a close relationship that is rooted in an unsupportive and uncaring universe; the only emotional support possible is the support that one person gives another.

- The metaphor of two knives in a night that "strikes sparks" suggests that the couple's relationship is at times confrontational and hostile because events and emotions in the normal course of living incite them to quarrel.

*3. *"Two stars" and "empty sky"* The metaphor of two stars suggests that the couple possesses beauty, brilliance, and vitality, all aspects of human potential. However, falling stars, which are burning out, symbolize the couple's inevitable mortality. The metaphor of the empty sky suggests that the universe is devoid of meaning.

4. *Order of stanzas* The location of the last stanza, which is the climax, must be fixed. The arrangement of the other four stanzas depends on personal taste, although there is a pairing of opposites between stanzas 1 and 2 (water and earth) and 3 and 4 (roots and knives, suggesting connection and separation). In addition, some readers may think there is a logical progression from striking sparks (stanza 4) to the "two stars falling" (stanza 5).

5. *Function of repetition* Repetition unifies the poem. The repetition of "Two bodies face to face" emphasizes that the poem is describing five aspects of a relationship. The repetition of "at times" conveys the variable aspect of any human relationship. The omission of "at times" in the last stanza emphasizes humans' inevitable mortality in a meaningless universe.

6. *Existentialist aspects* Against the poem's background of human mortality and an intrinsically meaningless universe, Paz implies that human relationships—with all their limitations—are the only source of soul-satisfying values in the universe. This attitude reflects the following characteristics of existentialism: Human beings must choose the values by which they will live, for the only certainties in life are suffering and death; in the absence of absolute values, human beings have the awesome freedom and responsibility to create their own individuality through their choices and their actions.

WRITING ABOUT LITERATURE

1. *Essay examining Paz's use of metaphor* (See **A.L.T.** questions 1, 2, and 3 above.) **AP**

2. *Creative writing: a poem about a relationship* Call students' attention to the suggestions and directions in the textbook assignment. **(P.L.J.)**

FURTHER READING

Paz, Octavio, *Early Poems; Blanco; A Tree Within; Collected Poems.*

Crossroads

CARLOS SOLÓRZANO

INTRODUCING THE PLAY

In *Crossroads* (also known as *Crossing*) Solórzano depicts life in the twentieth century as a time when human beings are isolated and emotionally starved in an impersonal and absurd world. Impossibility is possible, and surprise is an inherent part of life. Appearance is both real and illusory; those who are old in appearance are young in mind and heart.

The character called the Man misses a special moment because he cannot recognize, accept, and value that moment when it occurs. He is so committed to his preconceptions of what reality should be that he is unable to relinquish his illusions. He leaves in desperation, blaming the Flagman for his situation.

The intensity of the man's anger and desperation reflects his subconscious recognition of certain unpalatable truths. Life is often unpredictable, and reality often shatters illusions. True communication is often impossible because egoism constructs unbreakable walls. Factors such as age, sex, race, religion, and nationality create social barriers that even well-meaning people cannot overcome. Consequently people find themselves caught in webs, both those of their own spinning and those created by the values of their society.

With the Man, Solórzano paints a portrait of a self-deluding soul who would be a poignant figure if he were not completely self-centered. In contrast to the Man, the Woman engages the sympathy of the reader and the audience. She leaves filled with the sorrow and anguish of rejection, but having realized from the beginning that rejection was a possibility, she is prepared to continue living through her dreams and her correspondence.

Solórzano creates effective drama with three characters who converse in sparse dialogue on a bare stage. The Man's inability to recognize the Woman when he sees her produces many dramatic and verbal ironies. The themes of the play are dynamic. Life contains more than people expect. People must be open to broader ways of thinking; otherwise, like the Man, they may miss an important experience. Solórzano's choice of names for his characters, his setting, and his staging create a generic situation that becomes symbolic of life in the modern age.

Personal Literary Journal: Have you ever missed something of value because the experience that you had was so different from what you had expected that you were unable to appreciate it?

Literary Terms: characterization, foreshadowing, irony, paradox, setting, symbol, theme

COMPREHENSION QUESTIONS

1. *Who is the Man?* the Woman's pen pal
2. *Who does the Man wish would help him?* the Flagman

3. *How does the Man expect to recognize the person he's waiting for?* She will be wearing a white flower on her dress.

4. *Is the Man successful in his quest? Why or why not?* He fails because he refuses to see beyond the Woman's age.

5. *How does the Man feel at the end of the play? Why?* desperate—needing a loving relationship and longing for the woman he expected to meet

UNDERSTANDING THE PLAY: POSSIBLE ANSWERS

1. *Why the Man and the Woman do not have names* The Man and the Woman represent men and women in general, not particular individuals. Their plight is symbolic of the plight of all human beings. This treatment gives the play a broader focus and a more important message.

*2. *"They call me by many names"* Like the Man and the Woman, the Flagman does not represent a particular person or a person with a particular role in life. The Flagman is the detached bystander, one who is not interested in anyone else. He does not listen, he is not involved, and he does not care. He symbolizes the impersonal element in the universe.

3. *"The impossible is always true"* Students will probably agree with the Flagman's statement. One cannot predict eventualities such as illness and death or the ramifications of economic and political events. Factors interrelate in a multitude of ways, creating unforeseen results.

*4. *Why the Woman is afraid of finding the one she seeks* The Woman is afraid that reality will disappoint her. She has good reason to be pessimistic because she has been tempting young men with an old touched-up photograph of herself, and she knows that a great discrepancy exists between her actual appearance and the appearance that the young men expect. By ignoring the Man's presence, the Woman can keep alive her dream of a relationship between them.

5. *Why the Woman doesn't reveal identity to the Man* The Woman wants to protect herself from being rejected for being old and unattractive. She would rather that the Man think that he'd never met the person whom he expects.

   The Woman offers the Man the flower to see whether he will make the connection between the flower and her and whether he will give her a chance to be what he wants her to be.

*6. *Why the Man feels the woman he awaits must come* The Man is so desperate for a romantic relationship that his heart is fixed on the idea that this meeting will satisfy his needs.

7. *What the Woman's story reveals* The Woman's story reveals her loneliness and her desperate need to be accepted and loved. The Man's reaction to the story reveals his preoccupation with himself, which is so extreme that he does not realize that the Woman is talking about herself and that she is the woman he is so anxious to meet.

8. *Why the Man is angry at the end* The Flagman states the reality of the situation; the Man—beneath his anger—realizes that the Flagman is right. The Woman really is the woman the Man was searching for. On the surface, the

Man's anger is focused on the Flagman's double-talk. Beneath the surface, the Man is angry at the circumstances of his life, angry at the Flagman for reminding him of these circumstances, and angry at himself for pinning his hopes on an illusion.

*9. *The Man's final line* The Man's final line reveals the agony that results from his discovery. He cannot accept the reality of the Flagman's comments about the Woman's identity. He desperately wants his dreams to come true. He repeats "What the devil are you good for!" because he cannot face that the Flagman's purpose is to reveal reality.

10. *"One moment to recognize one another"* The Woman is referring to herself and the Man and their situation: For them, "now or never" probably reflects reality. In the Woman's view, the Man would have valued a relationship with her if he understood his need for companionship.

Most students probably will agree that a relationship can develop only when two people who are in contact with each other are both ready for the relationship. However, students may disagree about whether such an opportunity will occur only once.

11. *What the Man and the Woman learn from their experience* The Man reluctantly learns that appearance all too often belies reality and that reality destroys illusions. His desperation and anger at the end of the play reveal the shattering effect that this discovery has upon his psyche.

The Woman's experience confirms her suspicion that reality destroys illusions. These suspicions have led her to hide at home behind letters and old photographs.

12. *Themes* Possible themes:
   - The best-laid plans go awry.
   - One's expectations are often disappointed.
   - True communication between human beings is often impossible.
   - People find themselves caught in webs, both those of their own making and those created by the values of their society.
   - Barriers exist in our society and in the world that even well-meaning people find difficult to overcome.
   - By being too certain about what one wants, one can be blind to other interesting—but different—opportunities.

ANALYZING LITERARY TECHNIQUES: POSSIBLE ANSWERS

1. *Setting* The lack of a specific location is consistent with viewing the characters and action as symbolic. It adds to the timeless quality of the characters and the plot. Having fewer people around causes less intrusion and distraction and creates greater focus.

*2. *Role of the Flagman* The Flagman symbolizes the impersonal modern world. Many of his lines reveal this impersonality: "They all look alike"; "I can't know if someone I don't know has been around"; "that's not my job"; "it's not important."

The Flagman also acts as a foil for the Man, who responds in frustration by amplifying the Flagman's comments. The Man responds to the lines "they all look alike" and "what other one?" with a description of the expected woman.

In addition, the Flagman's philosophical remarks provoke an analysis of society. Examples include the following: "They all look alike" (focus on appearance; generalization about reality). "Everyone sells something" (cynical attitude about everyone's being motivated by self-interest). "That's very common. The contrary's also common" (contradictory nature of society). "He's (or she's) never coming" (inevitability of disappointed expectations). "The impossible is always true" (unpredictable nature of experience). "I saw the one that you aren't looking for, and the one you're looking for I didn't see" (ironic aspect of life).

3. *Why the Woman is old* The Woman's age is used to underscore the Man's confusion about appearance and reality. Because the Man values appearances, he cannot see beyond the Woman's physical attributes to recognize her essential character. He literally does not see the person with whom he has been corresponding and with whom he believes he is in love, even when she is standing right before him.

While relationships between older men and younger women are fairly common (and therefore generally accepted) in Western societies, relationships between older women and younger men are less common. The Woman's age provides a barrier for the Man because she is asking him to accept the unexpected. The Woman attempts to breach the barrier of her age in a number of ways—by providing him with a touched-up photograph, by veiling herself, and by making him close his eyes—but she is unsuccessful.

4. *Foreshadowing* The Flagman's comment "one can't know by just seeing a person whether it was the one who placed an ad in the newspaper" foreshadows the discrepancy between the Man's expectations and the reality of the Woman. Foreshadowing prepares for the dramatic irony.

*5. *Dramatic and verbal irony*

- Examples of dramatic irony include the following: The Man's meeting with the Woman "seems impossible" and actually becomes impossible because of the Man's expectations and the Woman's actual appearance. The Man tells the Flagman, "Perhaps she has passed by and you didn't see her"; but later the Man sees the Woman without recognizing her. The Flagman tells the Man, "One can't know by just seeing a person whether it was the one who placed an ad in the newspaper"; but later the Man cannot face the possibility that the Woman is the person he received letters and a photograph from.

- Examples of verbal irony include the following: The Man states, "She's the woman that I've been waiting for for many years"; whereas, because of her age and appearance, she is actually not the woman he is waiting for at all. The woman tells the Man, "Now I believe that she won't come," which is correct because the Woman has come but the woman whom the Man is expecting does not exist.

*6. *Symbolism* Examples of symbolism include the following: The Man and Woman, with their generic names, symbolize men and women. The Flagman symbolizes the impersonal modern world. The broken clock symbolizes timelessness. The dark stage symbolizes the characters' inability to see, recognize, and understand life. Light—which blinds the Man because he is unable to tolerate too much knowledge—symbolizes knowledge.

7. *Paradox* Paradoxes include the following: The impossible is possible. Life is at once rational and irrational. A person can be both young and old. Two people can converse with each other without communicating. People can be blind to opportunities.

8. *"A Sad Vaudeville"* Vaudeville is a form of stage entertainment where performers sing, dance, tell jokes, and enact skits. This play is vaudeville in that it is stage entertainment. It is sad in that communication, which is of prime importance to the Man and the Woman, cannot occur because they are unable to remove barriers that have been constructed by society and by themselves.

WRITING ABOUT LITERATURE

1. *Essay analyzing the Flagman's role* Call student's attention to the directions in the textbook assignment with regard to content and organization. (See **U.P.** questions 2 and 9 and **A.L.T.** questions 2 and 6 above.)

2. *Essay analyzing dramatic and verbal irony* Call students' attention to the directions in the textbook assignment with regard to content and organization. (See **U.P.** questions 2, 4, and 6 and **A.L.T.** question 5 above.) **AP**

3. *Creative writing: how this experience affects the Man's life* Call students' attention to the questions suggested in the textbook assignment. **(P.L.J.)**

FURTHER READING

Solórzano, Carlos, *Three Acts* (includes *The Puppets*).

Chess

ROSARIO CASTELLANOS

INTRODUCING THE POEM

"Chess" is a poem about the fragility of human relationships. Two lovers assume that their relationship is strong enough to withstand a competitive game. However, in the process of playing the game, their relationship changes from one of friendship to one of competition. The reader is left to wonder whether the friendship will be finished by the time the game is finished.

The objective of the game of chess is to use superior intelligence to defeat one's opponent. However, the game actually symbolizes any competitive situation that makes adversaries of friends, thus threatening their relationship.

Personal Literary Journal: Have you ever played a competitive game with a good friend? Would you run for a competitive office against a good friend? Why or why not? To what extent would your good feelings toward each other be threatened if there was a "winner" and a "loser" in your relationship?

Literary Terms: irony, symbol, theme

COMPREHENSION QUESTIONS

1. *What is the relationship between the two people?* friends; sometimes lovers

2. *Why do they decide to play chess?* to have fun; to share another experience

3. *What is the goal of the game?* to destroy the opponent

4. *What closing words reveal the game's power?* "annihilate the other one forever"

UNDERSTANDING THE POEM: POSSIBLE ANSWERS

1. *The game: anticipation and reality* What the speaker anticipates as good-hearted fun becomes cutthroat competition. The game becomes personal and serious rather than playful and enjoyable.

*2. *Competition as a risk to friendship* The last line, "annihilate the other one forever," implies that the outcome of the game will transfer into actual life. By spending so much time in an adversarial relationship, the two people will destroy their friendship.

*3. *Gender of players* Current research supports the view that preserving relationships is, in general, more important to women and that winning a competition is, in general, more important to men. This would mean that a chess game (or another competition) might be more threatening to two men or to a man in a male-female relationship than to two women.

*4. *Themes* Possible themes: Friendship and love are fragile and need support to thrive; competitive people need to anticipate the effect of their success on important relationships.

ANALYZING LITERARY TECHNIQUE: POSSIBLE ANSWERS

*1. *Chess as symbol* The chess game symbolizes any serious competition between two people in which each competitor invests an unusual amount of time or emotion trying to surpass the other. A chessboard is a traditional symbol for a battlefield. The game is an excellent choice for intellectual competition because the strategies needed to win require long training times.

*2. *Structure of poem* The three stanzas are a progression during which the friendship disintegrates. The first stanza sets forth the friendship and the expectation of enhancing it. The second stanza describes the process of enhancing the friendship—playing a chess game. The third stanza reveals the competitive level, the time devoted to the pursuit of winning, and the antagonism between the competitors. The final line creates a bridge between the world of the game and the lives of the competitors after the game has concluded. It implies that the competition will leave lasting scars on the competitors' friendship.

*3. *Irony* It is ironic that the friends play an intellectual game in the expectation that it will foster their friendship when, in fact, the game threatens their friendship.

WRITING ABOUT LITERATURE

1. *Essay analyzing structure* Remind students of directions in the textbook assignment related to symbolism and irony. Also remind them of the importance of quotations. (See **U.P.** question 4 and **A.L.T.** questions 1, 2, and 3 above.)

2. *Creative writing: conversation between chess players* Students may want to create two versions, one in which the man is the winner and one in which the woman is the winner. (See **U.P.** questions 2 and 3 above.) **(P.L.J.)**

FURTHER READING

Castellanos, Rosario, *A Rosario Castellanos Reader.*

A Very Old Man
with Enormous Wings

GABRIEL GARCÍA MÁRQUEZ

INTRODUCING THE STORY

In "A Very Old Man with Enormous Wings," García Márquez tells the charming story of a decrepit angel who suddenly falls into the yard of an ordinary Colombian villager and his wife. The angel is exploited as a curiosity and is mistreated by everyone in the village because he does not look or act as the villagers think an angel should. The author uses irony as a source of humor, for example, in the priest who cannot accept an angel that does not pass his test, the miracles, and the freak adapted from the Greek myth of Arachne.

Regardless of whether the very old man is an angel or an unusual and unfortunate human being, the story's power emanates from García Márquez's attitude toward the indifference, intolerance, and inhumanity of ordinary people. All the villagers are sadly deficient in their ability both to appreciate the greatest wonders in life and to treat the unfortunate with sympathy, kindness, and respect. The story has a powerful satiric bite in its critical statement about human values and prejudices.

Yet what would be a tragedy in the hands of Fyodor Dostoyevski has a silver lining in the hands of García Márquez. Through his comic vision the Colombian author achieves a precarious balance in his fiction: the depiction of a world without illusion, without nobility, and without hope of perfection juxtaposed with the optimistic belief in the human ability to survive despite an endless succession of overwhelming obstacles. The satiric elements are gentle and lighthearted rather than sharp and bitter, and at the end the winged creature grows new feathers and flies away. The reader is left with paradoxes: The impossible is possible; predictable situations are filled with surprises; people all too often are blind to the significance of experiences that are part of their lives.

Typical of García Márquez's fiction, his style is inseparable from his subject. The casual and simple style of the folktale is the perfect vehicle for his magic realism. The fantastic is treated in the same manner as the ordinary, and the fantastic and the ordinary are inseparably combined into the fabric of the whole. This "tale for children" reflects García Márquez's oral legacy from his grandmother.

Magic realism provides an imaginative and sophisticated way to achieve free expression in countries that are ruled by dictators. Often the wild humor of the magical aspects of these otherwise realistic stories satirizes an underlying political problem, criticizing society in a way that is so oblique that the criticism is acceptable in a repressive environment.

Personal Literary Journal: A well-known saying states that "you can't judge a book by its cover." To what extent, if any, have you found this saying to be correct when applied to human beings? Do you make an effort to get to know people who appear to be quite different from yourself? Why or why not?

Literary Terms: allusion, comedy, folktale, humor, irony, magic realism, myth, paradox, satire, theme, tragedy

COMPREHENSION QUESTIONS

1. *What does Pelayo find in the rear of his courtyard?* an angel or an old man with wings

2. *Where does he put what he found?* into a chicken coop

3. *What first makes the priest question the nature of Pelayo's guest?* The old man doesn't understand Latin, "the language of God."

4. *How do Pelayo and his wife profit from their guest?* They charge a five-cent admission, and they use the money to build a mansion.

5. *What diverts the audience from Pelayo's show?* the arrival of a woman who had been changed into a spider

6. *What is appealing about the new show in town?* Her show is cheaper, and her fate teaches people a lesson.

7. *What miracles does the angel perform?* The blind man grows three new teeth, the leper's sores sprout flowers, and the paralyzed man almost wins a lottery.

8. *What does the doctor's examination reveal?* The noises from the angel's heart and kidneys make the angel's recovery from chicken pox seem impossible; also, the angel's wings appear to be natural.

9. *Why do Pelayo and his wife fear their guest's death?* They don't know what to do with a dead angel.

10. *What happens to Pelayo's guest at the end of the story?* He grows new feathers and flies away.

UNDERSTANDING THE STORY: POSSIBLE ANSWERS

1. *Why the angel appears as an old man* The angel disguised as an old man is treated by everyone as a decrepit old man would be treated, thus revealing the dark side of human nature.

2. *Why the angel speaks like a Norwegian* The angel speaks a language that is not related to Spanish, and the villagers do not understand a word he says. They assume he is speaking the language of a remote country. They probably say he sounds like a Norwegian sailor because the Norwegians are famous sailors and he has come from the sea.

3. *How Pelayo and Elisenda feel about their guest* Pelayo and Elisenda do not like him because of his disgusting smell and his disreputable appearance. He does not fit their preconceived ideas about angels.

4. *Importance of Pelayo's guest being an angel* If an angel that wanted to test the true nature of human beings appeared as a decrepit, disgusting-looking human-type creature, the angel would see people reacting normally to him. However, people would be on their best behavior if the angel looked like an angel.

5. *Villagers' treatment of the angel* Their treatment reveals the villagers to be selfish, callous, cruel, and intolerant of anything that is different. Their inability to appreciate the angel's unique qualities reveals their inability to appreciate the wondrous aspects of life.

6. *The angel's abilities and inabilities* The angel's abilities and inabilities distinguish him from what the villagers expect an angel to be like. He neither looks nor acts in a way that is considered typical of angels, and the villagers cannot accept an angel who does not conform to their preconceptions.

7. *The person who comes closest to identifying the angel* The doctor, observing the angel scientifically, determines that the angel cannot be human because of his wings and because of the sounds from his heart and kidneys. Ironically the doctor is viewed more favorably than the priest, because the doctor's evaluation is not based on preconceived ideas.

*8. *Significance of the villagers' fascination with the spider-maiden* It is ironic that even though the villagers are religious, they are more interested in the angel as a freak than as an angel. They prefer the spider-maiden because they can visit her more cheaply, and they can understand her and therefore relate to her. Their attitude reveals lack of imagination, lack of wonder, and lack of understanding the abstract.

9. *Why the angel lives so long with Pelayo's family* Five to six years is long enough for Pelayo and Elisenda to become accustomed to the angel and to make an effort to relate to him. However, they do not. The angel accepts their behavior, in that he does not strike out against them. His departure—

apparently dependent on the condition of his wings—is as natural and unpredictable as his arrival.

10. *Narrator's attitude* The narrator treats the tale matter-of-factly, suggesting that the events are no more amazing than any other life events.

11. *Theme* Possible themes:

- You cannot judge a book by its cover.

- People are inclined to ignore or mistreat those who are different from themselves.

- People often do not see beyond their preconceived ideas (prejudices) when evaluating others.

ANALYZING LITERARY TECHNIQUE: POSSIBLE ANSWERS

1. *Comedy versus tragedy* Sources of humor include: the arrival of a strange creature; the various attitudes about his identity, including the reasons for the priest's doubts; the illnesses of those who come to be cured and the nature of the miracles that the angel performs; and the spider-maiden's tale of woe. Sources of sadness include the angel's treatment by the villagers.

   It appears that comedy prevails. With few exceptions, the angel accepts his situation; and when his wings have recovered, he sets off for a better life. García Márquez may intend to reveal the patience and fortitude of the downtrodden.

2. *Satire* Satire ridicules people and institutions and makes them laughable; its purpose is usually to promote reform. It is clear that García Márquez uses this device. The tunnel vision of the priest and the shallow values of the villagers are the prime examples of satire. No one makes an effort to deal with the creature as he is, and he suffers because he does not conform to preconceived ideas about what he should be like. The reader may conclude that it is better to be tolerant and imaginative than parochial, and better to be kind and considerate than callous and cruel.

3. *Folktale* Both the style and the content of García Márquez's story are reminiscent of a folktale. The style is simple, as if it were being told aloud; it sounds like a story that originated from an oral tradition. The villagers are common folk who must cope with a magical event, and they react with an appropriate lack of sophistication.

4. *Irony* Irony is related to the thematic content and the humor of the story. For example, it is ironic that an angel who fell to earth would be unrecognized, unappreciated, and treated like a freak. His decrepit appearance, the assumptions made about him, the priest's reasons for being unable to accept him, the villagers' preference for a different freak, and Elisenda's finding it hell (verbal irony) to have an angel living with them are all sources of irony.

*5. *Why "a tale for children"* The story would be appealing to children because of its folktale style and because of the myth of the spider-maiden. Children would enjoy the magical idea of an unidentified decrepit angel falling to earth, the humorous maladies of the people who come to be cured, and the bizarre miracles that the angel performs.

Children might not appreciate the humor of the religious allusions, and they might not understand that the behavior of the villagers symbolizes the inhumanity of human beings toward those who are different.

6. *Magic realism* This story is a good example of magic realism in that it blends the magical (an angel suddenly appearing in a small village, a young woman turned into a spider) with the real (the village and villagers, the parish priest, the chicken coop). The combination of the magical and the real is delightfully provocative.

7. *Paradox* Paradoxes include the following: The impossible is possible in life; life is both rational and irrational; people can be blind to the significance of their life experiences.

WRITING ABOUT LITERATURE

1. *Essay analyzing this story as "a tale for children"* Call students' attention to the directions in the textbook assignment. Remind them to use quotations to support their ideas and to explain the appeal of each aspect that they identify. (See **A.L.T.** question 5 above.)

2. *Essay analyzing the allusion to Arachne and the role of the spider-maiden* Students may wish to consult a book of mythology or a reference book to learn more about the Arachne myth. The villager's interest in the spider-maiden serves as a contrast to the villagers' malicious treatment of the angel. (See **U.S.** question 8 above.) **AP**

3. *Creative writing: a report from the angel* Call students' attention to the questions suggested in the textbook assignment. **(P.L.J.)**

FURTHER READING

García Márquez, Gabriel, *One Hundred Years of Solitude; Love in the Time of Cholera; Of Love and Other Demons; Leaf Storm and Other Stories; Collected Stories; Strange Pilgrims: Twelve Stories; Innocent Eréndira and Other Stories; No One Writes to the Colonel and Other Stories.*

1. *The main characters in "The Tree," "The Story from Rosendo Juárez," and "End of the Game" come of age in the course of these short stories. Whether through a process or through an epiphany, each character's life is changed by his or her discovery. For each story, describe the coming-of-age and the effect of the newfound realization on the main character.* Brígida comes of age in "The Tree" when the rubber tree that has given her solace from her unhappy marriage to Luis is chopped down, revealing the harsh reality of her life. As a result of this epiphany, she takes control of her life and happiness, and she divorces Luis. In "The Story from Rosendo Juárez," Rosendo comes of age through a series of events, especially the death of Luis Irala, that makes him realize the foolishness of life as a knife fighter. He realizes that his life is more important than his reputation. The narrator of "End of the Game" comes of age when she, Holanda, and Letitia end their favorite game because of a boy's reaction to Letitia's paralysis. Although the narrator has commented on Letitia's fortune in being able to read and in being allowed to lie around when others are doing chores, she now realizes the full effect of the paralysis on Letitia's life.

2. *Three poems in this unit—"Vicarious Love," "Two Bodies," and "Chess"— discuss aspects of intimate relationships. Compare and contrast the views of the loving relationships found in these three poems.* In "Vicarious Love," Sor Juana Inés de la Cruz maintains her belief that love is extremely delicate and that love's true joy is found in being loved the right amount. She contrasts her love with the love of "pretty women," who seek nothing but worship and admiration. Their love often comes from vanity, infatuation, and lack of mutual respect. In "Two Bodies," love and human relationships, though imperfect, provide sustenance in a universe devoid of meaning. Whether lovers are in harmony with each other, hostile toward each other, or indifferent toward each other, these relationships add value and significance to life. "Chess" insinuates that competition between two lovers, though started in fun, may ultimately have dire consequences for the couple. Love is depicted as a carefully arranged game that has rules and guidelines, which, if broken, may lead to competition and unhappiness.

3. *Gabriela Mistral and Pablo Neruda are both Chilean poets known for their use of language. Analyze how the poets use figurative language to convey meaning in the poems "Serene Words" and "The Word." Use examples from each poem to support your ideas.* In the lyric poem "Serene Words," Mistral illuminates the beauty of the world through figurative language such as "the wind blows a honeyed breath" (line 8) and "a lily can ensnare our gaze" (line 12). The metaphors and personification throughout "Serene Words" create vivid images rather than relate a story. The meaning of her poem—that the sadness and pain of life are overshadowed by life's beauty—is conveyed through these images. Neruda also relies on metaphors to pay homage to the power of language in "The Word." In the opening stanzas, he uses

metaphors such as "pain took to the roads" (line 10) to outline human plight and movement and to show that words accompany humans no matter where they go. His metaphors of the cup, the blood, and the water relate language to various aspects of the world—the cup because words hold meaning; the blood because words are an essential part of being human; and the water because language is liquid, both in sound and meaning.

4. *In their short stories and play, João Guimarães Rosa, Gabriel García Márquez, and Carlos Solórzano examine the nature of reality. What is reality in these pieces, and how does reality influence each story? Why might each author have portrayed reality as he did?* In "The Third Bank of the River," the nature of reality is based on the psychology of the main characters. When the father abandons his family to live on the river, his sanity is thrown into question. This affects the psychological makeup of the entire family, most notably of his son who never marries or leaves the town because he believes his father needs him. His reality centers on his father. García Márquez relies on magic realism to construct the reality of "A Very Old Man with Enormous Wings." The third-person omniscient narrator and the townspeople treat mystical and astonishing events as though they are commonplace. García Márquez's satiric bite and commentary on people's preconceived ideas, blatant cruelty, and fascination with spectacle draw on the fact that amazing events are treated so ordinarily. In *Crossroads*, reality is murky, varying depending on what a person chooses to see. This is highlighted by the Flagman's commentary, which conveys how impersonal the modern world seems. A person creates his or her own reality—by touching up photographs, as the Woman does; by ignoring what is known to be true, as the Man does in refusing to see who the Woman is; or by ignoring the needs of others, as the Flagman does. Each person must live with the reality that he or she creates.

North America

Special Request for the
Children of Mother Corn

ZUÑI (TRADITIONAL)

INTRODUCING THE POEM

"Special Request for the Children of Mother Corn" is a poem from a Zuñi mid-winter ritual in which a religious leader prays for the blessing of a life-sustaining corn crop. The poem reveals the Zuñi people's connections to the earth as the great mother of all that grows; the sun as the nurturing father; and the cobs of seed corn as the children of the Corn Maidens, the Zuñi's spiritual life-sustaining mothers. The poem presents many aspects of the natural world in human terms: the trees, whose arms break beneath the snow (lines 7–9); the earth mother, whose flesh cracks with cold (lines 11–12); the young corn, whose hands stretch out in a plea for rain (lines 22–23). Underlying the Zuñi prayer is the concept that the corn possesses a living spirit that is aware of the Zuñi's thoughts. The Zuñi pray for winter snow that will enable the corn to grow in the spring, but they recognize that growing corn will depend on luck as well as prayer.

Personal Literary Journal: When you need something that money cannot buy, such as love or good health, how do you get it?

Literary Terms: figurative language, metaphor, personification

COMPREHENSION QUESTIONS

1. *Why will the Zuñi be lucky if the winter brings snow?* The spring snowmelt provides the moisture necessary for a new corn crop.

2. *Why do the Zuñi call the various kinds of corn "our mothers"?* Corn sustains them as a mother sustains her children.

3. *What do the Zuñi call the sun?* father

4. *Who creates the rain?* "rain makers," or rain clouds

5. *How do the Zuñi intend to live?* with thoughts of appreciation for the corn

UNDERSTANDING THE POEM: POSSIBLE ANSWERS

1. *Function of poem* The Zuñi hope to receive a fine yield of corn by pleasing the Corn Maidens.

2. *Zuñi relationship to corn* The relationship of the Zuñi to corn reveals the importance of corn in the lives of the Zuñi. Corn is a nurturing mother. The Zuñi consider themselves intimately related to the natural world.

*3. *Meaning of lines 15–17* The corn kernels (seeds) are being planted in the earth.

4. *Significance of the final lines* The corn myth outlined in the introductory material reveals that the Corn Maidens disappeared and left the people without sustenance when the Zuñi did not show respect and appreciation for the Corn Maidens. The Zuñi do not intend to make this mistake again.

ANALYZING LITERARY TECHNIQUE: POSSIBLE ANSWERS

*1. *Personification* Personification conveys the feeling that all of life is related. Personifying the earth and the sun as mother and father emphasizes their nurturing aspects and reflects the dependence of the Zuñi on nature. The following are examples of personification: the trees as beings whose arms break beneath the snow (lines 7–9); the earth, whose flesh cracks with cold, as the great mother of all that grows (lines 11–12); the sun as a nurturing father (line 20); the young corn as a child whose hands stretch out in plea for rain (line 23); the cobs of seed corn as the children of the Corn Maidens (lines 26–27).

2. *Metaphor* Metaphors include "frost flowers"; "a fourfold robe / Of white meal"; and "a floor of ice." Opinions about the role of metaphor in the poem will vary.

WRITING ABOUT LITERATURE

1. *Essay analyzing the role of personification* Call students' attention to the directions in the textbook assignment with regard to content and structure. (See **U.P.** question 3 and **A.L.T.** question 1.)

2. *Creative writing: a special request for something of value* Call students' attention to the directions in the textbook assignment. **(P.L.J.)**

FURTHER READING

Allen, Paula Gunn, ed., *Song of the Turtle; Voice of the Turtle*.

Astrov, Margot, ed., *The Winged Serpent*.

Bierhorst, John, ed., *The Sacred Path*.

Highwater, Jamake, ed., *Words in the Blood*.

Swann, Brian, ed., *Coming to Light: Contemporary Translations of the Native Literatures of North America*.

Trout, Lawana, ed., *Native American Literature: An Anthology*.

Turner, Frederick W. III, ed., *The Portable North American Indian Reader*.

Vizenor, Gerald, ed., *Native American Literature: A Brief Introduction and Anthology*.

Witt, Shirley H., and Stan Steiner, eds., *The Way*.

Give Me the Splendid Silent Sun
WALT WHITMAN

INTRODUCING THE POEM

In "Give Me the Splendid Silent Sun," Whitman rhapsodizes about life and about the irony of his wish for the beauty, peace, and solitude of the country when he loves being part of Manhattan, the ultimate urban environment.

The power of the poem comes from both its content and its style. Whitman presents a striking contrast between what he thinks he wants in life and what he really wants. The content of the poem is romantic in its idealization of both the natural world and the urban world. From the many details that could be chosen to describe the country and the city, he selects only those that support his view of the universe as a joyful assortment of choices. Nature is charming, and the city is exciting.

With a poet's ear for sound, Whitman chooses words and phrases that reflect the contrast between the natural world and the urban world. He describes the natural environment in long flowing lines and ornate speech and then changes to short disconnected clauses and simple speech when he describes the city scene.

Whitman's repetitive sentence structure, in the form of detailed lists of appealing qualities, creates visual pictures of both rural beauty and metropolitan variety and complexity. The sheer mass of pictorial images gives the poem power. Whitman's repeated use of "Give me . . ." and "Keep your . . ." emphasizes the irony that is implicit in his desire to move from the country to the city.

Personal Literary Journal: Do you think that you would prefer living in the country or living in the city? What are the advantages of each location?

Literary Terms: apostrophe, connotative language, contrast, free verse, irony, paradox, realism, repetition, romanticism, tone

COMPREHENSION QUESTIONS

1. *Where does Whitman first think that he wants to live?* in the country
2. *What aspects of rural life does he find most appealing?* solitude and beauty of nature
3. *Where does Whitman realize that he really wants to live?* in the city
4. *What aspects of this environment does he find most appealing?* the variety and complexity of life on the streets

UNDERSTANDING THE POEM: POSSIBLE ANSWERS

1. *Whitman's view of nature* Whitman's presentation of life in the country is realistic; he provides many concrete details of nature. However, his overall view of nature itself is idealized and romantic. He omits all aspects of nature that are unattractive, unreliable, or harmful. He also omits mention of the human labor necessary to sustain life in the country.

2. *Whitman's view of urban life* Whitman's presentation of life in the city is realistic; he provides concrete details such as the tired old soldiers' noticing nothing as they march. However, his view of the city itself is even more idealized and romantic than his view of the country. He lists unattractive and painful aspects of urban reality as though they were positive characteristics. For example, he describes men marching to and from war, often dazed and wounded; but this sight does not diminish his pleasure of the city.

3. *Whitman's views* Opinions will vary. Some students will prefer the pastoral environment; others, like Whitman, will prefer the city with all its problems.

4. *Relation between 1865 and content* Manhattan's Broadway hosted parades of soldiers going off to fight in the Civil War and returning from the battlefield. Whitman recorded the trumpets and drums, the brigades, the clanking muskets, and the military wagons loaded with war gear. The tone of these passages reflects the closing stages of the war. The speaker is enjoying the sights and sounds.

ANALYZING LITERARY TECHNIQUE: POSSIBLE ANSWERS

1. *Advantages of free verse* By using free verse, Whitman is able to focus on his subject rather than his form. Writing in free verse permits longer sentences, greater variety of content within each line, and less predictability. Whitman is free to use whatever devices he wishes to create unity and achieve emphasis.

2. *Contrast* Whitman's use of contrasting details and contrasting words and phrases highlights the difference between the noisy urban environment and the tranquil rural environment.

3. *Apostrophe* Whitman uses apostrophe to address both the city (line 15) and Nature (line 21). In both examples, Whitman treats nonhuman entities as if they were listening to him. Apostrophe makes the city and Nature appear to be vital forces that are interacting with him.

4. *Irony and first line* It is ironic that Whitman chooses a tumultuous environment over a peaceful, beautiful environment. He chooses to live in the city despite its many reminders of the human price of war. The first line symbolizes Whitman's view of nature; he uses the line twice. The line has the ironic function of wishing for the joys of nature and then repudiating those joys.

5. *Paradox* It is paradoxical that Whitman finds the perfection and beauty of nature to be boring, but he feels enriched and enchanted by the raucous, turbulent, disquieting aspects of the city.

*6. *Repetition* Examples of repetition include the following:
   * Repeated sentence structure: Detailed lists of appealing qualities give cumulative power to the rural beauty and the urban variety.
   * Repeated phrases: "Give me . . ." emphasizes Whitman's need; "Keep your . . ." emphasizes Whitman's rejection of the country and the irony of his decision to go to the city.

7. *Tone* Whitman's tone is ebullient and joyous. He is enthusiastic about both nature and the city, but he prefers the city. He conveys his enthusiasm through the use of the phrase "Give me . . ." and by his lists detailing the delightful variation and complexity of the sights that he enjoys.

WRITING ABOUT LITERATURE

1. *Essay analyzing the use of repetition in the poem* Call students' attention to the directions in the textbook assignment. Remind them of the importance of using quotations to support their ideas. (See **A.L.T.** question 6 above.)

2. *Creative writing: a poem about the best place to live* Remind students to work from a list of reasons that support their choice and to use repetition for emphasis and effect. **(P.L.J.)**

FURTHER READING

Whitman, Walt, *Leaves of Grass; Complete Poems.*

My life closed twice before its close—

EMILY DICKINSON

INTRODUCING THE POEM

"My life closed twice before its close—" is a philosophical lyric. With eloquence and power, it expresses the devastating impact Dickinson experienced when she lost two people she loved, an impact that was intensified by her skepticism about the possibility of reunion after death. In a series of paradoxes, Dickinson equates the loss of two loved ones with a living death. So great were these losses that her "life closed twice before its close." A more conventional religious view would have led her to hope for reunion in heaven after death. However, Dickinson expresses uncertainty about one's fate after death. She states that parting, which occurs only in this life, "is all we know of heaven." Dickinson's ability to express heartfelt emotions in a lyric poem enables her to confront her traumatic life experiences and to accept her reactions to them.

Personal Literary Journal: Imagine that a person very dear to you has left your life. What impact would that loss have on your life?

Literary Terms: climax, connotative language, lyric, paradox, tone

COMPREHENSION QUESTIONS

1. *Why did the speaker's life close twice?* Two devastating events occurred.

2. *What might immortality reveal to the speaker?* a third devastating event

3. *What do we know of heaven, according to the poem?* only that heaven involves parting from this life

4. *What does the poem suggest we know of hell?* Experiencing the pain of parting is like experiencing hell.

5. *What attitude does this poem express?* skepticism about reunion in heaven

UNDERSTANDING THE POEM: POSSIBLE ANSWERS

1. "My life closed twice" The speaker has died emotionally twice before her physical death.

*2. *Immortality* The speaker is uncertain about the nature of immortality. It is possible that loved ones are not reunited after death, so she fears a third cataclysmic separation.

*3. *"Parting is all we know of heaven"* Many people believe that they will be reunited with their loved ones in heaven. The speaker does not know whether this is true. She is certain only of what she experiences in this life, which is that parting from loved ones is devastating.

*4. *"Parting is . . . all we need of hell"* The speaker does not know whether hell exists after death, but she is certain that hell exists in life. In her experience, parting from loved ones is hell on earth.

ANALYZING LITERARY TECHNIQUE: POSSIBLE ANSWERS

*1. *Connotative language* Dickinson uses connotative language to convey the devastating effect of the two events to which she alludes. Examples: "So huge, so hopeless to conceive" (line 5) and "Parting . . . heaven . . . hell" (lines 7–8).

*2. *Paradox* The following are examples of paradox:

- "My life closed twice" (line 1): The speaker has died twice emotionally while she continues to live physically; she is experiencing a living death.

- "Parting . . . heaven" (line 7): Heaven is generally considered a reward. The speaker states that all she knows for certain about heaven is that it requires separation from those who are living. This suggests that heaven is a punishment for those left behind.

- "And all we need of hell" (line 8): People believe hell is a punishment after death. Dickinson is saying that parting from a loved one is so torturous that it creates hell on earth.

3. *The last line as the climax* The last line dramatically conveys the devastation caused by two events in the speaker's life. It intensifies the emotion behind all the other statements.

4. *Tone* The tone is one of despair and devastation. Two cataclysmic events have occurred in the speaker's life, and conventional religion offers little comfort for her. She is afraid of another devastating separation.

WRITING ABOUT LITERATURE

1. *Essay analyzing Dickinson's use of paradox* Call students' attention to the suggestions in the textbook assignment. Remind students to use quotations to support their ideas. (See **U.P.** questions 1, 2, 3, and 4 and **A.L.T.** question 2 above.) **AP**

2. *Essay analyzing Dickinson's technique of compression* Call students' attention to the suggestions in the textbook assignment. (See **U.P.** questions 1, 3, and 4 and **A.L.T.** questions 1 and 2.)

3. *Creative writing: significance of the loss or the presence of a loved one* Remind students that they can write either poetry or prose. **(P.L.J.)**

FURTHER READING

Dickinson, Emily, "There's a certain Slant of light"; "Because I could not stop for Death"; "The Soul selects her own Society"; "I heard a Fly buzz—when I died"; "The Brain—is wider than the Sky."

Ile

EUGENE O'NEILL

INTRODUCING THE PLAY

Ile is the story of a man who must choose between his wife's well-being and his own self-respect. As the captain of a whaling ship, Captain Keeney possesses both wealth and reputation; but his self-esteem depends on his ability to be successful at his profession, which is acquiring whale oil (ile). When the play opens, he has been two years at sea, and his hunt for whales has been unsuccessful. Supplies are dwindling; the men are mutinous; and his wife, Annie, is on the verge of a mental breakdown. Captain Keeney must decide whether to return home or to continue his frustrating search. Shortly after subduing his men and reluctantly agreeing to his wife's heartfelt plea to return home, the ice opens and whales are spotted. He reverses his decision to return home and orders his men to prepare for the kill. Mrs. Keeney responds by losing her mind.

Thus, a well-intentioned man becomes a pawn of fate through a common failing in human nature, excessive pride. Captain Keeney loves his wife and attempts to care for her, but his personal investment in his career is more compelling. When pushed, he puts his wife's needs ahead of his drive to search for an elusive prey. However, when the prey is within his grasp, he becomes deaf to his wife's pleas. Courage, determination, and perseverance are heroic in moderation but tragic in excess. Captain Keeney's obsessive drive to acquire the whale oil regardless of the mind-set of his crew and his wife makes him a tragic figure.

Mrs. Keeney is a tragic figure in that she lacks the psychological strength to create meaning in her life when the outer worlds of marriage, town life, and nature do not support her needs. She is also tragic in a universal symbolic sense, the victim of a world that can be indifferent—and sometime even hostile—to human needs.

O'Neill places these two tragic characters in a situation that has no satisfactory solution. Regardless of whether Captain Keeney decides to continue searching for whales or return home, disaster will come to both him and Annie. His decision to continue his search causes Annie's insanity and robs him of his wife. However, he would have been miserable if he had chosen to sacrifice his goal to take Annie home. He could not live without self-esteem, and he would have hated his wife for being the cause of his private shame.

The character of Captain Keeney reveals O'Neill's love of Greek tragedy with its interplay between fate and the human personality. Like many a hero in Greek mythology, Captain Keeney's greatest strength becomes his greatest weakness, and he is compelled to act in such a way that he brings disaster into his life. As the captain of the whaling ship, Captain Keeney is a man of high social stature. The source of his excellence (the Greek concept of *aretē*) is his expertise as a captain; he always returns from his whaling voyages with a full load of whale oil. His pride in his success and his related fear for his reputation are both excessive (the Greek concept of *hubris*); they lead him to take action that is blindly reckless or rash (the Greek concept of *atē*) in that he continues to pursue whales despite the crew's temperament and his wife's emotional needs. The retribution (the Greek concept of *nemesis*) is his wife's insanity.

Ile differs from the classical Greek tragedy in that Captain Keeney knows what form the retribution will take before he makes his critical decision. Having precipitated his wife's insanity, he reacts with denial rather than with remorse. O'Neill thus reveals the destructive power of the psychological need to be awesome. Pride leads to callous behavior, which in turn leads to isolation from loved ones. The question of whether responsibility to oneself is more important than responsibility to one's family is as old as Greek myths and as modern as the vital contemporary conflict between the demands of career and the needs of family.

Personal Literary Journal: In what ways, if any, are your own needs and desires more important to you than the needs and desires of other members of your family? In what ways, if any, are your family's needs and desires more important to you than your own? Has a conflict ever occurred where a family member had to make a choice between what was best for that person and what was best for others in the family?

Literary Terms: climax, conflict, crisis, exposition, foreshadowing, irony, melodrama, paradox, repetition, setting, symbolism, theme, tone, tragedy

COMPREHENSION QUESTIONS

1. *What is important about the day on which the action occurs?* The sailors' two-year commitment is over.

2. *What is Captain Keeney's goal?* get whale oil (ile)

3. *What has the problem been with the voyage?* There have been no whales, so there has been no oil.

4. *What does Mrs. Keeney want her husband to do?* return home

5. *How does Mrs. Keeney feel about the voyage?* She hates it.

6. *What effort has the captain made to please his wife?* He brought an organ on board for her.

7. *What is the attitude of the seamen?* They threaten mutiny if the captain doesn't turn back.

8. *What reversal occurs?* Captain agrees to turn back, but the ice breaks to the north so he changes his mind. Whales are seen almost immediately.

9. *In the end, what does the captain do?* goes whale hunting

10. *In the end, what happens to Mrs. Keeney?* She goes insane.

UNDERSTANDING THE PLAY: POSSIBLE ANSWERS

*1. *Three major conflicts* The major conflicts include the following:

- the conflict between Captain Keeney and Annie
- the conflict between the captain and himself (an inner conflict between the wish to please himself and the wish to please Annie)
- the conflict between the captain and external forces (fate or nature)

The conflict between Captain Keeney and his crew is a minor conflict.

*2. *Power of the conflicts* The power of the three conflicts arises from the interdependence of the conflicts. All three conflicts involve Captain Keeney's drive to acquire whale oil and his sense of priorities.

*3. *Blame for Mrs. Keeney's condition* The blame for Mrs. Keeney's condition is shared between Mrs. Keeney herself and the captain. She was not happy home alone so she chose life at sea. The captain places his obligation to himself and his goals over his wife's needs and his love for his wife.

*4. *Sympathetic character* One strength of *Ile* lies in the balance O'Neill achieves between the two major characters. Both are admirable people. Mrs. Keeney's point of view is understandable before the whales are sighted, and the crew echoes her position. Captain Keeney's point of view is understandable after the discovery of the whales.

*5. *Wiser decision for Captain Keeney* If Captain Keeney gives in to his wife's needs, his self-esteem may suffer irreparable damage because his reputation depends on a successful voyage. If he ignores his wife's needs, he must live with the responsibility for her mental state. The tragedy may be that Captain Keeney cannot win either way.

*6. *Ability of characters to control their fate* The power of the play resides in O'Neill's substitution of human psychology for the Greek concept of fate. The characters are limited by their personalities. Those who can be flexible and adaptable fare better than those who are either obsessed (Captain Keeney) or passive (Mrs. Keeney).

7. *Seamen's reaction to Captain's decision* Because of their financial stake in a successful voyage, the seamen will support Captain Keeney once the whales are in sight.

8. *Themes* Possible themes:

- Personality determines fate.
- Acting in moderation (flexibility, modest goals) leads to a happier life.

ANALYZING LITERARY TECHNIQUE: POSSIBLE ANSWERS

1. *Function of Ben and the steward* The conversation between Ben and the steward provides the exposition. It reveals the underlying situation as the play opens, including the problem of finding whales and the effect of this problem on the temperaments of all onboard ship—the crew, Mrs. Keeney, and Captain Keeney.

2. *Foreshadowing* A source of *Ile*'s power resides in the inevitability of the outcome of drama. One example of foreshadowing occurs when Ben and the steward characterize Captain Keeney and Mrs. Keeney. It is clear what will happen to Mrs. Keeney if the captain continues the whaling expedition.

*3. *Fate* Fate takes two forms:
   - the force in nature that supplies whales after the captain has agreed to return home
   - the force within the captain that programs him to react as he does

   The whales are the catalyst for the tragedy that Captain Keeney brings upon himself.

4. *Connection between setting and tone* The setting—at sea in the Arctic, with its isolation, impenetrable ice, and gray skies—creates a tone of depression, frustration, and mounting hysteria.

5. *Crisis and climax* The crisis occurs when Captain Keeney decides to pursue the clear passage northward regardless of the effect of his action on his wife. The climax occurs when Mrs. Keeney loses her mind. The climax is intensified by the Captain's denial of his wife's condition, a denial made necessary because his actions were the precipitating factor in her insanity.

*6. *Captain Keeney as a tragic figure* Captain Keeney is compelled by his nature to act in a way that causes the insanity of Mrs. Keeney. His excellence (*aretē*) is his expertise as a whaling captain; he always returns from his voyages with a full load of oil. His excessive pride in his accomplishments (*hubris*) leads him to take the rash action (*atē*) of continuing to pursue whales in spite of the risk to his wife. The retribution (*nemesis*) is Mrs. Keeney's insanity. Captain Keeney knows what form the retribution will take before he makes the critical decision, but he denies both the possibility and the reality, and he shows no remorse.

*7. *Paradox* Paradoxes include the following:
   - Single-minded devotion to the immediate goal of achieving financial success can prevent people from realizing the ultimate goal of improving their lives.
   - People may base their attitudes and behavior on how they think others view them when in reality others view them quite differently or may not think about them at all.
   - A person whose emotional needs are not being met can be desperately unhappy despite economic security.
   - A person's greatest strength is often that person's greatest weakness.

8. *Symbolism* The world of the sea symbolizes the uncaring, hostile, unpredictable universe in which human beings live. The concealment and the exposure of the whales motivate Captain Keeney's behavior—which, in turn, causes Mrs. Keeney's depression and madness.

9. *Repetition* Repetition emphasizes the characterizations of Captain Keeney ("I got to git the ile!") and of Mrs. Keeney ("Take me home . . . I can't bear it. . . . I'll go mad."). Repetition also emphasizes the sense of inevitability.

WRITING ABOUT LITERATURE

1. *Essay analyzing Captain Keeney as a tragic figure* Call students' attention to the directions in the textbook assignment with regard to content. (See **U.P.** questions 1, 2, 3, 4, 5, and 6 and **A.L.T.** questions 3, 6, and 7 above.)

2. *Creative writing: a dialogue between another captain and his wife* Students should focus on the issue of responsibility to oneself and to others and on the roles of love and career in marriage. The attitudes of both the husband and the wife should be presented. **(P.L.J.)**

FURTHER READING

O'Neill, Eugene, *The Great God Brown; Mourning Becomes Electra; The Iceman Cometh; Long Day's Journey into Night*.

Soldier's Home

ERNEST HEMINGWAY

INTRODUCING THE STORY

"Soldier's Home" reveals the difficulty that a marine has when he returns home after World War I and tries to reenter the world that he left behind. Although the members of his family have not changed, he has become a different person. The title may be read in two ways, reflecting the double focus of the story: First, the soldier is home; and second, the home of the soldier—that is, that family of the soldier.

"Soldier's Home" is typical of Hemingway's work in that it tells the important story indirectly, by implication. The story focuses on a soldier (Harold Krebs) who is now at home. Although Kreb's war experiences are never depicted, Hemingway reveals the war's effect on Krebs. The surface story shows the important truths that cause Krebs to think, speak, and act as he does. However, Krebs is more than his past. The war has caused him to reevaluate the universe and his place within it. Krebs accepts himself, in this period of transition, as he readjusts to civilian life.

Krebs is a Hemingway hero. His war experiences have taught him that he lives in a universe that lacks meaning and order. On the battlefield, he witnessed a world where bad things happen to good people; he saw that people are not always punished for mistreating others. Krebs lost any valid source of outer direction—including his religion. He has become inner-directed, responding pensively and courageously to the world by creating his own strong moral code of behavior.

Possessing the self-knowledge and self-confidence of the typical Hemingway hero, Krebs knows that he had been a good soldier. He behaved properly and performed well as a marine on the battlefield, reacting with a self-imposed code of behavior that demanded self-discipline and expertise. He finds it ironic that he must tell lies about the war—lies that make him nauseous, cause him to want to forget the war, and make him lose his pride in himself as a good human being and as a good soldier.

Meanwhile, Krebs's parents and sister are ignorant of the significance of his battlefield experiences. They expect that the person who has returned is the same person who left, except that he is now two years older. They know nothing about his new worldview and code of ethics; and without these pieces, Krebs's attitudes, values, and behavior are an impossible puzzle.

With the passage of time, conflict between Krebs and his parents develops. Krebs's time of decompression is seen as laziness. His parents want him to work, marry, and start a family. Yet Krebs finds the idea of courting and marrying a woman "too complicated."

The crisis in the story involves the escalating conflict between Krebs and his mother (who also speaks for his father) over his mother's attitude toward her religion, which she regards as a fixed set of universal beliefs. To encourage Krebs to get a job, she tells him, "God has some work for every one to do. There can be no idle hands in His Kingdom." When Krebs honestly responds, "I'm not in His Kingdom," his mother rejects his point of view and replies, "We are all of us in His Kingdom."

When his mother pursues the issue of wanting him to "settle down to work," Krebs's noncommittal response leads her to ask him whether he loves her—implying that if he does, he will do what she wishes. To her surprise and sorrow, Krebs announces that he does not love her or anyone else. However, he quickly realizes that his mother is incapable of understanding him and that he has hurt her with his honesty. Therefore, he lies and tells her that he did not mean what he said. Then the crisis moves from bad to worse. Krebs's mother asks him to pray with her. He kneels; but when she asks him to pray, he responds honestly, telling his mother that he cannot even try to pray. To this, she responds, "Do you want me to pray for you?" To avoid the complications that the truth would cause, Krebs tells a second lie and permits his mother to pray for him. This becomes the climax of Krebs's experience at home, because it teaches him that his parents will never be able to accept and understand him. He realizes that as long as he lives with them, he will have to tell lies and make compromises to avoid the complications of their relationship.

Krebs makes an important decision: He resolves to leave home to pursue his independent goals. The story closes with Krebs's multifaceted resolution. He will get a job in Kansas City where he will be able to lead an independent and, therefore, a less complicated life. This decision will please his mother. However, to avoid confrontation with his father, Krebs decides that he will not comply with his father's wish that he visit his father's office. Having made these difficult decisions with ease, Krebs is free to enjoy what life has to offer. He will begin by going to watch his sister play baseball—because she wants him to and because he likes her.

The tone of this story is somber but positive. Krebs's experiences have convinced him that he cannot resume a life that is based upon the conventional religious values of his parents. On the other hand, neither can he resume the life of a fraternity boy. He has learned who he is and what he wants out of life, and he possesses the courage and self-confidence to reach out for what he wants.

Hemingway—in the style that he made famous—reveals character and setting through simple sentences (the way people usually speak); sparse but significant details; and repetition of words, phrases, and clauses (which are often variations of a theme). What is extraordinary about this story is the extent to which Hemingway's style conveys the dual nature and significance of the title "Soldier's Home." The medium is the message, and neither would be as powerful without the other.

Personal Literary Journal: Recall or imagine a situation where you left home, lived somewhere else for a period of time, and then returned home. (For example, you may have gone away to school or to a summer camp or visited a friend or relative.) What was it like to return home? To what extent did your experience away from home change your values, your attitude, or your perception of members of your family?

Literary Terms: characterization, climax, crisis, irony, point of view, resolution, theme, tone

COMPREHENSION QUESTIONS

1. *How had Krebs entered the war?* He had enlisted as a marine.

2. *How long was he away from home?* about two years

3. *How long has Krebs been home when the story takes place?* about a month

4. *Why does Krebs not like to talk about the war he has just fought in?* To get people to listen to him, he must lie about it.

5. *How does Krebs spend his time?* He sleeps late, reads, plays pool, and plays the clarinet.

6. *Why does Krebs prefer foreign girls?* With them, conversation was unimportant.

7. *What does Krebs like to read?* histories of the war he fought

8. *What is Krebs's father willing to do for him? Why?* His father is willing to loan him the family car, hoping that he will start to date girls.

9. *What do Krebs's parents want him to do?* get a job

10. *What does Krebs' father want him to do that he refuses to do?* meet his father at the office to discuss his future

11. *What does Krebs say that makes his mother cry?* He does not love her.

12. *How does Krebs resolve this issue?* He tells her that he did not mean what he had said.

13. *What does Krebs permit his mother to do for him?* pray for him

14. *Why does Krebs plan to go to Kansas City?* to get a job

15. *What does Krebs decide to do at the end of the story?* to watch his sister play indoor baseball

UNDERSTANDING THE STORY: POSSIBLE ANSWERS

1. *Interpretations of the title* "Soldier's Home" may be read as "the soldier is home" or as "the home of the soldier." The dual interpretation of the title reflects the dual focus of the story, which deals both with Krebs's return and with the home (the family) to which he returns.

*2. *Effect of the war experience* Krebs has been a soldier in World War I. He fought with courage and skill on the battlefield. He saw innocent men injured and killed. He discovered that life or death is the result of luck rather than skill or worth. He learned that bad things happen to good people and that death on the battlefield is an undeserved fate. Krebs's war experience changed his attitude and values.

3. *College and fraternity* Nothing in a well-written short story is accidental or irrelevant, and opening sentences have great significance. In the first sentence, Hemingway states that Krebs attended a Methodist college to introduce Krebs's religious background into the story. In the second sentence, Hemingway makes the point that before Krebs entered the war, he was just like all his fraternity brothers, sharing their values, their interests, and even their appearance. As the story goes on, it becomes apparent that Krebs's war experiences have caused him to become a different type of person— an inner-directed individual as opposed to an outer-directed fraternity boy— and the contrast is important.

4. *Delayed return home* Krebs enjoyed the additional year he spent in Germany. The photograph of Krebs in Germany shows that he was happy and apparently well adjusted. He spent time with uncomplicated women who did not ask him to discuss his attitudes and ideas. While Krebs was in Germany, he was able to avoid the complications of returning to the world he had left behind.

*5. *A Hemingway hero* Krebs reveals that he is a Hemingway hero when he thinks about feeling "cool and clear inside himself . . . when he had done the one thing, the only thing for a man to do, easily and naturally, when he might have done something else." He acknowledges to himself, "He had been a good soldier. That made a difference." However, the lies that he feels forced to tell about the war and about his behavior as a soldier— although unimportant—make him feel nauseous, because they are untrue or exaggerated.

   At home, Krebs's goal is for "his life to go smoothly," without telling lies or being misunderstood and without feeling conflict about his change in attitude and values. As a Hemingway hero, Krebs has the inner strength to cope with the difficult transition to civilian life and to leave home so he can be true to his own moral code of behavior.

6. *Coping with transition* Krebs deals with his return home by permitting himself to decompress. He needs time to readjust to the values, goals, and pace of life at home. He does so by sleeping late and pursuing activities

that he enjoys. He is determined to avoid complications with people so he avoids conversing with his parents and dating attractive girls.

7. *Krebs vs. Harold or Hare* Harold Krebs, who was called by his last name when he was a soldier, has come to define himself as the soldier that he was in the war. The name Krebs is used whenever Hemingway is reflecting on Krebs himself or Krebs's situation. However, Krebs's parents call him Harold, and his sister calls him by the nickname Hare. When his parents or his sister use his first name, they are referring to the Harold they knew before the war. On the surface, Krebs and Harold are the same person; in an important sense, however, they have become two different people.

*8. *Krebs's parents* Hemingway conveys the personality of Krebs's mother by what she says and by what Krebs says about her. She loves Harold, but she cannot understand that her Harold was changed by the war. She assumes the role of communicator—speaking on behalf of her husband—but she does not hear what Krebs tries to tell her. She is religious beyond doubt or question, viewing everyone as a member of God's kingdom.

Hemingway conveys the personality of Krebs's father (who never enters the story) by what Krebs's mother says about him and by how Krebs reacts to what his mother says. Krebs's father does not allow his life to be changed by the war. He wants his son to move on with life—as though the war had not happened—and does not want his newspaper to be mussed up. In his role as head of the family, he sends word that his son should see him at his office and that his son may use the family car for dating.

Krebs's parents represent the world that Krebs left behind when he went off to war; their attitudes and values represent the issues that Krebs must cope with as he returns to civilian life. Krebs must live and socialize with people who know nothing about the realities or the effects of war.

9. *Love* Krebs tells his mother that he does not love her or anyone else because loving someone creates complications. Krebs is currently self-absorbed. Because of his war experience, he is not ready to become involved with someone else's needs and wishes.

10. *Mother's prayer* When Krebs permits his mother to pray for him, he realizes that he will always need to lie to his mother because she will always make him feel guilty if he tells her the truth. Krebs realizes that he must leave home if he is to determine the course of his own life and to live according to the moral code that he has created.

11. *Helen* Krebs's relationship with Helen appears to be unchanged, despite his participation in the war. She is comfortable teasing him, and he is comfortable replying in kind. Hemingway puts Helen into the story to reveal that Krebs is still capable of being very much like he used to be, as long as what is being demanded of him is consistent with his autonomy and his moral code.

*12. *Decisions* The decisions that Krebs makes at the end of the story reveal that he has the self-confidence and courage to leave home and to begin a new life as a civilian. Krebs will get a job in Kansas City, where he can lead an independent and, therefore, a less complicated life. This decision will please his mother, which pleases him. He will not visit his father's office to discuss his future because he is determined to be inner-directed. He will watch Helen play indoor baseball because he likes her; because it is important to Helen that he be there; and because watching her game does not involve lies, complications, or consequences.

*13. *Themes* Possible themes:

- Living by one's own moral code gives a person significant control over his or her life.

- People may not be able to control what happens to them, but they can control their responses.

- To be true to oneself, a person needs to be autonomous and independent of the values and attitudes of the group.

- Remaining true to oneself takes courage, self-confidence, and determination.

ANALYZING LITERARY TECHNIQUE: POSSIBLE ANSWERS

*1. *Point of view* The story is told from Krebs's point of view. This is important because the point of the story is Krebs's adjustment from the world of war to the world of peace. Krebs's parents do not understand what he has experienced or how his experiences have changed him. A story told from their point of view would be very different.

*2. *Conflict* The conflict in this story is between Krebs and his parents. The issue is inner-direction versus outer-direction. The Harold whom his parents reared was outer-directed. His goal was to "be a good boy" for his parents. The Harold who returns is inner-directed. He has created his own code of values and behavior, and it is his goal to live by this code.

3. *Crisis, climax, and resolution* The story contains two crises. The first crisis occurs when Krebs tells his mother that he does not love her and then feels obliged to tell her that he did not mean what he said. The second crisis occurs when he permits his mother to pray for him. Both incidents involve lies on his part and denial by his mother.

The climax occurs when Krebs realizes that he will have to continue to lead a life of lies, with their "complications" and "consequences," as long as he remains at home. Krebs has slowly come to realize that his mother is incapable of realizing who he really is, incapable of accepting his point of view, and incapable of accepting that someone could be inner-directed.

The resolution is Krebs's decision to leave home and get a job in Kansas City. Being a Hemingway hero, he resolves to do "the one thing, the only thing for a man to do, easily and naturally, when he might have done something else."

*4. *Irony* It is ironic that Krebs has to lie about the war to have anyone listen to him. Lying destroys Krebs's pride in himself for having been a good soldier.

It is the inability of people to understand the psychological effect of war on a "Hemingway hero" that creates Krebs's experience once he returns home.

*5. *Simple sentence structure* Hemingway's short simple sentences attempt to capture the way people think and speak, as opposed to the way they write. Hemingway uses this style when he describes the photo taken in Germany, when Krebs is thinking about girls, and when Krebs has conversation with his sister and his mother. The description of the photograph imitates the eyes of a stranger looking at the photograph for the first time and seeing only what is obvious. Krebs's thoughts about girls emphasize what is important to Krebs. The two conversations reveal how Krebs relates to his sister and with his mother—both verbally and emotionally.

*6. *Detail* Examples of detail include the following:

- The description of two photographs reveals how a stranger would see Krebs, first as a member of a college fraternity and second as a marine.

- Krebs's description of the girls with their short haircuts, sweaters, "shirt waists with round Dutch collars," and "silk stockings and flat shoes" reflects Krebs's reaction to civilian life. He is content to watch pleasing patterns rather than to make any attempt to get to know an individual girl.

- The details of Krebs' breakfast—his mother's calling him to breakfast, his reading the newspaper while he eats, and his mother's attempting to discuss his future—mark the passage of time like a ticking clock.

*7. *Repetition* Hemingway uses repetition to convey Krebs's state of mind as he attempts to adjust to civilian life. Repetitive thought characterizes the way a person copes with needs, desires, or ideas that are very important. The more important they are, the more the person thinks about them. So it is with Krebs as he thinks about his need to tell lies, his interest in girls, and his desire to avoid anything that will be complicated.

8. *Tone* The tone of this story is both somber and positive. It is somber because Krebs, like many soldiers who have endured the horrors of war, cannot resume a life that is based upon the conventional values of his parents. On the other hand, the tone is positive because Krebs has changed from a fraternity boy to a Hemingway hero. He has learned who he is and what he wants out of life. He possesses the character, courage, self-confidence, and determination to reach out for what he wants and to become independent of the attitudes and values of others.

WRITING ABOUT LITERATURE

1. *Essay analyzing Krebs as a Hemingway hero* Call students' attention to the directions in the textbook assignment with regard to paragraphing and the use of quotations. (See **U.S.** questions 2, 5, 12, and 13 and **A.L.T.** questions 2 and 4 above.)

2. *Essay analyzing Hemingway's style* Aspects of Hemingway's style include details, repetition, and short simple sentences. Call students' attention to

the directions in the textbook assignment with regard to paragraphing and the use of quotations. (See **A.L.T.** questions 5, 6, and 7 above.) **AP**

3. *Creative writing: "Soldier's Home" from the point of view of either Krebs's mother or his father* Call students' attention to the directions in the textbook assignment. (See **U.S.** question 8 and **A.L.T.** question 1.)

4. *Creative writing: a story in which a character has a profound experience* Call students' attention to the directions in the textbook assignment. **(P.L.J.)**

FURTHER READING

Hemingway, Ernest, *The Complete Short Stories of Ernest Hemingway.*

The Hollow Men
T. S. ELIOT

INTRODUCING THE POEM

Written shortly after the end of World War I and prior to Eliot's conversion to Anglo-Catholicism, "The Hollow Men" is a psychological portrait of the modern age. Although it is Eliot's most pessimistic poem, its striking images and its rhythms make it among the most memorable of his works.

With lives that are devoid of meaning, the "hollow men" have ceased to exist in any creative sense. They live in a sterile world—a dead land of cacti and of stone images in a valley of dying stars. Eliot may be describing the world after a great war, or he may be referring to the world of bustling technology where people move through time like mindless robots. Either way, whatever has bound human beings to one another and has provided meaning in life no longer exists in this waste land. The "hollow men" have no past and no future, and they have a dismal present. They despair because they are paralyzed, or they are paralyzed because they despair. Either way, they symbolize passivity, sterility, and wasted life. Their world ends "not with a bang but a whimper." By using the word "we" in the opening lines of the poem ("We are the hollow men / We are the stuffed men"), Eliot invites readers to see their own reflections in his mirror.

Eliot was interested in Jungian psychology. The "hollow men" may allude to Jung's Shadow, that inherent part of each person's personality that "personifies everything that the subject refuses to acknowledge about himself and yet is always thrusting itself upon him directly or indirectly." According to Jung, "to become conscious of it involves recognizing the dark aspects of the personality as present and real."

The possibility of this interpretation is confirmed by Eliot's use of the epigraph about Kurtz from Conrad's *Heart of Darkness*. Mr. Kurtz, an educated European man, enters the heart of Africa to buy ivory. His sojourn far from the laws and customs that govern civilized peoples destroys his polished veneer and releases his primitive nature. As he dies, he thinks about his deeds among the Africans, recognizes the darkness that inhabits his own soul, and exclaims "The horror! The horror!"

Conrad believed that everyone harbors the capacity to lose self-restraint and to be evil. He thought that people could control their actions only when they looked deep within themselves and recognized their potential for evil, because people cannot deal with problems that they do not acknowledge. This epigraph implies that the "hollow men" need to look within themselves, acknowledge the emptiness of their values, and muster the courage to revitalize themselves. The power of the allusion to Kurtz resides in the contrast between Kurtz's self-knowledge and the "hollow men's" self-deception.

Like the Symbolists, Eliot wants readers to enter the world of the poem prepared for the unusual and the unexpected and prepared to feel more than they can logically understand. In "The Hollow Men," as in other poems, Eliot places familiar words in new contexts to express new ideas and emotions. The allusions he uses gain intense emotional power by emphasizing contrast rather than similarity. He deliberately juxtaposes symbols, verbal styles, emotions, past and present, and thought and action in a way that defies conventional logic but that fits the world within the poem. Finally, he repeats phrases or sentences to intensify the emotional content of the poem and to unify it.

Personal Literary Journal: What might lead a poet to describe human beings as "hollow"? What kind of world do you think hollow people would inhabit? To what extent, if any, do you view people alive today as hollow? Why?

Literary Terms: allusion, characterization, connotative language, contrast, epigraph, figurative language, Imagist, lyric, metaphor, oxymoron, paradox, parallelism, repetition, rhythm, Shadow, simile, Symbolism, theme

COMPREHENSION QUESTIONS

1. (I) *What adjectives does Eliot use to describe his characters?* hollow, stuffed

2. (II) *How does the poet feel about "death's dream kingdom" (line 20)?* afraid of it; wishes to avoid it

3. (III) *What words does Eliot use to describe the land of the "hollow men"?* dead; cactus; stone images

4. (IV) *What adjective describes his characters?* "sightless" (line 61)

5. (V) *What children's singing game does Eliot allude to?* "Here We Go 'Round the Mulberry Bush"

6. (V) *What prayer does Eliot allude to?* the Lord's Prayer

UNDERSTANDING THE POEM: POSSIBLE ANSWERS

1. *"Hollow"* "Hollow" epitomizes emptiness; the word itself sounds empty. The men are hollow because they live without values or beliefs; they do not think, feel, or act in any significant way.

*2. (I) *"Shape without form, . . . gesture without motion"* The description may suggest a ghost. Like the "hollow men" and the scarecrows, the form is human but dead. The image creates a contrast between appearance and reality, and it functions as an effective characterization of the "hollow men."

*3. (I, II) *"Death's other Kingdom"* and *"death's dream kingdom"* "Death's other Kingdom" may be the kingdom of the dead who have died as contrasted with the kingdom of the dead "hollow men" who are still alive. "Death's dream kingdom" may also refer to the kingdom of the dead who have died. It is better than the land of the living dead in that the sun shines, the trees live, and the wind sings there; voices are perceptible, not quiet meaningless whispers. It is worse than the land of the living dead because it is the land of eternal death, where death is inescapable, unchangeable, and final. The speaker does not want to die.

4. (III) *"Stone images"* It is possible that the "stone images" are modern buildings, houses of worship, or other material creations of the "hollow men." The "hollow men" are the living dead who live in a dead land. They live among the wonders of modern technology, and they worship the gods of wealth and material possessions. These materialistic values have replaced spiritual values such as love, kindness, sympathy, and generosity. In section III, Eliot states, "At the hour when we are / Trembling with tenderness / Lips that would kiss / Form prayers to broken stone" (lines 48–51).

5. (IV) *"Lost kingdoms"* According to Eliot, the people of the modern age have lost both the kingdom of the living and the kingdom of faith. The kingdom of the living has become the "hollow men's" dead "cactus land." The kingdom of faith lies beyond the "hollow men's" reach. The Shadow that controls their lives, blinding and paralyzing them, is the side of themselves that they do not acknowledge. They must recognize the Shadow and understand its nature before they can truly live.

6. (V) *"Life is very long"* The statement that "life is very long" provides the only hopeful note in the poem. There is possibility of change for the better. Yet at the end of the poem, even that hope is cut short by the paralysis that exists because of a lack of self-knowledge. Length of life does not insure change.

7. (I, V) *Connection between "Remember us . . . As the hollow . . . stuffed men" and "This is the way the world ends / Not with a bang but a whimper"* The "hollow men" are passive. "Lost / Violent souls" may act out in counterproductive ways, but the "hollow men" do not act out at all.

8. *Themes* Possible themes:
   • People must recognize what they have become if they are to change.
   • It is possible to be physically alive yet (because of a sterile life) figuratively dead.

ANALYZING LITERARY TECHNIQUE: POSSIBLE ANSWERS

1. *"Stuffed men"* "Stuffed men" is an appropriate metaphor for modern men and women because scarecrows (figures stuffed with straw) cannot think, talk, act, or relate to others. The metaphor suggests immobility and inaction rather than vitality.

*2. *Vision imagery* The "hollow men" are either empty or disguised (lines 31–36), so people who look at them "With direct eyes" (line 14) cannot see them.

The "hollow men" themselves also lack the ability to see: "The eyes are not here / There are no eyes here" (lines 52–53); "We grope together" (line 58); "Sightless, unless / The eyes reappear" (lines 61–62). The vision imagery supports the poem's theme of the inability to see purpose in life.

*3. *Allusion to "Here We Go 'Round the Mulberry Bush"* The mulberry bush symbolizes a fertile environment, while the prickly pear symbolizes the environment of the desert. Eliot's substitution of the prickly pear cactus for the traditional mulberry bush creates a contrast between the environment of the "hollow men" and the environment of the readers (as the readers see their environment). It is a terrifying reminder of how people can become accustomed to the lives they lead, regardless of what their lives may be.

The allusion to a children's song is also effective because children lack adult sophistication. They realize that they live in a sterile world, and their acceptance of this sterile world is frightening. The tone of the second verse of the dance is in striking contrast to the tone of the first verse; the second verse is as depressing as the first verse is cheerful. Having the children sing these lines increases the power of the poem's chilling prediction about the end of the world.

*4. *Mistah Kurtz* The power of the allusion rests in the contrast between Mr. Kurtz's self-knowledge and the "hollow men's" self-deception. Conrad believed that everyone has the capacity to lose self-control and to be evil and that people can control their actions only by looking deep within themselves and recognizing this potential for evil. Eliot's use of this epigraph implies that the "hollow men" need to look within themselves and learn from the emptiness that they find there.

*5. *Guy Fawkes* The power of this allusion rests in the similarity between Guy Fawkes and the "hollow men." Fawkes was a man of purpose who acted upon his convictions. Today his effigy is annually burned at a festive holiday celebration that has lost its connection with the real Guy Fawkes. The "hollow men" are figurative effigies (or scarecrows) of people who once lived with conviction and purpose.

*6. *Figurative language* Eliot uses oxymorons ("Shape without form, . . . gesture without motion" [lines 11–12]), similes ("rats' feet over broken glass" [line 9]), metaphors ("stuffed men" [line 2]), and allusions (Kurtz, Fawkes, the mulberry bush) to compare objects and ideas that are not usually compared. His allusions gain intense emotional power because they emphasize contrast rather than similarity. He deliberately juxtaposes one symbol with another (the prickly pear with mulberry bush), one verbal style with another (the Lord's Prayer with the children's singing game), one emotion with another ("Lips that would kiss / Form prayers to broken stone" [lines 50–51]), the past (Guy Fawkes) with the present, and thought with action (the Shadow and the Lord's Prayer with the children's ring dance) in a way that defies conventional logic but fits the world within the poem. An equally significant contrast exists between the poem's aural appeal and its somber subject matter.

7. *Sound devices* Repetition, parallelism, and rhythm reinforce the incantatory quality of the poem, a quality that is also reinforced by the children's rhyme and the lines from the Lord's Prayer. Eliot repeats phrases or sentences to unify the poem and to reinforce its meaning and its emotional content.

WRITING ABOUT LITERATURE

1. *Essay analyzing contrast* Call students' attention to the directions in the textbook assignment with regard to content and organization. (See **U.P.** questions 2 and 3 and **A.L.T.** questions 2, 3, 4, 5, and 6 above.) **AP**

2. *Essay analyzing the poem's relation to Jung's Shadow* When Eliot states that the "hollow men" have no eyes and are "Sightless, unless / The eyes reappear / . . . / The hope only / Of empty men" (lines 61–67), he is expressing the idea that the "hollow men" are blind to the kind of people that they have become (their sterile Shadow-selves) and that their only hope for improving the quality of their lives is to look within themselves and acknowledge the emptiness of their values. If self-knowledge would replace self-deception, the "hollow men" might be able to muster the courage necessary to revitalize themselves. However, the poem's ending makes this possibility seem unlikely.

   Call students' attention to the questions in the textbook assignment. (See **A.L.T.** question 2 above.) **AP**

*3. *Creative writing: theme on whether modern people are "hollow"* Call students' attention to the directions in the textbook assignment. **(P.L.J.)**

FURTHER READING

Eliot, T. S., "The Love Song of J. Alfred Prufrock"; *Murder in the Cathedral.*

Mother to Son
LANGSTON HUGHES

INTRODUCING THE POEM

"Mother to Son" is a mother's exhortation to her son to follow her example of facing life with effort and courage. It is clear from the mother's message that she possesses dignity and pride despite having had a difficult life and that she cares about how her son will choose to lead his life.

Hughes characterizes the mother through her speech patterns as well as by her advice. His use of free verse enables the mother to tell her situation in her own language and to achieve emphasis through the use of movement and pauses in the structure of her sentences.

Hughes achieves power and poignancy through the symbol of the stairway, a common feature in the urban dweller's apartment life. The stairway, which is necessary for traveling from one level to another, lends itself to being an extended metaphor. The difficulties on the steps represent real difficulties on the journey of life.

Personal Literary Journal: A popular saying states, "When the going gets tough, the tough get going." To what extent do challenges excite you, and to what extent do you find them discouraging? Explain your point of view.

Literary Terms: apostrophe, characterization, connotative language, contrast, figurative language, free verse, metaphor, symbol, theme

COMPREHENSION QUESTIONS

1. *What kind of life has the mother had?* difficult
2. *What is the mother's attitude toward life?* She keeps aiming high.
3. *What advice does she give her son?* Keep trying to reach your goals.
4. *What symbol does Hughes use to represent the mother's life?* a stairway
5. *What is Hughes's metaphor for an easy life?* a "crystal stair"

UNDERSTANDING THE POEM: POSSIBLE ANSWERS

1. *Background of the mother* It is clear from the mother's use of English that her knowledge is primarily from experience rather than from traditional education. The nature of the mother's life explains her goal of wanting to improve the life of her family and herself. It also explains her use of stairs as a metaphor. Living in an inner-city apartment building, she would have actually climbed stairs that were in the condition she describes in the poem.

2. *The mother's description of life* The mother wants the son to know that it is possible to succeed in spite of the many obstacles in their lives. He should follow her example and keep aiming to achieve his goals.

*3. *The mother's character* Her description of continuing to climb the stairway of life despite every kind of obstacle—both physical and psychological— reveals her to be a woman of dignity, courage, and perseverance. Her desire to communicate her values to her son reveals that she is loving and supportive and that she has high expectations for the son as well as for herself.

*4. *Themes* Possible themes:

   - A motivated person can overcome obstacles.
   - If at first you don't succeed, try again and again.
   - Parents can set good examples for their children.
   - Dignity, courage, and perseverance do not depend on economic status.

ANALYZING LITERARY TECHNIQUE: POSSIBLE ANSWERS

*1. *Stairway as a symbol* Life moves from youth to old age, and a stairway is one way of moving from one place to another. The stairway is particularly appropriate here because it is an inherent part of apartment living in most urban neighborhoods. In the mother's neighborhood, one might expect the stairway to be in poor condition. People walk down stairs as often as they climb up; however, the mother speaks only of climbing up. Her climb symbolizes her efforts to improve her life.

*2. *The stairway as an extended metaphor* Possible answers include:

  a) tacks and splinters: racial prejudice in the form of slurs, discrimination, and injustice

  b) "boards torn up": obstacles based on racial discrimination, lack of education, or lack of money

  c) "no carpet": difficult tasks with nothing to ease them

  d) landings: brief periods when life is easier

  e) turning corners: beginning new stages in the progress toward old goals

  f) being in the dark: being uncertain of the future—unsure of how to achieve one's goals and unsure of success

3. *Apostrophe* Hughes's use of apostrophe gives the impression that the son is listening to the mother's advice. The mother's communication is particular (addressed to a real person) and immediate (some kind of response will be forthcoming).

4. *Techniques for characterizing the mother* Hughes uses the following techniques to characterize the mother:

  • what she says—her desire to communicate her values to her son

  • what she does—her continuous climb up the stairway of life despite a variety of obstacles, physical pain, and psychological discomfort

  • how she says it—her use of English (See **U.P.** question 3 above.)

5. *Advantage of free verse* Free verse gives Hughes the freedom to let the mother speak in her own style. Her speech helps her convey who she is and how she lives. The structure of her sentences, with their movement and their pauses, conveys the progress of her life and emphasizes the low points ("tacks," "splinters," "boards torn up," and "bare").

WRITING ABOUT LITERATURE

1. *Essay analyzing the extended metaphor* Call students' attention to the directions in the textbook. (See **U.P.** question 4 and **A.L.T.** questions 1 and 2 above.)

2. *Creative writing: response from son to mother* Call students' attention to the directions in the textbook assignment. Students can choose to write a poem or a letter. **(P.L.J.)**

FURTHER READING

Hughes, Langston, *Selected Poems; The Best of Simple*.

A Worn Path

EUDORA WELTY

INTRODUCING THE STORY

"A Worn Path" is the story of Phoenix Jackson, an African American woman who undertakes an arduous journey to procure medicine for her grandson, as she always does whenever he needs the medicine. Phoenix is the most humane of humans, at one with herself and with the universe. She expects from others the respect that she herself has for the living world, and she usually receives it.

On one level, "A Worn Path" is the story of an old woman's love for her grandchild. Her devotion is dramatized by her experiences on the journey and by the gift she buys her grandson in the end. No obstacle—neither the infirmities of old age nor the vicissitudes of nature—can deter her, and no personal sacrifice is too great.

On another level, "A Worn Path" is an affirmation of life despite all its obstacles. In the course of her journey, Phoenix experiences a series of anticipated and unanticipated trials, all of which she accepts as a part of life. Although time has attacked her body, her spirit refuses to be daunted. Beyond Phoenix's acceptance of life and her ability to endure its trials is her joy of simply being alive. She loves having one more day in which to enjoy the sights, sounds, smells, and feel of the universe. The story ends with a symbolic affirmation of life as Phoenix goes off to spend her two precious nickels on a paper windmill for her grandson. She will hold the windmill high all the way home, and the reader is left imagining Phoenix's enjoyment of its color and movement.

Opinions differ as to whether Phoenix's grandson is still alive. Those who believe that the grandson is dead cite the following details. Once Phoenix enters the doctor's office, her personality becomes more complex. She has had no trouble responding to the people she has met on her journey, but now she appears deaf to questions about her grandson's health. She has come for medicine to relieve life-threatening symptoms. Although he swallowed lye two to three years ago and has not recovered, the doctor does not ask to examine him. Phoenix describes him as an infant rather than a young child. Finally, her statement that she and her grandson are all alone in the world suggests her need to deny his death and to create the illusion of his life.

For those readers who think that Phoenix's grandson is dead, the death intensifies the power of the story and the story's statement about the human condition. Phoenix, true to the spirit of the legendary bird that is reborn out of its own ashes, keeps herself alive by keeping her grandson alive. As long as she can continue to believe that he lives, her life will have love, companionship, and purpose.

Welty addresses the question of Phoenix's grandson in her essay "Is Phoenix Jackson's Grandson Really Dead?" (*The Eye of the Story: Selected Essays and Reviews*) because it is the question she was asked most frequently by students and teachers. In Welty's opinion, it does not matter whether the grandson is dead, and readers are free to have their own opinions. The story is told from Phoenix's point of view—and to Phoenix, he is alive. The journey is the focal point of the story, and the possibility that Phoenix would continue to make the journey even if her grandson was dead shows her love for him, her devotion to him, and her hope that he will continue to live. Welty states in another interview (*Listen to the Voices*), "It doesn't bother me one bit if someone interprets something in a different way . . . because you have to try to make it (the story) full of suggestions, not just one."

Personal Literary Journal: Have you ever been lonely? If so, what did you do about it? Do you know any older people who are lonely? What do they do about their loneliness?

Literary Terms: characterization, humor, setting, symbolism, tone

COMPREHENSION QUESTIONS

1. *Describe Phoenix Jackson* an old African American woman with a red rag tied around her head

2. *What is she doing?* walking a long way through the country into town

3. *Name one of her difficulties* She walks with cane, she has difficulty seeing, she catches her dress on a bush, she crosses a stream on a log, she crawls through a barbed-wire fence, and she is knocked down by a dog.

4. *What is her goal?* to get medicine for her grandson

5. *What is unusual about her goal?* Phoenix's grandson may be dead.

UNDERSTANDING THE STORY: POSSIBLE ANSWERS

1. *Factors compelling Phoenix's journey* Phoenix makes the journey to procure medicine for her grandson. Her need to have someone to care for motivates her.

*2. *Purpose of Phoenix's adventures* Phoenix's adventures and her running conversation with the environment define her character. They reveal her dignity (being careful not to tear her dress and asking to have her shoes laced), pride (seeing the humor of falling into the ditch), determination (walking over a log to cross a creek; crawling through a barbed-wire fence), courage (facing a ghost in the cornfield), cleverness (distracting the young man so she can pick up the coin), self-knowledge (recognizing her "theft" of the coin), sense of humor (greeting the white man from the ditch; laughing about the scarecrow), and unselfishness (coping with the obstacles of this journey so she can procure medicine for her grandson). Her determination, courage, and unselfishness make her a heroic figure.

3. *Significance of cake and scarecrow* The episodes of the cake and the scarecrow reveal that Phoenix's mind sometimes wanders and that she sometimes has trouble remembering where she is and what is happening. Her reaching out to touch the "ghost"—only to find it is a scarecrow—reveals her ability to return to reality. Phoenix's ability to laugh at herself reveals that she is still mentally sharp in many ways. It also reveals that she can see herself as someone else might see her.

4. *Meeting with the hunter* The young hunter is both insensitive and threatening. His "What are you doing there?" is unfeeling, considering that she

is lying on the ground because she has been knocked over by his dog. His admonition to her to return home might be interpreted as well-meaning, but it indicates that he does not understand that she could have a purpose for being so far from home; his remark about "old colored people" wanting to see Santa Claus is a derogatory stereotype. His question about her age is rude. Finally, his pointing the gun at Phoenix is a genuine threat.

Meeting the hunter is an important episode. It reveals many of Phoenix's character traits, and it foreshadows the kind of treatment she will receive from the attendant in the doctor's office.

5. *Changes in Phoenix's behavior at the doctor's office* Phoenix, who was relaxed and talkative, becomes stiff and silent. She develops a nervous twitch and appears to be deaf. The problem seems to be more than simply fatigue. It is possible that Phoenix is close to being aware of her grandson's true state and that her behavior reflects the strain of this realization.

6. *Attitudes of attendant, nurse, and doctor* The attitudes of those who work in the doctor's office reveal various levels of sensitivity and knowledge. The attendant, who does not know Phoenix, treats Phoenix like a stranger. The nurse, who knows Phoenix, is gentle and considerate. The doctor, who knows why Phoenix keeps returning for the medicine, permits Phoenix to have the medicine when she comes to get it.

7. *Phoenix's grandson: dead or alive?* Student opinion will differ as to whether Phoenix's grandson is dead or alive. Those who think he is alive will cite Phoenix's determination to succeed in her journey, her general ability to distinguish between fantasy and reality, her ease in acquiring the medicine from the doctor, and her plan to purchase a windmill. Those who think he is dead will cite the relationship between the nature of his symptoms and the possibility of recovery, the nurse's surprise that the boy's condition has not changed, the doctor's willingness to supply medicine without examining the boy or talking with Phoenix, and Phoenix's need to believe that her grandson is alive.

8. *Welty's attitude toward Phoenix* Welty is filled with sympathy and compassion for Phoenix. Evidence for this includes Phoenix's determination and spirit during the journey, her behavior in the doctor's office, and her intention to purchase a paper windmill.

ANALYZING LITERARY TECHNIQUE: POSSIBLE ANSWERS

1. *Technique of gradual revelation* Withholding information about the time of year and about the purpose of Phoenix's journey permits the reader to concentrate on Phoenix's character traits as the challenges of the journey reveal them. Withholding information about Phoenix's grandson enables the reader to know Phoenix before it becomes necessary to consider her mental state.

2. *Phoenix* The phoenix is a legendary bird that builds a pyre every five hundred years, burns itself to ashes, and then emerges alive and renewed to life. Phoenix renews her life by living for her grandson and meeting all

the challenges in her life. The grandson is also a phoenix symbol. In Phoenix's mind, he has emerged alive from death, that is, he has survived a life-threatening accident.

3. *The paper windmill as a symbol* The windmill—with its movement, color, and design—symbolizes Phoenix's enjoyment of life. For Phoenix, life is more than endurance and perseverance.

4. *Title* "A Worn Path" emphasizes the repeated ritualistic nature of Phoenix's journey; it focuses on the journey itself rather than on the purpose of the journey. The title symbolizes the nature of human life—a journey with trials, failures, and accomplishments—and the personality traits necessary for the journey to be successful.

5. *Welty's style* Welty's style gives the story an oral quality, making it read like a folktale. The simple and direct sentences reflect Phoenix's personality and her relationship with the world around her.

WRITING ABOUT LITERATURE

1. *Essay analyzing Phoenix as a heroic figure* Call students' attention to the directions in the textbook assignment with regard to content and organization. Remind them that both quotations and their own ideas are important. (See **U.S.** question 2 above.)

2. *Creative writing: reports from two different points of view* Call students' attention to the direction in the textbook assignment. Remind them to focus on an analysis of Phoenix and her grandson. **(P.L.J.)**

FURTHER READING

Welty, Eudora, *The Collected Stories of Eudora Welty.*

Day of the Butterfly

ALICE MUNRO

INTRODUCING THE STORY

"Day of the Butterfly" is the poignant story of the fragile friendship between two girls—Helen, the sensitive insider, and Myra Sayla, an outsider. With an eye for revealing detail, Munro vividly recalls the world of sixth-grade girls, where conformity reigns. Its rule is so tyrannical that even sensitive girls, like Helen, often feel forced to be cruel to outsiders. They lack the courage to be kind because they fear ridicule and they risk isolation from their group.

Like a shadow in the background is the story of Myra's six-year-old brother, whose need for her makes her different from the other girls. He, too, suffers from the rule of conformity. In fact, the power of this story emanates from its ability to remind readers of the ways in which conformity rules their own lives and the price that they, too, pay for social acceptance.

Helen narrates this story years after the event occurred. Her distance from the event enables her to be selective in the incidents and details that she presents and to move the story to its conclusion without extraneous details. Her distance from her younger self enables her to be objective in confronting her conflicting attitudes and emotions in a difficult social situation.

Personal Literary Journal: To what extent, if any, is it important to you to be like your friends in the way that you dress, speak, and act? To what extent, if any, do you try to be independent of the control of others?

Literary Terms: characterization, conflict, narrative perspective, paradox, theme

COMPREHENSION QUESTIONS

1. *What is Myra Sayla's problem?* She needs to care for her younger brother even while she is in school.

2. *Why do the sixth graders know Jimmy Sayla?* He enters their classroom when he needs Myra's help.

3. *What does Jimmy do at recess?* He stays inside if he is being punished, or he stays in the back porch with Myra.

4. *How is Jimmy treated by the other boys?* He is beaten up.

5. *What does Miss Darling ask the sixth-grade girls to do?* be nice to Myra

6. *What is Helen's position in the group?* She is accepted by the group, but she is somewhat of an outsider because she lives on a farm.

7. *What memorable event happens on Helen's walk with Myra?* Myra finds a butterfly brooch in the Cracker Jack; Helen gives the brooch to her as a gift.

8. *Why is Myra not in school?* She is in the hospital with leukemia.

9. *What does Miss Darling suggest doing?* celebrating Myra's birthday early at the hospital

10. *What important event occurs at the end of the girls' visit with Myra?* Myra gives Helen one of her birthday gifts.

UNDERSTANDING THE STORY: POSSIBLE ANSWERS

*1. *Conflict* The conflict occurs within Helen rather than between Helen and her group or between Helen and Myra. It involves whether to be nice to Myra. Helen feels ambivalent: Her instincts that she should be kind and friendly to an outsider confront her fears that the group will ridicule her or reject her. Helen's inner conflict is intensified by her perception of the tenuous nature of her own position in the group because she is a farm girl, not a town girl.

*2. *Relationship between Jimmy Sayla's problem and Myra's treatment* The group operates under the principle of contamination by association. Jimmy's bathroom problem contaminates Myra and makes her unacceptable to the group. Like Myra, Jimmy is an outsider, and he is persecuted by the other boys at recess. He has learned that if he misbehaves, he will be punished by being kept inside at recess; consequently, he misbehaves.

*3. *Why Jimmy and Myra are "uncommunicative"* Jimmy and Myra are "meekly, cryptically uncommunicative" so they will have as little contact with the other children as possible. They try to do nothing that will call attention to themselves for fear of being tormented when they are noticed. Being ignored is the best treatment that they can expect in school.

4. *Miss Darling's role in Myra's life* Some students may feel that asking the girls to be nice to Myra was inviting them to be insincere, callous, and cruel toward her. Others may feel that Myra's school experience is so painful that Miss Darling is obligated, as a caring teacher, to do her best to inspire the girls to be kinder.

*5. *Helen's concern about her school life* Because Helen lives outside of town on a farm, she dresses differently from the town girls and she brings a lunch pail. Her situation causes a conflict. Being different from the other girls, Helen is more sensitive to Myra's feelings and her plight. However, Helen also runs the risk of being socially rejected, so she is concerned about taking social risks, such as being friendly to an outcast.

*6. *Myra's birthday* Miss Darling, who is aware that Myra may not live until July, wants Myra to have a birthday party before she dies. The party becomes fashionable because Miss Darling will let only a select group of students go to the party. Gladys takes her desired role as leader; she can impress her peers with special knowledge because her aunt is a nurse.

*7. *Myra's gift to Helen* Myra reconfirms her friendship by giving Helen a gift in return for the butterfly brooch. At first Myra's gift is a source of concern for Helen, because Helen's acceptance of the gift implies a friendship with Myra that could be socially disastrous for Helen.

The intrusion of the real world outside the hospital reminds Helen that she will not become Myra's friend and that she has misled Myra by permitting the exchange of gifts. Helen convinces herself that she is free from the danger that Myra's gift presents.

*8. *Myra's reactions to party* During the party, Myra changes from being suspicious of a new experience that might disappoint her to being captivated by the event. Helen notices Myra's small private smile and her pride. However, the last lines of the story suggest that Myra, having been disappointed so often by her peer group, has permanently walled herself off from the others to protect herself. If this is true, she may forget about her gift to Helen and the implications of a friendship between them.

Since Myra would have been unaware of Helen's private misgivings about befriending Myra, the butterfly brooch and the birthday party may have been the high points of Myra's short life.

ANALYZING LITERARY TECHNIQUE: POSSIBLE ANSWERS

1. *Setting* The setting, an elementary school in the recent past, makes the story believable. Myra's status as an outsider is threatening to Helen, who must decide whether to risk her own status in order to be Myra's friend. The girls are eleven or twelve years old, an age where actions and feelings significantly influence future behavior. Helen would have been old enough to remember the details and emotions of this experience.

2. *The butterfly as a symbol* The butterfly symbolizes friendship; it is a reminder of a gesture of kindness made by Helen and accepted by Myra. Like a butterfly, Helen's friendship with Myra is ephemeral. Helen's uncertainty about the ramifications of befriending Myra is emphasized by Helen's relief that Myra does not wear the butterfly brooch.

3. *Narrative perspective* Helen, as an adult, narrates this story about an event from her youth. She is the center of consciousness, so the reader never knows the thoughts of the other characters. Her distance from the event enables her to be selective in the incidents and details that she presents and to avoid extraneous details that would distract readers' attention from her main point. Helen's distance from her younger self enables her to be objective in confronting her conflicting attitudes and emotions in a difficult social situation.

4. *Helen as reliable narrator* Helen's language and insights reveal her to be an adult. Her acknowledgment of her internal conflict—her feeling of vulnerability in her social group—presents her to the reader as being very human; she makes no effort to have the reader view her behavior as better than it was.

*5. *Paradox* It is paradoxical that good people (like Helen) can knowingly be callous and cruel.

WRITING ABOUT LITERATURE

1. *Essay analyzing what Munro reveals about human nature* Call students' attention to the directions in the textbook assignment. Students may discuss the following characteristics of human nature:

   - A person who feels insecure about acceptance in a group will be careful to conform to the group's expectations (Helen).

   - Outsiders develop defensive strategies to protect themselves from being hurt by the group (Myra).

   - The leader of a group knows what personal qualities must be demonstrated to maintain a position of leadership and uses ridicule against anyone who threatens that authority and control (Gladys).

   - A well-intentioned but unrealistic authority figure can do more harm than good (Miss Darling). (See **U.S.** questions 1, 2, 3, 5, 6, 7, and 8 and **A.L.T.** question 5 above.)

2. *Creative writing: a different ending* Call students' attention to the assignment in the textbook. **(P.L.J.)**

FURTHER READING

Munro, Alice, *Dance of the Happy Shades; The Progress of Love; Who Do You Think You Are?; Friend of My Youth.*

Hands

ANNE HÉBERT

INTRODUCING THE POEM

While Anne Hébert is better known for her novels than her poetry, her poems have garnered much critical praise. She began her writing career as a poet with the publication of *Les songes en equilibre* (meaning "dreams in equilibrium") in 1942; after writing several novels, she returned to publishing poetry with the volume *La jour n'a d'égal que la nuit* (*Day Has No Equal but the Night*) (1992).

The characters in Hébert's writings are often caught between the reality of their situations and their desire to live their lives. In subtle ways, the poem "Hands" shows this tension between what is and what could be—or what has been. In the poem, an elderly woman is reflecting on her life by looking at her hands. "The signs of the world / Are etched on her fingers"; in other words, her life has made its mark on her hands. Her hands are her connection between the person she has always been and the person she is now. She has worked hard to get to this place of "rest and love," and her sacrifices show on her "hands adorned with pain / Opened to the sun." Her hands are still restless—flashing like rays, never closed— as she reaches out for all that life still has to give.

Personal Literary Journal: Think about a scar or birthmark or other distinguishing physical feature that you have. How did you get this scar or mark? What story does it tell about you?

Literary Terms: figurative language, image, simile, tone

COMPREHENSION QUESTIONS

1. *What is the woman in the poem doing?* She is looking at her arthritic hands and flexing them.

2. *Why is she "strange"?* She is confused about what is her past life and what is her present life.

3. *What are the "deep markings"?* the scars and markings of many years of work, as well as the effects of arthritis

UNDERSTANDING THE POEM: POSSIBLE ANSWERS

1. *"She"* The "she" of the poem is an elderly woman.

2. *Sitting "on the edge of seasons"* She is caught between her past life and her present life.

3. *"Etched on her fingers"* "The signs of the world" are marked on her hands.

4. *"Us"* "Us" may refer to readers of the poem or to people watching the woman as she flexes her hands. "Us" most likely refers to younger people who are looking at the woman across the gap of a generation.

5. *"Ruthless offering"* The elderly woman has shown her love over the years by working hard; now her hands show the marks of all her work.

ANALYZING LITERARY TECHNIQUE: POSSIBLE ANSWERS

*1. *Figurative language* Examples of figurative language include:

- The simile "flashes her hands like rays" (line 2) leads the reader to think both of the sun's rays and of intense movement.

- The image "days on her hands" (line 5) describes the age of the skin on the woman's hands, implying that she is elderly.

- The image "signs of the world / Are etched on her fingers" (lines 9–10) shows how a lifetime of living has worked its way into the woman's features—particularly on her hands.

- The image "Weighing her down with massive wrought rings" (line 12) indicates either that the ordinary rings she wears have become too heavy for her hands or that the skin of her hands has wrinkled into "rings" around her knuckles, affecting her ability to move her hands.

- The image "hands adorned with pain / Opened to the sun" (lines 16–17) describes both the beauty and the anguish of age; the scars on the woman's hands are her badge of honor, yet a lifetime of work now causes her hands to be in constant pain.

2. *Tone* The tone of the poem is reflective; the poet is musing about the elderly woman and the significance of her hands.

*3. *Character* Even though the poet never describes the woman directly, the reader can understand the woman's character through the images in the poem. The woman is older; she is sitting "on the edge of seasons" (line 1), and her hands have "many deep markings" (line 11). The woman is confused by the worlds of past and present; "The days on her hands / Occupy and arrest her" (lines 5–6). The woman is generous; her hands are never closed (line 7), and her hands are a "ruthless offering" (line 15)—that is, she has sacrificed her hands to give to others, at the cost of pain to herself. The woman is peaceful; though she is in pain, her hands are "adorned" (line 16) and open so the sun's rays can offer her the goodness of life.

WRITING ABOUT LITERATURE

1. *Essay analyzing figurative language to reveal the woman's character* Remind students to use quotations from the poem to illustrate their points. (See **A.L.T.** questions 1 and 3 above.) **AP**

2. *Creative writing: physical marking reveals a character or life* Remind students to use figurative language to describe both the scar and the person's character. **(P.L.J.)**

FOR FURTHER READING

Hébert, Anne, *Day Has No Equal but the Night* (1994); *Anne Hébert: Selected Poems* (1987).

Roselily

ALICE WALKER

INTRODUCING THE STORY

"Roselily" is the poignant story of an African American woman who is marrying a man in order to lead a new life. Roselily is leaving rural Mississippi, where she has lived the life of a rural black woman in the Deep South. She has given birth to four children by four different fathers, none of whom married her. Economics has dictated her need to work; lack of education and opportunity have led her to work as a seamstress in a sewing plant, a job she is anxious to leave. For her children and herself, she wants respect and she wants a future. She wants freedom to find herself, and she wants to be loved.

Part of the story's power resides in Roselily's need to choose between two unattractive alternatives, her old life in Mississippi or a new life as a wife in Chicago. To remain is to relinquish her dreams of a better life for herself and her children; to leave is to take great risks. Her new husband is a Black Muslim. His religion differs from hers, and his values differ from hers. He is taking her to Chicago, far away from the only life she has ever known. She worries about being ignorant and backward in her new environment. Her new husband loves her, but he appears to be insensitive to her emotional needs. She may be exchanging one form of subjugation and tyranny (that of society) for another (that of a domineering husband)— but this time, she will be a stranger in the strange land of opportunity.

Walker's narrative technique enhances the power of the story. By presenting Roselily's stream of consciousness as she hears the parts of the marriage ceremony, Walker juxtaposes Roselily's past and future with her present. While Roselily remembers the past and worries about the future, the marriage ceremony moves forward and the future becomes reality.

Personal Literary Journal: How do you feel about the prospect of change in your life, such as moving or starting a new school? If you were to move, would you rather live in a small town or a big city? List some of the advantages and disadvantages of each location.

Literary Terms: characterization, contrast, figurative language, interior monologue, irony, narrative perspective (third-person limited omniscience), psychological realism, stream of consciousness, symbolism, theme

COMPREHENSION QUESTIONS

1. *What is occurring in Roselily's life?* She is being married.
2. *What is different about Roselily's husband?* his religion; his home (Chicago); his somberness
3. *What does Roselily want in life?* love and respect
4. *What is Roselily concerned about?* the life of her son, her marriage, and her future
5. *How does Roselily feel about what is happening?* ambivalent; curious, yet reluctant

UNDERSTANDING THE STORY: POSSIBLE ANSWERS

*1. *Roselily like cotton* Throughout her life, Roselily has been treated more like a commodity than a human being. Now she is "selling" herself for the best price, for what she hopes will be a better life. Just as "dry leaves and twigs" cannot be removed completely from cotton, so Roselily cannot be separated completely from her life experiences, her memories, and her ingrained attitudes.

2. *New husband's attitude toward marriage* Roselily's new husband supports the institution of marriage but not this particular religious ceremony. His religion (Black Muslim) is different from Roselily's.

3. *Weakness of father of Roselily's fourth child* That father did not stand by Roselily. He loved her enough to father her child and live with her through her pregnancy but not enough to leave his wife and marry her. He was ashamed to bring Roselily into his Northern life, believing that she could not master the skills he valued; and he had no wish to adapt to her Southern life. He is rearing their child at his home in the North, but he does not communicate about the child's well-being. Apparently, he does not have the courage to let that child know its real mother.

*4. *Importance of roots to Roselily* Roselily recognizes her ties to her past: her mother, her father, and her grandparents. She views herself as a totality that includes her past as well as her present and her future.

*5. *Why Roselily is marrying* Roselily's life is a closed book as long as she remains in Mississippi. She wants love, respect, opportunity for self-fulfillment, and a better life for her children. By marrying and moving to Chicago, she has more to gain than to lose. This marriage will remove her from her life in the rural South, where she must work at a job she dislikes, rear her children alone, and expect that her future and the future of her children will simply mirror the past. Even if her marriage fails, more job opportunities and a greater variety of people are available to her in Chicago.

*6. *Chicago may not be a new experience* Roselily's marriage and the Chicago experience may disappoint her. She may not find the happiness she seeks. Ironically, she may have no more control over her life in Chicago than she did in Missisisippi. Her decisions in her old life have been determined by economic necessity; her decisions in her new life may be determined by her husband. She may simply be substituting one kind of constraint for another.

*7. *Roselily's view of the preacher* The preacher represents acceptance of things as they are. His religion teaches him to advise turning the other cheek rather than striking out. He appears to be critical of Roselily's hopes and of her attempts to improve herself and her situation.

*8. *Why Roselily feels wrong* Roselily feels inadequate for the challenges she faces in her new life, and therefore she is afraid of what she is doing. The risks are real. Her new husband has different values, and their marriage may not survive these differences. Each of them seems to see the other more as an object or a symbol than as an individual. Roselily sees her new husband as a ticket to a better life. She has thought about freedom and opportunity, not about his personality.

Roselily's new husband sees Roselily as someone to love and to rescue. He appears to have more understanding of her condition than he does of her psychological being. Roselily may not be able to adapt to ways so different from those she has known. She may feel isolated and estranged, and she may be homesick for the comfort of the customary path. Her husband may not be able to understand her feelings and, therefore, may not be able to give her the emotional support that she needs.

*9. *Characterization of Roselily* Roselily is courageous. She is marrying a city man who has different values, and she is leaving home to start a new life in a distant city. She has also given one of her children to his father so that the child can have greater opportunities.

ANALYZING LITERARY TECHNIQUE: POSSIBLE ANSWERS

1. *Narrative perspective; psychological realism* Because the story is told through Roselily's thoughts, the reader has intimate knowledge of Roselily's situation and is able to sympathize with her. The story is organized around the minister's words at the marriage ceremony. Each group of words makes Roselily think about her past or her future. This narrative technique imitates the workings of the human mind. It is an effective technique given the circumstances (a wedding) and Roselily's situation (leaving her old life for a new life).

2. *Relationship between the marriage ceremony and Roselily's thoughts* The contrast between the preacher's words and Roselily's thoughts dramatizes the contrast between the world in which she has been living (that of a single woman in the rural South) and the precarious nature of her new marriage. The words of the wedding ceremony are juxtaposed with Roselily's thoughts: *"to join this man and this woman"* with ropes and chains, *"in holy matrimony"* with children born to previous relationships, *"if there is anybody . . ."* with the demands of her husband's religion, *"together"* with her isolation in a new home, and *"let him speak"* with her being so impatient that she did not ask enough questions.

3. *Contrast* Walker contrasts the South and the North, the country and the city, the old and the new, and the male and female view of women. The contrasts accentuate the tremendous change that is about to occur in Roselily's life. They enable the reader to identify with Roselily's ambivalent feelings of anticipation and regret. Roselily feels an affection for the unsophisticated life in the South despite its shortcomings. This has been the only life she has ever known.

*4. *Symbolism* Walker uses symbols of constraint. Examples include ropes, chains, handcuffs, religion, a yoke, a trapped rat, and quicksand. Roselily desires freedom from the constraints of a society that have limited her potential, and she thinks of the factors that have obstructed and will obstruct her opportunity to achieve self-fulfillment.

WRITING ABOUT LITERATURE

1. *Essay analyzing symbols of constraint* Call students' attention to the directions in the textbook assignment. Remind them to incorporate quotations into their analysis. (See **U.S.** question 7 and **A.L.T.** question 4 above.) **AP**

2. *Character sketch of Roselily* Call students' attention to the directions in the textbook assignment. Remind them of the importance of quotations. (See **U.S.** questions 1, 4, 5, 6, 7, 8, and 9 above.)

3. *Creative writing: a letter from Roselily describing her new life* Roselily may have either a negative or a positive experience. She may be accepted or rejected by her husband's friends. She may adapt to city life, or she may prefer the unsophisticated life of her Southern community. She and her husband may or may not have a satisfying marriage; they may or may not understand and support each other. **(P.L.J.)**

FURTHER READING

Walker, Alice, *Good Night, Willie Lee, I'll See You in the Morning: Poems; Revolutionary Petunias and Other Poems; The Color Purple; In Love and Trouble.*

1. *In this section, the Zuñi, Langston Hughes, Eugene O'Neill, Alice Munro, and Eudora Welty rely on symbolism to convey main concepts and images. Define* symbolism *and compare and contrast its use in three works. What is the symbolism in each piece, and how does it function within the work? What does it contribute to the meaning of the work? Use quotations to support your points.* The family imagery in "Special Request for the Children of Mother Corn" represents the nurturing role that corn plays in the Zuñi community and the link that the Zuñi see between corn and their own survival. The staircase in "Mother to Son" symbolizes life; the splinters, tacks, and spots of bareness symbolize life's hardships. The ice in *Ile* symbolizes Captain Keeney's emotional frigidity and coldness toward the desires of his wife and crew and their hopes to return to Homeport. The butterfly in "Day of the Butterfly" symbolizes the delicate friendship between Helen and Myra. Phoenix Jackson's brightly colored pinwheel in "A Worn Path" symbolizes her enjoyment of life, as earlier evidenced in her good humor along her walk.

2. *The main characters in "Soldier's Home" and "Hands" observe the differences between who they are and who they once were. How do Ernest Hemingway and Anne Hébert explore this theme, and how does the theme differ in each work? Does the age of each protagonist play an important role? Compare and contrast the role of change in these works. Use quotations to support your points.* The change in Hemingway's protagonist Krebs was caused by his experiences as a soldier in World War I. He has developed from the "good boy" he once was into a man trying to find his new place in life. In "Hands," a woman has been changed by age; the marks on her hands are signs of a long life. The differences are apparent: Krebs is frustrated and displaced, while the woman is contemplative and serene. The changes in Krebs's life are illustrated in his newly strained relationship with his parents and the differences between the attitude he had in college and the attitude he now holds. In "Hands," change is highlighted in the lines "She sits on the edge of seasons," "She is strange," and "The days on her hand / Occupy and arrest her." Students should outline their theses and provide textual support for their main points.

3. *The poems of Walt Whitman, Emily Dickinson, Langston Hughes, and T. S. Eliot provide excellent examples of connotative language. Define* connotative language *and analyze its use in three of the four poems. How does each poet use connotative language, and what does it contribute to his or her work? Compare and contrast the poems, using quotations to support your points.* Connotative language evokes images and feelings beyond the literal meaning of the words. Walt Whitman uses connotative language such as "Yet giving to make me glutted, enriched of soul, you give me forever faces" to convey the differences between emotions elicited by life in the country and in the city. Emily Dickinson captures the enormity of her pain and her feelings of helplessness in the face of separation through connotative language such as

"So huge, so hopeless to conceive." Langston Hughes's language—"For I'se still goin', honey, / I'se still climbin'"—captures the mother's wisdom and indefatigable spirit. T. S. Eliot evokes the desolation of an emotionally void generation through such language as "Our dried voices, when / We whisper together / Are quiet and meaningless."

4. *Many selections in the North America section explore personal values and the effect of these values on the protagonists' personal relationships and choices in life. Pick two pieces that examine values. Compare and contrast how the protagonist in each selection lives by his or her values. How are these values crucial to the plot and the themes of the work? Use quotations and examples to support your points.* In *Ile*, Captain Keeney's personal values lead him to ignore Annie's and the crew's wishes and needs. In "Roselily," the protagonist's values lead her to marry a man of a different religion and to move to Chicago so that her children can have a better life. In "Soldier's Home," Krebs's new values are different from those of his family; he no longer loves his family as he once did, and he cannot pray with his mother. Helen faces a conflict between her personal values and social acceptance in "Day of the Butterfly." Student essays should clearly outline the values of each protagonist and should support these values with textual evidence. Comparisons between selections should be clear and well written.

Great Britain and Ireland

A Woman's Message

ANONYMOUS

UNDERSTANDING THE POEM

"A Woman's Message," usually called "A Wife's Lament," is a powerful and poignant human cry from an age long past. The woman laments her fate and the fate of her husband as they live separately in exile. Her song reflects the harsh society in which she lives and repeats themes that play a prominent role in *Beowulf*: family treachery, the dependent and vulnerable position of women, and the hard lives of those who are at the mercy of an unfamiliar community.

In the narrative, the woman paints three striking pictures: first, a heart-rending description of her position as one who has lost love, friendship, safety, and hope; then, a devastating curse on the lord, her new master, who condemned her to exile; and finally, a view of her husband's life, which she describes as being as pitiful as her own. However, the wife is relating the story from her point of view. Her husband or his family might tell an equally interesting but different story.

The woman's fate was caused by her husband's treachery. She states that he cared more about committing his crime, despite the risk of punishment, than he cared about her. It is possible that his family sent him into exile with the hope of saving his life. The family may have advised him to travel alone to increase his chances for survival, and he may have accepted the advice either because he agreed with his family or because he no longer loved his wife. The wife states that she accepted her husband's exile over other choices because exile brought the possibility of a better fate.

The wife can only imagine her husband's fate as an exile, and she assumes that he is as lonely and miserable as she is. Other surviving Anglo-Saxon poems (particularly "The Seafarer," "The Wanderer," "The Husband's Message," and *Beowulf*) show various possible outcomes for the husband. He may have died at sea, been condemned to wander from one community to another as an outcast, been enslaved, or found a way to begin life anew in another community.

The anonymous poet's eloquence spans time and space. A series of oxymorons conveys the fact that the woman's life has become a paradox in which she has been "blessed with sorrow" and condemned to a "living death" in a convent. She lives with "wooden nuns" in earthen caves beneath oak trees in towns that are "bramble patches / Of empty pleasure." The common Norse metaphor of the loom, on which the strands of each mortal's life are woven into a pattern, combines with images of darkness (exile, evil plans) to create this stark portrait of an exiled woman for whom "the sun of protection and safety" has been denied.

Personal Literary Journal: What possible events in your life would bring you the most sorrow and suffering? What would sustain you in times of such stress?

Literary Terms: alliteration, center of consciousness, connotative language, elegy, figurative language, irony, lyric monologue, metaphor, narrative perspective, oxymoron, paradox, setting, soliloquy, theme, tone, unreliable narrator

COMPREHENSION QUESTIONS

1. *Where is the woman?* in a convent housed in underground caves

2. *Who sent the woman there?* a new lord, her master

3. *What happened to the woman's husband?* He was exiled from their community.

4. *What did the woman's husband do to deserve his fate?* He plotted a murder.

5. *What is the tone of the poem?* sad, angry, resentful

UNDERSTANDING THE POEM: POSSIBLE ANSWERS

1. *Most responsible for the woman's fate* (a) The woman's husband is responsible in that he has been exiled because he committed a crime. Although he was responsible for the care of his wife, he may have agreed to the separation. (b) The husband's family is responsible in that they may have suggested exile as a way for the husband to save his life and may have suggested that he go without his wife. They did not choose to protect the woman by taking her into the family home. (c) The woman's new lord is responsible in that he is the person who sent her to join the convent of "wooden nuns." (d) The woman herself is responsible only for her decision to leave her community and for her attitude toward her new situation.

2. *Aspects of life that make the woman most unhappy* (a) The woman's loneliness is a major cause of her unhappiness; however, she apparently has made little effort to make friends within her new community. (b) The woman's physical discomfort is probably not as important as her loneliness and her memories. (c) The woman may not be in much danger in that she is living in an established community of women. (d) The woman's memories are probably the most important cause of her unhappiness. Because the woman is always comparing the present with the past and the lives of her old friends with her own life, she makes no effort to adjust to her new situation.

3. *Why no names* The story is more personal and more powerful when it is told in the first person. Characters without names become universal.

4. *The woman's motivation to tell her story* Possible motives:

   - The woman's story is her identity; it defines and confirms who she is.
   - Telling the story helps the woman accept her new life; she concludes her story by pitying her husband as much as she pities herself.
   - By telling the story, the woman may win the sympathy and friendship of others.

5. *The poem transcends time and space* The poem is a powerful expression of human loneliness and suffering, two aspects of life that bridge time and space.

ANALYZING LITERARY TECHNIQUE: POSSIBLE ANSWERS

1. *Relationship between setting and theme* The setting is the woman's location in exile. Her separation from all that she loves is the cause of her suffering and sorrow.

2. *Function of contrast* The woman's awareness of the contrast between her past life and her present life causes her suffering. Her memories keep reminding her of all that she is missing. There is also a contrast between light and dark, which symbolizes the contrast between good and evil.

3. *The tone of the poem* The tone of deep sorrow and suffering is created through words such as "sorrow," "misery," "sadness," and "suffering" and through the connotative and figurative language that reinforces these emotions.

*4. *Poet's use of metaphor* The theme of the poem is that a life of exile is a life of sorrow and suffering. The metaphors that reinforce this theme include the following: "journeys into sorrow," "ravel out its misery," "darkness of exile droops on my life," "Seeking the sun of protection and safety," "exile as payment for hope," "our friendship's a fable that time has forgotten / And never tells," "bitter towns all bramble patches / Of empty pleasure," and "famished / Desires that leap at unquenched life."

5. *Both a lyric monologue and an elegy* The poem is a monologue in that it is a soliloquy in verse in which a woman reveals her thoughts, her attitudes, and some background information. It is a lyric monologue because it emphasizes the woman's emotions more than her story (which is why the woman reveals so few details about her past and present circumstances) and because figurative language is an important aspect of the poem. The poem is an elegy (a lament) in that it expresses great sorrow because of a great loss.

6. *Paradox in the poem* The woman's life has become a paradox, described by combinations of contradictory ideas. She describes her love as condemned to "a living death," her life as "blessed with sorrow," and her current location as being in "bitter towns all bramble patches / Of empty pleasure."

7. *Oxymorons* An oxymoron is a combination of paired words that combine incongruous and usually contradictory words. Oxymorons convey reality in a dramatic way. The following examples describe the paradoxes in the woman's life: "living death," "blessed with sorrow," and "empty pleasure."

8. *The woman's point of view; reliability of the narrator* By choosing to tell this story from the woman's point of view, the poet dramatizes the plight of women in Anglo-Saxon society. The first-person narrative technique conveys dramatic immediacy and power. It also adds a sense of mystery as the reader tries to discern the reality.

   The woman is a reliable narrator in that she is describing emotions that are real and justified. However, she may be an unreliable narrator because she is more concerned about expressing her feelings than relating a narrative, her description of her husband's situation may be inaccurate, and her depiction of her husband's family presents only the adverse effect his family has had on her own life. In addition, the woman may be unreliable with regard to her husband's situation.

9. *Irony* Examples include the following:
   - It is ironic that the woman's husband, who has sworn everlasting love, cares more about committing a crime than caring for his wife.

- The woman's depiction of her husband and his situation may be ironic. His love for her was not what he had promised her. It is possible that he was willing to go into exile without her and that he is faring very well in another community.

- It is also ironic that the woman is living so unhappily in a community of other women. The towns of "empty pleasure" may contain pleasure, but she finds no pleasure there.

10. *Alliteration and its contribution* The sound of an initial consonant is repeated in the second half of most lines, a typical stylistic device of Anglo-Saxon poetry. The technique creates a unified effect and oral appeal when the poetry is recited aloud.

WRITING ABOUT LITERATURE

1. *Essay analyzing the poet's use of metaphor* Call students' attention to the directions in the textbook assignment with regard to process, organization, and content. (See **A.L.T.** question 4.) **AP**

2. *Creative writing: the man's story of his journey in either prose or poetry* Call students' attention to the issues suggested in the textbook assignment. Remind them that they may express the man's point of view either in prose or poetry. If you read aloud "The Husband's Message," "The Seafarer," and "The Wanderer," your students will learn what can happen to a male who is exiled from his community, and they will enjoy more great Old English poetry. **(P.L.J.)**

FURTHER READING

"The Husband's Message"; "The Seafarer"; "The Wanderer"; *Beowulf.*

The Pardoner's Tale

GEOFFREY CHAUCER

INTRODUCING THE STORY

"The Pardoner's Tale" is a popular story because of its interesting characters and exciting plot. The selection is an excerpt; do not read the entire tale with your class unless you first read it carefully yourself and make appropriate deletions because the Pardoner makes many offensive remarks.

You may want to tell your students about the person who tells this tale. Chaucer accepts a world in which neither the people nor the institutions are perfect. A dishonorable person—such as the Pardoner—is still a human being, and no human being is completely evil. The Pardoner makes his living by preying on the weaknesses of others, yet he is such a masterful preacher that his formidable verbal and dramatic skills persuade people to lead good lives even while he walks off with their worldly wealth. The Pardoner is his own most tragic victim, for it is both ironic and sad that his inability to resist being greedy is as great as his ability to combat this temptation in others. Readers are free to decide to what extent the Pardoner's immoral actions are offset by his ability to motivate good behavior in others.

As part of his sermon, the Pardoner uses an *exemplum*, or parable (a story that teaches a moral), to show that greed is the root of evil. The original folktale of the three thieves had made its way into medieval Europe from the Orient by the 1300s. Because of its subject, it became a popular example in preachers' sermons. In "The Pardoner's Tale," Chaucer transforms the folktale into a miniature work of art through his treatment of setting and theme, his tightly knit plot, his use of conversation to reveal character, and his beautiful use of language. Death pervades every aspect of Chaucer's version, unifying all its elements. Chaucer's depiction of the old man is remarkable in two respects: the man's mysterious connection with Death and his poetic, evocative description of his search for Death. Not only is this story an integral part of the Pardoner's overall sermon, it is considered one of the best short stories in all of literature.

Personal Literary Journal: Have you ever been punished because your words or actions were improper or unkind? If so, to what extent has luck, rather than justice, been responsible for what has happened to you?

Literary Terms: allegory, characterization, foreshadowing, dramatic and verbal irony, parable, personification, theme

COMPREHENSION QUESTIONS

1. *Why do the three youths want to kill Death?* He has killed their friends.
2. *Whom do they meet on their way to the village?* an old man
3. *Why do the young men head toward the tree?* to find Death
4. *What do they find there?* a pile of gold
5. *What happens to them? Why?* They kill one another for gold.

UNDERSTANDING THE STORY: POSSIBLE ANSWERS

1. *How the old man knows the young men will find Death* The old man is psychologically astute; he realizes that the desire for wealth often motivates murder. The way the young men treat the old man reveals their potential for immoral behavior.

2. *Will all who find gold also find Death?* One opinion: All people are inherently greedy. Faced with sharing a fortune, some people will kill to become the sole possessor of the fortune. Others would either leave a fortune or share it.

3. *Why the young men think the old man is a spy* Possible reasons:
   - The old man is so old that he should be dead; therefore, he must be collaborating with Death.
   - The old man wants to exchange his age for youth, so he may want to kill them.
   - Death is already in the town; many people have recently died.

4. *Why the young men think they can kill Death* They are drunk, so they lack the power of reason and they are no longer aware of their limitations.

ANALYZING LITERARY TECHNIQUE: POSSIBLE ANSWERS

1. *The old man's identity; personification* Possibly the old man is the personification of Death. If so, he casts a longer and darker shadow than if he is simply an old man. Whether or not he is the personification of Death, his presence brings out the characters of the young men. The way they treat him predicts their response to the gold, which he may have put under the tree. The encounter between the old man and the three youths foreshadows how the tale will end. Personification intensifies and enhances its subject, making Death more real because it appears as a human.

2. *Irony* The old man knows what the young men do not know—that their search for Death will end in their own deaths. Even when planning one another's deaths, they do not expect to become victims themselves.

3. *Why no description of the first murder* The focus is the *triple* murder that was committed because of greed. Extraneous detail slows the pace and dilutes the impact.

4. *How the death of all three men is fitting* All are equally greedy and cruel and therefore equally deserving of their fate.

5. *Parable or allegory* A parable is a short story designed to teach a religious (moral) value. An allegory is a longer story designed to reveal truths about the human condition; it often has symbolic characters (such as Death) that represent abstract ideas. Greed, one of the seven deadly sins, is the subject of this tale. The theme and lesson: Those who succumb to the temptation of greed cause their own moral and physical destruction.

WRITING ABOUT LITERATURE

1. *Essay examining a view of justice* Students will need to start with a point of view and then defend it. They should use quotations to support their opening statement. **(P.L.J.)** ⒶⓅ

2. *Essay examining the role of Death* An example of a general statement: Death pervades "The Pardoner's Tale." Students should devote one paragraph to each aspect of the story they examine.

3. *Creative writing: tale for another pilgrim* Chaucer provides a fine opportunity to give students a great choice. With nineteen characters and four types of stories from which to choose, each student should find an interesting tale to write.

FURTHER READING

Chaucer, Geoffrey, other tales from *The Canterbury Tales*, such as "The Franklin's Tale" and "The Nun's Priest's Tale."

Much Ado About Nothing

WILLIAM SHAKESPEARE

INTRODUCING THE PLAY

Much Ado About Nothing is a provocative play about falling in love and being inner-directed. Although the play is considered to be a comedy, its tragic elements are impossible to ignore. Shakespeare was a mature and successful playwright by the time he wrote *Much Ado* in the latter part of 1598, and he clearly intended to communicate "something" important about human beings. The attitudes and behavior of the characters in a play—even in comedies—must be rooted in psychological realities or the characters and situations cease to seem real.

The Hero-Claudio plot is as old as *Chaereas and Kallirrhoe*, a Greek romance written by Chariton in A.D. 400. Shakespeare was certainly aware of the story; during the Renaissance, writers and dramatists in Italy, Spain, France, and Germany—as well as in England—had created versions of it. Shakespeare adapted the Hero-Claudio plot primarily from Matteo Bandello's version ("Timbreo and Fenicia," in *La Prima Parte de le Novelle del Bandello* [1554, in Italian; 1569, in French]). In Bandello's version, a rival for the heroine's love—not a villain—tricks the hero into believing that the heroine is unchaste. The hero witnesses the ruse alone, not with a companion, and he breaks his betrothal before the wedding ceremony is scheduled to occur, not at the ceremony. The heroine's father responds by defending his daughter's innocence, not by condemning her. Shakespeare also adapted details from the fifth canto of Ariosto's *Orlando Furioso* (1516, in Italian; 1566 and 1591, in English), where the heroine's maidservant dresses in her mistress's clothes and becomes an innocent accomplice in the deception.

One of Shakespeare's additions to the story is the powerful wedding (or church) scene, which has always troubled audiences, literary critics, and readers. The problem at the wedding is caused by the successful ruse—a common theme in folklore. All successful tricksters are expert analysts of society. Because they understand the attitudes and values of those they prey upon, they need only set the stage and their victims will fall into their trap. Don John's victims react just as he predicts they will. The ruse is successful because Don John and Borachio realize the importance that Don Pedro and Claudio (and Leonato) place upon honor and reputation—qualities that males in their society expect to find in one another.

Human beings are social creatures; they choose to live in groups, and they function as part of the societies in which they live. Societies, both ancient and modern, often expect their members to be primarily inner-directed or primarily outer-directed. Inner-directed people think for themselves, and they often choose to differ from others in their attitudes and behavior. In contrast, outer-directed people base their attitudes and behavior on what others—especially those whose favor they are trying to curry—view as socially desirable.

The aristocratic characters who take center stage in the play are outer-directed; their values are based on the views and expectations of others. This explains why Don Pedro and Claudio do not question the scenario that they observe from afar on a dark night, why Claudio waits until his marriage ceremony to attack his beloved's virtue, and why Leonato reacts by condemning his daughter and wishing for her death. The actions of these males are reprehensible. However, if we understand the values of the society in which these men live—the society that Don John criticizes early in the play—we can understand the factors that lead them to react as they do, despite the fact that they are basically good people.

The relational aspects of *Much Ado* are of prime importance in understanding this play. Through their conversations with each other, the characters reveal why a proved villain is able to achieve success so easily. The aristocratic male characters have a negative stereotypical view of females, and the men are anxious about the idea of marriage. They do not trust women because they fear female betrayal; yet, the one male who is betrayed is tricked by another male. The bachelors in *Much Ado* bond with one another to assert their sexual appeal and power over the females.

This stereotypical view of women has a twofold historical basis. Most women in Shakespeare's day were economically dependent on a male provider. A father often arranged for his daughter to marry a man who would provide for her economically. A financially secure husband was usually older—and sometimes far older—than his wife. Love, which was not a factor in marriage, might or might not develop with time.

Given the disparity in age between a young wife and her older husband, the young wife might be tempted by a young bachelor's flattery. Humorous stories were told of the creative ways a young wife and her bachelor lover would contrive to be alone together—and thus humiliate (cuckold) her old husband. (The word *cuckold*, which always refers to a man who has an unfaithful wife, derives from the cuckoo, a bird that lays its eggs in the nests of other birds.) People thought that horns, symbolizing the marital infidelity of a man's wife and thus the man's own dishonor, would sprout from the forehead of a cuckolded husband. However, the horns were always invisible because the dishonored husband would keep them concealed beneath his cap. Throughout *Much Ado*, the numerous cuckold jokes and the allusions to the cuckold's invisible horns express both the male's fear and distrust of women and his role as the conqueror of women. Some cuckold jokes, such as those in Act I, focus on the male as the victim of feminine wiles. Others, such as those in Act IV, focus on the bachelor as the virile cuckolder, the powerful bull and conquering hero.

Another basis for a man's stereotypical view of women was the custom for women of wealth to have their infants reared by wet-nurses until the children were ready to be weaned from the breast. Fortunate were the children whose wet-nurse lived with their family and remained with them until she died. However, some infants were "farmed out" to a young nursing mother who would be paid to feed and nurture these infants along with her own. When these children outgrew the need to be nursed, their parents would retrieve them. Some children were able to cope with the trauma of losing the only caregiver they had ever known; others were not so fortunate. Such a childhood trauma could lead an adult male to harbor a distrust of women. Although the man needed a woman's love, he would not permit himself to make an emotional commitment for fear the woman could not satisfy his need or would betray him by being unfaithful.

Most versions of the Hero-Claudio plot end happily. However, Shakespeare was one of the few writers to turn the story into a comedy. He created one subplot involving Beatrice and Benedick and another involving Dogberry and Verges. The characters of Dogberry and Verges were based on real people in Elizabethan England. In the following excerpt from a letter, Lord Burghley, one of Queen Elizabeth's principal ministers, describes the absurd conduct of the watchmen who stood about in every village. The letter reads as follows:

> Sir—As I cam from London homward, in my coche, I sawe at every townes end the number of x or xii, standyng, with long staves, and untill I cam to Enfeld I thought no other of them, but that they had stayd for avoyding of the rayne, or to drynk at some alehowse, for so they did stand under pentyces at ale howses. But at Enfeld fyndyng a dosen in a plump, when ther was no rayne, I bethought my self that they war appointed as Watchmen, for the apprehendyng of such as are missyng; and there upon I called some of them to me apart, and asked them wherfor they stood there? and one of them answered, "To take 3 yong men." And demandyng how they should know the persons, one answered with these wordes: "Marry, my Lord, by intelligence of ther favor." "What meane you by that?" quoth I. "Marry," sayd they, "one of the partyes hath a hooked nose." "And have you," quoth I, "no other mark?" "No," sayth they. And then I asked who apoynted them; and they answered one Bankes, a Head Constable, whom I willed to be sent to me. Surely, sir, who ever had the chardge from yow hath used the matter negligently, for these Watchmen stand so openly in plumps, as no suspected person will come neare them; and if they be no better instructed but to fynd 3 persons by one of them havyng a hooked nose, they may miss thereof. And thus I thought good to advertise yow, that the Justyces that had the chardge, as I thynk, may use the matter more circumspectly. (*Shakespeare Society Papers* I [1844], pp. 3–4.)

In *Much Ado*, Shakespeare is at his best in revealing the beauty and versatility of the English language. Words fascinate everyone—from aristocrats like Benedick and Beatrice who love to duel with them to a comedian like Dogberry who misuses them. Benedick declares, "if a man will be beaten with brains, a' shall wear nothing handsome about him" (V.iv.100–101). The play reminds students that they possess the priceless gift of language—the mark of intelligence.

Much Ado About Nothing, like many of Shakespeare's other plays, is the source of many famous sayings. Among them are the following—paraphrased, where appropriate, into modern English:

"as merry as the day is long" (II.i.37)
"speak all mirth and no matter" (II.i.256)
"speak plain and to the purpose" (II.iii.15–16)
"are good men and true" (III.iii.1)
"They are not the men you took them for." (III.iii.37–38)
"They that touch pitch will be defiled." (III.iii.44–45)
"some of us will smart for it" (V.i.109)
"I was not born under a rhyming planet." (V.ii.29–30)

Kenneth Branagh's film *Much Ado About Nothing* is superb. Those who see the film first find the play much easier to read. Those who read the play first find the film even more enjoyable.

Personal Literary Journal: Think about your attitudes and behavior. Do you make important decisions by yourself, or do you make decisions based on what your friends think is important?

Think about mistakes that you and your friends have made. How likely are you to err by judging a situation too quickly? How likely is it that your judgment of someone else's behavior is dependent on whether that person is your friend? How easily do you forgive a friend's mistreatment of you? How easily do you forgive your own misjudgment or treatment of a friend?

Literary Terms: alliteration, catharsis, characterization, climax, comedy (low and high), farce, figurative language (metaphor, simile, symbol), foreshadowing, irony (situational, verbal), malapropism, oxymoron, paradox, plot, poem, subplot, Shakespearean sonnet, soliloquy, theme, tone, tragedy, tragicomedy

COMPREHENSION QUESTIONS

1. (II.i.) *How do many of the principal characters pass the time during the week before the wedding?* They contrive to have Benedick and Beatrice fall in love.

2. (II.ii.) *Describe the plan to spoil the wedding.* Borachio suggests that Don John lead Claudio and Don Pedro late at night to observe a woman disguised as Hero as she is conversing with Borachio. Then Don John will tell Claudio and Don Pedro that Borachio is having an affair with Hero.

3. (II.iii.) *How do the principal characters carry out their scheme to have Beatrice and Benedick fall in love?* As Claudio, Don Pedro, and Leonato stand within earshot of Benedick, they discuss Hero's assertion that Beatrice loves Benedick. Likewise, within earshot of Beatrice, Hero and Ursula discuss Claudio's assertion that Benedick loves Beatrice.

4. (III.ii.) *How does Claudio respond to the villain's plan?* Claudio believes that Hero is unfaithful.

5. (III.iii.) *How is the villainous plot first discovered?* The watchmen overhear Borachio tell Conrade about the deception of Claudio and Don Pedro. First Borachio says that Margaret was disguised as Hero and then he relates the plan to slander Hero.

6. (III.v.) *What is the result of the conversation between Dogberry, Verges, and Leonato?* Leonato tells Dogberry and Verges to examine the prisoners and to bring him the testimony in writing.

7. (IV.i.) *What does the groom do at the wedding? How do the bride and her father respond?* Claudio accuses Hero of being unfaithful, and he refuses to marry her. She protests that she is innocent, but her father believes Claudio and Don Pedro and wants Hero to die.

8. (IV.i.) *What does the friar suggest?* The friar will hide Hero while Leonato spreads the word that she is dead.

9. (IV.i.) *What does Beatrice demand of Benedick, and how does he respond?* Beatrice demands that if Benedick loves her, he must kill Claudio. At first Benedick refuses, but then he declares that he will challenge Claudio to a duel.

10. (V.i.) *In the beginning of Act V, who accuses whom of what?* First Leonato accuses Claudio of slandering Hero; then Benedick does the same.

11. (V.i.) *How do Claudio and Don Pedro respond to Benedick's challenge?* They don't take him seriously; instead, they tease him about Beatrice.

12. (V.i.) *What news does Benedick reveal to Don Pedro?* Don John has fled from Messina.

13. (V.i.) *How is the villain's plot made public at last?* Borachio confesses to Don Pedro and Claudio.

14. (V.i.) *What two demands does the bride's father make to avenge Hero?* First, Leonato demands that a ceremony of mourning be held to proclaim Hero's innocence. Second, he demands that Claudio marry his niece, who looks just like Hero.

15. (V.iv.) *After the love plot is revealed, what proves that Benedick and Beatrice really love each other?* Claudio and Hero reveal the sonnets that Benedick and Beatrice have written about each other.

16. (V.iv.) *What happens to the villain?* Don John is caught. Benedick decides that he will punish Don John the next day—after the wedding festivities.

UNDERSTANDING THE PLAY: POSSIBLE ANSWERS

1. (I.i.) *Claudio's ideas for a wife* Claudio says his wife must be physically attractive, aristocratic by birth, and wealthy. His choice of Hero shows that he wants a wife who is subservient as well. His treatment of Hero in IV.i. shows that he wants a wife who possesses unquestionable virtue. These qualities reveal that Claudio is more interested in the social aspects of his marital arrangement than in the unique qualities that his wife may possess. Claudio always relies on the opinions of others—Benedick, Don Pedro, and Don John—to help shape his own.

2. (I.iii.) *Don John's motives* Don John can never claim an honorable name, social prestige, or financial security of property and money because he is a bastard son. He is prohibited from entering into a reputable marriage and having socially acceptable children. Thus, Don John cannot profit from being outer-directed, so he chooses to be inner-directed and to live as he chooses—inevitably as an outsider. (See lines 8–13 and 20–27.)

   Don John's feelings are the typical feelings of an outsider. He hates both his brother and Claudio because he is jealous of who they are and what they possess. On hearing that Claudio intends to marry Hero, Don John tells Borachio, "That young start-up hath all the glory of my overthrow: if I can cross him any way, I bless myself every way" (I.iii.49–50. See also II.ii.4–7.)

3. (II.i.) *Beatrice's conversations about marriage* Beatrice tells Leonato that she has no use for a husband (lines 21–24 and 26–31) and that marriage would

diminish her autonomy (lines 44–48). However, she also fears spinsterhood and its isolation (lines 246–48). Beatrice's arguments against taking a husband confirm to Leonato that she and Benedick are equally opposed to marriage. However, their talents, common interests, and shared phobia motivate their friends and family to contrive to bring them together.

4. (II.i.) *Why wedding is delayed* When Leonato accepts Claudio's proposal, the audience knows that Don John will not be satisfied that his first scheme against Claudio has failed and that he will contrive further to prevent Claudio's marriage. Moreover, the Beatrice-Benedick subplot, which has been all sound and fury, must be resolved. The week's delay before the marriage ceremony helps Don John and Don Pedro develop their respective schemes—Don John to destroy Claudio's marriage and Don Pedro to get a husband for Beatrice.

5. (II.ii.) *Why Borachio and Don John expect success* Borachio and Don John know that aristocrats place great emphasis on the esteem of others. Therefore, Borachio and Don John will emphasize the characteristics that are particularly important to their two victims—honor (Don Pedro) and reputation (Claudio). (See II.ii.25–30.)

6. (II.iii.) *Benedick's ideals for a wife; comparison with Claudio's ideals*

   a) Benedick's wife must be beautiful, wise, virtuous, wealthy, mild, and noble; she must be an able conversationalist and an excellent musician (lines 21–28). Benedick's ideas show that he is inner-directed. He will choose a wife who pleases him and who loves him. He has no need to solicit the opinions of others about her.

   b) Benedick's ideals are similar to Claudio's to the extent that they include beauty, wealth, and social position (hence the conversational and musical abilities). However, Benedick values intellect and judgment as well. Claudio is outer-directed, and Benedick is inner-directed.

7. (II.iii.) *Plot to deceive Benedick* First, Don Pedro, Leonato, and Claudio describe the intensity of Beatrice's love for Benedick, her inability to reveal her love because of Benedick's scorn, and the possibility that Beatrice will die to arouse Benedick's sympathy. Next, the three men speak of Beatrice's exemplary qualities—her sweetness, her virtue, and her wisdom. Last, the three men speak well of Benedick—of his being "a very proper man": wise, intelligent, and valiant—to motivate Benedick to live up to their opinion of him.

   Their conversation appeals to Benedick's self-esteem because he is flattered that Beatrice loves him. It appeals to his subconscious love for Beatrice; since discovering that Beatrice loves him, Benedick has not hesitated to requite her love. It appeals to his good nature; he realizes that Beatrice is suffering and that others pity her because of her love for him. Therefore, Benedick will not let Beatrice love him in vain; he declares himself "horribly in love with her."

Benedick is certain that "this can be no trick" (line 177) because he believes he is overhearing a private conversation among Leonato, Don Pedro, and Claudio. Leonato's presence and Hero's information about Beatrice add authenticity to their remarks.

8. (III.i.) (a) *Plot to deceive Beatrice;* (b) *the difference between the two plots*

   a) First, Hero and Ursula say that Don Pedro and Claudio have declared that Benedick loves Beatrice and that he deserves to have her; this is to engage Beatrice's attention and trust. Next, Hero and Ursula criticize Beatrice for being too proud, too disdainful of men, and too self-absorbed to love anyone but herself; this is designed to motivate Beatrice to change her attitudes and behavior. Finally, Hero and Ursula acknowledge that Beatrice is intelligent, and they describe Benedick as "So rare a gentleman"; this is to motivate Beatrice to acknowledge that she and Benedick are worthy of each other.

   Beatrice is flattered to hear of Benedick's love; however, she is disturbed to hear the criticisms that Hero and Ursula have spoken of her (lines 107–16). She apparently has had a previous unrequited involvement with Benedick (II.i.215–17), and now her pride will not permit her to love and trust him unless he has matured. However, Beatrice sees that her contempt for Benedick is self-defeating. She realizes that Benedick deserves her love, so she resolves to return Benedick's love.

   b) Beatrice's friends criticize her behavior toward men, but Benedick's friends voice no criticism of his behavior toward women. This double standard reflects the society in which Beatrice and Benedick live. The criticism helps Beatrice recognize that she lives in a man's world. If she wishes to keep Benedick's love, she must curtail her assertive words and deeds and submit—to some degree—to Benedick's needs and wishes.

9. (III.iii.) *Success of Don John's ruse* Claudio and Don Pedro should have questioned the validity of what Don John was revealing because they observed it "afar off in the orchard" (lines 116–19). The ruse is successful because of Don John's oaths, the darkness of the night, and Borachio's villainy (lines 121–25). Don Pedro's need to preserve his own honor prevents him from considering whether Borachio's testimony against Hero is valid.

10. (IV.i.) (a) *Claudio's public slander of Hero;* (b) *blame or pity Claudio*

    a) Claudio denounces Hero at their wedding ceremony because he belongs to outer-directed society where the greatest punishment is public shame. He does not consider questioning Hero privately or breaking their engagement quietly. By publicly denouncing Hero, Claudio is asserting his moral superiority. Claudio's tears (lines 149–50) reveal that he loves Hero and that he is accusing her because he feels that circumstances leave him no other choice. The audience must retain some sympathy for Claudio so they can accept the end of the play, where Hero marries him.

    b) Many people consider Claudio to be the most detestable character in *Much Ado*. Claudio, favored as he is by Don Pedro and Hero, has no reason to be cruel to Hero or her father. However, some people pity Claudio for his need to be outer-directed—for a lack of self-confidence so extreme that he bases his judgments about marriage on the opinions of others. Other pity him because he is Don John's victim and, therefore, he is not responsible for his behavior.

11. (IV.i.) *Leonato's response to Claudio's accusation* By condemning Hero, Claudio is also condemning her father and subjecting him to public shame. Leonato's immediate thought is for himself rather than for his daughter. This response reflects the common psychological concern, "How does this affect me? What will my friends think of me?" Leonato feels that he has no one to blame but himself for Hero's behavior (lines 126–35). He wishes for Hero's death and declares that he would even kill her himself to avoid the resulting shame, condemnation, and ostracism of society (lines 110–12; 116–39).

Shock plays a major role in Leonato's response. However, as time passes, his reason takes hold, and he becomes self-confident enough to trust his knowledge of his daughter and to believe in her innocence. However, his instinctive emotional response reveals the thin veneer of his trust in his daughter and possibly of his trust in women in general.

12. (IV.i.) *Margaret's silence* Margaret remains silent during the accusal because she innocently pretended to be Hero for the fun of it and now is too ashamed and terrified to confess her role in the ruse. She fears that she will lose her reputation, her job, and her home, and so she has no choice but to remain silent.

Margaret probably could not have saved Hero's wedding ceremony by contradicting the accusers because Leonato would have needed time to think the matter through. However, her public statement would have cast doubt on the testimony of the accusers. Because Margaret's confession would have saved the reputations of Leonato and Hero, she probably would have been forgiven.

13. (IV.i.) (a) *Benedick's role*; (b) *Beatrice's demand*; (c) *how Benedick proves his love*

   a) Beatrice tells Benedick that he is not the man to avenge Claudio's treatment of Hero (line 261). Benedick is not a member of Hero's family, and Claudio is a close friend of Benedick's. However, once Benedick confesses his love for Beatrice (line 262–63) and she confesses her love for him (lines 276–77), their new relationship enables Benedick to take on the responsibility of revenge.

   b) Beatrice's conversation with Benedick (lines 251–319) reveals that the man whom she would marry must be a man of principle and honor. Beatrice is asking Benedick to take her word about Hero's innocence even though Benedick is convinced that his friend Claudio would not intentionally make a false accusation. Beatrice is willing to risk Benedick's life to test his honor.

   c) Benedick proves his love for Beatrice by agreeing to challenge Claudio to a duel (line 316). His relationship with Beatrice is so important to him that he will separate himself from his male friends. Equally important to Beatrice, however, is Benedick's complete trust in her judgment that Hero is innocent.

14. (V.i.) *Claudio's responses to Hero's death* Claudio expresses neither sorrow nor regret upon learning that Hero has died. Leonato's charge that Claudio is a villain both surprises and enrages Claudio (lines 72, 77), particularly as Claudio would be the last to believe that he had fallen victim to Don John's wiles.

15. (V.i.) *Change in Benedick* Don Pedro and Claudio still view Benedick as the Benedick of the past, so they tease him about the idea of his marrying Beatrice (lines 115–87). To their amazement, their words do not affect Benedick. Faced with a new Benedick (lines 170–76), they can only think that Benedick "leaves off his wit" (is out of his mind) (line 183).

16. (V.i.) *Borachio's confession* Borachio confesses his villainy to Don Pedro (lines 206–16) because, faced with the death of Hero, he is ashamed of what he has done. The members of the watch have already recorded his confession.

17. (V.i.) (V.ii.) (V.iv.) *Claudio and Don Pedro's mistake* Opinions will vary about the extent to which Claudio and Don Pedro are correct when they tell Leonato, "Yet sinn'd I not, / But in mistaking" (V.i.244–45). Shakespeare, to make this play end happily, blames only Don John. However, today's readers are likely to agree with Leonato that Claudio and Don Pedro are also to blame: Both were more concerned about maintaining their social position and avoiding public embarrassment than they were about questioning Don John and evaluating the situation.

In the end, however, Leonato supports the innocence of Don Pedro and Claudio because they are his friends (V.iv.2–3). Once Hero's reputation— and therefore his own—has been restored, Leonato accepts their claim that they made a mistake.

18. (V.i.) (V.iv.) *Leonato's acceptance of Claudio* Leonato proceeds to have Hero marry Claudio because Leonato blames Don John rather than Claudio for the plot to sully Hero's reputation. Claudio's social position, his deferential attitude toward Leonato, and his penitent acts allow Leonato to feel that he was right in his original choice of Claudio and that he should honor his pledge to let Claudio marry Hero. Leonato does not solicit Hero's opinion in this matter because economic security rather than love was usually the basis for marriage. Moreover, in Elizabethan times, a father would not have asked his daughter's opinion about her marriage; Leonato cannot take the risk of having Hero disagree with his judgment, which would invite more public embarrassment.

19. (V.iv.) *Benedick's and Beatrice's love* Benedick and Beatrice are aware that they have been playing witty roles for their self-protection. Now they need to feel secure that these roles have masked their sincere mutual love.

20. *Marital success* Hero and Claudio could be happily married. Hero would be the ideal wife for a man of Claudio's time: subservient, supportive, and loving. For Hero, love may excuse all. However, for their marriage to succeed, both she and Claudio would have to view Claudio as Don John's innocent pawn.

   Although it appears that Claudio's accusation has changed neither Claudio nor Hero nor their relationship, it is possible that, beneath her sweet exterior, Hero might feel loved only for her beauty, wealth, and social position, and she might resent the way that Claudio has treated her.

   Benedick and Beatrice could be happily married because they are a fine match: loyal, supportive, intelligent, clever, fun-loving, and appreciative of each other. However, theirs would be a marriage of equals, and they would continue to demand much from each other—at a time when men expected to wield great authority over their wives. Their marriage would either be the richer for its reciprocity, or it would fall apart beneath this strain.

21. *Dogberry's similarity to Beatrice and Benedick* Dogberry is similar to Beatrice and Benedick in his love of language. All three characters view language as symbolic of their intelligence. It gives them a sense of superiority over their peers. All three characters are also alike in that they possess inner selves that are insecure and vulnerable; consequently, they use language as their suit of armor. They use words to protect themselves from the barbs of criticism.

   By creating Dogberry in a mold that resembles Beatrice and Benedick, Shakespeare unifies the play by providing an additional connection between the two subplots. The contrast between Dogberry's comical use of language and Beatrice's and Benedick's witty use of language enriches the importance of language and highlights these characters.

22. *Themes* Possible themes:

   - You can't judge a book by the cover (Beatrice's and Benedick's protestations about remaining single; the use of masks at Leonato's welcoming celebration).

   - Look before you leap—to conclusions (Don Pedro, Claudio, Leonato) or into marriage (Beatrice, Benedick, Claudio, Hero).

   - "The course of true love never did run smooth" (Claudio and Hero; Benedick and Beatrice).

   - "All's well that ends well" (double marriages; a villain who will be punished).

   - Seeing (or hearing) is believing (Claudio, who sees and hears Borachio, is tricked into rejecting Hero; Beatrice and Benedick, who hear their friends discussing them, are tricked into recognizing their love for each other).

   - Honorable but outer-directed people can be led to cruelty (Claudio's victimization by Don John and Borachio leads to Claudio's condemnation of Hero).

   - The existence of what is bad increases the appreciation of what is good (the effect of Claudio's treatment of Hero on Beatrice and Benedick).

ANALYZING LITERARY TECHNIQUE: POSSIBLE ANSWERS

1. *Structure of the play*

   a) (I.iii., II.i.) *Allusions to previous events* By alluding to, but not explaining, events that occurred before the play begins, Shakespeare accomplishes three important feats: He avoids a long opening exposition, he keeps the action moving forward to its climax, and he creates a series of slice-of-life situations. For example, Shakespeare does not mention the cause of Don Pedro's quarrel with Don John (I.iii.15–16), nor does he explain Beatrice's experience with Benedick (II.i.215–17).

   b) (III.v.) *Dogberry's visit* Dogberry's arrival both creates and relieves tension. His visit creates situational irony because the audience knows how important Dogberry's news is, yet Leonato cannot imagine the importance of the constable's visit. Dogberry's visit also foreshadows imminent doom because Leonato proceeds with the wedding, disregarding Dogberry's prisoners.

   However, when Leonato sends Dogberry to interrogate the prisoners (line 38–39), the audience knows that Leonato will learn of Don John's villainy and will accept his daughter's innocence.

   c) (IV.i.) *Hero's apparent death* Hero's apparent death does more than give Claudio the opportunity to mourn her death and his loss. It also provides time for Dogberry to examine the prisoners and for Leonato to hear the results of this examination, thus learning of Don John's scheme.

   d) (IV.i.) *Beatrice's charge to Benedick* In this play of words—too many words, incorrect words, clever words, and hurtful words—Beatrice's two words, "Kill Claudio" (line 282), stand out in their simple clarity. Beatrice speaks not only for herself and Hero but for the audience as well. The frustration and horror of watching a tragedy unfold while no one does anything—to prevent or avenge it—have been immense. Three men of honor have dishonored themselves, and one man has stood by and done nothing. Beatrice is the first person to react appropriately to Claudio's accusation. Her response conveys power and relieves tension. In Aristotelian terms, her charge to Benedick performs a catharsis (a purge of the emotions of pity and fear, as well as a release of tension).

   e) *The Dogberry subplot* The Dogberry subplot—discovering Don John's plot against Hero and informing Leonato of Don John's treachery—minimizes the tragic nature of the principal plot and makes it possible for the play to end happily. In addition, Dogberry's and Verges's attitudes toward their responsibilities as "the poor duke's officers" and their misuse of the English language infuse the play with a bumbling humor.

   f) *The Beatrice-Benedick subplot* The Beatrice-Benedick subplot parallels, contrasts with, and comments upon the love-and-marriage theme of the principal plot.

      • The genuine love of a mature inner-directed couple (Beatrice and Benedick) contrasts with the fabricated romantic love of an immature outer-directed couple (Hero and Claudio). Benedick's willingness to put his love for Beatrice before his love for his friend contrasts markedly with Claudio's rash rejection of Hero. The subplot brings romance—true romance—to the play.

- The Beatrice-Benedick romance is lively, clever, and humorous; it contributes vitality and humor to the play. Beatrice and Benedick are so appealing in their vulnerability and verbal sparring that their romance upstages the principal plot and keeps Claudio's slander of Hero from giving *Much Ado* a pervasive tragic tone.

- The subplot enables Shakespeare to criticize romantic love in a socially acceptable manner. The contrast between the two kinds of love makes his audience more appreciative of the weaknesses of romantic love and the strengths of mature love. Because the values present in the subplot criticize the values in the principal plot, the members of his audience are freer to come to their own conclusions.

g) (V.) *Climax of the three plots* All three plots reach their climax in Act V. In V.i., Dogberry produces written testimony revealing that Borachio and Don John are responsible for Don Pedro's and Claudio's false accusation of Hero. In V.ii., Benedick tells Beatrice that he has challenged Claudio to a duel, thereby proving his love for her. Then Benedick and Beatrice learn that their assumptions about Don John are correct. In V.iii., Claudio performs the public rites of mourning that clear Hero's name of slander and restore her unblemished reputation. Finally, in V.iv., Benedick tells Leonato of his love for Beatrice and their desire to marry. Meanwhile, Claudio pledges to marry his promised bride, only to discover that the bride is Hero herself. Thus Act V brings every plot to a happy conclusion and ties up all the loose ends. The cumulative effect is that this play has been "much ado about nothing" since "all's well that ends well."

h) (IV.iv.) *Benedick announces his desire to marry* The last scene of the play is the proper time for Benedick to announce his love for Beatrice. The announcement must come after Benedick has proved his love to Beatrice by challenging Claudio to a duel. Moreover, Benedick's and Beatrice's love affair is naturally part of the play's climax.

2. *Tone*

a) *Comedy or tragicomedy? Much Ado About Nothing* is considered a comedy, though a comedy with a problem. Both the high comedy that fuels the Beatrice-Benedick subplot and the low comedy that is attached to the Dogberry subplot are designed to create a play that is often very comic in tone. Shakespeare uses high comedy and low comedy to appeal to both literate and illiterate audiences and to the different tastes of theatergoers.

A tragicomedy combines both comic and tragic elements, but it has a happy resolution. With the two marriages in Act V, Shakespeare concludes *Much Ado* on a felicitous note. He gives the potentially tragic events a happy conclusion; they turn out to be nothing serious after all because no lasting damage occurs.

However, serious things are often said in jest, and through comedy Shakespeare may be inviting his audience to note how easily tragedy can occur when decisions are based on the opinions of others rather than on independent judgment. Outer-directed people may hurt others for their own gain or their fear of shame.

b) *High and low comedy* The battles of wits between Benedick and Beatrice are examples of clever, polished, sophisticated humor. Examples of high comedy include the following:

- Beatrice speaking about Don John: "How tartly that gentleman looks, I never can see him but I am heart-burned an hour after" (II.i.3–4).

- Benedick speaking about Beatrice: "Here's a dish I love not: I cannot endure my Lady Tongue" (II.i.211–12).

- from Benedick's soliloquy: "No, the world must be peopled. When I said I would die a bachelor, I did not think I should live till I were married" (II.iii.192–94).

- Benedick, to himself: "Ha! 'Against my will I am sent to bid you come in to dinner'; there's a double meaning in that" (II.iii.203–4).

Dogberry's constant misuse of language, his ideas about the watch, and his roundabout way of communicating are examples of coarse, unsophisticated humor. The inaccurate words that Dogberry chooses often sound similar to the appropriate words, but they are outrageously inappropriate in the context in which he is using them. Dogberry's and Verges's behavior often provides slapstick humor as well. Examples of this low comedy include the following:

- Dogberry's directions to the watchmen (III.iii.10–12, 14–20, 22–24, 27–29, 31–34, 40–42)

- the malapropisms and attitudes of the watchmen (III.iii.30, 70–71, 130–31, 138)

- the discussion of fashion between Borachio and Conrade (III.iii.77–112), which is ludicrous in the midst of Borachio's revelation of Don John's scheme

- Dogberry's taking "coxcomb" (IV.ii.57–58) and "ass" (IV.ii.61–63 and V.i.227) as compliments

- Don Pedro's imitation of Dogberry's report (V.i.198–200)

See the box at the end of this section for a guide to Dogberry's malapropisms.

c) *Tragedy* The following situations provide tragic elements to the play:

- Don John's and Borachio's scheme to prevent Claudio's marriage to Hero (II.ii.) is tragic because, until their plot is discovered, it destroys the virtuous reputation of an innocent maiden.

- Claudio's and Don Pedro's acceptance of Don John's scheme (III.ii.) is tragic because Claudio and Don Pedro are tricked into making a false public accusation that, until the truth is discovered, destroys the honor and reputation of an innocent maiden and of her family.

- Leonato's postponement of examining Dogberry's suspects (III.v.) is tragic because Leonato could have uncovered Don John's plot and saved his daughter and himself from public humiliation.
- Claudio's and Don Pedro's condemnation of Hero is tragic (IV.i.) because it is public.
- Leonato's reaction to this accusation is tragic because he believes it, rather than his daughter's character and her word.

3. *Foreshadowing* Examples of foreshadowing include the following:

- Beatrice's statement to Benedick "I thank God and my cold blood, I am of your humour for that: I had rather hear my dog bark at a crow than a man swear he loves me" (I.i.98–99) foreshadows that Beatrice and Benedick, who love verbal sparring about their disinterest in each other, will fall in love.
- Benedick's remark to Claudio "there's her cousin [Beatrice], an she were not possessed with a fury, exceeds her [Hero] as much in beauty as the first of May doth the last of December" (I.i.141–42) foreshadows Benedick's romantic interest in Beatrice.
- Don Pedro's three comments to Benedick—"I shall see thee, ere I die, look pale with love" (I.i.183); "In time the savage bull doth bear the yoke" (I.i.193); and "If Cupid have not spent all his quiver in Venice, thou wilt quake for this shortly" (I.i.200–201)—all foreshadow his plan to conspire with Claudio and Leonato to make Benedick fall in love with Beatrice.
- Don Pedro's plan to disguise himself as Claudio, create an "amorous tale," and woo Hero in Claudio's name (I.i.244–53) foreshadows Claudio's falling in love with Hero.
- Benedick's soliloquy condemning love (II.iii.7–29) foreshadows that he will fall in love with Beatrice.
- Hero's conversation expressing her anxiety about marriage (III.iv.5–28) foreshadows the trauma of Claudio's false accusation of Hero at their wedding.
- Leonato's request that Dogberry examine the prisoners himself (III.v.38–39) and Dogberry's response (III.v.40) foreshadow the exposure of Don John's scheme and the restoration of Hero's unblemished reputation.

4. *Verbal and situational irony* Many of the great moments of humor and tragedy in *Much Ado* occur because of Shakespeare's ability to create verbal irony. The following are examples.

a) *Verbal irony for comic effect*

- Benedick's protest to Beatrice "But it is certain I am loved of all ladies, only you excepted: and I would I could find in my heart that I had not a hard heart, for, truly, I love none" (I.i.93–95) and his protest to Don Pedro and Claudio against marriage "That a woman conceived me, I thank her . . . I will live a bachelor" (I.i.177–82) are so exaggerated that they become comic irony and foreshadow that Benedick will marry—most likely Beatrice.

- Comic irony is apparent in the extreme negativity of Beatrice's protest to Leonato "Not till God make men of some other metal than earth. Would it not grieve a woman to be overmastered with a piece of valiant dust? to make an account of her life to a clod of wayward marl? No, uncle, I'll none . . ." (II.i.44–47), which foreshadows Beatrice's eventual marriage.

- Benedick's protests to Don Pedro against the attractions of Beatrice "O, she misused me past the endurance of a block . . . so indeed all disquiet, horror, and perturbation follows her" (II.i.185–201) is another example of comic irony created through negativity and foreshadowing.

- Benedick's soliloquy against falling in love (II.iii.7–29) is comic irony because Benedick is criticizing Claudio for the faults that he himself will soon display.

- Comic irony is illustrated in Benedick's comment "I do spy some marks of love in her" (II.iii.195) because Benedick is misinterpreting her behavior.

- Benedick's declaration "This can be no trick. . . . When I said I would die a bachelor, I did not think I should live till I were married" (II.iii.177–94) is comically ironic in that Benedick quickly accepts the conversation he overhears about Beatrice's love for him and embraces all that he has been rejecting—namely, Beatrice and marriage.

- Dogberry's proud misuse of language is verbal irony used for comic effect. For example, Dogberry uses "ass" (IV.ii.61–63 and V.i.227) as a complimentary term, though Conrade intends it to be derogative.

b) *Verbal irony for tragic effect*

- Claudio's exclamation "Oh what men dare do! what men may do! what men daily do, not knowing what they do!" (IV.i.14–15) is tragically ironic. Claudio is referring to Leonato's unknowingly giving a sullied Hero to him in marriage; however, it is Claudio who does not know what he is doing when he slanders the innocent Hero.

- Don Pedro's support of Claudio's accusation (IV.i.82–89) is tragic because Don Pedro has accepted the scene that he has witnessed from afar in the dark and will slander a young woman from a family that he knows well—despite his previous experience with his step-brother's villainy.

c) *Verbal irony for humiliating effect* Leonato uses verbal irony in the following lines to criticize Don Pedro and Claudio: "Here stand a pair of honorable men" (V.i.236); "I thank you, princes, for my daughter's death"
(V.i.238); "Record it with your high and worthy deeds" (V.i.239); and
"'Twas bravely done" (V.i.240).

d) *Situational irony*

- Don Pedro, Claudio, and Leonato's conversation (II.iii.78–176) is
  ironic in that Benedick is unaware that he is overhearing the plot
  contrived to get him to love Beatrice.

- Benedick's conversation with Beatrice (II.iii.196–208), in which
  Benedick, having been duped by Don Pedro, reacts to Beatrice's words
  as if she were in love with him, is situational irony because Beatrice
  has yet to be duped by Hero and Ursula.

- Hero and Ursula's conversation (III.i.23–106) is ironic in that
  Beatrice is unaware that she is overhearing the plot contrived to get
  her to love Benedick.

- Dogberry's circuitous ramblings to Leonato (III.v.1–41) become the
  heralds of impending tragedy since the audience realizes that the
  imminent wedding ceremony and Leonato's ignorance of the significance of Dogberry's announcement will prevent Leonato from
  accompanying Dogberry to interview the two prisoners.

- Situational irony is illustrated in Leonato's reply to Borachio "I thank
  you, princes, for my daughter's death" (V.i.238) in that Leonato is
  intentionally stating the opposite of the truth, but his listeners
  respond as if he were speaking the truth.

- Claudio's hanging a scroll on Hero's tomb proclaiming her to be the
  innocent victim of slander (V.iii.1–21) is ironic in that Hero is
  actually alive.

5. *Deception as illusion* Much Ado is more about "noting" than "nothing," and
   some critics believe that that noting what others do was Shakespeare's point
   in writing the play. Plots set up to deceive people are the core of *Much Ado*.
   Don Pedro, Claudio, and Leonato contrive to trick Benedick into falling in
   love with Beatrice. Likewise, Hero and Ursula contrive to trick Beatrice
   into falling in love with Benedick. Don John and Borachio agree to a plot
   in which Margaret pretends to be Hero so Don Pedro and Claudio will
   be tricked into believing Hero's reputation is tarnished. Don John and
   Borachio's plot creates an illusion that appeals to Don Pedro's and Claudio's
   hidden fears. Because they are designed to appeal to the innermost wishes of
   Benedick and Beatrice, or the hidden fears of Don Pedro and Claudio, these
   plots succeed in that the characters respond as expected. Don Pedro and
   Claudio accept the illusion as reality, and they act upon it—nearly ending
   their hopes for happiness. However, for Benedick and Beatrice, who need
   help acknowledging their love for each other, illusion becomes reality.

Following are some examples where characters in the play deceive themselves or others:

- Benedick deceives himself about his feelings for Beatrice and his interest in marriage (I.i.93–95, I.i.177–82, II.iii.18–28).

- Beatrice deceives herself about her interest in marriage (II.i.44–48).

- Don Pedro initiates an important deception when he begins the plot to bring Beatrice and Benedick together (II.i.278–84).

- Borachio initiates an important deception when he plots to have it appear that Hero is having an affair with him (II.ii.25–37).

- Don Pedro, Claudio, and Leonato deceive Benedick when they enact Don Pedro's scheme to make Benedick fall in love with Beatrice (II.iii.78–168).

- Hero initiates an important deception when she, Margaret, and Ursula contrive to make Beatrice fall in love with Benedick (III.i.1–106).

- The friar initiates an important deception when he suggests that Leonato and the rest maintain that Hero died when she was accused by Claudio (IV.i.196–204).

- Leonato initiates an important deception when he commands Claudio to marry his niece in place of the dead Hero (V.i.256–62).

6. *Figurative language* Following are examples of metaphors and similes:

- The messenger's portrayal of Claudio as "doing, in the figure of a lamb, the feats of a lion" (I.i.11–12) is a metaphor that conveys action. The lamb symbolizes a young docile follower, whereas the lion symbolizes a mature commanding aggressor.

- Beatrice's depiction of Benedick as one who has "a new sworn brother" every month (I.i.54) leads to her simile of the hat—"he wears his faith [sworn friendship] but as the fashion of his hat; it ever changes with the next block [mold]" (I.i.56–57). The hat's being molded into a newer model symbolizes Benedick's inability to sustain a loyal long-standing relationship.

- The messenger's statement "I see, lady, the gentleman is not in your books" (I.i.58) and Beatrice's reply "No, and he were, I would burn my study" (I.i.59) are metaphors conveying the idea that Beatrice is studying Benedick. Beatrice's manipulation of this metaphor conveys the intensity of her dislike of Benedick; she would rather burn up her entire library than suffer Benedick's presence in a few of her books.

- Don Pedro's remark "What need the bridge much broader than the flood?" (I.i.241) is a metaphor that compares the number of words Claudio will need to woo Hero to the length of a bridge.

- Don John describes his position in society as that of an outsider. When he states "I had rather be a canker [a diseased plant] in a hedge than a rose in his [Don Pedro's] grace" (I.iii.20) he is making a comparison between two flowers—one an ugly diseased flower in a common hedge and the other a beautiful flower in a cultivated garden. He says that he prefers being the ugly flower in a common hedge.

- Ursula's metaphor "The pleasant'st angling is to see the fish / Cut with her golden oars the silver stream, / and greedily devour the treacherous bait" (III.i.26–28) conveys a scene in which Beatrice is a fish about to be caught by Hero's plot.

- Claudio's metaphor "the two bears will not bite one another when they meet" (III.ii.57–58) compares Beatrice and Benedick to two antagonistic, competitive bears who are engaged in conflict.

- Don Pedro's question to Claudio "Runs not this speech like iron through your blood?" (V.i.217) uses the simile of an iron weapon (a sword) to convey the deadly impact of the discovery that Don John and Borachio fabricated their account of Hero.

7. *Oxymorons* Claudio calls Hero "most foul, most fair" and "pure impiety, and impious purity" (IV.i.98–99). He uses oxymorons because only their incongruity can express the intensity of his emotions.

WRITING ABOUT LITERATURE

1. *Essay analyzing Benedick's character* Remind students to use quotations for their examples and to analyze Benedick's words and actions. Students should explain how each of their examples relates to their principal idea(s).

2. *Essay analyzing the ways in which the principal characters are outer-directed* Students should note Don John's speech in which he distinguishes himself from the members of Don Pedro's society. They should quote lines that reveal Don Pedro's humiliation in choosing Hero for Claudio. They should cite Claudio's dependence on Don Pedro, who is his superior, as well as Claudio's determination to punish Hero through his public accusation. Even Dogberry understands the outer-directed society in which he lives, which is why he wants everyone to learn that he is an ass.

3. *Essay analyzing Shakespeare's choice of title* Shakespeare may have titled this play *Much Ado About Nothing* because nothing bad happens despite the bad events in the play. Writers and artists often handle serious subjects by setting their stories in distant times or places or by presenting their stories as fantasies or comedies. In this play, Shakespeare may have used comedy to make a serious, even tragic, subject acceptable in his society. Unless he intended for the audience to see the seriousness of his subject, it is difficult to understand why he added tragic elements to a common humorous plot. Through comedy an audience can question, consider, and accept ideas that might otherwise be too threatening psychologically. However, while comedy pleases an audience, a writer may pay a great price for choosing this medium since comedy may trivialize human beings by robbing their words and deeds of significance.

Certainly this play deals with the issues of inner- versus outer-direction, the overwhelming need for social acceptance, and the existence of subconscious social prejudices. Don Pedro, Claudio, and Leonato are all outer-directed in their attitudes and behavior. They care more about the abstract concept of honor than about honorable actions, and thus their attitudes and behavior are self-centered. Their vulnerability to Don John and their treatment of Hero show that they view women with fear, distrust, and hostility.

Such snap judgments and acceptance of slander do occur today. Likely accusers are members of the majority—whether of race, religion, gender, nationality, or social class. Likely victims are members of the minority, who are viewed as outsiders. Many among the majority subconsciously distrust the minority, sometimes to bolster their own self-image.

4. *Essay examining the relationship between the subplots and the plot* Call students' attention to the directions in the textbook assignment.

5. *Essay on valuing only what is lost* Responses with regard to weather, wealth, health, and peace will vary.

6. *Creative writing: Hero's story from her point of view* Students might use the format of a diary, a conversation, or a letter to tell Hero's story. They should include Hero's thoughts and feelings as she contemplates her relationship with her father and with Claudio.

7. *Creative writing: Claudio's or Hero's story from a modern point of view* Students should include relationships that parallel the relationships Claudio and Hero have in the play. Remind students to use dialogue to reveal their character's personality, ideas, and values.

FURTHER READING

Shakespeare, William, *As You Like It; Romeo and Juliet; A Midsummer Night's Dream; Twelfth Night; The Taming of the Shrew; The Winter's Tale; Hamlet; Macbeth; King Lear; Julius Caesar; Richard III; Henry IV (Part I)*.

Line Number	Dogberry's Malapropisms	Translations
III.iii.		
line 2	*it were pity but they should*	it would be a pity if they did not
line 2	*salvation*	damnation
line 7	*desartless*	deserving
line 12	*nature*	nurture
lines 16–17	*no need of such vanity*	need of such skill
line 17	*senseless*	sensible
line 19	*comprehend*	apprehend
line 19	*vagrom*	vagrant
line 20	*stand*	halt, stop

line 22	*take no note of him, but let him go*	detain him
lines 23–24	*you are rid of*	you have captured
line 29	*tolerable*	intolerable
line 30	*rather sleep than talk*	neither sleep nor talk
line 59	*present*	represent
line 74	*vigitant*	vigilant
III.v.		
line 2	*confidence*	conference, confidential conference
line 3	*decerns*	concerns
line 3	*nearly*	closely
line 9	*blunt*	sharp
line 13	*odorous*	odious
line 15	*poor duke's*	duke's poor
line 16	*tedious*	generous, rich
line 20	*exclamation on*	acclamation, commendation of
line 24	*excepting*	respecting
line 35	*comprehended*	apprehended
line 36	*aspicious*	suspicious
line 40	*suffigance*	sufficient
line 46	*examination*	examine
line 51	*excommunication*	communication
IV.ii.		
line 1	*dissembly*	assembly
line 5	*exhibition*	commission
line 29	*eftest*	shortest, most convenient
line 45	*redemption*	damnation, perdition
line 54	*opinioned*	pinioned, bound
line 63	*piety*	impiety
V.i.		
line 189	*cursing*	accursed
line 225	*plaintiffs*	defendants
line 226	*reformed*	informed
lines 277–78	*a key in his ear, and a lock hanging by it*	a lovelock of hair

line 290	*restore you to health*	keep you in good health
line 291	*I humbly give you leave to depart*	I will depart
line 292	*prohibit*	permit

My Heart Leaps Up

WILLIAM WORDSWORTH

INTRODUCING THE POEM

"My Heart Leaps Up" is a celebration of Wordsworth's joyful appreciation of nature. He is delighted that he is able to perceive and appreciate the natural world with the mind of a child, open to nature's wonder and beauty. This faculty for appreciation ("natural piety") is so important that he would rather die than lose it.

Wordworth's style achieves his goal: the union of imagination with simple means of expression. Wordsworth believed adults should attempt to retain the attitudes toward nature that they had as children, namely, a sense of wonder and an appreciation of beauty. He conveys this complex philosophical idea through the use of paradox ("The Child is father of the Man"), and he expresses the joy of nature through his metaphorical use of the verb "leaps."

The theme of the poem, appreciation of nature, is important to all human beings. Beauty often surrounds people in small, apparently insignificant forms. Such beauty is easily missed by those who get lost in the larger events of their lives. Yet for those who remember to look outside themselves, appreciation of the various facets of nature enhances the experience of living. Nature provides a touch of beauty for people who may live in stressful or drab environments.

Personal Literary Journal: What role does an appreciation of nature play in your life? Have you always reacted to nature in the way that you do now? To what extent has an experience with nature had an effect on your life?

Literary Terms: metaphor, paradox, repetition, theme

COMPREHENSION QUESTIONS

1. *What does Wordworth love to behold?* nature, represented by the rainbow

2. *About how old is the poet when he writes this poem?* middle-aged

3. *What unusual statement does the poet make?* "The Child is father of the Man."

UNDERSTANDING THE POEM: POSSIBLE ANSWERS

1. *Important to poet* An appreciation of nature is important. Retaining a childlike sense of wonder about nature is especially important.

2. "The Child is father of the Man" An adult is a child grown up. A person's childhood experiences determine to a considerable extent how he or she reacts to later life experiences. Wordsworth applies this relationship to the appreciation of nature.

3. *Natural piety* *Piety* means "faithful devotion." *Natural piety* means "faithful devotion to nature."

4. *Theme* The appreciation of nature is a critically important aspect of one's life. A goal in life should be to preserve the view of the natural universe that one had as a child.

ANALYZING LITERARY TECHNIQUE: POSSIBLE ANSWERS

*1. *Paradox* "The Child is father of the Man" contradicts the usual way people think about the parent-child relationship. This formulation of the relationship reveals the unity within each person from childhood to old age and implies a cause-and-effect relationship between early life experiences and later reactions to those life experiences. Just as a parent teaches a child, the child may be seen as the teacher of the parent. The child views the world as a new and delightful experience, one that is filled with wondrous sights and events. Those who retain their appreciation of the wonder and beauty of the natural environment (and of life itself) lead rich lives.

2. *Poem in terms of Wordsworth's goals* The poem is a fine example of Wordsworth's goals. His subject is his powerful emotional reaction to nature, which he expresses in terms of his heart's leaping joyfully when he sees a rainbow. He also achieves remarkable success in using common language to describe a common sight in a way that expresses the spiritual relationship between human beings and nature. Except for the opening metaphor, Wordsworth avoids using figurative language.

   In addition, the paradox ("The Child is father of the Man") conveys a complex relationship in graphically simple terms. Wordsworth avoids adjectives and adverbs. The result is a philosophical theme that is presented in a simple and uncluttered form.

3. *Metaphor* The verb "leaps" effectively conveys life, vitality, excitement, and enjoyment. Animals leap with vitality; people leap with joy. Wordworth's leaping heart signifies his joyful reaction to the beauty in nature.

4. *Capitalization* The capitalization of "Child" and "Man" accomplishes two goals simultaneously: Wordsworth emphasizes both words and their meanings, and their meanings expand to represent all children and all adults.

5. *Repetition* The repetition of "so" expresses the continuity of Wordsworth's feelings throughout the three stages of his life.

WRITING ABOUT LITERATURE

1. *Essay on the paradox of the child's being the parent of the adult* Call students' attention to the questions in the textbook assignment. Remind them to support their ideas with specific examples. (See **U.P.** question 2 and **A.L.T.** question 1 above.) **(P.L.J.)**

2. *Creative writing: a memorable experience in nature* Remind students that they can choose to express their thoughts in either prose or poetry. Also reminder them to choose words that will help others see the sight or feel the experience.

FURTHER READING

Wordsworth, William, "The Daffodils"; "To the Cuckoo"; "The Solitary Reaper"; "Lucy"; "The World Is Too Much with Us"; "Ode: Intimations of Immortality from Recollections of Early Childhood."

Dover Beach

MATTHEW ARNOLD

INTRODUCING THE POEM

"Dover Beach" eloquently expresses the power of human love in a world made uncertain and uncaring by the loss of faith. The structure of the poem is modern; associative thinking leads the speaker from one stanza to the next. The poet looks out of his hotel-room window at the beach and the sea beyond. On this beautiful moonlit night, he listens to the sound of the waves as they ebb and flow over the pebbles on the shore. Their mournful sound reminds him of the fourth speech of the Chorus in *Antigone* (lines 656–77), where Sophocles compares the "roar, and low moaning" of the tide to the repetition of human sorrow and devastation. Sophocles's sad association leads Arnold to compare the ocean's tide to the tide of "the Sea of Faith," which is now retreating. Arnold concludes his poem with his vision of a world without faith and without peace, a world where the love of one human being for another is the only solace in an irrational universe.

Personal Literary Journal: To what extent, if any, do you need a support system in your life to help you cope with difficult circumstances? If you do, what is that support system?

Literary Terms: allusion, apostrophe, climax, connotative language, contrast, irony, metaphor, paradox, repetition, setting, symbol, theme, tone

COMPREHENSION QUESTIONS

1. *What is the speaker in this poem doing?* looking out the window at the seashore
2. *What time of day is it?* night
3. *Describe the sea.* calm; moonlit
4. *What does the speaker hear?* the sound of waves lapping on the shore
5. *What feeling does the sea evoke in the speaker?* sadness; melancholy
6. *What does the poet compare the sea to?* "the Sea of Faith"
7. *To whom is the speaker speaking?* the person he loves
8. *What does the speaker ask of the listener?* that they be true to each other

9. *At the end of the poem, how does the speaker describe the world?* a place without love, joy, peace, certainty, or help for pain

UNDERSTANDING THE POEM: POSSIBLE ANSWERS

1. *Why these thoughts are expressed* A beautiful view out the window sets off a chain of associations.

2. *The sea's characteristics* The ebb and flow of the waves on the shore have a mournful sound that is conducive to thinking about the following ideas:
   - timelessness and the universe before human life
   - an impersonal universe and the loneliness of the individuals in it
   - an awesome power that is beyond human control and the inherent insignificance and vulnerability of human beings in the universe
   - personal suffering or loss

3. *Thoughts about Sophocles* The Chorus in *Antigone* chants several philosophical passages that are famous for their eloquent expression of the nature of human life. Being well educated, Arnold was familiar with *Antigone* and was reminded of this passage when he heard the mournful sound of the waves.

4. *How the ebb of sea affects the speaker's outlook* The decline of religious faith leads Arnold to consider the plight of the world without faith. The result is a world without certainty, comfort, or peace. Only the enduring love of two people for each other can surmount the terror of realizing that faith is waning.

5. *How the ebb of faith is important for human relationships* As faith declines, human relationships become more important because they can provide the psychological support that is missing. For those who turn away from religion, human companionship and love can be the balm and glue of life.

6. *Possibility that the poem could be written today* The twentieth century was replete with events that would cause people to feel that they are alone in an uncaring universe: two World Wars, the Holocaust, a host of natural disasters, and rampant diseases—to name the most obvious.

7. *"A criticism of life"* "Dover Beach" is a criticism of life in that it is an evaluation of the human condition in the universe. It has philosophical overtones and universal implications.

ANALYZING LITERARY TECHNIQUE: POSSIBLE ANSWERS

1. *Setting* The setting provides the foundation for the structure of the poem. The ebb and flow of the sea's tide start in the present, reach into the past, and then become symbolic of the contemporary lack of faith.

2. *Apostrophe* Arnold's use of apostrophe personalizes the poem and confirms that the poem is an actual experience. As a real person stands looking out a window, he invites his companion to join him in the experience.

*3. *Contrast* Examples include the following:
   - Flow/ebb: The water flows in and out on the beach.

- Present/past: while looking out on Dover's beach, Arnold thinks of Sophocles, who also saw the ebb and flow of the tide as symbolic of human life.

- Dream/reality: The world that Arnold perceives is a dream; the real world has no positive characteristics.

- Faith/uncertainty: "The Sea of Faith" is waning, leaving uncertainty in its place.

- Peace/war: The world outside the window is tranquil; the world at large is filled with battles over religion, politics, and economics.

- Loving relationships/uncaring universe: The love between the poet and his companion (his wife) is all that can sustain them in an uncaring universe where tragedy is a reality in human life.

*4. *Relation of contrast to tone* One of the greatest sources of power in the poem is found in the contrast between the tone of optimism and tranquility in the opening stanza and the tone of pessimism and mindless hostility in the closing stanza.

*5. *Connection between contrast and paradox* Arnold's use of paradox involves the contrast between two simultaneous realities. The world that is perceived to be beautiful and full of promise (stanza 1) is the dreamlike vision of another reality—a world that is irrational, uncaring, changing, and threatening (stanza 5).

*6. *Relation of metaphor and symbol to contrast* Metaphor: "The Sea of Faith" contrasts with the current lack of faith, creating a contrast between a universe that offered intellectual certainty and emotional comfort and a universe that offers neither. Symbol: Night, at the end of the poem, symbolizes the lack of knowledge, understanding, and certainty.

*7. Antigone *passage and function of allusion* Arnold chose this passage because it is a famous philosophical statement about the nature of human life. Sophocles speaks of unceasing ruin, sorrows piling on sorrows without release, and hope and light destroyed by senseless words and raging passions. Arnold repeats these ideas in the last stanza.

*8. *Relationship between climax and theme* The climax states the theme—the love of one person for another is the only factor in life that enriches life and enables human beings to cope with life's inevitable tragedies.

9. *Connotative language* Examples include the following:

- "The sea is calm," "the moon lies fair," and "sweet the night air is" all connote beauty and peace.

- The "grating roar / Of pebbles," "the eternal note of sadness," and "the turbid ebb and flow / Of human misery" connote lack of harmony.

- "Melancholy . . . roar" and "drear / And naked shingles" connote a sad, bleak, barren environment.

- Joy, love, light, certitude, peace, and help for pain all connote the well-being that is missing in the world.
- "Ignorant armies clash by night" "on a darkling plain" "with confused alarms of struggle and flight" connotes the wanton destructiveness of human behavior in an irrational world.

10. *Repetition of "nor"* Arnold's repeated use of "nor" separates—and thereby emphasizes—each of the five qualities that are lacking in the world. The technique gives power to the stanza.

11. *Irony* It is ironic, and very sad, that a beautiful moonlit night would elicit such a string of pessimistic associations. Moments of beauty should be appreciated and treasured, for they make the tragedies bearable. It is also ironic that the world that seems to be so beautiful is, in Arnold's view, so irrational and painful.

WRITING ABOUT LITERATURE

1. *Essay analyzing how contrast reinforces the theme* Call students' attention to the suggestions in the textbook assignment. Remind them that the purpose of quotations is to support a point of view and that they should express their own analytic thinking. (See **A.L.T.** 3, 4, 5, 6, 7, and 8 above.) **AP**

2. *Creative writing: response to the Arnold's theme* Call students' attention to the suggestions in the textbook assignment. Remind them that they have a choice of points of view. Some people will support Arnold's view with numerous examples. Others will refute it with examples of their own.

FURTHER READING

Arnold, Matthew, "Thyrsis"; "The Scholar-Gipsy"; "The Forsaken Merman"; "Self-Dependence."

Sonnet 32

ELIZABETH BARRETT BROWNING

INTRODUCING THE POEM

Sonnet 32 is particularly appealing in that Barrett eloquently expresses doubts that are common to many people before they make a lasting emotional commitment. She finds it ironic that Browning has chosen to love her when he could find a younger, healthier, more attractive woman. She wonders whether he is acting so quickly that he will soon be sorry. By the end of the poem, she has accepted Browning's judgment, believing that his love has made her the person that he loves and that it is possible for two "great souls" to overcome physical imperfections and to unite with confidence.

The poem is based on the paradox that one who loves can make a plain-looking loved one beautiful or, as described in the central image of the poem, that a master musician can produce perfect music using an obsolete out-of-tune instrument. Barrett uses the simile of "an out-of-tune / Worn viol" (lines 7–8) to describe herself and the metaphor of "a good singer" (line 8) to describe Browning. At the end of the poem, Barrett unites the contrasting musical strands, stating that "master-hands" can bring forth "perfect strains" from "instruments defaced" and that "great souls, at one stroke, may do and dote" (lines 12–14).

Contrast is a major technique in the poem. It establishes the disparity between the speaker's view of herself and the lover's view of her. Barrett carries the contrast through the first eleven lines of the poem. The end of the contrasts in the last lines of the poem marks the speaker's acceptance of her lover's point of view. Her changed attitude is the climax of the poem.

Personal Literary Journal: Have you ever felt unworthy of the love of someone whom you admire, or have you known someone who felt unworthy of your affection and attention? What caused you or the other person to feel inadequate?

Literary Terms: alliteration, climax, contrast, figurative language, irony, metaphor, paradox, rhyme, simile, sonnet, tone

COMPREHENSION QUESTIONS

1. *What bothers the speaker about her lover's oath?* His oath may have been made too quickly.

2. *What does the speaker expect might happen?* Her lover will be sorry and change his mind.

3. *What does the speaker compare herself to?* an old out-of-tune, defaced viol

4. *What does the speaker conclude about her attitude?* The speaker is unfair to her lover if she does not trust his love.

5. *What is the tone of the conclusion?* optimistic

UNDERSTANDING THE POEM: POSSIBLE ANSWERS

1. *The speaker's doubts* The speaker believes that she is too old, unattractive, and out-of-date for him.

2. *The speaker's reluctance to accept love* The speaker is concerned that her lover has fallen in love too quickly and that he will soon tire of her or find her lacking in qualities that are important to him. If this happens, she will be hurt.

3. *How the speaker's attitude wrongs her lover* The speaker decides that she must accept what her lover sees in her. She recognizes that what he sees is a part of her that she has not seen in herself. Not trusting his love is unfair.

4. *The speaker's conclusion* The speaker concludes that two mature people who are right for each other may know it soon and with certainty.

5. *Importance of effort in a relationship* The critical ingredient in a relationship is the attitude of both partners (their "great souls") and the quality of their love, not their age, physical appearance, or length of acquaintance.

ANALZYING LITERARY TECHNIQUE: POSSIBLE ANSWERS

*1. *Contrast* Contrast establishes the disparity between the speaker's view of herself and her lover's view of her. Barrett carries the contrast through the first thirteen lines of the poem. Examples include the following:

- the constant sun versus the inconstant moon (lines 1–2)
- "thine oath / To love me" versus "slacken all those bonds [of love]" (lines 1–3)
- "Quick-loving" versus "quickly loathe" (line 5)
- "out-of-tune / Worn viol" versus "a good singer" (lines 7–8)
- "snatched in haste" versus "laid down at the first ill-sounding note" (lines 9–10)
- "did not wrong myself" versus "placed / A wrong on thee" (lines 11–12)
- "perfect strains" versus "instruments defaced" (lines 12–13)

*2. *Extended metaphor* Barrett uses the simile of an out-of-tune viol to describe herself and her relationship to Browning, whom she describes metaphorically as "a good singer." The extended metaphor built on these figures of speech symbolizes her view of their relationship. Examples include the following:

- the singer would "spoil his song" with the "out-of-tune / Worn viol" (lines 7–9)
- an instrument "snatched in haste, / Is laid down at the first ill-sounding note" (lines 9–10)
- "perfect strains may float / 'Neath master-hands, from instruments defaced" (lines 12–13)
- "great souls, at one stroke" (line 14)

3. *Relationship of climax to sonnet structure* The climax occurs at the end of the sonnet, in the last sentence (the last three lines). It presents a change of attitude, one that unites the contrasting strands of the rest of the poem. The speaker decides that "master-hands" can bring forth "perfect strains" from "instruments defaced" and that "great souls, at one stroke, may do and dote."

4. *Relationship of tone to sonnet structure* The tone changes from one of skepticism (in the first ten lines) to one of confidence (in the remaining four lines).

*5. *Consonance, assonance, and rhyme* Sound devices help to unify the poem. They make the lines read smoothly and musically, thus reinforcing the poem's central musical metaphor. Examples include the following:

- Repeated open consonants and spirants (f, l, m, n, s, and r sounds) give the lines a rolling, flowing sound.
- Repeated vowel sounds, especially long vowels ("the sun rose on thine oath / To love me, I looked forward to the moon" [lines 1–2]) add to the musical softness of the poem.

- The use of near rhyme (oath/troth/loathe/wroth; moon/soon/one/tune) softens the chiming, singsong effect of repeated perfect rhyme.

WRITING ABOUT LITERATURE

1. *Essay analyzing figurative language* Call students' attention to the directions in the textbook assignment. Remind them to use quotations from the poem. (See **A.L.T.** questions 1, 2, and 5 above.) **AP**

2. *Creative writing: a response from the lover* Remind students that they may choose the form of their response.

FURTHER READING

Browning, Elizabeth Barrett, *Sonnets from the Portuguese; Aurora Leigh.*

The Old Stoic
EMILY BRONTË

INTRODUCING THE POEM

Emily Brontë's eloquent personal plea for freedom and for the courage to endure all trials reveals the values that sustained her to the day of her death. In her poem, as in her life, she rejects the goals that many people value: love, wealth, and fame. Brontë's creed is confirmed in the "Biographical Notice of Ellis and Acton Bell," which was included in the second edition of *Wuthering Heights.* There Currer Bell (Charlotte Brontë) describes Emily Brontë's nature, the lack of recognition for her poetry and her novel, and the courageous way she faced the ravaging effects of tuberculosis. Emily Brontë's creed is also confirmed by how she chose to live her life—walking in solitude on the moors, seeking the company of only her sisters, and persevering in her writing despite the unfavorable reception her work received.

Stoicism is based on the thoughts of the Greek philosopher Zeno, who lived about the turn of the third century B.C. Stoics believe that human beings are obliged to reject the appeals of pleasure, devote their lives to good works, and accept their fate with courage. Brontë's wish for the courage to endure and her rejection of love, wealth, and fame coincide with the stoic's indifference to pain and pleasure. However, she substitutes a passion for liberty for the stoic's commitment to duty.

Part of the poem's appeal is its musical quality. Brontë achieves this through rhythm (iambic tetrameter, alternating with iambic trimeter) and rhyme.

Personal Literary Journal: What do you need to have a happy life? What would you sacrifice in life to have what you value?

Literary Terms: connotative language, contrast, lyric, metaphor, rhythm

COMPREHENSION QUESTIONS

1. *What does the speaker value lightly?* riches

2. *What does the speaker scorn?* love

3. *What dream has vanished?* the desire for fame

4. *What does the speaker pray for?* to keep her heart; to be free

5. *What does the speaker want through life and death?* a free soul; the courage to endure

UNDERSTANDING THE POEM: POSSIBLE ANSWERS

1. *Values of the speaker* The speaker values liberty more than anything else—more than wealth, love, and fame.

2. *Other insights into the speaker* The poem also reveals that the speaker is aging, which suggests that the speaker's stoicism may derive from experience, perhaps disappointing experience. The speaker is concerned about maintaining her integrity even beyond the grave.

ANALYZING LITERARY TECHNIQUE: POSSIBLE ANSWERS

*1. *Contrast* The speaker emphasizes the importance of liberty by comparing her passion for liberty with her rejection of the love, wealth, and fame that most people value.

2. *"Chainless soul"* The metaphor in the last stanza of a "chainless soul" creates a visual picture of a free spirit, both in life and death. This is the liberty that the speaker passionately values. She prays for it in the second stanza, after having stated in the first stanza that she has no interest in any other aspect of life.

3. *Ballad meter and rhyme scheme* The seven-stress lines of ballad, or hymn, meter (iambic tetrameter, alternating with iambic trimeter) combine with the regular *abab* rhyme scheme to give the poem a soothing musical quality. Ballad meter connects the poem with traditional oral forms of poetry. It contributes to the poem's simplicity and directness.

4. *Connotative language* Brontë's use of connotative language gives the poem its power. "Laugh to scorn" (line 2) reveals the ease with which the speaker dismisses love from her life. "A dream / That vanished" (lines 3–4) conveys the transitory nature of the speaker's wish for fame. "Liberty" (line 8), by not being more specific, is open to each reader's interpretation. "Give me" (line 8) combines the directness of a command with the passion of a desire. "I implore" (line 10) conveys great depth of feeling.

5. *Lyric poem* This is a lyric poem because the poet is expressing personal feelings in a form that is short, complete in itself, and musical in quality.

WRITING ABOUT LITERATURE

1. *Essay analyzing Brontë's use of contrast* Remind students to support their ideas with quotations. (See **A.L.T.** question 1 above.) **AP**

2. *Creative writing: how the speaker became a stoic* Remind students that they are free to choose both the content and the form of this work. Students may wish to experiment with ballad meter, a fairly easy-to-write poetic form. **(P.L.J.)**

FURTHER READING

Brontë, Emily, "Remembrance"; "No Coward Soul Is Mine"; "The Prisoner"; *Wuthering Heights*.

Goblin Market

CHRISTINA ROSSETTI

INTRODUCING THE POEM

"Goblin Market" operates on two levels. On the surface, it is the delightful heroic story of the triumph of love over adversity. Lizzie's love for her sister Laura is so great that after Laura has been poisoned by eating the tempting but forbidden goblin fruit, Lizzie conquers her fears and subjects herself to the powers of the evil goblins to save Laura's life. By courageously withstanding temptation and stoically enduring the goblins' taunts and abuse, Lizzie returns with the antidote for the poison.

Beneath the surface, "Goblin Market" is the story of the triumph of self-control over temptation. Woven into its texture are two biblical themes. The first, from Genesis, involves the loss of innocence by succumbing to the temptation to eat forbidden fruit. The second, from the New Testament, involves the Christ-like salvation of a sinner through love and suffering.

Also woven into the texture of "Goblin Market" are interesting psychological themes. The sisters share all of life's experiences, with one critical exception. Laura functions as Lizzie's Shadow or doppelgänger in that she represents Lizzie's unrestrained self, the part of Lizzie that is willing to be curious and to experiment despite the risks. In contrast, Lizzie "thrust a dimpled finger / In each ear, shut eyes and ran" from the goblin men (lines 67–68). The relationship between Lizzie and Laura may be viewed as symbolizing an internal conflict within one person—a conflict between two diametrically opposed inclinations, those that are rational and viewed by the self as "good" and those that are irrational and viewed by the self as "evil."

To use the terminology of Albert Guerard, "Goblin Market" may be seen as the soul-satisfying "solitary spiritual journey" or "night journey" of a person who is dealing with an inner conflict between good and evil. Her Lizzie-self first abdicates; she runs in fear from the goblin men's temptations and lets her Laura-self indulge her curiosity and experience the disastrous tempting fruits. Then her Lizzie-self musters her courage and proves that she possesses the qualities necessary to save her Laura-self by confronting and resisting the goblin men's temptations. As a result, her Lizzie-self can triumphantly claim a double victory. She has saved the life of her Laura-self and has proved that her Lizzie-self no longer needs to fear temptation. Through the night journey, the person who has been experiencing the inner conflict heals herself of her internal division and emerges as an integrated personality.

The plot, character development, and thematic material of "Goblin Market" reveal the poem to be similar to an allegory in that it can be understood on two levels: on the surface, a simple narrative; beneath the surface, a tale with a moral. Lizzie's actions on Laura's behalf reveal the power of a person's love to support and enrich the life of a loved one. The goblins' fruits reveal two paradoxes: First, evil (their fruit) may appear to be attractive and benign; second, actions that are pleasurable may also lead to corruption and death. Finally, as Lizzie learns, one can combat evil only by confronting it; ignoring evil simply perpetuates it.

"Goblin Market"—with its rhythms, rhymes, and repetitions—asks to be read aloud. Its lists of details regarding tempting fruits and evil goblin men enrich the imagination. The stylistic highlight may be Rossetti's technique of emphasizing each significant dramatic point in the story by means of a series of remarkable similes.

Personal Literary Journal: To what extent, if any, do you consider present pleasure worth the possibility of future pain? If you are a person who avoids temptation, what methods do you use to achieve this goal? Do you find that it is better for you to avoid the tempting situation or to confront it?

Literary Terms: allegory, alliteration, conflict, connotative language, contrast, doppelgänger, fairy tale, figurative language, foreshadowing, irony, metaphor, narrative, night journey, onomatopoeia, paradox, parallelism, repetition, rhyme, Shadow, simile, symbol, theme

COMPREHENSION QUESTIONS

1. *To whom do the goblin men call?* young women and girls
2. *When do the goblin men sell their wares?* morning and evening
3. *What do the goblin men sell?* fruit
4. *What is Laura's attitude toward the goblin men?* curious
5. *What is Lizzie's attitude toward the goblin men?* fearful
6. *Who is Jeanie?* a girl who died after eating goblin fruit
7. *What is unusual about the cost of goblin fruit?* Money is not accepted; payment must be something from oneself.
8. *What does Laura do?* Laura eats goblin fruit and begins to die.
9. *How does Lizzie respond?* Lizzie brings goblin fruit juice to Laura and cures her.
10. *What is the concluding idea in the poem?* A sister is one's best friend.

UNDERSTANDING THE POEM: POSSIBLE ANSWERS

1. *Goblin men's customers* The goblin men are only interested in corrupting innocence; thus, they have no interest in women who have eaten their fruits or who are married.
2. *Payment for wares* The goblin men do not sell their fruit for financial gain. Their payment is corruption. When Laura pays with a lock of hair and a tear (lines 126–27), she is literally and symbolically paying a personal price for choosing evil. She is losing not only her hair, but also her innocence.
3. *Jeanie's fate* Before Laura consorts with the goblin men, she knows about Jeanie's fate. Laura simply disregards all prior knowledge and experience and acts as she chooses, without concern for the consequences. She has

become blind to the reality that the goblin men are evil and that they are deaf to her conscience and to Lizzie's admonitions.

4. *Lizzie's inner conflict and its resolution* Lizzie, who has chosen never "to listen and look" for goblin men, must choose between her fear for her own personal safety and her love for her sister. Lizzie's love for Laura gives Lizzie the courage to suppress her fears and seek the goblin men.

*5. *Lizzie's courage and heroism* Lizzie's initial courage is supported by her determination not to let the goblin men's evil contaminate her. She keeps the image of Jeanie at the forefront of her mind to help her resist the goblin men's temptations. She keeps the image of Laura at the forefront of her mind to help her tolerate the goblin men's physical abuse.

Lizzie, who has earlier trained herself not to look at what is tempting but evil, now summons the ability not to feel the assault of evil. Her motivation and self-discipline enable her to submit stoically until the goblin men give up torturing her. Lizzie's heroic qualities include her courage, determination, perseverance, stoicism, and purpose, which is for the benefit of someone other than herself.

6. *Nature of the goblin fruit* Rossetti's treatment of the goblin fruit implies that whether a substance is a poison or an antidote is determined by the intention of the person using it. The goblin men's evil purpose contaminates their fruits, but Lizzie's purpose transforms the nature of the fruit from evil to good.

7. *Nature of evil* Rossetti makes the following implications about the nature of evil:

- Evil can appear in the guise of something harmless or good (delicious goblin fruit).

- Actions that are enjoyable can lead to corruption and death (eating goblin fruit).

- Evil intent can corrupt what would otherwise be good (the goblin men's contamination of the fruit).

- Anyone who disregards rational thought, gives in to emotion, or lives without moral restraint consorts with evil (Laura's loss of innocence by meeting with the goblin men and eating their fruit).

*8. *Themes* Possible themes:

- Evil can appear disguised as attractive and benign.

- A person can combat evil only by confronting it.

- Evil intent can corrupt what would otherwise be good.

- Taking personal risks and suffering for the good of someone else is heroic behavior.

- To give in to temptation is to risk hurting oneself.

ANALYZING LITERARY TECHNIQUE: POSSIBLE ANSWERS

*1. *Goblin men* The goblin men and their fruit symbolize temptations that lead to behavior that is harmful to oneself or to others. Examples include smoking, alcohol abuse, drug abuse, and promiscuous or irresponsible sexual activity.

*2. *Fairy tale* Like a fairy tale, "Goblin Market" contains a heroic confrontation with evil, supernatural figures (goblin men), and a symbolic relationship to human experience. However, the moral focus of the symbolic relationship in "Goblin Market" (note its many moral themes) is characteristic of an allegory.

3. *Night journey* Both Laura and Lizzie experience night journeys. Laura's night journey is negative, causing her to lose her innocence and to begin wasting away. Lizzie's night journey is positive. By courageously confronting the temptations that she has fearfully avoided, Lizzie proves to herself that she no longer needs to fear the temptations because she is strong enough to resist them. (Her concern for her sister motivates her to overcome her fears.)

4. *Foreshadowing* Jeanie's story foreshadows what will happen to Laura if Lizzie does not intervene.

*5. *Sound devices* The effect of this poem depends largely on sound devices. Rossetti employs irregular metrical and rhyme schemes. While most lines have four stresses, some lines have three stresses and others have only two. The poem is not arranged into couplets or quatrains—any number or combination of lines can rhyme, and sometimes rhyme is only suggested, as in the lists of fruits. The irregular metrical and rhyme schemes contribute to the poem's fairy-tale-like effect and create a singsong quality characteristic of children's rhymes. The poem is pleasing when read aloud.
   Examples of sound devices include the following:

   - Alliteration: "Crouching close together / In the cooling weather, / With clasping arms and cautioning lips" (lines 36–38); "Plums on their twigs; / Pluck them and suck them,— / Pomegranates, figs" (lines 360–62); "Mauled and mocked her" (lines 428–9).

   - Assonance: "Do you not remember Jeanie, / How she met them in the moonlight" (lines 147–48); "Poor Laura could not hear; / Longed to buy fruit to comfort her, / But feared to pay too dear" (lines 309–11).

   - Onomatopoeia: "She heard a voice like voice of doves / Cooing all together" (lines 77–78); "Puffing and blowing, / Chuckling, clapping, crowing, / Clucking and gobbling" (lines 333–5).

   - Repetition: "Come buy, come buy" (throughout the poem); lists of goblin fruits (such as lines 5–14); descriptions of goblin men (such as lines 71–76); chains of similes, especially to describe Laura and Lizzie (such as lines 82–86). (See also question 6 below.)

*6. *Figurative language* Rossetti employs chains of images for dramatic effect to highlight significant points in the narrative:

   - "Like a rush-imbedded swan . . . When its last restraint is gone" (lines 82–86) conveys the dangerous extent of Laura's curiosity.

- "Sweeter than honey . . . flowed that juice" (lines 129–31) conveys the delicious nature of goblin-fruit.
- "Like two pigeons in one nest . . . gold for awful kings" (lines 185–91) conveys the close relationship between the two sisters.
- "Like a lily in a flood . . . Mad to tug her standard down" (lines 409–21) conveys Lizzie's determined and courageous stand against the assaults of the goblin men.
- "Her locks streamed like the torch . . . a flying flag when armies run" (lines 500–506) conveys the power of the antidote to invade Laura's body.
- "Like the watch-tower of a town . . . She fell at last" (lines 514–21) conveys the great battle between the antidote and the poison in Laura's system.

WRITING ABOUT LITERATURE

1. *Character sketch of Lizzie as a hero* Call students' attention to the directions in the textbook assignment. (See **U.P.** question 5 above.)

2. *Essay analyzing Rossetti's treatment of a theme* Call students' attention to the directions in the textbook assignment. Remind them to use quotations to support their ideas. (See **U.P.** question 8 and **A.L.T.** question 1 above.)

3. *Creative writing: a fairy tale* Call students' attention to the directions in the textbook assignment. Remind them of their choices with regard to content, style, and form. (See **U.P.** question 8 and **A.L.T.** questions 1, 2, 5, and 6 above.) **(P.L.J.)**

FURTHER READING

Rossetti, Christina, "A Birthday"; "Echo"; "Uphill"; "When I Am Dead, My Dearest"; "In an Artist's Studio"; "Remember."

An Outpost of Progress

JOSEPH CONRAD

INTRODUCING THE STORY

"An Outpost of Progress" is an adventure story about the fate of two ordinary Belgians who become ivory traders in central Africa. On one level, the story is a bitter indictment of colonialism and the slave trade. Kayerts and Carlier are typical of the white traders who entered central Africa under Belgian rule. Ostensibly bringing the fruits of civilization with them, they destroy the environment, and they, in turn, are destroyed by the environment. Like many men whom Conrad observed on his own Congo journey, they exploit Africans for their own financial gain. Without civil law and public opinion to guide their behavior, they lack the inner resources to behave honorably and responsibly.

On a deeper level, Conrad's tale reveals the dual nature of human beings. What Conrad will call the "heart of darkness," G. H. Schubert (in *The Symbolism of Dreams*, 1814) calls the doppelgänger—a second passionate self that haunts the rational self. Carl Jung calls this subconscious self the Shadow; he describes it as "a living part of the personality" that "personifies everything that the subject refuses to acknowledge about himself and yet is always thrusting itself upon him directly or indirectly." Jung also explains that "to become conscious of it involves recognizing the dark aspects of the personality as present and real," which a person usually does through dreams. In literature the process by which this discovery occurs has become known as the night journey. Albert Guerard, in discussing Conrad's works, describes the night journey as "an essentially solitary journey involving profound spiritual change in the voyager" and explains that the particular experience and the nature of the psychological change vary with each voyager.

Conrad reveals how the civilized veneer falls away from people who, when their survival is threatened, lack the internalized moral values to sustain their humanity. With no understanding of the consequences, Kayerts and Carlier move from untidiness to total laziness and from an acceptance of Makola's immoral behavior to a participation in that behavior. In time they not only blindly aid Makola's bartering workers for ivory, but they accept the ivory even though it was obtained by selling human beings into slavery. With this deed, they forfeit their souls; however, they are not aware that their behavior is now governed by their basest instincts.

When Kayerts realizes that he has murdered his unarmed friend, he attempts to rationalize his behavior. When this attempt fails, he must acknowledge the reality of his dark inner self. His recognition of his doppelgänger or Shadow marks the culmination of his night journey. He is already filled with self-hatred, and the arrival of the delayed supply boat, bringing with it the judgment of society, is more than he can tolerate. He commits suicide. The captain finds Kayerts hanged, with his swollen tongue extended—perhaps symbolizing the dead man's disdain for a civilized culture that failed him in his time of need.

Makola may be the most interesting character in that he is a civilized African native who has also become completely amoral in this isolated environment. He, too, lacks the inner convictions that would enable him to be a man of honor. Not only does he despise and manipulate Kayerts and Carlier because they are white traders, he despises the station's African workers and is willing to sell them into slavery to obtain ivory. When Conrad says that Makola "cherished in his innermost heart the worship of evil spirits," he has more in mind than local tribal deities.

In "An Outpost of Progress," Conrad moves from one form of literary realism to another. For most of the tale, he achieves realism in a traditional manner by having the story controlled by an omniscient, impersonal narrator. However, once Carlier threatens to show Kayerts who is the master—even if Carlier must kill Kayerts—Conrad switches to a realism that is psychologically oriented. With Kayerts's response to Carlier, the narrative perspective is limited to Kayerts's perceptions. As an effective bridge between the two types of narration, Conrad chooses to remain with third-person narration rather than switch to first-person narration.

A particularly important factor in "An Outpost of Progress," as in Conrad's other works, is the relationship of the setting to the plot and the theme. It is Kayerts and Carlier's physical, social, and emotional isolation in the Congo jungle that leads them to discard their civilized veneer and surrender to their basest instincts. Conrad depicts that environment with special care to convey the debilitating intensity of the sun, the dark density of the forest with its mysterious noises and rhythms, and the shroudlike blanket of fog that covers the dead.

Note: The word *nigger,* conventional in Conrad's time, has been changed to *native* without damage to the meaning of the story.

Personal Literary Journal: To what extent, if any, would you lead a different life if you were alone and no one cared what you did or did not do? What values would you keep? What values would you discard?

Literary Terms: characterization, doppelgänger, existentialism, foreshadowing, impressionism, interior monologue, irony, limited omniscience, modernism, narrative perspective, night journey, setting, Shadow, symbol, theme, unreliable narrator

COMPREHENSION QUESTIONS

1. *How does Makola feel about Kayerts and Carlier?* He despises them.
2. *What happened to the first chief of the station?* He died of fever.
3. *What is Kayerts and Carlier's job?* managing the ivory trade and the trading station itself
4. *What is the major problem of this station?* It is isolated, and it is not profitable.
5. *What makes Kayerts and Carlier like each other?* their fear of being alone
6. *What does Gobila do for Kayerts and Carlier?* He gives them friendship and food.
7. *What ends their relationship with Gobila?* On the night Makola sells the station workers into slavery, some of Gobila's men are also carried away, and one man is shot.
8. *What do Kayerts and Carlier argue about at the end?* sugar for their coffee
9. *How does this argument end?* Kayerts murders Carlier.
10. *What does the Director find upon his arrival?* Kayerts has hanged himself.

UNDERSTANDING THE STORY: POSSIBLE ANSWERS

*1. *Incapability of Kayerts and Carlier* Both Kayerts and Carlier are incapable of independent thought and action. Without supervision, they resort to indolence. Their lack of commitment and their laziness contribute to their eventual moral decay.

2. *Courage and principles belong to the crowd; contact with primitive nature brings trouble to the heart* Many people permit their values and behavior to be governed by society. When primitive forces come in contact with a person's hollow inner core, that person's intellect and honor may surrender to uninhibited passions. The situation is dangerous because neither the exterior

controls of group opinion and law nor the internal controls of conscience exist to control immoral behavior or to prevent the loss of a civilized veneer.

3. *Gobila's ideas and attitudes* Gobila's misperception of the white ivory traders parallels the traders' misperception of the Africans. A cultural chasm exists between the traders and Gobila.

*4. *Makola as Henry Price* Makola demonstrates how the supposedly admirable goal of "civilizing" Africans can be misguided. Makola's identification with European customs and accomplishments suggests that isolation corrupts black Africans just as it does white Europeans. Despite Makola's "civilized" veneer, he lacks moral values, and he uses others as objects to fulfill his own desires. The white Europeans despise his aspirations, and they treat him no differently than they treat other Africans.

*5. *Makola's discomfort* Makola doesn't want Kayerts and Carlier to learn the nature of his dealings with the armed men. He despises the agents, and he manipulates them for his own ends. He gives them reason to fear their own deaths, and he raises the question in Kayerts's mind of the cause of the first agent's death.

*6. *Kayerts and Carlier's responsibility for slave trade* Kayerts and Carlier let Makola manipulate them. They try to avoid being suspicious; they condemn Makola's behavior without making an effort to restrain him; and finally they rationalize their acceptance of Makola's ivory as the "Company's ivory." As a result, Kayerts and Carlier lose all restraint and all vestiges of civilized values. In the absence of internal and external controls, they become increasingly vulnerable to moral decay.

*7. *Cause of fight* On the surface, the rules about using sugar cause the fight between Kayerts and Carlier. The underlying causes of the fight are the loss of self-respect, the loss of respect for others, and the loss of respect for authority and rules.

Kayerts and Carlier have changed psychologically beyond recognition. Neither man realizes who he himself is, nor does he recognize who the other has become. A person who does not acknowledge that the doppelgänger or Shadow is part of his or her personality risks being controlled by the doppelgänger. Once the Shadow or doppelgänger controls a person's behavior, that person loses control. Thus, Kayerts shoots an unarmed man who has been his friend.

*8. *Fear* Fear plays the following roles in the story:

- Kayerts and Carlier fear death from the dangers of the sun and from illness because they believe that the first station manager died from a tropical fever.

- Makola threatens Kayerts and Carlier with reminders of the first station manager's death. He continues to instill fear of the sun and of fever in them so he can control them.

- By the end of the story, Kayerts and Carlier have become so different and so afraid of each other that Carlier is able to threaten to shoot

Kayerts and Kayerts is able to kill Carlier without noticing that Carlier is unarmed.

*9. *Kayerts's attitude toward death and life* Before Kayerts kills Carlier, Kayerts is aware that he has lost his moral bearings. Now he also realizes that he has lost his only friend. While he can still choose to behave courteously today, he has lost his confidence in tomorrow, and he fears for his survival. Human life, including his own, has lost its value. Therefore, he advocates amorality as a value.

After Kayerts murders Carlier, his fear of his own death and his horror of his deed combine to make him oblivious of his murder of Carlier.

*10. *Effect of Makola's comment* Makola makes Kayerts question the real cause of the first agent's death. Makola's apparent knowledge and his complete control of the situation cause Kayerts to fear Makola.

*11. *Why Kayerts commits suicide* Kayerts commits suicide because he cannot live with himself and he cannot live in society. He cannot tolerate being judged and condemned for what he has become.

12. *Theme* The primary theme: Know thyself—it is important to have strong internalized values so that one can be true to oneself when faced with competing values or the absence of external values.

ANALYZING LITERARY TECHNIQUE: POSSIBLE ANSWERS

1. *Relationship between setting and plot* Kayerts and Carlier's physical, social, and emotional isolation from civilization leads them to discard their civilized veneer. To convey how the location where Kayerts and Carlier live and work erodes their attitudes and behavior, Conrad depicts the debilitating intensity of the sun, the dark density of the forest with its mysterious noises and rhythms, and the shroudlike blanket of fog that covers the dead.

2. *Significance of the title* The title is ironic. The outpost has been established in the name of civilization and progress, but it is an outpost of regressive, unciv-ilized behavior and of disintegrated values. Conrad finds that these "pioneers of trade and progress" do nothing except harm the Africans and themselves.

*3. *Makola's role* Makola's behavior reveals that isolation affects both whites and Africans in the same way. Makola encourages the greed of the agents and helps to destroy the men and their principles.

4. *Foreshadowing* Examples of foreshadowing include the following:

- The untidiness of the agents foreshadows their laziness, lack of discipline, and lack of self-restraint.

- The phrase "more white men to play with" foreshadows Makola's encouraging the agents' greed and self-destruction.

- Carlier's replanting the cross and hanging on it foreshadows Kayerts's use of the cross to commit suicide.

- The agents' loading their revolvers to cope with the "bad men" foreshad-ows Carlier's threatening to shoot Kayerts and Kayert's shooting Carlier.

5. *Crisis and climax* The crisis in the story is the point where Kayerts and Carlier accept the ivory that Makola acquired by selling the station workers and some of Gobila's people into slavery. The immediate result of the action is the loss of Gobila's help, which, in turn, increases their fears for safety and survival. The climax, Kayerts's murder of Carlier, is directly related to these fears, given the disintegration of their personalities and of their relationship and the scarcity of their provisions.

*6. *Narrative perspective* Once Carlier threatens to shoot Kayerts, the omniscient narrative perspective ends. While the narrative stays in the third person, the remainder of Kayerts's experiences are told from Kayerts's limited point of view. The change creates suspense because the reader must rely on a narrator who is unreliable because he does not understand everything. The limited omniscient point of view creates immediacy because the reader experiences Kayerts's perceptions directly.

*7. *Kayerts's night journey* The climax of Kayerts's rule by his doppelgänger or Shadow is his murder of Carlier, who is unarmed. When Kayerts realizes that he has murdered his unarmed friend, his attempt to rationalize his behavior ultimately fails. He must then acknowledge the reality of his dark inner self. This recognition marks the culmination of his night journey. Being unable to tolerate the person he has become and unable to face society and take responsibility for his actions, Kayerts commits suicide.

WRITING ABOUT LITERATURE

1. *Essay analyzing the role of fear* Call students' attention to the directions in the textbook assignment. (See **U.S.** question 8 above.) **(P.L.J.)** **AP**

2. *Essay analyzing of Kayerts's progressive psychological disintegration* Call students' attention to the directions in the textbook assignment with regard to prewriting and to content. (See **U.S.** questions 1, 6, 7, 8, 9, 10, and 11 and **A.L.T.** questions 6 and 7 above.)

3. *Creative writing: Makola's point of view* Call students' attention to the directions and suggested questions in the textbook assignment. (See **U.S.** questions 4 and 5 and **A.L.T.** question 3 above.)

FURTHER READING

Conrad, Joseph, *Heart of Darkness*; "The Lagoon"; *The Secret Sharer*; *Lord Jim*; *The Nigger of the Narcissus*.

The Lake Isle of Innisfree

WILLIAM BUTLER YEATS

INTRODUCING THE POEM

"The Lake Isle of Innisfree" masterfully conveys Yeats's love and nostalgia for the Irish countryside where Yeats spent his childhood. In a captivating rhythm that begs to be read aloud, he paints a word picture of a beautiful pastoral scene: a simple cabin on a small island where the only noises are the birds, the crickets, and the bees, and the lake water lapping the shore. His depiction of the simple beauties of nature in lovely summer weather connote a sense of luxuriant peace—a tonic for the poet, now an adult living in a crowded, noisy, drab city. The lazy hypnotic feeling of the poem is conveyed not only by content but also by style. The rhythm sings soothingly, and the repeated words give a sense of familiarity. Rhyme and alliteration, with consonant sounds from the first half of a line repeated in the second half, provide continuity and an enhancement of the poem's musical quality.

The Symbolist influence in the poem is revealed in Yeats's ability to make his picture of Innisfree reflect and communicate his emotional yearning. On a symbolic level the pastoral details symbolize the sense of inner peace, tranquility, freedom, and ease that the idea of Innisfree creates.

The poem also has many romantic qualities, such as Yeats's focus on his own state of mind, his feeling of nostalgia for a simpler life, his emphasis on the sensuous elements of nature, and his lyrical style.

Personal Literary Journal: Have you ever been to a place you would love to return to? List details about the place that appeal to you. If you are fond of your home, you may use it as an example.

Literary Terms: alliteration, contrast, figurative language, repetition, rhyme, rhythm, setting, tone

COMPREHENSION QUESTIONS

1. *What is the first thing that the speaker will do on Innisfree?* build a cabin
2. *What appeals to the speaker about Innisfree?* peace; beauty of nature; solitude
3. *Who will live on Innisfree with the speaker?* no one
4. *Where does the speaker hear the lake water lapping?* deep in his heart, or echoed in his heartbeats
5. *Where is the speaker when he narrates this poem?* in the city; on a road or sidewalk

UNDERSTANDING THE POEM: POSSIBLE ANSWERS

1. *The speaker thinks of Innisfree* The drab streets and sidewalks of the city make the speaker think of the country and nature.
2. *The speaker's current life* The speaker's thoughts of Innisfree reveal that he prefers the island to the city. He misses all of the qualities that he associates with Innisfree: solitude, nature, peace, simplicity, and quietness.

ANALYZING LITERARY TECHNIQUE: POSSIBLE ANSWERS

1. *Contrast* The speaker's thinking about Innisfree when he is standing on a road or on the pavement implies that he longs for the country when he is in the city. The detailed description of Innisfree implies a series of opposites that would describe the speaker's current environment.

*2. *Tone* The tone is one of tranquility. It is conveyed by the sights and sounds of Innisfree and by the poetic techniques of rhythm, rhyme, alliteration, and repetition.

*3. *Figurative language* Examples include the following:

- "Bee-loud" (line 4) cleverly describes the quiet noise level of the island.

- "Peace comes dropping slow" (line 5) conveys a mood of languor. In a way, the description alludes to the movement of honey being procured from the beehive. The words, therefore, contribute unity to the poem.

- "Veils of the morning" (line 6) conveys the atmosphere of early morning mist; it complements the midnight atmosphere described as "a glimmer" and the noon atmosphere described as "a purple glow" (line 7).

*4. *Sound devices* Rhythm, repetition, alliteration, and rhyme help to unify the poem. The poem begs to be recited aloud because of its musical appeal. The sounds connect with one another through repeated words ("I will arise and go now"; "dropping"; "hear"), repeated consonants ("have," "hive," "honey"; "glimmer," "glow"; "lake," "lapping," "low"), and rhyme (*abab*).

WRITING ABOUT LITERATURE

1. *Essay analyzing the poem as romantic* Although romanticism was no longer in vogue, the poem reflects the following romantic qualities:

- the speaker's emphasis on his own emotions (longing)

- his view that civilization is a burden (implied in the contrast between the city streets and the world of nature)

- his nostalgia for a simpler place

- his emphasis on nature (beans, bees, birds, and a misty atmosphere)

- his emphasis on the sensuous elements of nature (sights and sounds)

- the relaxed lyrical structure of the poem (its rhythm and arrangement of sounds)

(See **A.L.T.** questions 2, 3, and 4 above.) **AP**

2. *Creative writing: favorite place to live* Call students' attention to the directions in the textbook assignment. Remind them that they can use their imagination and that details are important. Some students may wish to write in verse. **(P.L.J.)**

FURTHER READING

Yeats, William Butler, "An Irish Airman Forsees His Death"; "An Acre of Grass"; "A Coat"; "The Wild Swans at Coole"; "Sailing to Byzantium"; "Among School Children"; "The Second Coming."

Araby

JAMES JOYCE

INTRODUCING THE STORY

A bazaar is the focal point for this story about the loss of a young boy's childish innocence. In just a few pages, Joyce takes the reader from the beginning to the end of the boy's short but intense infatuation with his friend's older sister. "Araby" is more than a jolting initiation that reveals the pain that often accompanies personal growth. It suggests all experiences in which reality is disappointingly different from one's hopes and dreams.

Joyce chooses the narrative perspective of an older narrator, a narrator who remembers a painful experience, reconstructs it selectively step by step, and then enhances its significance by alluding to religious images. The wording and structure of each sentence have been so painstakingly crafted that every aspect of the story is more significant than it initially appears to be.

An important characteristic of Joyce's style is his use of the epiphany. The term means "showing forth." The Christian feast of Epiphany marks "the divine made visible to human eyes"; it commemorates the infant Jesus' revelation to the Magi. In Joyce's *Stephen Hero* (1944), Stephen explains an epiphany as "the most delicate and evanescent of moments" in which, in an insignificant event, the observer intuits "a sudden spiritual manifestation, whether in the vulgarity of speech or of gesture or in a memorable phase of the mind itself."

At the end of "Araby," the trivial conversation between the young lady and the two young men is the ordinary event that provides an epiphany for the young boy. His romantic concept of the sacred nature of love abruptly collapses before the harsh reality of casual and common flirting. The bazaar, that place of "Eastern enchantment," becomes a place of total disillusionment. The boy now feels that his behavior has been ridiculous. Realizing that his childish illusions have no basis in the real world, he is engulfed by anguish and anger.

Personal Literary Journal: Have you ever been infatuated with someone? How did your infatuation begin? Was the object of your admiration aware of your feelings? How were you treated, and how did you feel about the way your were treated? How did your infatuation end? What were your final feelings? Was this a memorable experience? Why?

Literary Terms: allusion, contrast, epiphany, figurative language, foreshadowing, imagery, narrative perspective, symbolism

COMPREHENSION QUESTIONS

1. *What is Araby?* a bazaar; a fair for the sale of goods for charity

2. *Why does the boy go to Araby?* to buy a gift for his friend's sister whom he has a crush on

3. *Why isn't he successful?* He arrives so late that most stalls are closed.

4. *What emotions does he feel at the end of the story?* anguish; anger

5. *What causes him to feel this way?* He overhears a conversation that makes him feel young and foolish about his crush.

UNDERSTANDING THE STORY: POSSIBLE ANSWERS

*1. *Effect of the conversation on the boy* The trivial banter between the young woman and the young men makes the boy aware that he has idealized his feelings and his relationship with his friend's sister.

*2. *Anguish and anger* The boy suffers from the loss of his great love and from the loss of his idealized view of love. He is embarrassed by his naiveté and is angry at himself for being so foolish. He is also angry at life for being different from his dreams. As an adult, he remembers the experience because of its importance in his life—his fall from illusion into reality caused such great anguish and anger that he was no longer the same person.

*3. *Initiation, rite of passage, or loss of innocence* The narrator's use of religious symbolism and the boy's anguish and anger reveal that this experience had the significance of a rite of passage. He is now a more mature person in that he knows more about himself and the world in which he lives.

ANALYZING LITERARY TECHNIQUE: POSSIBLE ANSWERS

1. *Narrative perspective* Joyce uses the perspective of an older person who is relating an experience from his childhood. A younger person probably would choose different details and express them in simpler language. A much older person might have outgrown his interest in the significance of the experience. By relating the experience in retrospect, the narrator can exercise selective memory and omit extraneous details. A mature narrator can use complex language and sentence structures and can add religious imagery to his rendition of the experience.

*2. *Religious allusions and symbolism* Religious allusions symbolize the nature and intensity of the boy's feelings. The words "litanies," "chalice," "prayers and praises," and "adoration" and the comparison of the silence in the hall to the silence in "a church after a service" reveal the pure and sacred nature of his love. The "fall of coins" onto a salver as men are "counting money" symbolizes the secular world of Araby and the foolishness of the boy's love. Like Jesus, who angrily drove the merchants and moneychangers out of the temple, the boy is appalled and repelled by those who destroy what he has considered to be scared.

*3. *Foreshadowing* The following examples foreshadow the failure of the boy's expedition and of his romantic expectations:

- the disparity between the ages of Mangan's sister and the boy
- the late arrival of the boy's uncle
- the boy's ride to Araby on a deserted train
- the dark, silent hall in which the bazaar is being held
- the lone remaining seller's lack of interest in a boy of his age

*4. *Purpose of the boy's late arrival* The late hour means that most stalls will be closed, fewer people will be present, and no distractions will ameliorate the boy's uncomfortable situation. Single details stand out: the commercial aspect of the bazaar, the meager choice of gifts, and the young woman's attitude toward the boy.

*5. *Contrast* Joyce constructs this story around the gap that exists between the illusions and the reality of the boy's world. Examples of contrast include the following:

- The dullness of the real houses on North Richmond Street contrasts with the color and excitement that the boy imagines he will find at Araby. This colorful image contrasts with the dark, empty bazaar that the boy finds upon his late arrival.

- The young age of the boy contrasts with the older age of Mangan's sister. This disparity foreshadows the collapse of the boy's illusions about a romantic relationship.

- The boy's romantic and religious conceptions of love contrast with the silly behavior of the young lady and the young gentlemen at the bazaar. This glimpse of reality causes the boy's illusions about love to collapse.

6. *Epiphany* The trivial conversation between the young lady and the two young men at the bazaar is the ordinary event that provides an epiphany for the young boy. His romantic concept of the sacred nature of love abruptly collapses before the harsh reality of casual and common flirting. He realizes that his illusions have no basis in the real world.

WRITING ABOUT LITERATURE

1. *Essay on the* Irish Times *quotation* Call students' attention to the poem and the directions in the textbook assignment. Remind them that the explanations of the quotations are what make each student essay unique. (See **U.S.** questions 1, 2, and 3 and **A.L.T.** questions 2, 3, 4, and 5.) **AP**

2. *Essay analyzing contrast* Call students' attention to the directions and suggestion in the textbook assignment with regard to content and organization. (See **A.L.T.** question 5 above.) **AP**

3. *Creative writing: retelling the story from the boy's point of view* Call students' attention to the directions and suggestions in the textbook assignment. Remind students to write with the eyes, ears, and interest of a boy. The details, language, and sentence structure should all be those that a teenage boy would use. **(P.L.J.)**

FURTHER READING

Joyce, James, *Dubliners:* "Eveline" and "The Dead"; *Stephen Hero; A Portrait of the Artist as a Young Man.*

1. *In many of the selections in this unit, one person's love for another is tested. Analyze the crises in three selections. Explain how the characters (or the speakers) prove (or fail to prove) their love and how their actions affect their relationships.* In Shakespeare's *Much Ado About Nothing,* many characters are tested. When Claudio is presented with "evidence" of Hero's unfaithfulness, he fails the test by believing Don John instead of trusting his fiancée; he later proves his mettle when he agrees to marry Leonato's niece sight unseen. Likewise, Leonato believes his daughter's accusers rather than Hero herself, but he, too, comes to believe in Hero's innocence. Beatrice stands her ground and believes in her cousin's virtue. Benedick initially balks at Beatrice's charge to "Kill Claudio"; but when he realizes her seriousness, he challenges Claudio to a duel. Fortunately, the truth is discovered before he has to follow through with his challenge, but his intentions have been proved. In "Goblin Market," Lizzie shows her love for her sister, Laura, by standing up to the goblin men and bringing home the juices of the fruit that Lizzie needs to recover from her almost-fatal encounter with the goblin fruit-sellers; for the rest of her life, Laura sings Lizzie's praises. In Sonnet 32, Elizabeth Barrett Browning admits her fears of being loved and works through these fears so she can accept her fiancé's love. In "Araby," the boy wants to prove his devotion to Mangan's sister by bringing her something from the bazaar that she cannot attend; although he overcomes numerous obstacles to get to the bazaar, his attempts to purchase something fail, and he realizes his love is vain.

2. *The plots of "A Woman's Message," "The Pardoner's Tale,"* Much Ado About Nothing, *and "An Outpost of Progress" are marked by trickery or deception. Select two of these works and discuss the purpose of the deception in each work. What is the outcome of the trickery? What does the trickery contribute to the work?* The speaker of "A Woman's Message" was tricked by her husband's family, and she anguishes over the course of her life. After her husband committed murder, his family convinced her to live in exile in a convent full of "wooden nuns." The Pardoner tells of "three young roisterers" who are tricked first by Death and then by one another in "The Pardoner's Tale." Death tricks them by leading them to a fortune that will turn them against one another. Although they are seeking to kill Death, he tricks them into killing one another. Two of the friends trick the third upon his return from town. However, he had already poisoned the wine that they would drink when they toasted their success. In *Much Ado,* both the plot and the subplot revolve around deception. In the main plot revolving around the wooing of Hero, Don Pedro woos Hero in Claudio's name; Don John deceives Claudio and Don Pedro about Hero's virtue; and after Claudio's accusation, Hero pretends to be dead until the truth comes out. Meanwhile, in a more light-hearted deception, Don Pedro and the rest join forces to trick Benedick and Beatrice into loving each other. While all eventually ends

well, the pain and sorrow accompanying the main plot's deceptions are significant, and one has to wonder about marriages that begin with so much trickery behind them. In Conrad's "Outpost of Progress," the Managing Director deceives Kayerts and Carlier about their prospects at the trading station; Makola deceives the hired hands into being traded for ivory; and Kayerts and Carlier deceive themselves about their abilities to manage the station and eventually about their acceptance of the ivory trade. The consequences become fatal when the veneer of civilization wears off and the characters' true personalities are revealed.

3. *William Wordsworth, Matthew Arnold, and William Butler Yeats demonstrate a strong connection with nature in their poems. Using quotations from each poem, analyze how nature informs each poet's actions or beliefs.* In "My Heart Leaps Up," Wordsworth stresses the spiritual bond between humans and nature with lines such as "My heart leaps up when I behold / A rainbow in the sky." Throughout the poem, he relates his belief in the importance of connecting with nature. In "The Lake Isle of Innisfree," Yeats longs for a simpler life in a natural setting. He hears nature, with its "lake water lapping with low sounds by the shore," calling him in the city, and he believes that he will find peace by leaving the city and moving to the country. In "Dover Beach," Arnold recounts an ominous response to nature. The ebb and flow of the waves of the sea remind him of Sophocles and "the turbid ebb and flow / Of human misery." The natural scene reminds him of the grief and alienation of human life and inspires him to cling to his wife in the face of such uncertainty.

4. *The setting plays an important part in many of the selections in this unit. Analyze how the setting affects the speaker's perspective in three selections. Use quotations from each selection to support your analysis.* Students may choose to describe and analyze the fantastical woodland glen of "Goblin Market," the hostile environment of "An Outpost of Progress," the dungeonlike cavern of the woman in "A Woman's Message," the contrasting city pavement and island cabin in "The Lake Isle of Innisfree," or the tranquil yet ominous moonlit beach in "Dover Beach."

SELECTED BIBLIOGRAPHY

THE MEDITERRANEAN

General

Bye, Charles Rowan. *Ancient Greek Literature and Society*. New York: Doubleday/Anchor, 1975. (Sappho, Sophocles)

Dudley, D. R., ed. *The Penguin Companion to Literature. Vol. 4: Classical and Byzantine.* New York: Penguin, 1969.

Hadas, Moses. *A History of Greek Literature*. New York: Columbia University Press, 1965. (Sappho, Sophocles)

Howatson, Margaret, ed. *The Oxford Companion to Classical Literature*. 2nd ed. New York: Oxford University Press, 1989.

Rimanelli, Giose, and Kenneth J. Atchity, eds. *Italian Literature: Roots and Branches*. New Haven: Yale University Press, 1976.

Akhenaton

Breasted, James Henry. *The Dawn of Conscience*. New York: Scribner's, 1976.

Budge, E. A. Wallis. *Egyptian Religion*. New York: Penguin, 1988.

———. *The Gods of the Egyptians or Studies in Egyptian Mythology*. 2 vols. New York: Dover, 1969.

Pritchard, James B. *Ancient Near Eastern Texts Relating to the Old Testament*. 3rd ed. with Supplement. Princeton: Princeton University Press, 1969.

David

Alter, Robert, and Frank Kermode, eds. *The Literary Guide to the Bible*. Cambridge: Harvard University Press, 1987.

Frye, Northrop. *The Great Code: The Bible and Literature*. San Diego: Harcourt, 1983.

Sandmel, Samuel. *The Hebrew Scriptures: An Introduction to Their Literature and Religious Ideas*. New York: Oxford University Press, 1978.

Schneidau, Herbert N. *Sacred Discontent: The Bible and Western Tradition*. Berkeley: University of California Press, 1976.

Sappho

Campbell, David A., ed. *Greek Lyric, Vol. 1: Sappho and Alcaeus*. Cambridge: Harvard University Press, 1990.

Dover, Kenneth J., ed. *Ancient Greek Literature*. New York: Oxford University Press, 1980.

Lattimore, Richmond, ed. and trans. *Greek Lyrics*. Rev. ed. Chicago: University of Chicago Press, 1960.

———. *Sappho*. Chicago: University of Chicago Press, 1970.

Sophocles

Bloom, Harold, ed. *Sophocles*. New York: Chelsea House, 1990. (Critical essays)

Kaufman, Walter. *Tragedy and Philosophy*. Princeton: Princeton University Press, 1968.

Kitto, Humphrey D. *Greek Tragedy, A Literary Study*. 3rd Rev. ed. New York: Routledge, 1966.

Knox, Bernard M. W. *The Heroic Temper: Studies in Sophoclean Tragedy.* Berkeley: University of California Press, 1965.

———. Introduction to *The Three Theban Plays.* New York: Viking, 1982.

———. *Word & Action: Essays on the Ancient Theater.* Baltimore: Johns Hopkins University Press, 1980.

Vickers, Brian. *Towards Greek Tragedy: Drama, Myth, Society.* London: Longman, 1973.

Gaius Valerius Catullus

Catullus, Gaius Valerius. *Catullus: The Poems; Edited with Introduction.* Edited by Kenneth Quinn. London: Macmillan; New York: St. Martin's Press, 1970.

Garrison, Daniel H. *The Student's Catullus.* Norman: University of Oklahoma Press, 1989.

Havelock, Eric Alfred. *The Lyric Genius of Catullus.* New York: Russell & Russell, 1967.

Ross, David O., Jr. *Style and Tradition in Catullus.* Cambridge: Harvard University Press, 1969.

Small, Stuart G. P. *Catullus, A Reader's Guide to the Poems.* Lanham: University Press of America, 1983.

Wheeler, Arthur Leslie. *Catullus and the Traditions of Ancient Poetry.* Berkeley: University of California Press, 1974.

Shmuel HaNagid

Carmi, T. *The Penguin Book of Hebrew Verse.* New York: Viking Press, 1981.

Goldstein, David. *The Jewish Poets of Spain, 900–1250.* Harmondsworth: Penguin, 1971.

HaNagid, Samuel. *Jewish Prince in Moslem Spain: Selected Poems of Samuel Ibn Nagrela.* Translated by Leon J. Weinberger. Tuscaloosa: University of Alabama Press, 1973.

Dante Alighieri

Bergin, Thomas G. *A Diversity of Dante.* New Brunswick, NJ: Rutgers University Press, 1969.

Bloom, Harold, ed. *Dante.* New York: Chelsea House, 1986. (Critical essays)

Freccero, John. *Dante: The Poetics of Conversion.* Cambridge: Harvard University Press, 1988.

Haller, Robert S., ed. *Literary Criticism of Dante Alighieri.* Lincoln: University of Nebraska Press, 1974.

O'Donoghue, Bernard. *The Courtly Love Tradition.* Manchester, Eng.: Manchester University Press, 1982.

Quinones, Ricardo J. *Dante.* Boston: G. K. Hall, 1985.

Emilia Pardo Bazán

Pattison, Walter Thomas. *Emilia Pardo Bazán.* New York: Twayne Publishers, 1971.

Luigi Pirandello

Bloom, Harold, ed. *Luigi Pirandello.* New York: Chelsea House, 1989. (Critical essays)

Cambon, Glauco, ed. *Pirandello: A Collection of Critical Essays.* New York: Prentice, 1967.

Starkie, Walter. *Luigi Pirandello, 1867–1936.* Berkeley: University of California Press, 1965.

Federico García Lorca

Campbell, Roy. *Lorca: An Appreciation of His Poetry.* New York: Haskell House, 1971.

Duran, Manuel, ed. *García Lorca: A Collection of Critical Essays.* Englewood Cliffs: Prentice, 1962.

Gershator, David, ed. and trans. *Federico García Lorca: Selected Letters.* New York: New Directions, 1984.

Gibson, Ian. *Federico García Lorca: A Life.* New York: Pantheon, 1989.

Nazim Hikmet

Göksu, Saime, and Edward Timms. *Romantic Communist: The Life and Work of Nazim Hikmet.* New York: St. Martin's Press, 1999.

Naguib Mahfouz

Mahfouz, Naguib. "The Conjurer Made Off with the Dish." Translated by Denys Johnson-Davies. *Egyptian Short Stories.* Three Continents Press, 1978.

———. "The Conjurer Made Off with the Dish." Translated by Denys Johnson-Davies. *The Time and the Place and Other Stories.* New York: Doubleday, 1991.

CONTINENTAL EUROPE

General

Bloom, Harold, ed. *German Poetry: The Renaissance Through 1915.* New York: Chelsea House, 1990. (Critical essays)

Brée, Germaine. *Twentieth Century French Literature: 1920–1970.* Translated by Louise Guiney. Chicago: University of Chicago Press, 1983. (Sartre, Camus)

Friedman, Maurice. *Problematic Rebel.* Chicago: University of Chicago Press, 1970. (Dostoyevsky, Kafka, Camus)

Glicksberg, Charles I. *The Tragic Vision in Twentieth-Century Literature.* Carbondale: Southern Illinois University Press, 1963. (Kafka, Camus, Sartre)

Quennell, Peter, and Tore Zetterholm, eds. *An Illustrated Companion to World Literature.* London: Orbis, 1986.

Seymour-Smith, Martin, ed. *The New Guide to Modern World Literature.* New York: Peter Bedrick Books, 1985.

Simmons, Ernest J. *Introduction to Russian Realism: Pushkin, Gogol, Dostoyevski, Tolstoi, Chekhov, Sholokhov.* Bloomington: Indiana University Press, 1965.

Hans Christian Andersen

Conroy, Patricia L., and Sven H. Rossel, eds. and trans. *The Diaries of Hans Christian Andersen.* Seattle: University of Washington Press, 1991.

———. Introduction to *Tales and Stories by Hans Christian Andersen.* Seattle: University of Washington Press, 1980.

Fyodor Dostoyevsky

Bloom, Harold, ed. *Fyodor Dostoyevski.* New York: Chelsea House, 1989. (Critical essays)

Dostoyevsky, Anna. *Dostoyevsky: Reminiscences.* Translated by Beatrice Stillman. New York: Liveright, 1975.

Frank, Joseph. *Dostoyevsky: The Seeds of Revolt, 1821–1849.* Princeton: Princeton University Press, 1976.

———. *Dostoyevsky: The Years of Ordeal, 1850–1859.* Princeton: Princeton University Press, 1986.

———. *Through the Russian Prism: Essays on Literature and Culture.* Princeton: Princeton University Press, 1990.

Jackson, Robert L. *The Art of Dostoyevsky: Deliriums and Nocturnes.* Princeton: Princeton University Press, 1981.

Mochulsky, Konstantin. *Dostoyevsky: His Life and Work.* Translated by Michael Minihan. Princeton: Princeton University Press, 1967.

Schuster, M. Lincoln, ed. *A Treasury of the World's Great Letters: From Alexander the Great to Thomas Mann.* New York: Simon & Schuster, 1968.

Wellek, René, ed. *A Collection of Critical Essays.* Englewood Cliffs: Prentice, 1962.

Leo Tolstoy

Bloom, Harold, ed. *Leo Tolstoy*. New York: Chelsea House, 1986. (Critical essays)

Christian, R. F., ed. and trans. *Tolstoy's Diaries*. 2 vols. New York: Macmillan, 1985.

———. *Tolstoy's Letters*. 2 vols. New York: Scribner's, 1978.

Matlaw, Ralph E., ed. *Tolstoy: A Collection of Critical Essays*. Englewood Cliffs: Prentice, 1967.

Rowe, William W. *Leo Tolstoy*. Boston: Hall, 1986.

Simmons, Ernest J. *Introduction to Tolstoy's Writings*. Chicago: University of Chicago Press, 1969.

Wasiolek, Edward. *Critical Essays on Tolstoy*. Boston: Hall, 1986.

Henrik Ibsen

Fjelde, Rolf, ed. *Ibsen: A Collection of Critical Essays*. Englewood Cliffs: Prentice, 1965.

Gray, Ronald D. *Ibsen: A Dissenting View*. Cambridge, Eng.: Cambridge University Press, 1980.

McFarlane, James W. *Ibsen and Meaning: Studies, Essays, and Prefaces, 1953–1987*. Chester Springs, PA: Dufour Editions, 1989.

Meyer, Michael. *Ibsen: A Biography*. New York: Penguin, 1985.

Rose, Henry. *Henrik Ibsen: Poet, Mystic & Moralist*. New York: Haskell House, 1972.

Selma Lagerlöf

Gustafson, Alrik. *A History of Swedish Literature*. Minneapolis: University of Minnesota Press, 1961.

———. *Six Scandinavian Novelists*. Princeton: Princeton University Press, 1940.

Anton Chekhov

Chekhov, Anton. *Short Stories*. Critical Edition. Edited by Ralph E. Matlaw. New York: Norton, 1979.

Hellman, Lillian, ed. *The Selected Letters of Anton Chekhov*. Translated by Sidonie K. Lederer. New York: Farrar, 1984.

Jackson, Robert L., ed. *Chekhov: A Collection of Critical Essays*. Englewood Cliffs: Prentice, 1967.

Karlinsky, Simon, and Michael Heim, eds. and trans. *Anton Chekhov's Life and Thought: Selected Letters and Commentary*. Berkeley: University of California Press, 1976.

Pritchett, V. S. *Chekhov: A Spirit Set Free*. New York: Random, 1988.

Simmons, Ernest J. *Chekhov: A Biography*. Chicago: University of Chicago Press, 1970.

Troyat, Henri. *Chekhov*. Translated by Michael Heim. New York: Fawcett, 1988.

Colette

Cottrell, Robert D. *Colette*. New York: Ungar, 1974.

Lottman, Herbert R. *Colette: A Life*. Boston: Little Brown, 1991.

Phelps, Robert. *Belles Saisons: A Colette Scrapbook*. New York: Farrar, 1978.

———, ed. *Earthly Paradise: An Autobiography of Colette Drawn from Her Lifetime Writings*. Translated by Herma Briffault. New York: Farrar, 1966.

———, ed. *Letters from Colette*. New York: Farrar, 1980.

Rainer Maria Rilke

Rilke, Rainer Maria. *Letters to a Young Poet*. Translated by Stephen Mitchell. New York: Random, 1986.

Peters, H. Frederic. *Rainer Maria Rilke: Masks and the Man*. Staten Island, NY: Gordian Press, 1977.

Rose, William, and G. Craig Houston, eds. *Rainer Maria Rilke: Aspects of His Mind and Poetry*. Staten Island, NY: Gordian Press, 1970.

Franz Kafka

Bloom, Harold, ed. *Franz Kafka*. New York: Chelsea House, 1986. (Critical essays)

Brod, Max. *Franz Kafka: A Biography*. New York: Schocken Books, 1963.

———, ed. *The Diaries of Franz Kafka: 1910–1913*. Translated by Joseph Kresh. New York: Schocken Books, 1987.

———, ed. *The Diaries of Franz Kafka: 1914–1923*. Translated by Martin Greenberg. New York: Schocken Books, 1987.

Emrich, W. *Franz Kafka: A Critical Study of His Writings*. Translated by Sheema Zeben Buehne. New York: Ungar, 1968.

Flores, Angel. *The Problem of the Judgment: Eleven Approaches to Kafka's Story*. Staten Island, NY: Gordian Press, 1977.

Glatzer, Nahum N., ed. *I Am a Memory Come Alive: Autobiographical Writings of Franz Kafka*. New York: Schocken Books, 1976.

Heller, Erich, and Juergen Born, eds. *Letters to Felice*. Translated by James Stern and Elizabeth Duckworth. New York: Schocken Books, 1988.

Janouch, Gustav. *Conversations with Kafka*. Rev. ed. Translated by Goronwy Rees. New York: New Directions, 1971.

Pawel, Ernst. *The Nightmare of Reason: A Life of Franz Kafka*. New York: Farrar, 1984.

Tauber, Herbert. *Franz Kafka: An Interpretation of His Works*. New York: Haskell House, 1969.

Anna Akhmatova

Akhmatova, Anna. *Anna Akhmatova and Her Circle*. Compiled by Konstantin Polivanov. Translated by Patricia Beriozkina. Fayetteville: University of Arkansas Press, 1994.

Chukovskaia, Lidiia Korneevna. *The Akhmatova Journals, 1938–1941*. Vol. 1. Translated by Milena Michalski, Sylva Rubashova, and Peter Norman. Evanston: Northwestern University Press, 2002.

Hingley, Ronald. *Nightingale Fever: Russian Poets in Revolution*. New York, Knopf, 1981.

Nayman, Anatoly. *Remembering Anna Akhmatova*. Translated by Wendy Rosslyn. New York: Henry Holt, 1991.

Jean-Paul Sartre

Kaufmann, Walter, ed. *Existentialism from Dostoyevsky to Sartre*. Magnolia, MA: Peter Smith, 1984.

Kern, Edith, ed. *Sartre: A Collection of Critical Essays*. Englewood Cliffs: Prentice, 1962.

Suhl, Benjamin. *Jean-Paul Sartre: The Philosopher as Literary Critic*. New York: Columbia University Press, 1973.

Albert Camus

Camus, Albert. *The Myth of Sisyphus and Other Essays*. New York: Knopf, 1955.

Bloom, Harold, ed. *Albert Camus*. New York: Chelsea House, 1990. (Critical essays)

Cruickshank, John. *Albert Camus and the Literature of Revolt*. Westport, CT: Greenwood, 1978.

Thody, Philip. *Albert Camus: A Study of His Work*. New York: St. Martin's Press, 1989.

AFRICA

General

Beier, Ulli, ed. *Introduction to African Literature*. London: Longman, 1979.

Cook, David. *African Literature: A Critical View*. London: Longman, 1977.

Heywood, Christopher. *Aspects of South African Literature*. London: Heinemann, 1976.

———, ed. *Perspectives on African Literature*. London: Heinemann/University of Ife Press, 1971.

Kesteloot, Lilyan. *African Writers in French: A Literary History of Négritude*. Philadelphia: Temple University Press, 1974. (Dadié, Senghor)

Killam, G. D. *The Writing of East and Central Africa*. London: Heinemann, 1985.

———, ed. *African Writers on African Writing*. London: Heinemann, 1973. (Achebe, Gordimer)

Klein, Leonard S., ed. *African Literatures in the 20th Century: A Guide*. New York: Ungar, 1986. (Achebe, Dadié, Gordimer, Paton, Senghor, Soyinka)

Lang, D. M., ed. *The Penguin Companion to Literature: Vol. 4: Oriental and African*. Baltimore: Penguin, 1969.

Larson, Charles R. *The Emergence of African Fiction*. Rev. ed. Bloomington: Indiana University Press, 1972. (Achebe, Senghor, Soyinka)

Moore, Gerald. *Twelve African Writers*. Bloomington: Indiana University Press, 1980. (Achebe, Senghor, Soyinka)

Morrel, Karan L., ed. *In Person: Achebe, Awoonor & Soyinka*. Austin: University of Texas Press, 1975.

Mphahlele, Ezekiel. *The African Image*. Salem, NH: Merrimack Book Service, 1972.

Olney, James. *Tell Me Africa: An Approach to African Literature*. Princeton: Princeton University Press, 1973. (Achebe, Dadié, Soyinka)

Roscoe, Adrian. *Mother Is Gold: A Study in West African Literature*. Cambridge, Eng.: Cambridge University Press, 1971. (Achebe, Senghor, Soyinka)

Seymour-Smith, Martin, ed. *The New Guide to Modern World Literature*. New York: Peter Bedrick Books, 1985.

Dahomey (Traditional)

Courlander, Harold. *A Treasury of African Folklore*. New York: Crown, 1974.

Rothenberg, Jerome, ed. *Technicians of the Sacred: A Range of Poetries from Africa, America, Asia, Europe & Oceania*. Berkeley: University of California Press, 1985.

Trask, Willard R., ed. *The Unwritten Song: Poetry of the Primitive and Traditional Peoples of the World*. Vol. 1. New York: Macmillan, 1966.

Alan Paton

Paton, Alan. *Towards the Mountain*. Magnolia, MA: Peter Smith, 1988. (Autobiography, Vol. 1)

———. *Journey Continued: An Autobiography*. New York: Macmillan, 1990. (Vol. 2)

Callan, Edward. *Alan Paton*. Rev. ed. Boston: Hall, 1982.

Léopold Sédar Senghor

Vaillant, Janet C. *Black, French, and African: A Life of Léopold Sédar Senghor*. Cambridge: Harvard University Press, 1990.

Doris Lessing

Lessing, Doris. Preface. *African Stories*. New York: Simon & Schuster, 1981.

———. *A Small Personal Voice: Essays, Reviews, Interviews*. New York: Random, 1975.

Bloom, Harold, ed. *Doris Lessing*. New York: Chelsea House, 1986. (Critical essays)

Brewster, Dorothy. *Doris Lessing*. Boston: Twayne, 1965.

Pickering, Jean. *Understanding Doris Lessing*. Columbia: University of South Carolina Press, 1990.

Sprague, Claire, and Virginia Tiger. *Critical Essays on Doris Lessing*. Boston: Hall, 1986.

Nadine Gordimer

Gordimer, Nadine. *Introduction to Selected Stories*. New York: Viking, 1976.

Bazin, Nancy T., and Marilyn D. Seymour. *Conversations with Nadine Gordimer*. Jackson: University Press of Mississippi, 1990.

Cooke, John. *The Novels of Nadine Gordimer: Private Lives—Public Landscapes*. Baton Rouge: Louisiana State University Press, 1985.

Chinua Achebe

Achebe, Chinua. *Hopes and Impediments: Selected Essays*. New York: Doubleday, 1990.

Killam, Gordon D. *The Novels of Chinua Achebe*. London: Heinemann, 1969.

Wole Soyinka

Soyinka, Wole. *Aké: The Years of Childhood*. New York: Random, 1989.

———. *Ìsarà: A Voyage Around "Essay."* New York: Random, 1989.

———. *Myth, Literature and the African World*. Cambridge, Eng.: Cambridge University Press, 1976.

Jones, Eldred Durosimi. *The Writing of Wole Soyinka*. 3rd ed. Portsmouth, NH: Heinemann, 1988.

Maduakor, Obi. *Wole Soyinka: An Introduction to His Writing*. New York: Garland, 1987.

Moore, Gerald. *Wole Soyinka*. New York: Holmes and Meier, 1972.

Bessie Head

Barnett, Ursula A. *A Vision of Order: A Study of Black South African Literature in English (1914–1980)*. Amherst: University of Massachusetts Press, 1983.

ASIA AND THE SOUTH PACIFIC

General

Aston, W. G. *A History of Japanese Literature*. Rutland, VT: Charles E. Tuttle, 1972.

Barks, Coleman. *The Hand of Poetry: Five Mystic Poets of Persia: Translations from the Poems of Sanai, Attar, Rumi, Saadi, and Hafiz*. New Lebanon: Omega Publications, 1993.

Giles, Herbert A. *A History of Chinese Literature*. Rutland, VT: Charles E. Tuttle, 1973.

———. *The Classical History of Chinese Literature*. 3 vols. Albuquerque: Gloucester Art, 1985.

Gowen, Herbert. *A History of Indian Literature*. New York: D. Appleton, 1931.

Keene, Donald. *Dawn to the West: Japanese Literature in the Modern Era. Fiction*. New York: Holt, 1984.

———. *Japanese Literature. An Introduction for Western Readers*. New York: Grove, 1955.

———. *The Pleasures of Japanese Literature*. New York: Columbia University Press, 1988.

———, ed. *Modern Japanese Literature from 1868 to Present Day*. New York: Grove, 1956.

Lang, D. M., ed. *The Penguin Companion to Literature: Vol. 4: Oriental and African*. Baltimore: Penguin, 1969.

Lau, Joseph S. M., et al., eds. *Modern Chinese Stories and Novellas: 1919–1949*. New York: Columbia University Press, 1981. (Lu Hsün, Ting Ling)

Liu, James J. *Chinese Theories of Literature*. Chicago: University of Chicago Press, 1979.

Rawlinson, Hugh G. *India: A Short Cultural History*. New York: Praeger, 1952.

Rimer, J. Thomas. *Modern Japanese Fiction and Its Traditions: An Introduction*. Princeton: Princeton University Press, 1986.

Rushdie, Salman, and Elizabeth West, eds. *Mirrorwork: 50 Years of Indian Writing*. New York: H. Holt and Co., 1997.

Seymour-Smith, Martin, ed. *The New Guide to Modern World Literature*. New York: Peter Bedrick Books, 1985.

Ueda, Makoto. *Modern Japanese Writers and the Nature of Literature*. Stanford: Stanford University Press, 1976.

Wright, Arthur E., and Denis Twitchett. *Perspectives on the T'ang*. New Haven: Yale University Press, 1973. (Li Po, Jiang Fang)

Yamanouchi, Hisaaki. *The Search for Authenticity in Modern Japanese Literature*. Cambridge, Eng.: Cambridge University Press, 1978.

Li Po

Liu, James J. *The Art of Chinese Poetry*. Chicago: University of Chicago Press, 1983.

Waley, Arthur. *The Poetry and Career of Li Po*. Winchester, MA: Unwin Hyman, 1951.

Yohannan, John D., ed. *A Treasury of Asian Literature*. New York: New American Library, 1956.

Rumi

Harvey, Andrew. *Teachings of Rumi*. Boston: Shambala, 1999.

Iqbal, Afzal. *The Life and Work of Jalal-ud-din Rumi*. London: Octagon Press, 1983.

Nicholson, Reynold A., ed. *Rumi: Poet and Mystic (1207–1273)*. Oxford: Oneworld, 1995.

Wines, Leslie. *Rumi: A Spiritual Biography*. New York: The Crossroad Pub., 2000

Nguyen Binh Khiem

Durand, Maurice M., and Nguyen Tran Huan. *An Introduction to Vietnamese Literature*. Translated by D. M. Hawke. New York: Columbia University Press, 1985.

Rabindranath Tagore

Tagore, Rabindranath. *Collected Poems and Plays*. New York: Collier Books, 1993.

Chakravarty, Amiya, ed. *A Tagore Reader*. Edited by Amiya Chahravarty. Boston: Beacon/Macmillan, 1971.

Dutta, Krishna, and Andrew Robinson, eds. *Rabindranath Tagore: An Anthology*. New York: St. Martin's Press, 1997.

Yeats, W. B. *Prefaces and Introductions. The Collected Works*. Vol. VI. Edited by William H. O'Donnell. New York: Macmillan, 1989.

Katherine Mansfield

Magalaner, Marvin. *The Fiction of Katherine Mansfield*. Carbondale: Southern Illinois University Press, 1971.

Meyers, Jeffrey. *Katherine Mansfield: A Biography*. New York: New Directions, 1980.

Murry, John Middleton. Introduction to *The Short Stories of Katherine Mansfield*. New York: Ecco Press, 1983.

O'Sullivan, Vincent, ed. *Katherine Mansfield: Selected Letters*. New York: Oxford University Press, 1989.

O'Sullivan, Vincent, and Margaret Scott, eds. *The Collected Letters of Katherine Mansfield*. 2 vols. New York: Oxford University Press, 1984, 1987.

Tomalin, Claire. *Katherine Mansfield: A Secret Life*. New York: Knopf, 1988.

Lu Hsün

Lu Hsün. *A Brief History of Chinese Fiction*. Translated by Hsien-yi Yang and Gladys Yang. Westport, CT: Hyperion, 1990.

Huang Sung-K'ang. *Lu Hsün and the New Culture Movement of Modern China*. Westport, CT: Hyperion, 1975.

Průšek, Jaroslav. *The Lyrical and the Epic: Studies of Modern Chinese Literature*. Bloomington: Indiana University Press, 1980.

Ryūnosuke Akutagawa

Yu, Beongcheon. *Akutagawa: An Introduction*. Detroit: Wayne State University Press, 1972.

Yasunari Kawabata

Petersen, Gwen B. *The Moon in the Water: Understanding Tanizaki, Kawabata, and Mishima*. Honolulu: University Press of Hawaii, 1979.

Shen Congwen

Shen Congwen. *Recollections of West Hunan*. Translated by Gladys Yang. Beijing: China Publications Centre, 1982.

Ting Ling

Barlow, Tani E., with Gary J. Bjorge, eds. *I Myself Am a Woman: Selected Writings of Ding Ling*. Boston: Beacon, 1989.

Feuerwerker, Yi-tsi M. *Ding Ling's Fiction: Ideology and Narrative in Modern Chinese Literature*. Cambridge: Harvard University Press, 1982.

Hsu Kai-Yu, ed. *Literature of the Peoples' Republic of China*. Bloomington: Indiana University Press, 1980.

CENTRAL AND SOUTH AMERICA

General

Anderson-Imbert, Enríque. *Spanish American Literature: A History*. 2 vols. Detroit: Wayne State University Press, 1976.

Bassnett, Susan, ed. *Knives and Angels: Women Writers in Latin America*. London: Jed Books, 1990.

Bloom, Harold, ed. *Modern Latin American Fiction*. New York: Chelsea House, 1990. (Critical essays)

———. *Modern Spanish and Latin American Poetry*. New York: Chelsea House, 1990. (Critical essays)

Foster, David William, and Virginia Ramos Foster, eds. *Modern Latin American Literature*. 2 vols. New York: Ungar, 1975.

Franco, J. *An Introduction to Spanish American Literature*. Cambridge, Eng.: Cambridge University Press, 1971.

Gallagher, David P. *Modern Latin American Literature*. New York: Oxford University Press, 1973.

Garfield, E. Picon. *Women's Voices from Latin America: Interviews with Six Contemporary Authors*. Detroit: Wayne State University Press, 1985.

Gonzáles Echevarría, Roberto. *The Voice of the Masters: Writing and Authority in Modern Latin American Literature*. Austin: University of Texas Press, 1985.

Harss, Luis, and Barbara Dohmann, eds. *Into the Mainstream: Conversations with Latin American Writers*. New York: Harper, 1967.

King, John. *On Modern Latin American Fiction*. New York: Hill & Wang, 1989.

Martin, Gerald. *Journeys Through the Labyrinth: Latin American Fiction in the Twentieth Century*. New York: Verso, 1989.

Meyer, Doris, ed. *Lives on the Line: The Testimony of Contemporary Latin American Authors*. Berkeley: University of California Press, 1988.

Monegal, Emir Rodríguez, ed. *The Borzoi Anthology of Latin American Literature: From the Time of Columbus to the Twentieth Century*. New York: Knopf, 1977.

———. *The Borzoi Anthology of Latin American Literature: The Twentieth Century—From Borges and Paz to Guimarães Rosa and Donoso*. New York: Knopf, 1977.

Ortega, Julio. *Poetics of Change: The New Spanish-American Narrative*. Translated by Galen
D. Greaser. Austin: University of Texas Press, 1984.

Seymour-Smith, Martin, ed. *The New Guide to Modern World Literature*. New York: Peter
Bedrick Books, 1985.

Solé, Carlos A., ed. *Latin American Writers*. 3 vols. New York: Scribner's, 1989.

Torres-Rioseco, Arturo. *The Epic of Latin American Literature*. Berkeley: University of
California Press, 1964.

Ward, Philip, ed. *The Oxford Companion to Spanish Literature*. Oxford: Oxford University
Press, 1978.

Sor Juana Inés de la Cruz

de la Cruz, Sor Juana Inés. *A Woman of Genius: The Intellectual Autobiography of Sor Juana
Inés de la Cruz*. Translated by Margaret Sayers Peden. Salisbury: Lime Rock Press, 1987.

Ashby, Ruth, and Deborah Gore Ohrn. *Herstory: Women Who Changed the World*. New
York: Viking, 1995.

Kirk, Pamela. *Sor Juan Inés de la Cruz: Religion, Art, and Feminism*. New York: Continuum,
1998.

Paz, Octavio. *Sor Juana, or, The Traps of Faith*. Translated by Margaret Sayers Peden.
Cambridge: Belknap Press, 1988.

Gabriela Mistral

Bates, Margaret. *Introduction to Selected Poems of Gabriela Mistral*. Edited and translated by
Doris Dana. Baltimore: Johns Hopkins University Press, 1971.

Castleman, William J. *Beauty and the Mission of the Teacher: The Life of Gabriela Mistral of
Chile*. Smithtown, NY: Exposition Press, 1982.

María Luisa Bombal

Adams, M. Ian. *Three Authors of Alienation*. Austin: University of Texas Press, 1975.

Jorge Luis Borges

Agheana, Ion T. *The Meaning of Experience in the Prose of Jorge Luis Borges*. New York:
Peter Lang, 1988.

———. *The Prose of Jorge Luis Borges: Existentialism and the Dynamics of Surprise*. New
York: Peter Lang, 1984.

Alazraki, Jaime, ed. *Borges and the Kabbalah and Other Essays on His Fiction and Poetry*.
Cambridge, Eng.: Cambridge University Press, 1988.

———. *Critical Essays on Jorge Luis Borges*. Boston: Hall, 1987.

Bell-Villada, Gene H. *Borges and His Fiction: A Guide to His Mind and Art*. Chapel Hill:
University of North Carolina Press, 1981.

Bloom, Harold, ed. *Jorge Luis Borges*. New York: Chelsea House, 1986. (Critical essays)

Cortínez, Carlos, ed. *Simply a Man of Letters: Papers of a Symposium on Jorge Luis Borges*.
Orono: University of Maine Press, 1982.

Friedman, Mary Lusky. *The Emperor's Kites: A Morphology of Borges' Tales*. Durham, NC:
Duke University Press, 1987.

Monegal, Emir Rodríguez. *Jorges Luis Borges: A Literary Biography*. New York: Dutton, 1978.

Sturrock, J. *Paper Tigers: The Ideal Fictions of Jorge Luis Borges*. Oxford: Oxford University
Press, 1978.

Wheelock, Carter. *The Mythmaker: A Study of Motif and Symbol in the Short Stories of Jorge
Luis Borges*. Austin: University of Texas Press, 1969.

Yates, Donald A. *Jorge Luis Borges: Life, Work, and Criticism*. Fredericton, New Brunswick,
Canada: York Press, 1985.

Pablo Neruda

Neruda, Pablo. *Memoirs*. Translated by Hardie St. Martin. New York: Farrar, 1977.

———. *Passions and Impressions*. Translated by Margaret Sayers Peden. New York: Farrar, 1983.

Bloom, Harold, ed. *Pablo Neruda*. New York: Chelsea House, 1989. (Critical essays)

de Costa, René. *The Poetry of Pablo Neruda*. Cambridge: Harvard University Press, 1982.

Duran, Manuel, and Margery Safir. *Earth Tones: The Poetry of Pablo Neruda*. Bloomington: Indiana University Press, 1981.

Santí, Enrico Mario. *Pablo Neruda: The Poetics of Prophecy*. Ithaca, NY: Cornell University Press, 1982.

João Guimarães Rosa

Vincent, Jon S. *João Guimarães Rosa*. Boston: Twayne, 1978.

Julio Cortázar

Alazraki, Jaime, and Ivar Ivask, eds. *The Final Island: The Fiction of Julio Cortázar*. Norman: University of Oklahoma Press, 1978.

Alonso, Carlos J. *Julio Cortázar: New Readings*. Cambridge, Eng.: Cambridge University Press, 1998.

Standish, Peter. *Understanding Julio Cortázar*. Columbia: University of South Carolina Press, 2001.

Stavans, Ilan. *Julio Cortázar: A Study of Short Fiction*. New York: Twayne Publishers; London: Prentice Hall International, 1996.

Octavio Paz

Paz, Octavio. *The Bow and the Lyre*. Translated by Ruth L. C. Simms. Austin: University of Texas Press, 1973.

———. *Convergences: Essays on Art and Literature*. Translated by Helen Lane. San Diego: Harcourt, 1987.

Fein, John M. *Toward Octavio Paz: A Reading of His Major Poems, 1957–1976*. Lexington: University Press of Kentucky, 1986.

Ivask, Ivar, ed. *The Perpetual Present: The Poetry and Prose of Octavio Paz*. Norman: University of Oklahoma Press, 1973.

Wilson, Jason. *Octavio Paz*. Boston: Hall, 1986.

———. *Octavio Paz: A Study of His Poetics*. Cambridge, Eng.: Cambridge University Press, 1979.

Rosario Castellanos

Ahern, Maureen, ed. and trans. *A Rosario Castellanos Reader: An Anthology of Her Poetry, Short Fiction, Essays, and Drama*. Austin: University of Texas Press, 1988.

Dauster, Frank. *The Double Strand: Five Contemporary Mexican Poets*. Lexington: University Press of Kentucky, 1987.

Meyer, Doris, and Margarite Fernandez-Olmos. *Contemporary Women Authors of Latin America: Introductory Essays*. New York: Brooklyn College Press, 1984.

Gabriel García Márquez

Bell-Villada, Gene H. *García Márquez: The Man and His Work*. Chapel Hill: University of North Carolina Press, 1990.

Bloom, Harold, ed. *Gabriel García Márquez*. New York: Chelsea House, 1989. (Critical essays)

Foster, David W. *Studies in the Contemporary Spanish-American Short Story*. Columbia: University of Missouri Press, 1979.

Janes, Regina. *Gabriel García Márquez: Revolutions in Wonderland*. Columbia: University of Missouri Press, 1981.

McGuirk, Bernard, and Richard Cardwell. *Gabriel García Márquez: New Readings*. Cambridge, Eng.: Cambridge University Press, 1987.

McMurray, George R., ed. *Critical Essays on Gabriel García Márquez*. New York: Ungar, 1977.

McNerney, Kathleen. *Understanding Gabriel García Márquez*. Columbia: University of South Carolina Press, 1989.

Minta, Stephen. *García Márquez: Writer of Colombia*. London: Cape, 1987.

Ortega, Julio, ed. *Gabriel García Márquez and the Powers of Fiction*. Austin: University of Texas Press, 1988.

Williams, Raymond L. *Gabriel García Márquez*. Boston: Hall, 1984.

NORTH AMERICA

General

Bloom, Harold, ed. *The Critical Perspective: Vol. 9: Emily Dickinson to Lewis Carroll*. New York: Chelsea House, 1989. (Critical essays)

Ellmann, Richard, and Robert O'Clair, eds. *The Norton Anthology of Modern Poetry*. 2nd ed. New York: Norton, 1988.

Hart, James D., ed. *The Oxford Companion to American Literature*. New York: Oxford University Press, 1983.

Untermeyer, Louis, ed. *Modern American Poetry*. New York: Harcourt, 1950.

Zuñi (Traditional)

Cushing, Frank Hamilton. *Zuñi Breadstuff*. New York: Museum of the American Indian/Heye Foundation, 1974.

Dutton, Bertha P. *American Indians of the Southwest*. Rev. ed. Albuquerque: University of New Mexico Press, 1983.

Green, Jesse, ed. *Zuñi: Selected Writings of Frank Hamilton Cushing*. Lincoln: University of Nebraska Press, 1979.

Scully, Vincent. *Pueblo: Mountain, Village, Dance*. Chicago: University of Chicago Press, 1989.

Stevenson, Matilda Coxe. *The Zuñi Indians: Their Mythology, Esoteric Fraternities, and Ceremonies (1901–1902)*. Glorieta, NM: Rio Grande Press, 1985.

Tedlock, Dennis, and Barbara Tedlock. *Teachings from the American Earth: Indian Religion and Philosophy*. New York: Liveright, 1976.

Walt Whitman

Allen, Gay W. *The New Walt Whitman Handbook*. New York: New York University Press, 1987.

———. *The Solitary Singer: A Critical Biography of Walt Whitman*. Chicago: University of Chicago Press, 1985.

Bloom, Harold, ed. *Walt Whitman*. New York: Chelsea House, 1985. (Critical essays)

Miller, Edwin H. *Walt Whitman's Poetry: A Psychological Journey*. New York: New York University Press, 1968.

———. *Walt Whitman's "Song of Myself": A Mosaic of Interpretations*. Iowa City: University of Iowa Press, 1989.

———, ed. *Selected Letters of Walt Whitman*. Iowa City: University of Iowa Press, 1990.

Emily Dickinson

Bloom, Harold, ed. *American Women Poets.* New York: Chelsea House, 1986. (Critical essays)
———. *Emily Dickinson.* New York: Chelsea House, 1985. (Critical essays)
Budick, E. Miller. *Emily Dickinson and the Life of Language: A Study in Symbolic Poetics.* Baton Rouge: Louisiana State University Press, 1985.
Diehl, Joanne F. *Dickinson and the Romantic Imagination.* Princeton: Princeton University Press, 1981.
Franklin, R. W., ed. *The Master Letters of Emily Dickinson.* Amherst: Amherst College Press, 1986.
Johnson, Thomas J., ed. *Emily Dickinson: Selected Letters.* Cambridge: Harvard University Press, 1985.

Eugene O'Neill

Bloom, Harold, ed. *Eugene O'Neill.* New York: Chelsea House, 1987. (Critical essays)
Bogard, Travis. *Contour in Time: The Plays of Eugene O'Neill.* New York: Oxford University Press, 1988.
Bogard, Travis, and Jackson R. Bryer, eds. *Selected Letters of Eugene O' Neill.* New Haven: Yale University Press, 1988.
Gelb, Arthur, and Barbara Gelb. *O'Neill.* Rev. ed. New York: Harper, 1974.
Griffin, Ernest. *O'Neill: A Collection of Criticism.* New Haven: Yale University Press, 1976.
Törnqvist, Egil. *A Drama of Souls: Studies in O'Neill's Super-Naturalistic Techniques.* New Haven: Yale University Press, 1969.

Ernest Hemingway

Baker, Carlos. *Ernest Hemingway: A Life Story.* New York: Macmillan, 1988.
———. *Hemingway: The Writer as Artist.* Princeton: Princeton University Press, 1972.
———, ed. *Ernest Hemingway: Selected Letters: 1917–1961.* New York: Macmillan, 1989.
Bloom, Harold, ed. *Ernest Hemingway.* New York: Chelsea House, 1985. (Critical essays)
Brooks, Van Wyck. *Writers at Work:* The Paris Review *Interviews.* Second Series. New York: Viking, 1965.
Burgess, Anthony. *Hemingway and His World.* New York: Macmillan, 1985.
Meyers, Jeffrey. *Hemingway: A Biography.* New York: Harper, 1986.
———, ed. *Hemingway: The Critical Heritage.* New York: Routledge, 1982.

T. S. Eliot

Bloom, Harold, ed. *T. S. Eliot.* New York: Chelsea House, 1985. (Critical essays)
Frye, Northrop. *T. S. Eliot: An Introduction.* Chicago: University of Chicago Press, 1981.
Headings, Philip R. *T. S. Eliot.* Rev. ed. Boston: Hall, 1982.
Kenner, Hugh, ed. *T. S. Eliot: A Collection of Critical Essays.* Englewood Cliffs: Prentice, 1962.
Kirk, Russell. *Eliot and His Age: T. S. Eliot's Moral Imagination in the Twentieth Century.* La Salle, IL: Sugden, 1984.
Leavis, F. R. *The Common Pursuit.* London: Hogarth, 1984.
Olney, James, ed. *T. S. Eliot: Essays from the Southern Review.* New York: Oxford University Press, 1988.

Langston Hughes

Barksdale, Richard K. *Hughes: The Poet and His Critics.* Chicago: American Library Association, 1977.
Bloom, Harold, ed. *Langston Hughes.* New York: Chelsea House, 1990. (Critical essays)
Emanuel, James A. *Langston Hughes.* Boston: Hall, 1967.
Jemie, Onwuchekwa. *Hughes: An Introduction to the Poetry.* New York: Columbia University Press, 1985.

Eudora Welty

Welty, Eudora. *The Eye of the Story: Selected Essays and Reviews*. New York: Random, 1990.
———. *One Writer's Beginnings*. Cambridge: Harvard University Press, 1984.
Bloom, Harold, ed. *Eudora Welty*. New York: Chelsea House, 1986. (Critical essays)
Brans, Jo. *Listen to the Voices: Conversations with Contemporary Writers*. Dallas: Southern Methodist University Press, 1988.
Devlin, Albert J. *Eudora Welty: A Life in Literature*. Jackson: University Press of Mississippi, 1987.
———. *Eudora Welty's Chronicle: A Story of Mississippi Life*. Jackson: University Press of Mississippi, 1983.
Vande Kieft, Ruth M. *Eudora Welty*. Rev. ed. Boston: Twayne, 1987.

Alice Munro

Martin, W. R. *Alice Munro: Paradox and Parallel*. Lincoln: University of Nebraska Press, 1987.

Anne Hébert

Russell, Delbert W. *Anne Hébert*. Boston: Twayne, 1983.

Alice Walker

Walker, Alice. *In Search of Our Mothers' Gardens: Womanist Prose*. San Diego: Harcourt, 1984.
———. *Living by the Word: Selected Writings: 1973–1987*. San Diego: Harcourt, 1989.
Bloom, Harold, ed. *Alice Walker*. New York: Chelsea House, 1990. (Critical essays)

GREAT BRITAIN AND IRELAND

General

Allen, Walter. *The Short Story in English*. New York: Oxford University Press, 1981.
Allison, Alexander W., et al., eds. *The Norton Anthology of Poetry*. New York: Norton, 1975.
Drabble, Margaret, ed. *The Oxford Companion to English Literature*. New York: Oxford University Press, 1987.
Gilbert, Sandra M., and Susan Gubar. *The Madwoman in the Attic: A Study of Women and the Literary Imagination in the Nineteenth Century*. New Haven: Yale University Press, 1979.
Unterrneyer, Louis, ed. *Modern British Poetry*. San Diego: Harcourt, 1950.
———, ed. *A Treasury of Great Poems: English and American*. New York: Simon & Schuster, 1955.

Geoffrey Chaucer

Bowden, Muriel Amanda. *A Reader's Guide to Geoffrey Chaucer*. New York: Farrar, Straus, 1964.
Braddy, Haldeen. *Geoffrey Chaucer: Literary and Historical Studies*. Port Washington: Kennikat Press, 1971.
Brewer, Derek, ed. *Geoffrey Chaucer*. Athens: Ohio University Press, 1975.
Burrow, John Anthony, ed. *Geoffrey Chaucer: A Critical Anthology*. Harmondsworth: Penguin, 1969.
Gardner, John. *The Life and Times of Chaucer*. New York: Knopf, Random House, 1977.
Nardo, Don, ed. *Readings on the* Canterbury Tales. San Diego: Greenhaven Press, 1997.
Pearsall, Derek Albert. *The Life of Geoffrey Chaucer: A Critical Biography*. Oxford: Blackwell, 1992.
Phillips, Helen. *An Introduction to the* Canterbury Tales: *Fiction, Writing, Context*. New York: St. Martin's Press, 1999.
Rudd, Gillian. *The Complete Critical Guide to Geoffrey Chaucer*. New York: Routledge, 2001.

Saunders, Corinne, ed. *Chaucer*. Oxford: Blackwell Publishers, 2001.

Schoeck, Richard J., and Jerome Taylor, eds. *Chaucer Criticism: An Anthology*. South Bend: University of Notre Dame Press, 1960.

William Shakespeare

Shakespeare, William. *Much Ado About Nothing*. In *The Yale Shakespeare*. Edited by Wilbur L. Cross and Tucker Brooke. New York: Barnes and Noble, 1993.

―――. New York: Dover, 1994. Reprint from *Works of William Shakespeare*. Vol. 2. London: Macmillan, 1891.

―――. *Shakespeare: The Complete Works*. Edited by G. B. Harrison. New York: Harcourt Brace, 1948.

―――. *The Arden Shakespeare*. Edited by A. R. Humphreys. New York: Routledge, 1988. Reprint of London: Methuen, 1981.

―――. *The New Cambridge Shakespeare*. Edited by F. H. Mares. Cambridge, Eng.: Cambridge University Press, 1988.

―――. *Shakespeare: Signet Classic*. Edited by David L. Stevenson. New York: Penguin, 1989.

―――. *The Folger Library Shakespeare*. Edited by Louis B. Wright and Virginia A. LaMar. New York: Washington Square Press, 1964.

Auden, W. H. *Much Ado About Nothing*. *Lectures on Shakespeare*. Princeton: Princeton University Press, 2000.

Barton, Anne. Introduction to *Much Ado About Nothing*. Edited by Herschel Baker, et al. *The Riverside Shakespeare*. Vol. 1. Boston: Houghton Mifflin, 1974.

Bate, Jonathan, ed. *The Romantics on Shakespeare*. New York: Penguin, 1992.

Bloom, Harold. *Shakespeare: The Invention of the Human*. New York: Penguin Putnam, 1998.

Charlton, H. B. *Shakespearean Comedy*. London: Methuen, 1979.

Goddard, Harold C. *Much Ado About Nothing*. *The Meaning of Shakespeare*. Vol. 1. Chicago: The University of Chicago Press, 1951.

Harrison, G. B. Introduction to *Much Ado About Nothing*. *Shakespeare: The Complete Works*. New York: Harcourt Brace, 1948

Hays, Janice. "Those 'soft and delicate desires': *Much Ado* and the Distrust of Women." In *The Woman's Part: Feminist Criticism of Shakespeare*. Edited by Carolyn Ruth Swift Lenz, Gayle Greene, and Carol Thomas Neely. Urbana: University of Illinois Press, 1983.

Heffner, Ray L., Jr. "Hunting for Clues in *Much Ado About Nothing*." In *The Meaning of Shakespeare*. Vol. 1. Edited by Harold C. Goddard. Chicago: University of Chicago Press, 1970.

―――. "Hunting for Clues in *Much Ado About Nothing*." In *Teaching Shakespeare*. Edited by Walter Edens, Christopher Durer, Walter Eggers, Duncan Harris, and Keith Hull. Princeton: Princeton University Press, 1977.

Lewis, Anthony J. *The Love Story in Shakespearean Comedy*. Lexington, Kentucky: University Press of Kentucky, 1992.

Muir, Kenneth. *Much Ado About Nothing*. *The Sources of Shakespeare's Plays*. New Haven: Yale University Press, 1978.

Neely, Carol Thomas. "Broken Nuptials: *Much Ado About Nothing*." In *Broken Nuptials in Shakespeare's Plays*. Urbana: University of Illinois Press, 1993.

Ornstein, Robert. *Shakespeare's Comedies: From Roman Farce to Romantic Mystery*. Newark: University of Delaware Press, 1986.

Park, Clara Claiborne. "As We Like It: How a Girl Can Be Smart and Still Popular." In *The Woman's Part: Feminist Criticism of Shakespeare*. Edited by Carolyn Ruth Swift Lenz, Gayle Greene, and Carol Thomas Neely. Urbana: University of Illinois Press, 1983.

Rossiter, A. P. *Much Ado About Nothing*. In *Shakespeare: The Comedies: A Collection of Critical Essays*. Edited by Kenneth Muir. Englewood Cliffs, New Jersey: Prentice Hall, 1965.

Rowse, A. L. *Much Ado About Nothing*. In *Prefaces to Shakespeare's Plays*. London: Orbis, 1984.

Slights, Camille Wells. *Shakespeare's Comic Commonwealths*. Toronto: University of Toronto Press, 1993.

Stauffer, Donald A. "The Garden of Eden." In *Shakespeare's World of Images: The Development of His Moral Ideas*. Bloomington: Indiana University Press, 1966. Reprint of Norton, 1949.

Stevenson, David L. Introduction to *Much Ado About Nothing*. New York: Penguin (Signet Classic), 1989.

Van Doren, Mark. *Shakespeare*. Garden City, New York: Doubleday Anchor, 1953.

Westlund, Joseph. *Shakespeare's Reparative Comedies: A Psychoanalytic View of the Middle Plays*. Chicago: University of Chicago Press, 1984.

Williamson, Marilyn L. *The Patriarchy of Shakespeare's Comedies*. Detroit: Wayne State University Press, 1986.

William Wordsworth

William Wordsworth and the Age of English Romanticism. New Brunswick, NJ: Rutgers University Press, 1987.

Alan, G., ed. *The Letters of William Wordsworth: A New Selection*. New York: Oxford University Press, 1985.

Bloom, Harold, ed. *The English Romantic Poets*. New York: Chelsea House, 1986. (Critical essays)

———. *William Wordsworth*. New York: Chelsea House, 1985. (Critical essays)

Durrant, Geoffrey H. *William Wordsworth*. Cambridge, Eng.: Cambridge University Press, 1969.

Frye, Northrop. *A Study of English Romanticism*. Chicago: University of Chicago Press, 1983.

Hartman, Geoffrey H. *The Unremarkable Wordsworth*. Minneapolis: University of Minnesota Press, 1987.

———. *Wordsworth's Poetry: 1787–1814*. Cambridge: Harvard University Press, 1987.

Moorman, Mary, ed. *The Journals of Dorothy Wordsworth*. Oxford: Oxford University Press, 1971.

Elizabeth Barrett Browning

Forster, Margaret. *Elizabeth Barrett Browning: A Biography*. New York: Doubleday, 1989.

———. *The Life and Loves of a Poet*. New York: St. Martin's Press, 1990.

Schuster, M. Lincoln, ed. *A Treasury of the World's Great Letters: From Alexander the Great to Thomas Mann*. New York: Simon & Schuster, 1968.

Emily Brontë

Bloom, Harold, ed. *The Brontës*. New York: Chelsea House, 1987. (Critical essays)

Frank, Katherine. *A Chainless Soul: The Life of Emily Brontë*. Boston: Houghton, 1990.

Gerin, Winifred. *Emily Brontë*. Oxford: Oxford University Press, 1972.

Taylor, Irene. *Holy Ghosts: The Male Muses of Emily and Charlotte Brontë*. New York: Columbia University Press, 1990.

Christina Rossetti

Bloom, Harold, ed. *The Pre-Raphaelite Poets*. New York: Chelsea House, 1986. (Critical essays)

Rosenblum, Dolores. *Christina Rossetti: The Poetry of Endurance*. Carbondale: Southern Illinois University Press, 1986.

Rossetti, William M., ed. *Family Letters of Christina Georgina Rossetti, with Some Supplementary Letters and Appendices*. New York: Haskell House, 1969.

Joseph Conrad

Conrad, Joseph. *Heart of Darkness*. Critical Edition. Edited by Robert Kimbrough. New York: Norton, 1971.

———. 1897 Preface to *The Nigger of the "Narcissus."* Critical Edition. Edited by Robert Kimbrough. New York: Norton, 1979.

Bloom, Harold, ed. *Joseph Conrad*. New York: Chelsea House, 1986. (Critical essays)

Dowden, Wilfred S. *Joseph Conrad: The Imaged Style*. Nashville: Vanderbilt University Press, 1970.

Guerard, Albert J. *Conrad the Novelist*. Cambridge: Harvard University Press, 1958.

Karl, Frederick R. *Joseph Conrad: The Three Lives*. New York: Farrar, 1979.

———, and Laurence Davies, eds. *The Collected Letters of Joseph Conrad*. 4 vols. Cambridge, Eng.: Cambridge University Press, 1983–1990.

Meyers, Jeffrey. *Joseph Conrad: A Biography*. New York: Scribner's, 1991.

Watt, Ian. *Conrad in the Nineteenth Century*. Berkeley: University of California Press, 1979.

William Butler Yeats

Yeats, William Butler. *Autobiography of William Butler Yeats: Consisting of Reveries over Childhood and Youth*. New York: Macmillan, 1988.

Bloom, Harold. *Yeats*. New York: Oxford University Press, 1972.

———, ed. *W. B. Yeats*. New York: Chelsea House, 1986. (Critical essays)

Domville, Eric, and John Kelly, eds. *The Collected Letters of W. B. Yeats. Vol. I: 1856–1895*. New York: Oxford University Press, 1986.

Ellmann, Richard. *a long the riverrun*. New York: Knopf, 1989.

———. *The Identity of Yeats*. Oxford: Oxford University Press, 1964.

———. *Yeats: The Man and the Masks*. Rev. ed. New York: Norton, 1978.

James Joyce

Joyce, James. *Dubliners*. Critical Edition. Edited by Robert Scholes and A. Walton Litz. New York: Penguin, 1985.

———. *Stephen Hero*. New York: New Directions, 1955.

Bloom, Harold, ed. *James Joyce*. New York: Chelsea House, 1986. (Critical essays)

———. *James Joyce's Dubliners*. New York: Chelsea House, 1988. (Critical essays)

Ellmann, Richard. *James Joyce*. Rev. ed. New York: Oxford University Press, 1982.

———, ed. *Selected Letters of James Joyce*. New York: Viking, 1975.

Gifford, Don. *Joyce Annotated: Notes for Dubliners and A Portrait of the Artist as a Young Man*. Rev. ed. Berkeley: University of California Press, 1982.

Torchiana, Donald T. *Backgrounds for Joyce's Dubliners*. Boston: Allen & Unwin, 1986.